3 0117 03062 7323

the
Unoffic
Guid

Windows
Vista™

GW00546202

Derek Torres and Stuart Mudie

BICENTENNIAL
1807
WILEY
2007
BICENTENNIAL

Wiley Publishing, Inc.

Unofficial Guide® to Windows Vista™

Published by

Wiley Publishing, Inc.
111 River Street
Hoboken, NJ 07030-5774
www.wiley.com

For general information on our other products and services or to obtain technical support please contact our Customer Care Department within the U.S. at (800) 762-2974, outside the U.S. at (317) 572-3993 or fax (317) 572-4002.

Wiley also publishes its books in a variety of electronic formats. Some content that appears in print may not be available in electronic books. For more information about Wiley products, please visit our web site at www.wiley.com.

Library of Congress Control Number: 2006939454

ISBN: 978-0-470-04576-3

Manufactured in the United States of America

10 9 8 7 6 5 4 3   1

Page creation by Wiley Publishing, Inc. Composition Services

In loving memory of Ann D. Gray, you are gone but never forgotten
To my family and friends
— Derek Torres

To Ellie and Justine, with love
— Stuart Mudie

Acknowledgements

Derek Torres

I'd like to first thank my good friend co-author, Stuart Mudie, for contributing four chapters to this book. This book certainly is richer thanks to his help. I'd also like to thank my wife, Céline, and our two lads for putting up with my seven day work weeks so that I could complete my writing. Special thanks to our brilliant team at Wiley, including our acquisitions editor Jody Lefevere (thanks for yet another opportunity to undertake a labor of love), our project editor Beth Taylor, and our technical editor Jim Kelly. I'd like to thank my agent, Lynn Haller, for her dedication and hard work. Thanks to my parents, family and friends who've helped along the way. I'd also like to thank both Arnaud and Alan, who put me on the path to writing.

Stuart Mudie

Thanks to Ellie and Justine, for everything, and in particular for their patience and support during the writing of this book; my parents Marion and Bill Mudie, for all their love and encouragement, without which I wouldn't be where I am today; my co-author Derek Torres, for his friendship over the years and in particular for getting me involved in this project in the first place; Lucia Holguín Diego, whose father might one day tell her why; my agent, Lynn Haller, for her hard work and dedication; and our editors Jody Lefevere, Beth Taylor and Jim Kelly, and all the other fine folks at Wiley.

Credits

Acquisitions Editor
Jody Lefevere

Project Editor
Beth Taylor

Technical Editor
James F. Kelly

Copy Editor
Beth Taylor

Editorial Manager
Robyn Siesky

Vice President & Group Executive Publisher
Richard Swadley

Vice President & Publisher
Barry Pruett

Project Coordinator
Adrienne Martinez

Graphics & Production Specialists
Beth Brooks
Jonelle Burns
Jennifer Mayberry
Heather Ryan
Amanda Spagnuolo

Quality Control Technician
Brian H. Walls

Proofreading
Laura L. Bowman

Indexing
Richard Shrout

Book Interior Design
Lissa Auciello-Brogan
Elizabeth Brooks

Wiley Bicentennial Logo
Richard J. Pacifico

About the Authors

Derek Torres is a technical communicator and author. He is the co-author of *The Unofficial Guide to Windows XP* and is the author of *ASP.NET 2.0: Your visual blueprint for developing Web applications*. He is also a contributor to Microsoft's Work Essentials Web site and Windows Vista Expert Zone. When he's not writing, he enjoys traveling, gastronomy, and doing nothing. He is currently based in Washington DC and tracks his activities at www.derektorres.net.

Stuart Mudie is a Scot living in Paris, France. A professional communicator since 1995, he has worked with numerous companies in the IT and Telecommunications sectors in such fields as mobile applications and services, Web content management systems, and business intelligence. He has been blogging regularly about all of this (and also about food, wine, languages and music, just a few of his other loves) since 2001 at www.blethers.com.

Contents

It's not every day that Microsoft releases a new operating system, so it's with great pleasure that we offer you the *Unofficial Guide to Windows Vista.* Though it seems like this operating system would never see the light of day, it's finally here and we think you're going to like what you see.

If you are already using Windows Vista, we hope that this book will help you navigate the ins and outs of the latest addition to the Windows family. If you're considering buying Windows Vista, we hope that this book will make your decision easier before taking those first steps.

This book is, in a way, the continuation of the *Unofficial Guide to Windows XP.* Not everything in Windows Vista changed, so you may notice that some sections in this book remain the same from the Windows XP version. However, any new or updated features are completely rewritten to give you the most up-to-date information possible.

Microsoft received a lot of bad press in the run up to the Vista release; some of this criticism was well-deserved, while at other times it seemed to come from people who had little knowledge of what a software development cycle is like. Our goal in this book is to give you the good, the bad, and everything in between. Being neither pro-nor-anti-Microsoft, we like to think that we've praised the good things and spared no punches where Redmond got it wrong. All things considered, we believe Microsoft has put out a solid operating system that will please many users, especially technically-oriented users. Our hope is to show you perhaps a different way of doing things, or simply just a quick tip to help you become more productive.

We have strived to make this book as technically accurate and up-to-date as possible. Every care was taken to represent the very latest information. However, it's important to note that this book was written during the Beta 2 through RC (Release Candidate) stage of Windows Vista development. Any last minute information that is available after publishing can be found on our companion Web site at www.unofficialvista.com.

One final note before we begin — keep in mind that this is version 1.0 of a major operating system. If you've been around software shops as long as we have, then you know that 1.0 doesn't mean that it's perfect. Vista still has bugs, glitches, and other annoyances. These will all be worked out over time; in the meantime, sit back and enjoy everything Vista has to offer.

Making the most of this book

Every book in the Unofficial Guide series offers the following four special sidebars that are devised to help you get things done cheaply, efficiently, and smartly.

1. **Hack:** Tips and shortcuts that increase productivity.

2. **Watch Out!:** Cautions and warnings to help you avoid common pitfalls.

3. **Bright Idea:** Smart or innovative ways to do something; in many cases, this will be a way that you can save time or hassle.

4. **Inside Scoop:** Useful knowledge gleaned by the author that can help you become more efficient.

Installation, Configuration, and Customization

PART I

GET THE SCOOP ON...
The history of Windows Vista ▪ What's new in Vista ▪
What Microsoft did right and wrong ▪ Members of the
Vista family ▪ Pricing Vista

The Road to Windows Vista

After several years of chatter, rumors, leaked information, and random hearsay, Windows Vista is finally here! This highly anticipated unveiling is the first major release for home users since Windows XP in 2001. It also promises to feature more of what users want and more of what they need, including enhanced security, which has never been one of Microsoft's perceived strong points.

In this chapter, we go back to school for just a bit and review our history: How did we get to Windows Vista and where is Microsoft going with it? More importantly, we help you decide for yourself whether or not now is the time for you to make the move to this long overdue operating system!

A brief history of Windows Vista

Several years ago, word of the next Windows operating system tentatively entitled "Longhorn" made its way across the Internet. Amateur Web sites and bloggers all loved sharing their thoughts about how the new Windows OS would work. Fast forward to July 22, 2005, and Microsoft reveals that they are preparing a new operating system that is called Windows Vista (named, curiously, for a pub in British Columbia, Canada).

However, Windows Vista was never supposed to be the topic of IT water cooler conversations or even a major release like Windows 95 or Windows XP. In fact, it was

3

originally meant to be an intermediary release between Windows XP and Windows "Vienna" (or Blackcomb). As deadlines were missed, as often happens in the software field, Windows Vista started to implement features of Windows Vienna, and it grew into something it was never meant to be, which is a full-fledged major operating system release and not just an upgrade.

Windows Vista was officially named the next release by Microsoft, while Microsoft Vienna has been relegated to a release date not worth publishing. As time went on, Vista continued to implement features intended for Vienna. However, as Microsoft tried to include as many features as possible for this release, there was some concern that reliability, simplicity, and scalability would all be sacrificed for new features. As a result, Microsoft scaled down some of their new features for the Vista release. One of the biggest casualties was the new WinFS feature. WinFS, or Windows Future Storage, is a data storage and management system that runs on a relational database (which is a database that uses a relational model and runs on RDBMS software). For more information on WinFS, check out http://msdn.microsoft.com/data/winfs/.

Development of Microsoft Vista using the Windows Server 2003 code base was soon underway. After months and months of work, Vista Beta 1 (Build 5112) was released to a select group of testers including MSDN and TechNet members.

Microsoft then started the CTP program (Community Technical Preview) that allows Beta testers and MSDN members to download and install builds. The CTP program is a monthly program that offers a "snapshot" of Windows Vista's current status. In February 2006, Microsoft released the February CTP, which was the first feature-complete version of Windows Vista. Microsoft soon after released an intermediary build that took into consideration initial feedback from the February CTP.

In March 2006, Microsoft announced that it would be delaying the Microsoft Windows Vista release. As you can imagine, there was a lot of speculation about the reason for the delay and rumors were rife that the product was not up to quality standards. Of course, anyone who was a Windows Vista tester knew this to be unlikely as the Beta builds were relatively stable and feature-complete. Microsoft's decision was more likely based on a combination of marketing and quality concerns. In fact, Microsoft decided to implement a two-tier rollout plan: Those with volume licensing agreements would be able to upgrade first, and the general public would then receive Windows Vista.

As a result of this delay, the next CTP would now be released at the end of May 2006 instead of April 2006. This is the first CTP that is considered a Beta 2 equivalent. This version is available through the Customer Preview Program, which allowed the general public to freely download the operating system and give it a try. This was a win-win situation; users who were curious to try out the software could do so without having to pay for it, and Microsoft could use their customer base to test their product for them.

Microsoft continued to issue monthly CTP releases until the final release date. Post Beta 2, Microsoft released a July CTP to a select audience, and then released a Pre-RC1 (Release Candidate) at the end of August. This Pre-RC1 version was greeted very warmly by the tech community, especially from a number of industry notables who were very critical of the post Beta 2 builds. Just several days after the Pre-RC1 release, Microsoft released the RC1 build (5600), which is the version we used when writing this book.

Windows Vista will be made available in November 2006, according to the current schedule, to volume licensed businesses before being released to the general public in January 2007.

Throughout this period, quality control and stability of the Beta-level builds was a major concern of analysts and testers alike. Many professionals felt that the Beta-level CTPs simply were not stable enough to proceed to a final build candidate. As a result, there were a number of professionals (who really were pro-Vista) who advocated for delaying Windows Vista yet again in order to iron out all the bugs before releasing it to the public. The fact that CTP builds had varying quality (some releases were stable, while others were buggy) and consistency made gauging the true status of Vista hard to determine. Fortunately, things seemed to take a turn for the better performance-wise with the Pre-RC1 edition.

Microsoft as a company also took a number of public relation hits during the summer of 2006. Ongoing litigation with the European Union saw Brussels levy a massive fine against Microsoft, which didn't help already slipping stock prices. In July, Bill Gates announced that in 2008 he would stop his day-to-day activities at Microsoft and hand over the reins to Steve Ballmer and Ray Ozzie. Microsoft also incurred delays with the long anticipated Microsoft Office 2007 release. Finally, a top executive who was fairly visible in the public eye was released or quit under mysterious circumstances. All of these reasons, combined with the specter of yet another Vista delay, pointed to a general feeling of concern and negativity surrounding Microsoft and their upcoming releases.

What's new in Windows Vista?

As you can imagine, Microsoft pulled out all the stops when putting together their wish list for Windows Vista. From features to security, there's something for everyone in the first incarnation of Windows Vista. For example, the first time we installed Windows Vista on our machines, we immediately thought of Linux and Mac OS X and how these users would appreciate the look and feel of their respective operating system. FireFox users will undoubtedly notice how Microsoft "borrowed" from the FireFox user interface in Internet Explorer 7.

Users will be pleased with Microsoft's latest offering — some new features are overhauled existing features and others are completely new! This section doesn't mention every new feature in Windows Vista, but it gives you a good idea of what awaits you! Each feature we describe in the following paragraphs is discussed in greater detail in various parts of the book.

Working with the Vista interface

Are you a home user? If so, some of the new features may impress you, while others will confuse you. For example, one of the first things you notice is that the ubiquitous Start button is now relegated to history's trash bin. Once the lynchpin of the entire Windows user interface, it is now replaced by a Windows "orb," for lack of a better expression. Despite the change in physical representation, this is still referred to as the Start menu. Users may also be surprised to find out what is hiding from them behind the Windows orb, as the appearance of the Start menu changes drastically in Windows Vista. These changes are covered in far greater detail in Chapter 4. Personally, our first reaction to seeing Windows Vista was "the menus are dark!" Also new is the navigation style of the Start menu; the days of this menu expanding to fill your entire screen are gone.

The new Welcome Center window appears at startup (yes, you can disable it). You can find extensive system information (see Figure 1.1). The bottom portion of the Welcome Center contains extra information such

Watch Out!

Not every feature is available in every edition of Windows Vista. Rather than start every paragraph with edition information, we provide a table at the end of this chapter that features new Windows Vista features and in what editions you can find them.

as Internet shortcuts, information on Vista, setting up various Vista features, and so on. It also features some self-promotion, whereby you can access or download a number of new Windows Live services.

The notification bar at the bottom-right side of the screen also appears differently than in XP. Although it has many familiar icons, it does include some new icons, including how your Internet connection appears. The dialog boxes in Vista now appear with a metallic, yet transparent, look about them. In fact, it reminds us quite a lot of Mac OS X dialog boxes and windows. It also reminds us a lot of Linux; two of Microsoft's biggest detractors now find themselves with a competitor that really is not so different from them in a number of ways.

Figure 1.1. The Microsoft Vista desktop.

If you are Aero-ready, you're going to be bowled over by how cool Windows Vista looks. It's well worth the extra hardware to check out this new desktop experience. From transparency, to interactive mouse pointers, to much improved window toggling options, Aero is a massive improvement that finally brings Microsoft into the twenty-first century. For example, in the taskbar, you can get a glimpse of what is in the application, file, or folder by placing your mouse over the taskbar icon. A real-time representation of its contents appears as a thumbnail above the taskbar. All this and more, thanks to Aero. If you aren't Aero compatible, this feature will not work; the standard alt text appears instead.

Folders and directories also have a refreshed look in Microsoft Vista (see Figure 1.2). These elements are much more icon oriented than in past versions of Windows. Although this is generally an improvement over Windows XP, adjusting to folders and directories make take some time. Folders now include powerful search features, such as preloaded saved searches for easy, on-the-fly searches with amazingly fast results. An embedded Favorites menu enables you to switch to other folders quickly. A new toolbar and navigation bar allow you to navigate with ease. Windows' Documents, Pictures, and Music folders in Windows Explorer are also color-coded in Vista, so that you can set them apart from other folders. Strangely enough, the video folder keeps the standard yellow color.

The Control Panel is also revamped in this new release. If you switch to the Classic mode, you can see exactly what we mean. (We discuss several new options later in this chapter.) The Control Panel can admittedly look a bit overwhelming at first; you may feel lost among the new icons and themes. However, as you familiarize yourself with Windows Vista, you see that everything is in its logical place. The use of links to help you find specific tasks is particularly helpful; now that we've been using it for a while, we find it quite helpful.

Finally, Windows offers *gadgets*, which are customizable mini-applications that facilitate certain user tasks. The Windows sidebar organizes your gadgets into an easy-to-use tool. Microsoft has created three different types of gadgets: desktop, Web, and device. For Windows Vista, you can use desktop gadgets. Web gadgets are for use with Web sites, such as start.com, while device gadgets run on external displays. Gadgets can be used on your desktop or on the Sidebar. You can also use them in conjunction with the start.com Web site. Currently an incubation experiment (meaning that it's not quite ready to go), this Web site lets you configure

Inside Scoop

Gadgets are designed to be used interchangeably among the environments. For example, you could use a Web gadget with the Windows Vista Sidebar.

an online version of the Sidebar using gadgets. Start.com, while a pretty neat idea, isn't the most visibly attractive site on the Internet. In fact, its rather bare-bones look might turn off a few users. Nevertheless, it's another option on the table if you want to use gadgets.

These gadgets, which we discuss in greater detail in Chapter 4, can be created either in DHTML (Dynamic Hypertext Markup Language) or a .NET language (for example, C# or VB.NET).

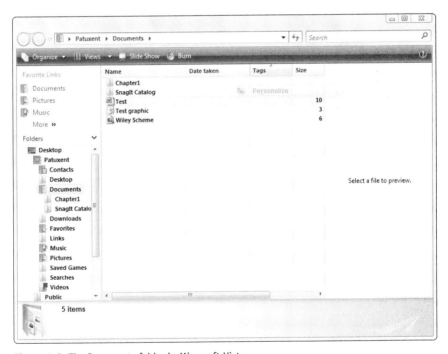

Figure 1.2. The Documents folder in Microsoft Vista.

Control Panel

As mentioned earlier in this chapter, the content and the look and feel of the Control Panel have changed extensively in Windows Vista (see Figure 1.3). The Vista Control Panel now integrates the Windows Explorer framework. Although you can still choose either the new or the Classic Control Panel mode (à la XP), it has a new color scheme and number of new system icons. This makes configuring your computer even easier. If you open one of these menus/icons, you find a whole series of subject-related (category-based) settings that you can choose from. These settings are detailed in descriptive terminology that makes it easier for users to understand exactly what they're getting into. Additional options appear on the left side of these windows that allow you to select from other related settings and services.

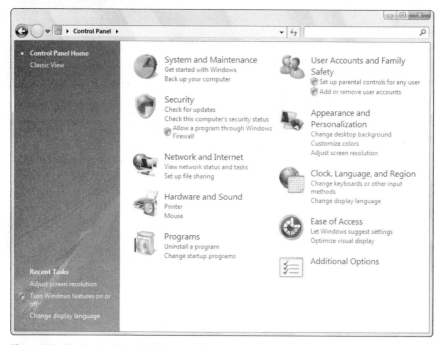

Figure 1.3. The Control Panel is bigger and better in Windows Vista.

Searches

Windows Vista has added two new controls to its search feature: Instant Search and Enhanced Column Headers. The Instant Search feature is found in the Start menu (as detailed in the next paragraph), while the Enhanced Column Headers facilitates how data is displayed. These features are detailed in Chapter 4.

Inside Scoop

Using the Instant Search, not only can you find Start menu applications by typing the first letters, you can also find hidden files as well as system files. This is helpful, for example, when calling the Microsoft Management Console.

When you click the Windows orb, you can see the Instant Search box at the bottom of the menu. You can insert just about anything, including a part of a filename or a property, and click the Search icon. To make things easier, you can even add keywords to file properties for future recall. In many ways, the Instant Search box makes up for the now defunct Run features. We've also seen this feature referred to as the Live Search. You can also use this search in the Control Panel to quickly locate what you're looking for.

Windows Vista also features a new tool called Search Folders. The name is a little confusing because you don't use this feature to search file folders; you use it to save search criteria for later use. Using the Search Folders tool, you can go back and perform another search using previously defined criteria. Windows Vista features a number of preloaded "saved" searches. By clicking them, you receive virtually instantaneous results.

XPS support

Microsoft created its response to Adobe's PDF standard; XPS (XML Paper Specification) is a static document format that can be used in Windows Vista. In Vista and its applications, you can print to the Microsoft XPS Document Writer, which appears by default in Vista Print windows.

The need for XPS is debatable. Microsoft had planned on creating a PDF filter in Microsoft Office, which would have let users save Word documents as a PDF directly from the Save window. Unfortunately, due to legal reasons, this feature was removed and Microsoft XPS becomes Microsoft's de facto cross-platform document reader and writer.

Live Icons

Remember the bland, ugly icons of Windows past? Vista now offers Live Icons (provided you have the right graphics hardware). These icons still represent files and their type; however, unlike the standard icon, these icons literally display a true view of the actual file. If you have a Word file icon, you can see text of the first available file. If it's a graphic, a thumbnail of the graphic appears in the folder icon (see Figure 1.4).

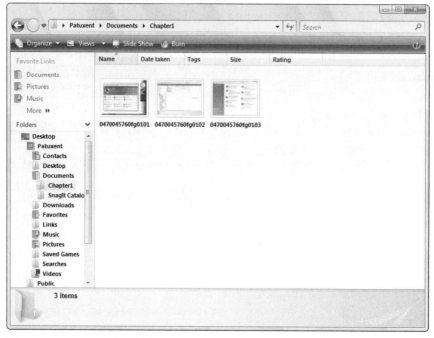

Figure 1.4. Live icons make folder browsing a little less boring.

Borders

In past versions, moving and resizing windows was difficult because of how svelte windows and dialog box borders are. Borders and headers of windows and dialog boxes in Aero are now wider so that you can move folders with ease. This feature change isn't as readily apparent in the Vista Basic environment.

Performance

The folks in Redmond clearly did their homework when it came to re-defining performance. And this is why we applaud Microsoft for righting some past wrongs. On the other hand, it's clear that innovation suffered at times due to focus on performance and security updates. So, what's new in terms of performance enhancements?

First and foremost, installation is considerably faster than previous versions of Windows. Startup time is also considerably faster. For example, we've noticed that it often takes two to three minutes for Windows XP to load everything and become functional. With Windows Vista, it took approximately 40 seconds from startup to being fully operational.

Another performance enhancement is the new Sleep feature. Sleep is a state somewhere in between Standby and Hibernate. Sleep can "wake up" as quickly as a computer set in Standby, but it also better protects data and consumes less battery power as if it were in Hibernate. How sleep works depends on your computer; if it is a desktop, the computer saves any open files or applications to both RAM and to the hard drive. On a laptop, it saves this information to RAM and then transfers it to the hard drive when battery power starts to wane.

The new SuperFetch feature tells Windows Vista to notice which applications you use the most and to store them into memory. As a result, recall is considerably faster. This is a marked improvement over previous behavior; for example, once you boot your computer, launching an often-used application could take a while or it might crash. The SuperFetch feature stores this application into memory so that it can launch the application at startup or post-crash quickly. In Windows XP, launching an application can be a tediously slow experience.

There are also EMD (external memory device) technology and hybrid hard drives to consider. When running Windows Vista, you can increase memory capacity by adding a USB flash drive as an EMD.

Hybrid hard drives are also new and compatible with Windows Vista. They contain an on-board flash memory buffer. Windows Vista uses this drive for major tasks, such as startup, hibernate, and faster reboots. These will eventually be a "strongly recommended" or even required piece of hardware of mobile users. We say eventually because hybrid

Watch Out!

If you add a USB flash drive as an EMD, keep in mind that the increased capabilities are only available so long as the USB drive is still plugged in. Once you remove it, the computer goes back to its original configuration.

drives are not intended to hit stores in the United States until June 2007 (date subject to change). As far as we know, these drives are only available for laptops.

Sidebar and gadgets

As discussed in the previous section and earlier in this chapter, the Windows Vista Sidebar and gadgets are a very important part of this release. The Windows Sidebar gives you direct access to your gadgets, thereby saving you time and finger energy and increasing productivity.

The Windows Sidebar sits on your desktop much like the Office Sidebar, where you can put often-used gadgets "in" it and easily call them back when necessary (see Figure 1.5). It works well with standard monitors and is ideal for widescreen monitors.

The gadgets, or mini-applications, are small, yet helpful applications that easily integrate into your Windows Vista experience. Though Windows ships with several gadgets on board; you can also download some over the Internet. They can be used with your desktop or used when using such Microsoft Web sites as Live.com.

Figure 1.5. The Windows Sidebar.

Ease of Access Center

Microsoft has improved its accessibility options through the creation of the Ease of Access Center. It allows you to set up accessibility tools from a single location, making Windows available for everyone. You can access it from the Control Panel or even enable accessibility features from the logon screen. One intriguing new feature is the speech recognition feature, which lets you teach your computer to recognize your voice so that you can control your computer vocally instead of using your mouse and keyboard.

Introducing Internet Explorer 7

Undoubtedly one of the most noticeable new features in Microsoft Windows Vista is the long-anticipated Internet Explorer 7. Even if you have not yet installed Windows Vista, you can get a taste of Microsoft's follow-up to IE 6 because it is also available for Windows XP. From the moment you launch the application, it's hard to miss several new features from the very minute you launch the browser.

For example, you can now search multiple search engines from the user interface (see Figure 1.6). In the options menu adjacent to the search box, you can easily select a new default search provider from a pretty extensive list. In fact, you can even take care of shopping from this menu by selecting one of many online boutiques. This list of search providers and boutiques includes such heavyweights as Yahoo!, AOL, Google, Amazon, MSN, Lycos, Target, and even the Weather Channel!

In what we interpret to be a nod to Firefox, Internet Explorer 7 also features tabs.

Instead of having to open up a new browser window, you can simply open up a new tab and work within the same window (see Figure 1.7). Unlike its competitor, you can also right-click the tab and perform basic tasks (close one or more tabs, refresh a tab, or create a new tab).

Internet Explorer 7 also makes cleaning up easier. A one-button cleanup feature clears passwords, temporary files, and caches. This new feature lets you clear pretty much anything quickly, which is a change from past versions.

You can also subscribe to RSS (Really Simple Syndication) feeds directly from Internet Explorer 7. This feature is useful for frequent blog readers who do not have enough time to read blog updates — RSS brings the updates to you.

Figure 1.6. The Internet Explorer 7 search provider list.

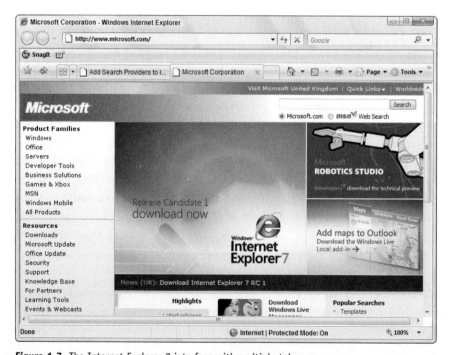

Figure 1.7. The Internet Explorer 7 interface with multiple tabs open.

Bright Idea

For more information on phishing, check out the Wikipedia entry at http://en.wikipedia.org/wiki/Phishing or visit the Anti-Phishing Working Group at www.antiphishing.org/.

Another great feature is the new anti-phishing feature that protects users from sites that might be phishing sites. Phishing is an attempt to commit fraud over e-mail. A user is asked to click on a link purporting to be a legitimate site, but really the site is bogus and is designed to solicit and store personal details that can then be used for nefarious reasons.

Improved security

Microsoft Windows Vista offers a number of new security features that are sure to please users. For example, Windows integrated their Windows AntiSpyware application — now called Microsoft Defender — into Windows Vista. Defender scans and protects your computer from dangerous spyware and other harmful applications that can infiltrate your computer.

The User Account Control is another improved feature in Windows Vista that is designed to protect you and your family while online by using the Parental Controls (see Figure 1.8). Parents can use this feature to prevent their children from accessing certain applications or accessing inappropriate Web sites. You can create limited accounts for children, for example, that prevent them from installing new software.

The improved firewall that ships with Windows Vista is now a bi-directional firewall. In other words, the firewall scans both incoming and outgoing data flow. This is an improvement over the Windows XP firewall, which only monitored incoming data. It also remedies a major concern with respect to Microsoft and safety. Currently, most firewalls available on the market offer bi-directional protection. Even Microsoft detractors will laud this major security improvement.

Windows BitLocker™ is another new Vista feature that helps you increase system security. When activated, it encrypts your entire hard drive. By using a special key that you generate (and save to an external media device, such as a flash drive), you can "unlock" your computer. This feature is particularly helpful if your computer is lost or stolen.

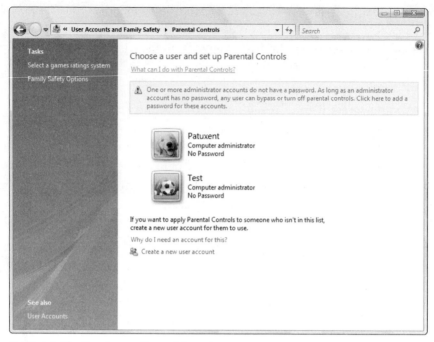

Figure 1.8. The User Account Parental Controls.

Creating backups

Windows Vista has improved backup capabilities that make backing up data safer and easier. There are now several levels of backup as well as protection from hardware failure.

Two new backup features include Windows Backup and the Volume Shadow Copy that up until now was only available in versions of Windows Server. The Windows Backup feature now features a new wizard that you can use to schedule backups. Because most of us tend to forget about backing up our machine due to life's daily activities and stresses, you can simply program when Windows should automatically back up your files. The Volume Shadow Copy, on the other hand, is a new backup feature that lets you save files at a specific point in time so that you can easily recall them in the event of file corruption or deleted file. Vista also suggests that you perform a backup the first time you launch Vista after installation; this is available from the notification area.

Windows Vista also features an improvement to the application called System Restore (see Figure 1.9). Unlike in Windows XP, you can now create a Shadow Copy (see Figure 1.9), which is a backup copy of a file or folder taken like a snapshot at a particular point in time. This way, you can call back a restore point from a specific time.

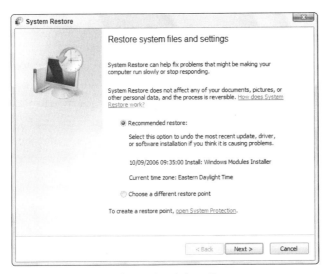

Figure 1.9. The Backup feature in Windows Vista.

Synching data

The new Data Sync feature is designed to let users synchronize data between multiple computers, between a computer and a server, and between your computer and handheld devices. While this will facilitate your life by making sure your PDA and laptop have the same information, it is important to note that Windows Vista does not integrate any third-party sync tools. For example, if you wish to sync your Palm Pilot, you will need to make sure you have the proper software from the manufacturer so that you can sync it with Windows Vista.

Speech recognition

As mentioned earlier in the Ease of Access section, Windows Vista now makes it possible to use speech recognition software to work with your computer using your voice. Using commonly used applications, you can dictate documents or e-mails or even fill out forms. Speech recognition is part of the Section 508 legislation in the United States that required software to be readable (in other words, compatible with several reader standards) for speech recognition software.

Windows SideShow

Windows SideShow (see Figure 1.10), not to be confused with SlideShow, is a new technology designed for laptops that allows users to store important information, such as contacts or e-mails. You can even listen to your favorite tunes using the Windows Media Player through SideShow. This information can then be displayed using a secondary (built-in) display without having to power up your computer. This is a feature for mobile computers only; however, most laptops currently available in retail stores do not have this secondary display. This display is usually no more than several inches by several inches in size.

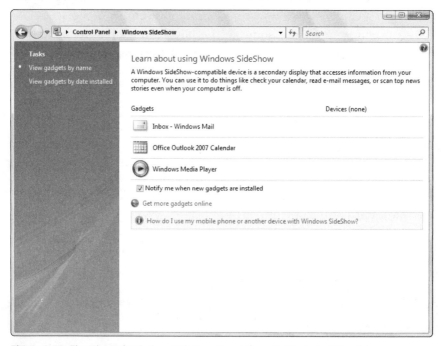

Figure 1.10. The Microsoft Windows SideShow is set through the Control Panel.

Windows multimedia

Windows Vista features new multimedia features and updates. What was formerly called Windows Movie Maker is now the Windows DVD Maker.

Depending on your edition of Vista, you can watch or record live television. Windows Media Player 11 also ships with Windows Vista releases (unless you reside within the European Union).

Windows Update

Okay, this feature is not new but rather an improvement over the version in Windows XP. The Windows Update feature now is certainly more low-key; for example, you can tell it to automatically update you computer without the intrusive dialog boxes that appear in Windows XP. You can perform Windows Update (see Figure 1.11) either running as a background application or as a primary application before installing your updates. Critics maintain that Windows uses an archaic Web-based updater; however, we dispute such a notion. Unlike Windows XP, which required Internet Explorer to download updates, Windows Vista lets you do everything from a window without having to use your browser.

This overview highlights some of the new features that await you in Microsoft Windows Vista. These features, as well as others, are detailed in their respective sections throughout this book.

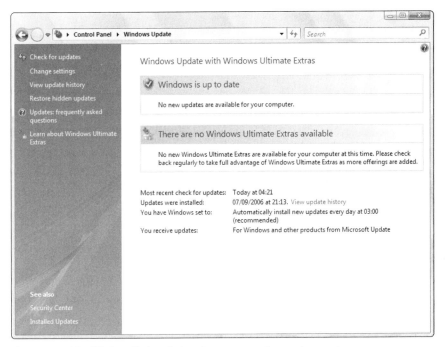

Figure 1.11. The Windows Update feature keeps your system up to speed.

Other applications

Windows Vista features some new goodies, most of which are detailed later in this book. For those who are tired of the same old toys, Vista has included some new games in its repertoire. The Outlook Express mail client is now replaced by Microsoft Mail, which is really the same product with a new name although it does feature some new, albeit very necessary, security tools. Windows Meeting Space is a new online collaboration tool that enables you to work remotely and share files with other users.

It also features several other low-level applications, like Calendar and Contacts, whose functions are fairly obvious. These are basically freebie apps that don't add much value to Vista since they are often replaced with more powerful applications, for example, Microsoft Office.

Windows Vista also features a Media Center (Ultimate edition) that lets you access pretty much every source of existing multimedia, if you have the hardware to do it. In other media news, Vista now has a Microsoft venture called URGE (see Figure 1.12), which is akin to Apple's iTunes. Finally, Microsoft continues Marketplace, which is a Microsoft portal that allows you to buy Vista-ready equipment from third-party vendors.

Figure 1.12. URGE, Microsoft's foray into digital music sales.

The many editions of Windows Vista

Not surprisingly, Windows Vista is available in a number of different versions that are really focused on a specific type of user. In fact, six different

Watch Out!

Do not attempt to run 64-bit Windows on a 32-bit computer; it will not work. If you are not sure if your computer is 32-bit or 64-bit, it's a safe bet that you are running a 32-bit computer.

editions are available, all of which come in 32- and 64-bit formats (with the exception of the Windows Vista Starter, which we discuss later in the chapter).

The new editions are Windows Vista Starter, Windows Vista Home Basic, Windows Vista Home Premium, Windows Vista Business, Windows Vista Enterprise, and Windows Vista Ultimate.

What? Well, you certainly can't say that Microsoft didn't leave you any choice when it comes to picking your Vista (and if you think this list is impressive, wait until you see the list of Office 2007 editions!). But, which one is right for you?

Picking the right version will not be a difficult choice, simply because as a consumer you only really have three options: Home Basic, Home Premium, and Ultimate.

Deciding on which of the three to go for is easy; simply ask yourself a few questions, such as "Is multimedia important to me?", "Will I need to create a small office network at home?", "How old is my PC?", or "Do I really just need an OS to run my computer?"

Let's take a closer look at each version and find the right Vista for you.

Windows Vista Starter

The Starter edition is, if you are reading this book, an edition you will most likely never, ever see. In an effort to combat the spread of pirated and counterfeit software, Microsoft created the Starter edition that is only available in countries that have "emerging market" status.

The Starter edition is severely limited in terms of functionality; in fact, you can only open up to three windows at a time. This is also the only Windows Vista edition that does not have a 64-bit version; it can only be used in 32-bit. Quite frankly, this version is a bare-bones version of Windows Vista and would not do heavy-duty users much good.

One can surmise that the idea behind the Starter edition is to try and prevent software piracy. Unfortunately, software piracy will probably never go away; however, by releasing Starter editions, software companies might be taking a big step toward reducing piracy since this version is slated to be considerably cheaper than other versions of Windows Vista. Of course, once software pirates see what the Starter edition is missing, they will most likely be back to old tricks with any of the following editions!

Windows Vista Home Basic

The Home Basic edition is the equivalent of the Windows XP Home edition. This edition is probably the best, or most practical, edition for your typical home user.

The Home Basic edition is a no-frills operating system that has a nice balance of features and security that are more than suitable for most home users. The Basic edition, like all Vista editions, includes most of the new features that are now available in Vista. However, there is one notable exception, the Aero Glass theme that you will read about in Chapter 4 is not available in Home Basic, but there is an Aero interface, albeit one that is not transparent.

Windows Vista Home Premium

If you have to think of an XP equivalent for Home Premium, I guess you could say that it's like a little bit of Home Basic and a whole lot of Windows XP Media Center Edition. Home Premium has all the features found in Basic, but it also features new multimedia features, such as HDTM support and DVD authoring. It also features the Aero Glass theme that Basic does not offer.

Home Premium also features all of the Media Center Edition features, in addition to the two listed above. If you are lucky enough to find someplace with an Xbox 360 in stock, you can also connect Home Premium to the console for use in multiple rooms.

Windows Vista Business

The first in the line of "big boys," Windows Vista Business is the modern-day equivalent of XP Professional. If you used Windows XP Professional, Windows Vista Business is the most similar edition.

Business edition prides itself on being ideal for all size deployments, but the justification for such a statement is not quite clear. It looks like Professional has been rebranded as Business in order to put more emphasis on how Windows can improve your business acumen (a debatable point) as well as offer more professional-level system tools — such as spyware blockers, new backup technologies, and the new Small Business Resources. Curiously, the one missing feature here is still the elephant in the room — where is the on-board antivirus software?

This is the first Vista edition to offer Windows Server domain support and a new version of IIS (Internet Information Services), neither of which are available with the Home versions.

It also features improved organizational features so that you can better run your business.

Windows Vista Enterprise

The Vista Enterprise edition is the older cousin to the Business edition. As far as your average user is concerned, they will not ever have access to the Enterprise edition. In other words, if you buy your operating systems, you will not be using the Enterprise edition. The Enterprise edition is not available for retail purchase, nor is it available as an OEM (meaning that computers shipped with Microsoft Windows operating systems will not have this version).

However, if you work for a large company or one that uses a significant number of Windows licenses, it is possible that you may use this edition of Microsoft Vista. If this is you, then this is what you need to know about Vista Enterprise: It features a multilingual user interface and is bundled with Virtual PC as well as a new drive encryption feature.

If you work in a multilingual or international environment, you can use the Enterprise edition to change the language or dialog boxes and menus on the fly. Using the Virtual PC feature, you can emulate a "foreign" operating system in order to run applications. Finally, the Windows BitLocker™ Drive Encryption helps protect data in case your computer (especially laptops) is lost or stolen. Curiously, this new data protection feature is not available in Vista Business. If you want it, you'll need to pony up the dough and buy the Windows Vista Ultimate edition.

Windows Vista Ultimate

The Vista Ultimate edition is the total package for the home user that needs that extra bit of power. We preface this section by saying that if you do not have a powerful, souped-up PC, then this edition is not for you. A true multimedia powerhouse, this edition is really suited to gamers or PC home-theater fans.

Watch Out!

Microsoft Windows Vista is shipping on a DVD, as it is easier than CD-ROM due to data size limitations. While the media may look the same, you must have a DVD-ROM player on your computer in order to install Windows Vista. If you are using a simple CD-ROM drive, the CD cannot be read. If you have an older machine, please refer to your computer documentation to verify the capacity of your ROM drive.

Ultimate edition mixes the best of both Home Premium and Business features and adds a few more toys: a new DVD-ripping feature, a tool that tweaks game performance, and podcasting support. Microsoft does not use the term podcasting, however — it has been reborn as blogcasting.

How it will ship

Microsoft is shipping the three retail versions (Home Basic, Home Premium, and Ultimate) on a single DVD. If you do not have a DVD-ROM drive, we believe that Vista will also be made available on a multiple-CD set, though it is worth noting that every pre-sale source lists only DVD versions of Windows Vista. If you are planning on using Premium or Ultimate, you can enter an unlock code through the Control Panel.

Should I make the jump to Windows Vista?

This is basically a rhetorical question; here's another. Can you really afford not to make the jump? Bad questioning aside, both of these questions can be answered with a short answer: Yes.

All things considered, the learning curve for Windows XP users making the upgrade to Windows Vista is not significant if switching between equivalents. Windows XP Home users upgrading to Windows Vista Home Basic should not have much trouble getting used to the new features and layout. Former XP Home users looking to upgrade to Windows Vista Ultimate may have a steeper learning curve as there are more technologically "heavy" features in this edition of Vista. The primary changes for most users to adapt to are simply the change in the Start menus and how things are displayed.

You may have noticed that within the past year, more and more software applications required at least the use of Microsoft Windows XP SP2. As Windows Vista becomes more and more mainstream (read: as more and more people are comfortable with installing or upgrading to a new

Watch Out!

Some people, especially businesses that must upgrade a number of computers in order to run Microsoft Vista, are hesitant to install the first release of an operating system. Given the important role an OS plays in the operation of a computer, Microsoft surely recognizes this and would probably not release a product that is not ready to see the light of day. If you have doubts, you can always wait until a subsequent release, such as Service Pack 1, to make the jump.

operating system), more and more applications will be available that are built on Vista technology. For example, you could run Microsoft Office 2007 on Windows XP SP 2, but why? The software was designed to use Vista's display and search features. Most peripheral developers now have Vista-compatible drivers available for their products. Fortunately, Windows Vista does a pretty good job of installing those drivers during Vista installation.

Eventually, there will come a point in time where you will have to make the jump or switch to another operating system. Even the most loyal fans of Windows 3.11 and Windows 95 saw the writing on the wall and switched when it was time.

Ultimately, we feel that most users will be happy with Windows Vista and the new features and security that it provides. If you don't believe me, the next 600 or so pages are here to convince you.

What Microsoft did right

Microsoft definitely pulled out all the stops when it came to designing and releasing Windows Vista. From the beta, Microsoft did an overall good job in communicating with partners and releasing remarkably stable beta builds for review and testing. We also appreciate how Microsoft maintained transparency throughout the early stages of Microsoft Vista development.

One of the first things Microsoft did right is Internet Explorer 7. This new and very improved Web browser clearly intended to fix previous wrongs by putting more emphasis on security and personal protection. This includes the new anti-phishing tool that helps crack down on phishing sites. One of the biggest compliments that we can give Internet Explorer 7 is that it looks like its developers were greatly inspired by its free competitor, FireFox. Similar features include the use of tabs to a one-stop cache/history clearing button, not to mention search engines available from the application interface. For a brief period of time, IE7 launched with two open tabs — your home page (www.msn.com by default) and the Windows Live Web site. Fortunately, this was quickly corrected so that only the home page appeared. Overall, you may personally prefer another browser; it's hard to argue that IE7 isn't an improvement over IE6.

Another reason to celebrate Microsoft Vista is the new anti-spyware application called Microsoft Defender. Finally catching up and responding to one of the biggest security threats to home users in recent years, Microsoft finally released an "in house" application that checks for and removes dangerous spyware from your machine. If you are unfamiliar with spyware and its risks, it is software that can display pop-ups (advertisements) or track user actions and collect personal data or modify personalized settings in Windows.

Defender is designed to sit in the background and monitor your computer in real-time; should Spyware or any other malicious software cause a security breech, Defender asks you to take action. You can also program Defender to scan your computer at your leisure. You can manually update the latest spyware definitions from the application interface or set the application to download updates as they become available.

Yes, Microsoft already has an existing anti-spyware application called Microsoft Windows AntiSpyware, but this application never left beta status and was never integrated with a Microsoft Windows release. Defender is the next version of Microsoft Windows AntiSpyware and is integrated with Microsoft Vista.

The improved firewall is another positive security enhancement as it offers bidirectional support — it monitors both inbound and outbound data. Surprisingly, it has taken Microsoft a longer time that I would have hoped to offer this rather basic firewall feature, but it's better late than never! The disk encryption feature (BitLocker™ Drive Encryption) is a nod to PGP, which has offered such protection for years, but it is also a welcome addition to the Windows Vista family, if you buy the right edition.

Microsoft has also improved its search functions by including a new desktop search feature. This new search function is lightning fast compared to the Windows XP search function. If you are connected to a Microsoft Vista network, you can also expand the search to include computers on the Vista network.

Aero is also a really cool feature or environment; however, it's value depends on how much you use your computer or are willing to spend on it. Its enhanced visualizations make the long hours we log on our computers worth the extra hardware.

Finally, Windows greatly improves the installation process. What used to take well over an hour depending on how powerful your computer is now takes approximately 35 minutes to install and minutes to set up once installed.

Microsoft spent a lot of time playing catch-up with the Windows Vista release. Where innovation may not be the number one priority in this release, it definitely corrects a fair amount of past wrongs, which shows that Microsoft has its head pointing in the right direction.

What Microsoft got wrong

Microsoft is not totally out of the dog house, despite the many stellar qualities of this Vista release. For example, despite the focused look on improved security, Microsoft has never put out one of the most glaringly missing tools: an antivirus software application. Although it may seem that the market may be fairly covered, this has not stopped Microsoft from putting out competitive software in the past. Although you can always sign up for Windows OneCare (a pay subscription service that offers antivirus protection, firewall, and so on), it would have been nice to see it in Microsoft Vista. This is especially true because Windows OneCare is currently only available for Windows XP, though there is currently a Beta version now available for Windows Vista.

While Microsoft is commended in the previous section for correcting previous wrongs or oversights, it is still a shame that there was not room left over for more innovative features. For example, one particularly exciting feature, the WinFS file server, which was originally slated to be part of Microsoft Vista, has been shelved for this release.

The biggest negative surrounding Windows Vista is without a doubt Microsoft's inability to manage PR and communications involving the operating system. Unfortunately, Microsoft always seemed to be reacting to a problem — be it personnel, development, or marketing — instead of getting in front of the problem. As a result, there was quite a bit of concern as to the health of the company on numerous occasions throughout 2005 and 2006. Microsoft's ongoing litigation in Europe and rumblings in Asia didn't help the company's image as they worked to get Vista out the door. The head of Microsoft's operating systems group left just prior to the RC1 release; which didn't seem to affect dates, but neither did it add to perceived company stability.

Another concern is potential computer limitations. For example, one of the authors of this book is running 768MB of RAM with a Pentium 4 processor, and the memory seems barely sufficient. We would not recommend running Microsoft Vista without at least 1GB of RAM on board, despite Microsoft's insistence that 512MB is adequate. Most new computers are currently shipping with at least 512MB of RAM on board, but the minimum is rarely enough to get by let alone take full advantage of resources. If you are lacking in memory, you can go to a more Classic look under Vista to free up system resources, but you want nice and pretty like everyone else, and not to have to pay money for the same old looking Windows, right?

This is a legitimate problem because Windows Vista will make a significant number of computers obsolete. Why? Well, the memory might not be so much a problem as other pieces of hardware, such as video cards. For example, your computer needs to support the Windows Vista Display Driver Model if you want to enjoy the new Aero theme.

In terms of graphics, unless your graphics processor supports DirectX9-level shaders, you cannot take advantage of the 3D accelerated elements. Older graphics cards do not support this, nor do a lot of modern laptops. If you do decide to upgrade your graphics card, you need to re-look your entire computer. If you are using an older or low-end computer, you might not have an AGP or PCI-Express slot (the equivalent of a souped-up PCI slot on your motherboard that is designed for high-quality graphics cards). You may also need to buy a power supply to handle the video card requirements.

So, yeah, many new or recent computers will be able to run Windows Vista, but you do run a significant risk of feature loss. This is particularly a problem in countries outside the United States where hardware or new computers are considerably more expensive, especially due to high local taxes. Microsoft's proposed workaround to the above problems is to simply buy a new Windows Vista-ready computer to replace your old one. Are people ready to spend a lot of money on a new or revamped computer now, especially when Windows XP is a tried and true operating system that has worked fine over the past few years? Are local economies conducive to consumers' spending on new computers and parts?

Two other issues have caused alarm among users, but these are not universally shared concerns. The first is the price: There have been a number of rumblings online and at the water cooler about the pricing scheme. Speaking to the communication problems we mentioned earlier in this section, the Windows Vista pricing information "leaked" to Canadian press and then appeared on the Amazon.com Web site. This pricing information is given in the following section. Given the cost of buying some of the on-board features, such as PGP to replace the disk encryption or third-party DVD ripping software, prices seem to be relatively fair, though certainly not cheap. The second issue is the increased integration of DRM (Digital Rights Management), which involves the protection of audio and video copyrights. This issue is discussed in greater detail in the Windows Media section.

Other members of the Vista family

There is more to the Windows Vista family than meets the eye or is covered in this chapter. In fact, Vista rears its head in a number of different fashions. Not all versions are available for all users and not all versions will necessarily be available at the time of the general release currently planned for January 2007.

Microsoft Windows Vista 64-bit

With the exception of the Starter edition, Windows Vista is available in 64-bit for all other editions. Essentially a recompiled version of the standard 32-bit Vista, this edition provides increased performance and reliability while running natively with a 64-bit processor.

This version is probably not necessary for most home users, but rather developers and other information technology professionals. You can also expect that, for this reason, it will probably be considerably more expensive than the standard 32-bit versions.

Microsoft Windows Vista N

Microsoft also has several versions of Vista N, which is a marketing way of saying "for the European market." After a number of years of legal wrangling during the Windows XP days, Microsoft agreed to release a special version of the Windows operating system in the European Union without the Windows Media Player. Of course, there is no price reduction for this Media Player–less Windows.

Please note that this version is not available outside of the European Union. At the time of writing, there were some renewed concerns in the EU about Microsoft's dominance and how the court's judgments' were being applied. At the moment, no other changes have been made to the N version.

Perhaps not ironically, no major retailers shipped units with Windows XP N on board and sales were dismal. Windows Vista N is likely to have the same result; it exists to satisfy a court requirement.

Windows Vista Tablet PC edition

Are Tablet PCs the Next Big Thing? Some people think so, and several vendors have developed specialized hardware that acts like an electronic version of a notebook. The Tablet PC edition of Windows Vista is still in the works from what we have understood, but Microsoft is remaining quiet about it. What we do know is that most Vista editions are compatible with Tablet PC.

Tablet PC features are currently available in every edition, except Start and Home Basic. We have read of successful installations and uses of the various CTP releases on Tablet PC. However, at this point in time, no release date has been made public for a Tablet PC–specific release. In the interim, use one of the Windows Vista editions supporting the use of Tablet PC.

Choosing the right edition

Table 1.1 contains a non-exhaustive list of various features in Windows Vista and in what edition(s) you can find them. Please note that we didn't include Windows Vista Home N and Windows Vista Business N in this table. These editions, available only in Europe, are the same as their standard counterparts, with the exception of the missing Windows Media Player 11 application. European users wishing to use this application will have to download it directly from the Microsoft Web site.

The Starter edition is also excluded from this list; most readers enjoying this book will not have access to it. For a complete list of features by edition, you should check out the Windows Vista Product Guide. This list is currently available for Beta 2 at `www.microsoft.com/downloads/details.aspx?FamilyID=bbc16ebf-4823-4a12-afe1-5b40b2ad3725&DisplayLang=en`.

Table 1.1. Features in editions

Feature	Home Basic	Home Premium	Business	Enterprise	Ultimate
User Account Control	*	*	*	*	*
Windows Security Center	*	*	*	*	*
Windows Defender	*	*	*	*	*
Windows Firewall	*	*	*	*	*
Parental Controls	*	*			*
Windows ReadyDrive	*	*	*	*	*
Service Hardening	*	*	*	*	*
Windows ShadowCopy			*	*	*
Encrypting File System			*	*	*
Virtual PC Express				*	*
Windows BitLocker				*	*
Windows Anytime Upgrade	*	*	*		
Aero interface		*	*	*	*
Instant Search	*	*	*	*	*
Windows SuperFetch	*	*	*	*	*
Windows ReadyBoost	*	*	*	*	*
Windows Media Player 11	*	*	*	*	*
Windows Movie Maker	*	*	*	*	*
Windows DVD Maker		*			*
Premium games		*	*	*	*
Windows Fax and Scan			*	*	*
Tablet PC		*	*	*	*
Windows SideShow		*	*	*	*
PC to PC Sync		*	*	*	*

continued

Table 1.1. *continued*

Feature	Home Basic	Home Premium	Business	Enterprise	Ultimate
Remote Desktop	Client only	Client only	*	*	*
Offline files and folders			*	*	*
Roaming user profiles			*	*	*
Internet Information Server (IIS)			*	*	*
Windows Media Center		*			*
Speech Recognition	*	*	*	*	*
XPS Document support	*	*	*	*	*
Network diagnostics	*	*	*	*	*
Windows Mail	*	*	*	*	*
Windows Calendar	*	*	*	*	*
Themed slide shows		*			*
Internet Explorer 7	*	*	*	*	*
Accessibility settings	*	*	*	*	*
Dual processors	*	*	*	*	*
Xbox 360 support		*			*
Scheduled file backup		*	*	*	*
Windows Vista Basic interface	*	*	*	*	*

Pricing Windows Vista

The Windows Vista pricing scheme has the potential to be confusing. Although the prices are pretty straightforward, it is easy to see how users can be confused when buying supplemental licenses and have to pick the type of additional license. Each license grants the use for a single computer; you can also buy additional licenses for a slightly discounted price.

When we say slightly, we mean slightly! The additional license is approximately $20 to $40 less than an upgrade license. It is our understanding that one license is for a single computer and not up to three computers, which is often the case with software.

Table 1.2. lists the suggested retail prices; they are what you will most likely pay at major retail stores. Of course, if you are buying a new computer with Windows Vista installed, the price of the operating system is included in the cost of the computer. We suspect that most users will be able to take advantage of some sort of upgrade; we discuss upgrade compatibility in Chapter 2.

Table 1.2. Pricing editions

Edition	Full version	Upgrade price	Additional license	Additional upgrade license
Windows Vista Home Basic	$199.00	$99.95	$179.00	$89.95
Windows Vista Home Premium	$239.00	$159.00	$215.00	$143.00
Windows Vista Business	$299.00	$199.00	$269.00	$179.00
Windows Vista Ultimate	$399.00	$259.00	$359.00	$233.00

If you do buy Windows Vista from a retail outlet, be sure to verify that exactly what you are buying corresponds to your needs. We advise you to

▪ Determine what edition of Windows Vista you need.

▪ Verify upgrade compatibility and determine if you need a full release or an upgrade.

▪ If you need an additional license, verify, based on the previous step, if you need an additional full installation or upgrade license.

Just the facts

▪ Windows Vista is Microsoft's latest operating system, due in late 2006 or early 2007. It features five different editions.

■ Windows Vista features a number of new features, including the Aero environment.

■ The Start menu is dramatically different in Windows Vista.

■ There are a number of different Windows Vista versions beyond the usual standard edition; these include Windows Vista N and 64-bit versions.

■ Some features are only available in certain editions; consult the table in this chapter or the Microsoft Web site to make sure that you by the right edition if you need a particular feature.

Preparing for Installation

Chapter 2

Here's a piece of good news for you, Windows users. Even though Vista is packed with new features, there's one thing that becomes shorter and easier: Windows installation.

The bad news is that your computer may be obsolete. The good news, on the other hand, is that if your computer is compatible for running (and taking advantage of) Windows Vista, you can most likely install Vista in approximately 35 minutes (originally, Microsoft was shooting for 15–20 minutes). The installation time has decreased with each CTP release; it is currently approximately 20 minutes or so. In fact, you'll find that you spend more time making sure that your computer is Vista compatible than you do actually installing it!

Fortunately, installing the Windows operating system has become a relatively straightforward process that is fairly easy to complete without having to break anything. Although it's not as easy as clicking Setup and sitting back, it's not far from being that.

Installation options

Windows Vista can be installed several different ways, depending on your current configuration. As Windows Vista grows older and starts putting out Service Packs, the list of available installation options will evolve.

Custom installation

A custom installation is a completely bare-bones installation of Windows Vista onto a blank hard drive. Don't be misled by the name, it's really just a standard installation. The custom installation performs a clean installation, meaning that it writes over everything. With a custom installation (see Figure 2.1), you decide where to install the operating system or where to make changes to your drives or partitions.

Figure 2.1. The Windows Vista Installation Screen.

If you opt to perform a custom installation, the state of your current data and hard drive is up for discussion. In theory, Windows backs up your existing version of Windows in another folder; this includes your User profiles and their respective folders. What it all comes down to is this: Back up everything of value before you attempt a Windows Vista installation. Keep in mind that you most likely must re-install any applications, so make sure your installation software is handy before installing Vista! Even though a backup is created, you should act as if you are starting over and won't have this backup from which to extract your personal files.

One of the nice features now available in Windows Vista is the fast setup technology that enables you to install Windows Vista within 35 minutes — with only a single reboot and very little work on the part of the user.

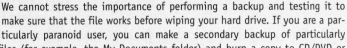

Watch Out!

We cannot stress the importance of performing a backup and testing it to make sure that the file works before wiping your hard drive. If you are a particularly paranoid user, you can make a secondary backup of particularly important files (for example, the My Documents folder) and burn a copy to CD/DVD or store it on an offsite server (for example, on your ISP account's server).

Installing Windows has never been faster (or easier) and will certainly please many users (unless you are like me and counted on using that hour or so to run errands or have lunch).

A custom installation is always preferable to an upgrade because it allows you to start with a fresh slate. Of course, running a custom installation means that you are ready to lose the content of your hard drive and create any necessary partitions. If you are uncomfortable about doing that kind of thing, we would highly recommend buying a copy of Symantec's Partition Magic software that lets you handle both operations very easily and comfortably. For more information on this product, please visit `www.symantec.com/home_homeoffice/products/system_performance/pm80/index.html`.

Upgrade

An upgrade installation is simply an upgrade of your existing operating system with Windows Vista. If you perform an upgrade installation, Windows Vista uses your existing Windows operating system as a base and installs Vista onto your hard drive. The upgrade installation is the type that Microsoft recommends (see Figure 2.2), assuming your previous version of Windows allows for an upgrade. If you are moving to Windows Vista from a non-Windows operating system, you will need to perform a Custom installation.

Any applications or documents currently found on your installation hard drive are saved and can be accessed. Although not the cleanest installation of the bunch, it is a safe installation that guarantees the integrity of your existing files and documents.

Unlike a custom installation, you must run the Vista upgrade directly from your current Windows operating system and not boot your computer from the Vista DVD. The autorun splash screen looks slightly different from the Custom installation splash screen; for example, you can perform a compatibility test before you attempt the upgrade. Once you start the installation, Windows Vista runs a second compatibility check on your computer to make sure that your hardware is compatible with Windows Vista. If any red flags are raised, Windows alerts you to the hardware in question. If you have any incompatible software on your computer, Vista requires you to uninstall it and to start the installation process over again. If any incompatible hardware is essential for the user, he may consider the next installation option: dual boot installation.

Upgrade installations are commonly used and are safe to perform. Like we said for Custom installations, performing a full backup of your current system (preinstallation) and testing its validity before proceeding with installation is a necessary step. Vista also lets you transfer files to another computer from the splash screen before you start installation.

These types of installations are of value to users who want the best of both worlds. They will have the Windows Vista operating system, but the familiarity of having their applications and documents exactly where they were before. You may have to spend some time reorganizing your folders, or replacing icons on your desktop.

The next two types of installations: dual boot and network are technically not available on the installation type menu during installation; however, you can perform them through a Custom installation.

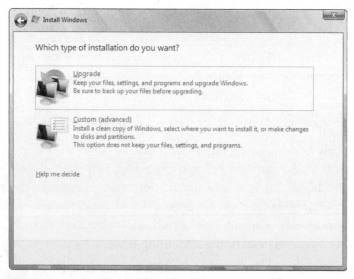

Figure 2.2. The Windows Vista Upgrade option.

Dual boot installation

You may be surprised to know that you can actually run two different, independent operating systems on a single computer. If you have a secondary partition or another hard drive, you may opt to perform a dual boot installation. A dual boot installation is when you have more than one operating system on your computer. For example, you may wish to run Windows XP on your primary (main) partition (hard drive), which is your boot drive and install Windows Vista on your secondary partition or a second hard drive (non-bootable).

This installation is performed exactly like a custom installation; however, you must be careful not to install it on the disk where the other operating system is currently installed. After you do this, you can select the desired operating system when you boot up your computer.

When you turn on your computer, a screen displays the available operating systems and asks you to select one. You can access applications from the drive of the other operating system provided that the applications are compatible. For example, you should be able to access Windows XP applications, while Linux applications cannot be opened under Windows Vista.

The dual boot installation can be a bit tricky; if you are not comfortable with setting up a second operating system on your machine, please ask a computer professional to help you. However, if you do opt for this installation, it can be very helpful to have two different operating systems on your computer. You can safely keep all of your existing hardware and toggle to your other operating system should it not be compatible with Windows Vista.

If you plan on installing a dual boot configuration on your computer using Vista, there are a couple of other salient points that you should consider before going forward:

- Do not install Windows Vista on a compressed volume (unless it is NTFS compressed).

- If you are running Windows Vista and Windows NT on the same computer, do not using NTFS as the only file system type.

- Install each operating system on its own partition.

- Use a different computer name for each installation if you are on a domain.

Watch Out!

Before attempting a dual boot installation, be sure to make a complete backup of your existing personal files and operating system. You should also make sure that you have CD backups of any installed software in case you must re-install.

Network installation

Although it is not explicitly mentioned during the installation procedure, you can still perform a network installation of Vista. If you want to install Windows Vista on multiple computers, you can make the software available over a network for users to install. Doing this is particularly easier than in the past because Windows Vista is stored in a single file (as a disk image), albeit a very large one.

You can also perform an upgrade installation, which is similar to a new installation (as described briefly in the above paragraph). In this case, the user inserts a media disc to install the operating system on his or her computer. Unlike during a new install, the user has no questions to answer or settings to set; the user's old settings are brought over to the new machine.

If you are using Windows Vista at home for personal use, it is unlikely that you would use a network installation unless you have created a true home network. This installation is primarily for system or network administrators in a corporate environment.

Other installation options

If you are worried about making the jump to Windows Vista because it is still brand new, you can try the virtual option. By using software such as VMWare or Microsoft's Virtual PC (an Express version is included in several editions of Windows Vista), you can create a virtual hard drive and install a custom installation of Windows Vista in a virtual environment (see Figure 2.3). By doing so, you have all the benefits of running the

Watch Out!

Using Virtual PC or VMWare may require specific hardware requirements. For more information on using either of these applications, and how to install Windows Vista using them, please refer to the manufacturer's Web site or documentation.

operating system from your machine without the dangers of potentially overwriting or otherwise breaking your computer.

This is a good way to try out Windows Vista without the hassle of performing a new or upgrade installation and then having to remove it from your system if you prefer to go back to your old operating system. It also has the benefit of letting you toggle between two different operating systems with the Alt + Tab key combination.

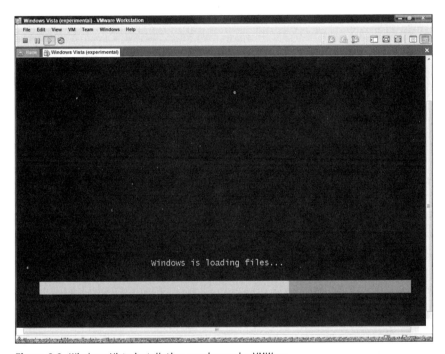

Figure 2.3. Windows Vista installation running under VMWare.

Buy a new computer, get Vista free

In this everchanging economy, everyone is looking for a deal. Here's some free advice: Want a free copy of Windows Vista? Buy a new computer!

Before you take us too seriously, here is our explanation. As Windows Vista starts to roll out, computer manufacturers will start to release Windows Vista compatible machines. Before you write these machines off as a marketing ploy, it may be a good idea to compare the cost of one of these machines to the cost of any eventual hardware upgrades your

What does it all mean?

Microsoft very cleverly came up with two types of Vista-ready computers: Vista Capable (see Figure 2.4) and Vista Premium. As you can see, both sound nice, but one clearly sounds better.

A computer that is Vista Capable means that it has enough juice to run Windows Vista. The operative word is, of course, "run." It can install the software, run Vista applications, and function properly. However, it does not meet the requirements to take advantage of all of Vista's features (notably the more high-tech ones). That, of course, is reserved for the other kind of computer: Vista Premium.

A Vista Premium computer has it all. Not only does it meet the requirements to run Vista, it exceeds them. If your PC is certified Vista Premium, you can take advantage of such features as Aero.

computer may require. For starters, you may want to visit Microsoft's Get Ready Web site at www.microsoft.com/windowsvista/getready/default.mspx. This Web site has just about everything you need to know to prepare for Vista's arrival. It features the Vista Upgrade Advisor that determines whether you're ready for Vista or you have some upgrading to do. Buying a new computer is also the easiest way to guarantee that you have a computer that is compatible with Windows Vista and to be sure that you are Aero-ready (if that is your intent).

Another great source of information is the Hardware Compatibility List (HCL). If you read the (HCL), which is a list of hardware devices that have successfully proven to be compatible with Windows Vista, then you know that this is one demanding operating system. Hardware, which in the past may have been considered high-performance, may simply not be up to par for Windows Vista.

At the time of writing, the first Windows Vista-ready computers are just now becoming available (also known as Vista Capable or Vista Premium). This means that the computer is strong enough for you to run Windows Vista on it; it does not mean that Windows Vista is already installed.

However, you can be sure that these computers will have the necessary motherboard power, processor speed, video card, and RAM requirements to not only run Microsoft Vista comfortably, but also to take full advantage of its features (such as the Aero environment).

Figure 2.4. The Microsoft Windows Vista Capable logo.

There really is no easier way of guaranteeing that your machine is 100 percent compatible with Vista out of the box unless it has the Vista Capable logo. Not only can you be sure that your hardware is compatible with Vista, but you can be sure that on-board software is also compatible with Vista and that you have the most up-to-date drivers for these applications.

Are there any disadvantages of buying a Windows Vista–compatible machine? That depends more on the user than the machine! One early concern is availability. Currently, you won't be able to purchase Windows Vista in retail stores until January 2007. We suggest shopping for a computer with the hardware compatibility list (or minimum requirements) in hand.

There are also a number of hassles involved with a new computer — be it a Windows Vista compatible machine or not. For example, computer manufacturers (particularly popular brands) tend to install considerable amounts of trial software. Often this software works for a short period of time and then requires you to pay for it if you want to continue using it. In addition to increasing the final cost of your computer, many times you find that you really do not want some of this software. As a result, you could have a considerable amount of unused icons on your desktop and your icon tray. Because some of this software loads at

Bright Idea

Before buying a new computer, find out if it (or its hardware) is Windows Vista Capable. For more information on this, please visit either www.microsoft. com/whdc/winlogo/default.mspx or www.microsoft.com/ technet/windowsvista/evaluate/hardware/vistarpc.mspx startup, valuable computer resources are used. As a result, you may spend a great deal of time uninstalling some of this software. For more information on this, turn to Chapter 4.

If you are a home user, you may want to consider purchasing your computer at a local retail store for the post-sale or technical support options that accompany the sale. Although it is harder to select or build your computer à la carte, you have a better chance of finding on-site or quality technical support. Buying online can be hit or miss depending on if you buy from a heavy hitter (like Dell or Gateway) or if you are going through a smaller company. An online vendor calling itself Joe's Tire and Computer is less likely to have a robust technical support plan than the heavy hitters. If you buy from a local retail store, you may be able to have on-site or at-home repair included in your warranty, which saves you the time of having to ship back your computer to the manufacturer (which can take several weeks to repair, not including the day or two it takes to receive the airway bill to ship the computer back).

There is always the option of using the Windows Marketplace (see Figure 2.5). The Marketplace is a Microsoft initiative that lets you buy

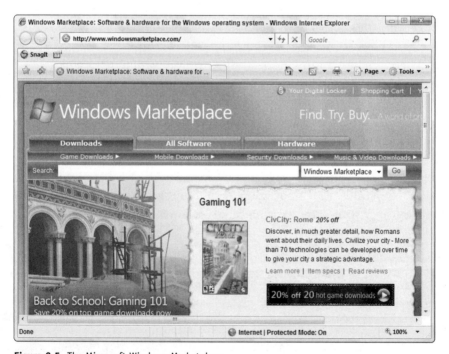

Figure 2.5. The Microsoft Windows Marketplace.

Microsoft-endorsed products from third-party merchants through a Microsoft portal. In other words, you can go to the Web site (www.windowsmarketplace.com/Content.aspx?ctId=366) and select the material you want. If you decide to buy it, you are forwarded to the third-party site where you can configure and purchase. You can also buy digital cameras, software, drivers, and so on. The advantage of buying through Marketplace is that you are guaranteed to find Vista Capable and Premium machines.

Upgrade your existing computer

If you are one of those folks who really does not feel like spending an exorbitant amount of money to replace a computer, perhaps for financial reasons or because you recently bought the computer you have, then you are certainly not alone! You can upgrade your computer in areas that might be lacking instead of replacing it.

Deciding whether to upgrade or replace your computer does not have to be a difficult decision. The biggest determining factor in this decision is the age of your computer. Most likely, any computer purchased over two years ago is not worth upgrading. The cost of material can still be relatively expensive, so if you need to upgrade memory, hard drives, video cards, and motherboard, you quickly arrive at the price of a whole new system! In some cases, replacing one piece of hardware may require you to replace another piece of hardware so that they are compatible! Table 2.1 illustrates the minimum requirements necessary for you to use Windows Vista.

Table 2.1 represents the most recent information available from Microsoft concerning minimum, recommended, and ideal requirements. These guidelines should be treated like the bare minimum requirements that they are, especially for the hard drive and memory requirements. If possible, it would be best to have at least 1GB of RAM installed. If you cannot support 1GB of RAM, you may want to use a USB

Watch Out!

When determining whether or not your computer is truly an "upgrade" candidate, you must be realistic. Any machine older than two years is probably worth replacing, as opposed to upgrading. When considering an upgrade, it is best to aim higher than the minimum requirements.

Watch Out!

Before making any upgrades to your computer, please visit the Microsoft Web site to make sure your system is compatible. For a current list of compatible processors, please visit www.microsoft.com/technet/windows vista/evaluate/hardware/entpguid.mspx#EHC.

drive as virtual memory to speed up your system. For your hard drive, try to allow for 20GB installation space just to be on the safe side. Of course, these numbers also depend on which edition of Windows Vista you are running, as well as which features you install post-installation (you cannot select which features to include during installation, this is all done post-installation).

Table 2.1. Windows Vista requirements

Component	Minimum	Vista Capable	Vista Premium
Processor	800 MHz 32-bit (x86) or 64-bit (x64) processor	800 MHz 32-bit (x86) or 64-bit (x64) processor	1 GHz 32-bit (x86) or 64-bit (x64) processor
RAM	512MB	512MB	1GB
Hard Drive	20GB (15GB available)	20GB (15GB available)	40GB (15GB available)
Graphics	N/A	DirectX 9 capable with 64MB memory	Aero-compatible card with 128MB memory
Display	SVGA (800x600)		
Optical Drive	CD-ROM drive	CD-ROM	DVD-ROM
Audio	N/A	N/A	Audio capable
Internet	N/A	N/A	Internet access

By comparison, Windows XP required only 64MB of RAM and 1.5GB hard drive space. Of course, Windows XP and Vista are not really comparable in terms of capabilities, so naturally, the required system resources are greater (especially in terms of memory and disk space).

The true cost of Windows Vista

As you can see from this chapter, Windows Vista is clearly a big jump up from Windows XP — especially in terms of resources necessary to run it!

The cost of moving to Windows Vista clearly goes beyond the price of buying the software. Unless you are buying a Windows Vista–certified machine, there is a very good chance that a large number of users will be required to upgrade at least one component of their computer. If you are upgrading memory, buy a larger DIMM (512MB or 1GB) because most computers have two memory slots; this in turn means greater cost than if you bought a smaller-capacity DIMM.

The risk of having to do a major computer upgrade or even replacing a computer (especially if it was purchased relatively recently) could be a potential roadblock to Windows Vista sales for a number of current Windows users. In many countries, exorbitantly high sales tax rates may very well prevent a large number of users from spending the money necessary to either upgrade or replace their computer, and buy the Windows Vista software.

Microsoft's selected media choice isn't totally clear at the moment. We have heard of both DVD and CD-ROM versions of Windows Vista. Most online retailers are currently only offering the DVD version of Windows Vista. According to hardware requirements, a DVD-ROM is only necessary if you want to be Vista Premium Ready. Perhaps it's an ill-advised assumption on the part of Microsoft that every computer shipped these days has a DVD-ROM on board. However, we guarantee you that if you buy a budget computer or an I-can't-believe-this-price computer from a major retailer, it most likely has a standard CD-ROM

Watch Out!
Once you determine appropriate compatibility with Windows Vista, please read all third-party documentation carefully before attempting to install any hardware or software.

drive. If you are installing from a DVD, Windows Vista checks in at over 2GB. Obviously, the Windows Vista installation file can only fit on a DVD-ROM, thus the need for the appropriate drive on your machine (unless you are performing a network installation). Fortunately, DVD-ROM drives have dropped drastically in price as of late (you can probably buy one starting at $40 or $50) and can be installed in minutes.

We cannot stress how important it is for you to fully analyze your Windows Vista needs before going out and upgrading or buying a new system. Besides the cost of buying equipment, you also run the risk of high maintenance fees if you have to take your computer to the shop in order to have upgrades installed. You also have the hassle of potentially being without your computer for an extended period of time. Analyze what you are looking for in Windows Vista, and how it will improve your experience, and then measure that against the state of your computer.

Use your existing hardware

Should you decide to perform an upgrade from Windows XP to Windows Vista (for more information on installation, please read Chapter 3), there is one major task you should perform that can be done in one or two ways:

- Use the Upgrade Advisor
- Use the Hardware Compatibility List

If you are deciding to use what you already have, you should make sure that everything is compatible with Windows Vista. To start, visit the Microsoft Web site to make sure your basics are compatible — processor, graphics processor, and so forth. You can currently view this list at www. microsoft.com/technet/windowsvista/evaluate/hardware/ entpguid.mspx#EHC.

Of course, if you are feeling brave, or are sure that your computer is up to the challenge, you can perform the upgrade installation. As we discuss later, the Windows Vista installer does a system compatibility check and alerts you to any hardware or software that might not work with Windows Vista.

If it turns out that a particular piece of hardware is incompatible with Windows Vista, but it must absolutely stay because you use it, you may want to consider a dualboot installation that was discussed earlier in this chapter. This option allows you to use the functionality of both operating systems. Just keep in mind that this particular hardware cannot be used in Windows Vista; you have to boot using the other operating system in order to access and use it.

If you are going to use your existing hardware, you may want to also consult the HCL or Get Ready Web site discussed earlier in this chapter. This is similar to the list mentioned in the link earlier in this section. This is your roadmap to hardware that is compatible with Windows Vista; if your material is on this list, your machine should work without any red flags. However, if it is not on this list, there is no guarantee that it will work, as stated earlier. Although Microsoft does not explicitly state that the non-listed hardware will not work, it is not guaranteed to work and therefore not recommended. The Get Ready Web site also has the Upgrade Advisor to guide you through upgrade preparations.

Before you start upgrading hardware left and right, do an analysis of your needs and price out parts. In many cases, it may be cheaper to buy a new computer. Even if it is cheaper to actually buy new hardware, you also need to evaluate whether or not you are tech savvy enough to install it. While installing extra RAM is easy enough, installing a motherboard can be a time-consuming procedure, and one that comes with certain risks. For example, it is easy to short a motherboard by touching it with static build-up. The cost of labor can drive the true cost of actual hardware upgrades considerably higher.

The Upgrade Advisor is an excellent tool that answers two crucial questions for you: Is my computer Vista compatible? What edition of Windows Vista is best for me? This is a quick download that performs a full analysis of your computer; it also asks you to rate your system priorities and what you plan on doing with your computer. Based on your information, the Upgrade Advisor suggests the best edition for you. It also rates your hardware, letting you know areas where you could upgrade to enjoy the full Vista experience. This wonderful feature is discussed later in this chapter.

Watch Out!

If you decide to use non-recommended hardware or hardware not on the HCL, you agree to do so at your own risk. It is highly unlikely that any warranties would apply if using such equipment were to cause your computer to stop working.

The Windows Vista hardware compatibility list

For every Windows release, Microsoft puts out a list of hardware that has successfully completed a battery of tests and is officially deemed "compatible" with that version of Windows. Any hardware that is on the list is guaranteed to work with Windows Vista. Hardware not on this list may or may not work.

Should you perform an installation with incompatible hardware, you run the risk of an unsuccessful installation or problems running Windows Vista once installed. To avoid the problems we discussed earlier in this chapter, consult the Hardware Compatibility List (HCL) on the Microsoft Web site. Currently, you can find it at the following address: www.microsoft.com/technet/windowsvista/library/plan/ed1 e3b7d-5ea7-4ad3-be3f-af29f7b48dde.mspx?mfr=true.

Collecting information about your computer

This section is primarily for people who have bought a computer with Windows Vista already installed. Windows Vista is just as helpful as Windows XP in terms of letting users know what is on their machine. Staying abreast of what is on your machine is important for a number of reasons. If you are thinking about upgrading a particular component of your computer (hard drive, graphics card, memory), you can use the System Information feature to analyze devices that might be good upgrade candidates. Having this information handy can be really helpful for diagnosing problems when using Windows Vista. Even though Windows Vista is pretty intelligent and insists on running tests when errors occur, personal knowledge has no equal; do not rely on the computer alone to handle all potential errors or incompatibility issues.

Using the System Information feature

The System Information program has the same purpose as in Windows XP; it gathers and prints out system information so that you know exactly

Bright Idea

If you are using hardware that is not on the HCL, you may wish to check the third-party vendor's Web site and see if a Windows Vista–compatible driver is available.

what is on your computer (see Figure 2.6). The report is pretty exhaustive and might take several pages to print out. Also, keep in mind that a lot of the data is rather technical and might not always be of interest to you. This information is helpful when troubleshooting problems.

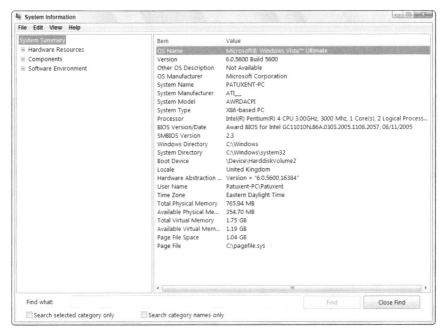

Figure 2.6. The System Information window.

The System Information feature, like in Windows XP, is found in the System Tools folder under Accessories from the Windows menu. The only real change in the Windows Vista version of this handy little application is the interface. Aesthetically, the Windows Vista version is much, much nicer. After you select System Information from the Windows menu, it may take a few seconds to load as it loads and refreshes your system data. When it is ready, a flurry of information related to your computer is displayed. You may then print the information from the File menu.

Putting the numbers together

If you bought your computer from a vendor, you should make a list of all your hardware and their subsequent model numbers. When upgrading your system, the list comes in handy when checking to see if your hardware is compatible or whether you need to update your drivers. This goes for your motherboard, video card, sound card, CD/DVD drive, and network cards, too. Unfortunately, you may need to crack open your computer and look inside and find the specific component in order to find its model number.

Dealing with firmware when working with hardware

Some hardware devices have device-specific code called firmware embedded in them. Firmware enables features and functions so that operating systems can make the best of the hardware. Devices that often have firmware are motherboards (for example, the BIOS, or basic input-output operating system, is the "brain" of the motherboard), CD/DVD drives, and networks. Sometimes video cards also have firmware. Be sure to check with each device's manufacturer to see if updated firmware is available for your device.

Determine device driver versions

Device drivers are hardware-specific code used by the operating system so that it can interact, manage, and control the hardware's functions. Windows Vista features device drivers for a large number of hardware devices available, while some new ones may be available on the Windows Update site. Be sure to check with the device manufacturer to see if new drivers are available for use with Windows Vista. By RC1, almost every driver required on our computers was available and installed during installation.

What's your (file) type?

If you are upgrading from Windows XP, you may recall that you could use one of three file system types: FAT, FAT32, and NTFS; however, you most likely are using NTFS. If your last upgrade has been a while, a file

---

 Watch Out!

If you incorrectly update or change a device driver's firmware, you may completely disable it, rendering it useless. If you download new firmware, be sure to follow the manufacturer's instructions carefully. If this is something you are not comfortable doing, by all means, have a computer professional help you.

system is how directories and files are organized and how they interact with the operating system.

In Windows Vista, the two FAT file systems are supported, but it is much better for you to use the NTFS file system because it handles access control, encryption, and compression; all of which are unavailable in the FAT systems. For more information on this, see Chapter 14.

Internet settings

In today's electronic age everyone from preschool children to grand-mothers are online. Internet connectivity is arguably the most important function of a computer. No one is buying these blazing fast machines to play solitaire! Regardless of whether you are using a national provider, a local ISP, or your company's network, you should have all the necessary connection information so that you can set up your computer properly (see Figure 2.7).

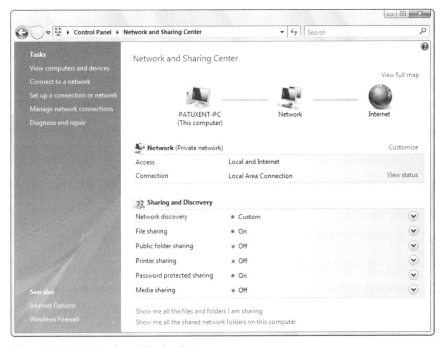

Figure 2.7. The Network and Sharing Center.

This information may already be available on your computer, or you may need to see your system administrator (if this is a professional computer or if you are connecting to an office network). If you already have Windows Vista installed:

1. Click Start ⇨ Control Panel, and then click Network and Sharing Center.

2. Click View status under Network.

3. Scroll down the list and then select the Internet Protocol (TCP/IP) item if it is not already selected (shown in Figure 2.8). Make sure the check box stays selected; otherwise, you will disable the Internet connection. Click Properties.

Figure 2.8. The Local Area Connection Properties window.

Write down all the information in the Internet Protocol (TCP/IP) Properties dialog box. This may not be all the information you may need. Dialup users need the dialup access information, including account

Watch Out!
You may notice that the image in Figure 2.8 contains the IPv6 protocol. This version is newly supported in Windows Vista.

name, password, and server settings (see Figure 2.9). Cable modem users may require PPPoE (Point-to-Point Protocol over Ethernet) modem and account logon settings. If you have any questions, call your Internet service provider (ISP) or refer to the ISP's Web site support section for help in collecting this information.

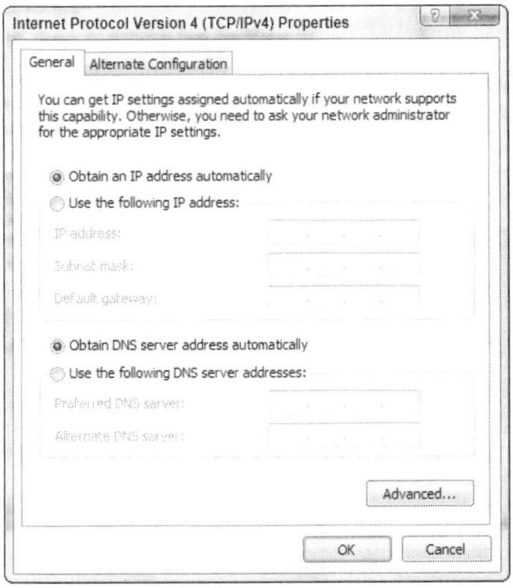

Figure 2.9. The Internet Protocol Properties window.

The Upgrade Advisor

Instead of using an upgrade wizard, Microsoft instead developed the Vista Upgrade Advisor (see Figure 2.10). This tool is designed to help users or companies test their computers for Vista upgrade readiness. This battery of tests includes system information, application compatibility, current devices, and hardware configuration to help you decide which edition to use, as well as determine any hardware weaknesses.

It's also a nice tool for home users to use as well! You can download it from the Windows Vista Get Ready Web site (www.microsoft.com/windowsvista/getready/default.mspx). The Upgrade Advisor is a quick download, which you then install and run!

When you start the Upgrade Advisor, it displays a list of various features or user experiences as checkboxes. For example, if you are interested in using the Aero environment, or are interested in mobile computing, you can click the corresponding check boxes. The Upgrade Advisor helps you decide which edition is right for you; the suggested edition appears at the bottom of the window based on your selections. The next screen displays any suggested hardware upgrades. The following screen displays a driver report by selected experience. You can ultimately save or print the Upgrade Advisor's report.

This is the easiest way to figure out which Vista is right for you as well as how your computer stacks up. For users who want a quick analysis of their computer without having to compare their computer against the HCL, this is definitely the way to go.

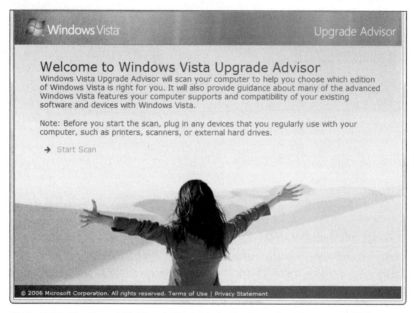

Figure 2.10. The Upgrade Advisor is the best way to determine Vista compatibility.

About activation and registration

Like versions that came before it, Windows Vista lets you register your copy of Windows Vista and requires you to activate your software. There is a major difference between these two procedures.

Windows Vista registration is an optional procedure where you provide user information to Microsoft (such as name, address, e-mail) in

Bright Idea

Before you install Windows Vista, make sure that you read the terms of your license agreement to see how many computers can use the same copy of Windows.

order to receive product support or updates, as well as any other Windows news. This procedure can be done online and in no time. (At the time of this book's writing, the Web site for Windows registration is not yet available.) Registering Windows Vista is a great way to stay up to date with the latest Vista information.

Activation, on the other hand, is a mandatory procedure that is required in order to use Windows Vista. Activation is how Microsoft verifies the validity of your copy of Windows Vista via the Windows Genuine program and that the license agreement is followed. After you install Windows Vista, you have a 30-day window to activate your software either by telephone or online. If you do not, some Windows Vista features will stop working until you activate the software. For example, you can no longer create new files or save existing files.

Generally, once you activate your software, you will not need to activate it again. However, if your computer undergoes "major surgery" (for example, you change a hard drive and memory at the same time) or if you reformat your hard drive or you are hit by a virus, you may need to reactivate. In this case, simply use the same product key as before.

To activate your copy of Windows Vista, the best way to go about it is to click the auto-activation option during installation; this automatically activates Windows Vista for you. Of course, you can also do this manually by going to Help and Support and doing a search on "activation." You can easily find a link to the Windows Activation window (see Figure 2.11). Otherwise, you can go to Start, Control Panel, System, and then scroll down to the Windows Activation section. This part of the System page indicates whether or not your copy has been activated. If not, you are prompted to activate your copy of Windows Vista. If so, it says "Windows is activated" and provides the Product ID number. A link is available if you need to change your product key. Once your copy of Windows Vista is activated, a dialog box appears indicating that activation was successful and that your copy is genuine.

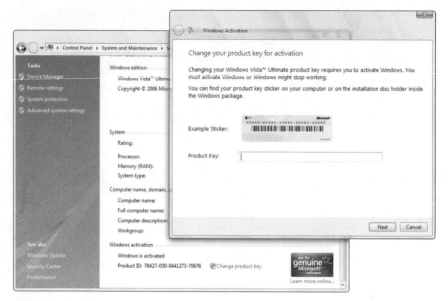

Figure 2.11. The Windows Vista Activation window.

Product activation is something that we suggest you do on your first day just so you will get it out of the way. Otherwise, you may forget and never get around to it. Plus, it's such an effortless procedure that it will be over and done with before you realize it!

Windows Genuine

Windows Genuine, aka the Windows Genuine Advantage, is a Microsoft requirement in order for you to use their operating systems. We say requirement because up until July 2006, this was optional.

The logic behind Windows Genuine is a noble one; users must authenticate their copy of a Windows operating system in order to use it. You have 30 days from the installation date to authenticate your copy; if you do not authenticate it within this time frame, various operating system features are disabled until you can no longer use the applications.

Many users tried to circumvent this; indeed, many people were offended by Microsoft's actions for several reasons, including privacy issues. However, such circumvention is highly discouraged as the Digital Millennium Copyright Act in the United States could apply in some cases.

As mentioned earlier, there have been privacy concerns arising that the program acts as spyware, reporting back to the mothership on a daily basis. Microsoft has denied any nefarious uses of the Genuine Advantage program. Whether or not you trust Microsoft's motives in this matter, the fact remains that you pretty much need to authenticate your copy of Windows if you expect to use it. If not, many people in the IT community have a fairly good idea of their other options!

Upgrading your current version of Windows

We discussed how to go about upgrading your computer to Windows Vista, but we haven't mentioned the more pragmatic side of upgrading, which is software compatibility!

Let's assume that you are running an earlier version of Windows. While we all remember the fanfare with which they shipped, the following versions of Windows are no longer supported:

- Windows 98
- Windows 98 Second Edition
- Windows ME

These versions now join Windows 3.11 and Win 95 in the trash bin. If you are currently running any of the above versions of Windows, the bad news is that there is no upgrade for you. You will need to buy and install a full copy of Windows Vista.

For those of you who can upgrade, which should be a majority of Windows users, Microsoft's upgrade plan is slightly confusing and definitely illogical. It's important to read this section carefully before upgrading to Vista.

First of all, there are two types of upgrade installations:

- In-place upgrade (Upgrade)
- Clean install (Custom)

The in-place upgrade is a true upgrade installation, whereby you can save your current applications, files, and Windows settings. They are simply transferred from the old version of Windows to Vista.

The clean install upgrade means that you are essentially wiping your hard drive and performing a fresh installation. If you use this installation type, you must first perform a backup of your files and un-earth your installation CDs before going forward. If you don't perform a backup, you can kiss those files goodbye!

Table 2.2 shows your upgrade availability to various editions of Vista from supported earlier versions of Windows.

For example, if you are currently running Windows XP Professional, you can only upgrade to a high-end edition of Windows Vista. Ironically, Windows XP Home lets you perform an in-place installation to any edition. Of course, some operating systems, like Windows 2000, require a clean install regardless of which edition of Vista to which you plan upgrading.

Table 2.2. Upgrade availability of Vista editions

	Home Basic	Home Premium	Business	Ultimate
Windows XP Professional	Clean install	Clean install	In-place install	In-place install
Windows XP Home	In-place install	In-place install	In-place install	In-place install
Windows XP Media Center	Clean install	In-place install	Clean install	In-place install
Windows XP Tablet PC	Clean install	Clean install	In-place install	In-place install
Windows XP Professional x64	Clean install	Clean install	Clean install	Clean install
Windows 2000	Clean install	Clean install	Clean install	Clean install

If you learned anything in this chapter

At the risk of sounding like a broken record, we will go ahead and dedicate a separate section to this one piece of advice that bears repeating:

Always perform a full backup of your data before attempting to perform an installation or upgrade, or formatting your drive.

Yes, it is time consuming; no, it is not fun, but you will feel much better knowing that your wedding pictures are safe in the confines of a backup drive rather than lost for good because an hour seemed like too much time to spend waiting for a backup to complete.

Just the facts

- To run or install Windows Vista, you can either use your current computer if it has the necessary hardware configuration or you can buy a Vista Capable certified computer.

- Be sure to consult the Upgrade Advisor, Windows Hardware Compatibility List (HCL), or Microsoft Get Ready Web site to make sure your current hardware configuration is compatible with Windows Vista.

- Use the System Information feature to view a list of current hardware and keep a list of current model numbers and/or firmware.

- Although registering your copy of Windows Vista is optional, activating is not. Activate your software as soon as you install it.

- Always make a backup of your computer before attempting an upgrade or custom installation. You may wish to keep a special CD just for your documents or extremely important files, in addition to your backup.

GET THE SCOOP ON...
Preparing hard drives and partitions ▪ Deciding on a file
system ▪ Installing Windows Vista ▪ Logging on to a
domain or workgroup ▪ Uninstalling Windows Vista

Installing Windows Vista

T he moment of truth is upon us! After all the preparation, research, and verification, you now must take the big leap and install Windows Vista. Installing your operating system can be a very important lesson in seeing exactly what your computer is made of and how it works. If you are preparing for a new install, you start anew and enjoy a fresh start. Any spyware, unused software, and excess files are deleted and you work from a fresh slate. If you are performing an upgrade, you have the security of knowing that all your old files and documents are still there.

You can take heart in knowing that installing Windows is no longer an afternoon-long process where you had to wait and guess when you needed to come back to validate a dialog box. Windows Vista installation can now be done within 35 minutes and does not ask a lot of questions prior to installation.

However, before you begin, there are still a few questions you must ask yourself and answer before you begin your installation. In this chapter, we help you prepare and answer those questions before tackling the various kinds of installations available to you.

Hard drives and partitioning

Before you install Windows Vista, take a minute to check out the state of your hard drive. How do you plan on installing Windows Vista? Will you be performing an upgrade installation and using a single, primary hard drive? Will you perform a new installation and use a single, primary hard drive? Perhaps you are going to add a secondary hard drive and add Windows Vista to this hard drive and use a dual boot configuration? Or, perhaps you bought a new computer and decided to reinstall Windows Vista after you format your hard drive. Will you leave the hard drive as a single, large partition, or will you break it into two or three smaller drives (partitions)?

Many computers bought out of the box at a retail store feature a single hard drive where you store all your applications, data, and files. If you are using an "older" computer (remember, this is Windows Vista so it cannot be too old!), it is likely that you may have upgraded it by adding a second or third hard drive. Personally, we find it easier throwing a new hard drive into a computer than reformatting and reinstalling software or files to a single hard drive.

A very important thing to remember, and it can admittedly be confusing, is the difference between a drive and a partition. Mistaking the two items can be a very costly error! Unfortunately, during installation, Microsoft kind of assumes you know what the difference is between the two.

Your hard drive is akin to a filing cabinet, while the partition is much like the drawer in the filing cabinet. When installing Windows Vista, you must tell it which filing cabinet and drawer should be used to house the operating system.

As we mentioned earlier in this chapter, many new computers feature an entire hard drive set up as a single partition. Although this is not such a bad thing, you may find it much more convenient to have a partitioned hard drive — that way your 100GB hard drive is now drive C: and D:, one with 25GB and the other 75GB. By doing this, you can put your operating system on C: and put your data and applications on drive D. Regardless of what breakdown you choose, we definitely do not recommend leaving your large disk as a single partitioned drive.

Watch Out!

During setup, Windows uses "destructive partitioning" to edit a drive's partition table. If you make a change, you have irretrievably lost your old partitions and all the data on them. To avoid this, try using Symantec's PartitionMagic to safely manage partitions prior to installation.

Watch Out!

Partitioning can be a complicated and potentially dangerous affair. Even though Microsoft tells you that this can all be done from a command line (a prompt), only advanced users should attempt this. More unfamiliar users should either do this using third-party software designed to work with partitions or should seek a computer technician's assistance.

Keep it simple!

If you grew up in the United States, you are most likely familiar with the expression "Keep it simple, stupid!", or KISS. Gratuitous insult aside, it is very good advice for readers at home who are contemplating their new or upgrade installation.

Windows Vista features a number of ways to configure your hard drives, file systems, or partitions. These tools were built in for different technologies that are required in different situations.

Windows is designed to work in a number of different fashions: on a diskless workstation, as a session within Terminal Services, or as a platform for legacy application support. Creating a RAID (Redundant Array of Inexpensive Disks), creating mount points, and working with dynamic drives can all enhance your Windows experience and maximize your computer's power. For more information on these features, read Chapter 14.

But, alas, with great power comes great responsibility, and with Windows flexibility comes complexity! There is no benefit to a system improvement if it is difficult to understand, implement, or troubleshoot. If you are a home user, you most likely will not use any advanced options; corporate users may use some of them, but they are most likely already configured by your system administrator.

If this is your first time working with the Windows Vista installation process, take it easy and keep it simple. As you become more familiar with Vista, and after reading this book, you should be ready to implement some of the features above, such as working with multiple drives and configuring partitions. For now, have fun and keep it simple!

If you ask most people who work with computers about partitions, most would agree that a two-partition hard drive is better than a single partitioned drive. In case of performing backups, it is much easier and cleaner to back up a drive that is purely data and application files, as opposed to a drive that also has operating system files on it.

For custom installations, the general rule of thumb is to divide a drive into two partitions: one-third for an operating system and two-thirds for data and application files. If you want to use a dual-boot configuration, we suggest buying a second hard drive rather than using a second partition so that your operating systems are completely separate. By doing so, you are minimizing the risks of having two operating systems on a single hard drive. Technically, you can have two operating systems on two partitions on a single drive, but we prefer to err on the side of caution.

Of course, if you are performing an upgrade installation to Windows Vista, you have fewer options. These installations are typically performed in the existing partition where the previous operating system is installed. You need to do this if you are to maintain existing applications and settings information.

If you are a new user or feel intimidated by computers, do not worry! Many of these concepts seem intimidating or as if they are life-defining decisions, but it is not that bad! However, we must stress that when in doubt, please consult this book, the Microsoft Web site, or a computer technician to help you out.

Shedding the fat: Viva NTFS

If you are preparing for an upgraded installation to Windows Vista, you must first back up and see what kind of file system you are using in your current version of Windows: FAT, FAT32, or NTFS. If you are currently running Windows 9x or Windows Me (Millennium), you are probably using FAT or FAT32. NTFS is more common on Windows NT or Windows 2000. If you are running Windows XP, you can use any of these three file systems, but are most likely using NTFS.

Windows Vista only supports NTFS file systems, but this is a good thing. There are several reasons for this. First and foremost, you gain the benefits of access control, encryption and compression, event auditing, and the use of dynamic disks. None of these important features are available on a FAT system. Although these benefits might not seem tangible

Inside Scoop

Converting FAT to NTFS requires some additional space on your hard drive. The size varies depending on a number of factors; allow up to 500 additional megabytes for conversion.

to many users, administrators who maintain company computers on a network will appreciate these elements.

If you are running a custom installation, Windows Vista tells you that it cannot install to a non-NTFS partition. You can either manually convert the partition to NTFS or select another NTFS partition.

For upgrade installations, you can choose to convert an existing FAT32 partition to NTFS during the install process. This adds an additional reboot to the system, but otherwise does not affect setup.

Installing Windows Vista: Custom installation

The moment of truth has arrived! Before you start, we recommend that you run through the installation checklist in the appendices. Doing this walks you through the steps to make sure you covered all your bases before proceeding with the installation.

One of the nicest things about the Windows Vista installation is that it should take no more than 35 minutes and a single reboot. Yes, you read correctly. Gone are the days of reading "installation will take anywhere from one hour to a couple hours. . . ."

Be mindful that you might not be able to perform a custom installation on your computer. If you bought a new computer, it most likely comes with a "restore disc" or a CD-ROM (or in this case DVD-ROM) called Windows Vista. This disc most likely contains an image of your operating system with applications that are preselected and preinstalled by the manufacturer. So, if you run the setup program, it installs everything the manufacturer wants you to have. This might not always be to your liking, especially if some applications are incompatible with ones you would like to install.

One such example is that you want to use Big Software Anti-Virus on your new laptop; unfortunately, your laptop comes with Symantec Norton Anti-Virus (and a trial version at that!). Because you cannot customize your restore disc (and tell the computer which applications to install and which not to install), you can only uninstall Norton and then

When free is more expensive than it sounds

With so many bargains out there, computer manufacturers are throwing everything but the kitchen sink at you to entice you to buy. These little enticements are in the form of bundled software that is included with your computer.

Let's not get too excited about this great deal! Any software given away with a new computer falls into one of three categories: shareware, trial versions, and stripped-down versions. Shareware is software that was developed for the public domain and is either free or requests a small financial contribution (usually made via PayPal) to the developer. You do not see a whole lot of shareware on new computers, but stranger things have happened. Trial versions of software are very common; this kind of software is a fully-functioning version of an application for a limited time. Once the trial period expires, you either have a dead application on your machine or you have to pony up the cash and buy a license key in order for it to work. The license key turns off the "time bomb" that is activated when a program expires. This type of software is found predominantly in anti-virus or firewall software. Stripped-down versions of software are delineated by the addition of lite or express; in other words, they have limited features enabled.

Depending on the type of work you do on your computer, you may be satisfied with the software described above. For example, Microsoft Works may be perfectly sufficient for some users. Whatever you decide, do not feel locked into using the software that comes with your computer. If you require higher-performance software that has the features you need, you may need to spend a little above and beyond what you spent on your new computer.

install Big Software. However, be advised that some manufacturers may consider this enough to void your customer support agreement.

If you want to avoid this problem, or if you need to install Windows Vista on another computer, buy a copy of Windows Vista. By buying another copy, you can be sure that you are properly using your licenses and avoid any hassles when trying to perform an installation.

Bright Idea

It may be a good idea to browse the "What to know before installing Windows" link from the Vista Installation window before performing the installation. Often, software companies discover late-breaking information or problems that are too late to document in the help systems. That information, as well as any solutions, is frequently published in the Release Notes.

The following instructions are based on the assumption that you are installing a genuine, retail edition of Windows Vista. To perform a custom installation, follow these steps:

1. Insert your Windows Vista DVD-ROM, boot your computer, and wait until it loads.

    A custom installation must originate as a boot disk and cannot be performed directly from your existing Windows operating system.

2. Select your desired language, time, currency format, and keyboard layout (Figure 3.1) from the installation window. Click Next.

Figure 3.1. The Windows Vista Installation screen lets you select a number of formats settings.

3. Click Install now to begin (Figure 3.2).

    You can also view important pre-installation information or repair your computer from this splash screen.

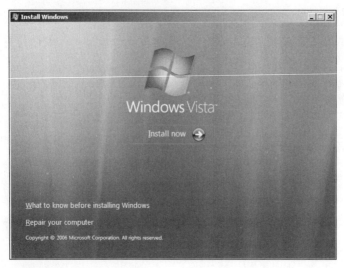

Figure 3.2. Important decisions are made from the Installation splash screen.

4. Enter your product key (Figure 3.3).

   This key can be found on a sticky label found on your DVD case or with your Windows Vista packaging. The product activation key is five sets of five alphanumeric characters; it must be successfully entered before you can continue installation. If you have any questions about what activation is, there is a link to a page in this window that explains the process.

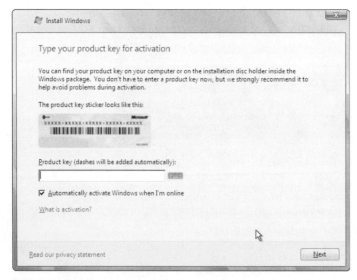

Figure 3.3. The Windows Vista product activation key window.

Bright Idea

Think about selecting the Automatically activate Windows when I'm online check box. By doing so, you can rest assured that your Windows Vista is indeed genuine and automatically activated for you. If you do not select this box, you will have to manually do it. Remember that activation must occur within the first 30 days after installation.

5. The Microsoft License Agreement is the next screen. To be honest, most people never read these. However, it is not a bad idea to do so especially in this new era where companies want more and more personal information. When you have finished reading it, you should accept the terms in order to continue the installation. As you might imagine, declining to accept the terms of the license agreement cancels the installation.

6. The next screen (the installation type screen) is where everything starts to fork depending on your choice (see Figure 3.4). In this particular case, we are going to perform a Custom (advanced) installation. For more information on what a Custom installation is, please refer to Chapter 2.

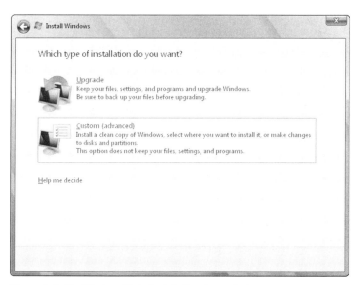

Figure 3.4. The Windows Vista installation type window.

Inside Scoop

If you check the Automatically activate Windows when I'm online box and your computer crashes during installation, try the installation again without checking this box.

7. Now you select your installation hard drive — specifically, your installation partition (see Figure 3.5). The window displays each partition for each hard drive. It includes the partition capacity, available partition space, and the type of drive. You can also install a device driver that accesses your hard drive (if you have SCSI drives, for example). To do this, click Load Driver and follow the instructions. If you are concerned that the information displayed is out of date, simply click Refresh.

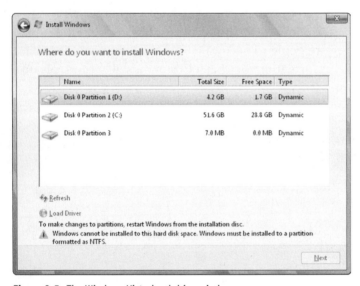

Figure 3.5. The Windows Vista hard drive window.

8. The installation process begins and should last approximately 35 minutes. Your computer reboots automatically during the installation procedure. If you need to cancel the installation for any reason, click the red button at the upper-right side of the window.

Your computer will reboot and continue installation for a relatively short amount of time. Windows Vista loads for the first time and asks you to set up your environment. To do so, follow these steps:

1. Choose a name and password for your computer. Click Next.

   The password is optional, but it's a good idea. If you choose to pass-word protect your computer, you'll need to re-type it for security purposes.

2. The next screen lets you set up a distinct name for your PC and also lets you choose your background picture. Type a computer name and select a background. Click Next.

   The name of your computer is the name that will appear on net-works. A limited selection of background pictures is available. You can always change it later using the extensive collection in the Control Panel.

3. The next screen lets you determine how Windows Vista works with updates. Select update preferences and click Next.

   We recommend using Use recommended settings.

4. Select time and date settings and click Next.

   The default settings are based on your initial language and format selections set at the beginning of the installation.

5. Select your current location (see Figure 3.6).

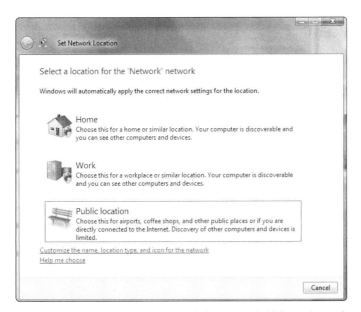

Figure 3.6. The current location screen helps you set initial security settings.

The current location feature is used to select default security settings, such as whether or not your files are visible to other users.

6. Click Start.

Congratulations! When your computer applies your settings, Windows Vista loads and you're home! Chapter 4 details your first steps with Windows Vista and how to customize your Vista experience.

Installing Windows Vista: Upgrade installation

The other common installation type is the Upgrade installation, which is also Microsoft's suggested installation type. As discussed earlier, the

---

Upgrade anytime, almost anywhere!

Back in the day, Windows used to be a single edition. You needed an operating system, and Microsoft gave it to you: Windows 3.11, Windows 95, Windows 95 2nd Edition, Windows 98, Windows Me, and so on. If you worked in large company, you may have used something called Windows NT. As time went on, Microsoft started giving us choices in the form of Windows XP Home and Windows XP Professional. As Bob Dylan said, the times, they are a-changin'.

With the release of Windows Vista, there are a number of different editions that are available for users (for more information on these editions, please refer to Chapter 1). However, Microsoft is making it easier for you to upgrade if you are not convinced that the current edition you are using is the right one for you.

In the Control Panel, there is a new feature called the Windows Anytime Upgrade. Using this feature, you can decide whether you want to switch to Vista Home Premium or Vista Ultimate. To make a well-informed decision, there is a side-by-side comparison of the different versions.

If you decide that an upgrade is right for you, Windows takes you to a third-party retailer Web site to purchase your license (activation key) where you can then go to the Activation page and add a new activation key.

This is a pretty neat idea from Microsoft; kudos to them for not stepping on their retailers and OEM partners by selling direct to customers.

Upgrade installation is a good idea if you want your file structure and data to remain the same and simply want to change your operating system. It is also ideal for users who are not comfortable setting configurations or making decisions about hard drives. Before you start your installation, get the facts by clicking What to know before installing Windows (see Figure 3.7).

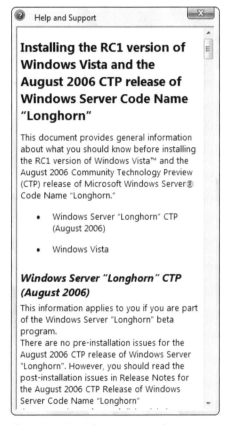

Figure 3.7. Read the important release notes to get late-breaking information.

Unlike the Custom installation, this installation takes approximately 80 minutes, which is a huge difference from the Custom installation. This takes us back to Windows XP installation; hopefully this is something that Microsoft will improve. The installation splash screen is somewhat different. (See Figure 3.8.)

Figure 3.8. The Windows Vista setup screen is slightly different for upgrade installations.

The following instructions are based on the assumption that you are installing a genuine, retailed edition of Windows Vista. To perform an upgrade installation, follow these steps:

1. From your current operating system, run the Windows Vista DVD.

2. When the splash screen appears, you can check compatibility or transfer files from another computer (see Figure 3.9). Once ready, click Install now from the Installation window.

3. Choose whether or not to upgrade installation information.

4. Click Upgrade.

Vista performs another compatibility check (see Figure 3.10).

Windows Vista follows the same procedure as the Custom installation from this point. Please refer to the Custom installation section for more information on continuing your upgrade.

Watch Out!

The upgrade installation can only be run from an upgrade compatible operating system (see Chapter 2). You cannot boot your computer using the installation DVD to perform an upgrade.

Figure 3.9. You can also transfer files from another computer.

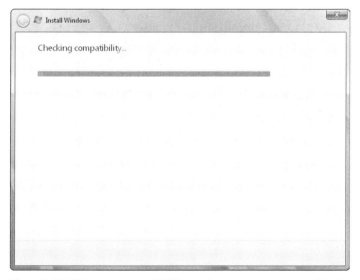

Figure 3.10. Vista runs a compatibility check to make sure your machine is ready for Vista.

Watch Out!

Vista will let you know if you have any incompatible software on your computer. If you do, you must exit the installation and remove it before being able to continue.

Installing Windows Vista: Network installation

A network installation is something that you are not likely to perform if you use your computer for basic at-home use; however, if you have a home office or a small office, you may need to perform a network installation.

This type of installation uses a shared installation file stored on your network. This can be a major time-saver for system administrators because instead of having to carry an installation CD around and manually install Vista on each computer, you can store the installation files once on a network and each computer can then install Vista using these shared files.

During a network installation, the setup program is executed across the network, and the files are copied to the local computer. In order to do this, you must have administrator access to select options or complete information during installation.

If you consider cloning or using Microsoft's RIS (Remote Installation Services, used with Windows Server), keep in mind that this is not the same thing as a network installation. If you use cloning or using RIS, you make a copy of an existing operating system and its application, store it centrally, and then image it (that is, place a copy of the original files) onto network computers. The downside to this is that it contains the needed drivers and hardware details for a specific computer; in other words, it cannot be imaged onto just any computer on the network. For example, an image from a computer with a Pentium processor cannot be used on a computer with an AMD processor. Conversely, network installations are performed individually for each computer every time.

Bright Idea

Keep a list of the necessary license keys with you; remember that each computer that installs Windows Vista from the network will need either its own license number or a license from a volume of licenses.

The hidden gotcha of network installs

In theory, a network installation is really only useful for upgrade scenarios. The reason is fairly simple: You need network drivers and a Microsoft network client in order to connect to a shared folder containing the installation files. Whether you are running Windows 9x or Me, Windows NT, 2000 or XP, you are safe, because you already have the drivers and client installed and can connect to a shared folder on the network.

If you are running a bare-bones PC, most likely, none of this support is installed, which makes connecting across a network difficult when networking is not installed and/or supported.

Utilities that create a "universal" boot floppy for connecting to Microsoft network shares are available on the Internet. Be sure that these utilities have been updated for use with Microsoft Windows Vista.

As we mentioned earlier, the person responsible for the network installation needs to make sure that she has the appropriate license keys for the number of installations performed. Simply being able to make the installation file available on a shared network drive does not mean that you are free to install Windows Vista on every computer on the network. Retail, upgrade, or OEM licenses are good for a single installation on a single computer. Even if you create a network installation, you are required to have a valid license for every copy of Windows Vista you run on your network.

Inside Scoop

Microsoft will eventually release a service pack for Vista. When it is available and you wish to do a network install, you can install it by creating a temporary folder on the same shared folder detailed above. Copy the service pack in this folder. From a command window, change directories to the temporary folder. Type the name of the executable plus the instructions, for example, sp1.exe /integrate: <path\sharename>, to integrate it into Windows Vista for new installations. If Vista is already installed, simply install the Service Pack.

If you have more than a couple of machines, you should contact a reseller for information on purchasing additional licenses. You may also need to purchase Client Access Licenses (CALs), which are required for connections to Windows Servers. This is most often a scenario in larger companies or corporate environments. Microsoft volume licensing programs do not apply if you have fewer than five computers to manage, so many home or SOHO (small or home office) users must rely on standard pricing for their copies of Windows Vista.

The following instructions show you how to copy the Windows Vista installation file to a network drive:

1. Copy the contents of the Windows Vista CD to a shared folder on your network.

2. Point the desired computer to the shared folder on the network and click setup.exe (the shared folder must have previously been mapped to a drive letter by the administrator).

3. Install the Windows Vista upgrade as indicated earlier in this chapter. Activate your copy of Windows Vista using a valid license key.

If you are using Windows Vista at the office, most likely your systems administrator or a colleague from the IT department will handle network installations. Most IT technicians are usually wary about letting users handle network installations (or anything dealing with the network). If you are a home user, this is a relatively easy process, though it is unlikely you will perform such an installation unless you run a small office out of your office. If you are performing a SOHO network installation, please refer to Chapter 6 for more information on sharing folders and directories.

Installing Windows Vista: Dual booting with Windows

As we discussed earlier in this chapter, a dual boot installation can be a worthwhile compromise if you have a powerful enough computer. If you have a dual boot configuration, Windows gives you the choice at startup of selecting between installed operating systems.

Dual boot, also known as side-by-side, installation is a great way for you to test Windows Vista without losing the comfort and safety of a working

Giving your system the (multi) boot

There are a number of reasons that we have discussed for why you might want to have multiple operating systems on your computer: security, maintaining legacy applications, hardware compatibility, testing, or just fiddling around.

There are a number of ways to get this done, depending on your budget or how important this really is to you. The cheapest way (assuming you already have all the hardware) is just to use multiple drives or partitions and just install operating systems to your machine. You can modify the boot.ini file, while letting the Windows boot manager figure out what is installed. (At time of writing, Microsoft had not added any articles to the Knowledge Base on performing a dual boot with Windows Vista.)

Alternately, you can drop a little cash and buy specialized software that was designed to be a standalone boot manager. Such software includes Symantec's PartitionMagic (Sound familiar? It also includes BootMagic, the boot manager!). For more information, visit the Symantec Web site at www.symantec.com. Other options include OSL2000 at www.osloader.com; Masterbooter at www.masterbooter.com; and Boot-US at www.boot-us.com. These applications are reasonably priced; please see their respective Web sites or retailers for pricing specifics. Please note that versions for Windows Vista may not be available until Vista is available publicly or soon after.

Your fancy, high- falootin' option is to use virtual machine software. Virtual machines create a sandbox on your machine (separating it from the rest of your data and files) where you can safely run another operating system. By using a virtual machine, you can easily roll back changes or remove the operating system from your machine. Two popular choices are VMWare's VMWare Workstation or Microsoft's Virtual PC. For more information on either of these, please visit their Web sites. If you decide to run virtual machine software, please consult the user documentation before installation or running a second operating system.

installation. It also lets you keep your old installation in case compatibility issues preclude moving to Windows Vista with all your hardware and software.

There are three ways to create a dual boot system; two of these are highly recommended, while the other is not. The recommended methods are to install Windows Vista onto a second hard drive installed on your computer, or to install Windows Vista into an empty partition on an existing hard drive. Regardless, do not install Windows Vista onto the same partition as your existing Windows installation. Why is this method a bad idea? Application files within the same partition are altered when you boot between the two systems. By doing so, your applications and the operating system will become unstable and eventually unusable. The only reason that you would ever want to do this is for troubleshooting. In most cases, the other operating system is so corrupted that the machine will no longer boot. The same-partition install lets you boot back into the computer and commence data recovery measures.

To create a dual boot installation:

1. Follow the steps in the "Installing Windows Vista: Custom installation" section earlier in this chapter.

2. Select a new drive or a different partition on the drive where the current operating system is installed.

3. Continue installation as illustrated in the "Installing Windows Vista: Custom installation" section.

Watch Out!

Dual boot installation can only be done using a new installation. Because the upgrade installation does not allow for selecting drives or partitions, this is not a viable option.

Inside Scoop

If you install Windows Vista using VMWare Workstation on a blank partition, you must use the Diskpart utility at the command prompt (Shift + F10) and do the following: select disk 0 and then create partition primary. Reboot your virtual machine and then continue installation. Failure to do so provokes an error and halts the installation process.

Installing Windows Vista: Dual booting with Linux

Many people, from business folks to regular folks, are adopting Linux as a free desktop replacement. Linux has plenty of features that appeal to users: the ability to configure just about every aspect of the operating system, the free, high-quality applications available for it, the lack of susceptibility to viruses and worms that love to attack Microsoft products, and the desire to avoid the "Microsoft Tax." Perhaps some of these reasons apply to you; if so, perhaps you may want to give Linux a shot?

The term Linux is used generically to define a complete package of programs, including the core operating system and applications. In reality, Linux is simply the kernel that makes the operating system work. What most people really mean when they say Linux is a distribution (or distro) configured to meet various goals. There are hundreds of distros available, and new ones are built every day. Some focus on security, some focus on gaming, and some try to be a better Microsoft than Microsoft. To see what distros are available, browse the site www.distrowatch.com, which lists some distros that you may have heard of and quite a few that you probably haven't!

Dual booting with a Linux distro can be a pain in the backside at times. This difficulty arises due to the Microsoft boot manager's deliberate design to recognize only operating systems that come from Microsoft. If you install a Linux distro followed by Windows Vista, you will find that the boot.ini file does not list the Linux distro and you now have no way to boot into Linux. Both Linux boot managers (GRUB and LILO) recognize Windows and will provide a way to boot into it, but if you then boot into Windows Vista and at some point install a service pack, it will clobber your Linux boot manager and you'll be back to playing around with Linux boot manager settings.

You can still set up your computer for dual booting with a complete version of Linux on a partition on your hard drive. Most Linux distros

Inside Scoop

The term "Microsoft Tax" is a pejorative expression frequently heard in the computing world to describe Microsoft's licensing scheme, in terms of fees and restrictions.

Bright Idea

When you buy a new computer, you can ask for one that does not have an operating system on it. This allows you to save money by not paying licensing fees for the operating system or all those other preinstalled applications you never use (Microsoft Works, we're looking in your direction).

come with HOWTO files that explain how to set up a dual boot environment with Windows, though the HOWTOs can vary in quality and comprehension. As you might imagine, Microsoft does not provide any instructions on how to do this. In fact, the Microsoft Knowledge Base includes articles only for how to remove Linux. Clearly Microsoft doesn't want you receiving other suitors for your attention; whether you appreciate Redmond's concern for your computer's choice of operating system is for you to decide.

Because the dual boot procedures differ from distro to distro, a step-by-step dual boot or multiboot guide will not be provided here. The Linux community, on the other hand, hasn't taken the dual boot challenge lying down. Several major distros have created live CDs that you can boot from and that load a preconfigured version of Linux into RAM; by doing this, no partitions or files on your hard drive are ever touched. If you have a broadband or DSL connection, you can download and burn a distro to a CD or DVD and run Linux from your CD or DVD drive. You can also order a live CD or DVD from various vendors at a nominal cost.

The most popular live versions are Knoppix (www.knoppix.org), Mandriva Move (formerly Mandrake LiveCD) (www.mandriva.com/en/individuals/products/move), and the Novell SUSE (pronounced "SOO-suh") Professional Live DVD (www.novell.com/products/linuxprofessional/index.html). The Knoppix version shown in Figure 3.11 is particularly adept at detecting your hardware and presenting you with a working desktop at boot time, courtesy of sophisticated installation scripts.

Live CDs are a fantastic way to dual boot with Linux, see what all the fuss is about, and leave your existing operating system intact and untouched. With Knoppix, if you like what you see, you can issue commands that will install the live CD onto your computer into a dual boot configuration (or, if you're willing, as the only operating system). Because Linux is so flexible and configurable, you may find yourself running Linux more often than Windows.

Figure 3.11. The Knoppix distro is clean, colorful, and easy for Windows users to work with.

Logging on to a domain or workgroup

Windows Vista is a slight departure from past versions for users that run over a domain or workgroup. When you first log on to Windows Vista, you will notice that there is no box for a domain or workgroup.

Logging on to a domain or workgroup is quite simple: Because there is nowhere to input the domain, just enter the domainname\username as the username and the domain password as the password.

Windows Vista will run the logon script, connect to network drives, and manage permissions.

Uninstalling or removing Windows Vista

You can uninstall or remove a copy of Windows Vista a number of ways. The easiest and cleanest way of doing this is by first performing an upgrade installation. By doing so, you can simply go to the Control Panel and remove the operating system upgrade. When you install an operating system upgrade, certain files are left on your computer in case you need to "roll it back" (uninstall the upgrade). This is convenient if you have compatibility issues with your existing applications and need to regain any lost features or functionality.

> **Watch Out!**
>
> If you perform this type of uninstallation, keep in mind that all your Windows Vista files, applications, and data will be permanently deleted.

Even though Microsoft clearly wants you to upgrade to Windows Vista, you also need to make sure that this particular point in time is good for you. Microsoft, despite many of their wonderful qualities, makes it very difficult to take steps back in the past. In other words, once a new operating system releases, you should abandon any previous versions. Of course, that's not always possible for myriad reasons that we covered earlier in this chapter. So, in order to avoid a potentially messy uninstall, perhaps a dual boot might be the right choice for you.

There is still hope for you yet if you performed a new install! This method is slightly more dangerous or "less clean" than an upgrade removal. To do this, put the installation disc of your desired operating system, let's say Windows XP, into your drive. Reboot your computer with the Windows XP install disc and start the installation process. Choose a "clean install" that should be performed on the same partition/drive as the Windows Vista installation. The Windows XP installer will format the hard drive and then perform a clean installation of Windows XP.

If you are trying to roll back an eventual Windows Vista service pack installation, you can simply go to the Control Panel and remove the service pack like any other application.

Just the facts

- Run through the Windows Vista installation check list that is found in the appendices.
- Decide which type of installation is right for you: new, upgrade, virtual machine, or dual boot.
- Prepare your hard drives for your desired installation; this involves creating the necessary partitions or formatting disks.
- Be careful when uninstalling your Windows Vista operating system.

GET THE SCOOP ON...
Welcome Center ▪ Aero theme ▪ Desktop basics ▪
Windows Sidebar ▪ Online help ▪ Ease of Access ▪
Gadgets ▪ Themes ▪ Automatic Updates

Managing the Windows Desktop

Congratulations! Yes, now that the hard part is out of the way, you can jump right in and get your hands dirty and start exploring Windows Vista. Installation wasn't that bad, now was it? All that is in the past, so let's take a look at some of the many features the Windows desktop affords us in Windows Vista.

After Windows Vista loads for the first time, you may notice some striking differences and some neat features designed to make your experience more comfortable, easy to manage, and fun. If you have the proper graphics capabilities, Aero will make these differences come alive, almost literally! In this chapter, we will walk you through the Windows desktop, including the items mentioned at the top of this page, as well as a few other surprises!

Meet the Welcome Center

Ever the hospitable host, Windows Vista loads the Welcome Center on startup, shown in Figure 4.1. If it does not appear, you can launch it from the Welcome Center icon in the Control Panel. If you want it to appear every time, simply check the "Run at startup" box near the lower-left corner of the page.

Figure 4.1. The Windows Vista Welcome Center.

The Welcome Center is where your Windows Vista experience begins. It features a wide array of information that may be helpful to you. The top section of the screen features basic system information such as which Windows Vista edition you are using, processor type (and speed), onboard memory, video adapter, and your computer name. If that has simply whet your appetite for more information, you can click the Show More Details link , which brings you to the System section of the Control Panel (shown in Figure 4.2). This page really doesn't offer much more in the way of new information, but it does allow you to do or view certain things: view your product ID and operating system processor (32 or 64 bit), and change computer name settings. You can also see your system rating to see how compatible your computer is with Windows Vista, as well as find out more about Genuine Windows.

Back in the Welcome Center, 14 other options or services are available in the bottom half of the window. These options are

- View your computer details
- Register Windows
- Access the Control Panel

- Connect to the Internet

- Set up the Windows Media Player

- Add new users

- Add a printer

- Personalize Windows

- What's new in Windows Vista (for your edition)

- Windows Easy Transfer

- Windows basics

- Windows Vista Demos

- Ease of Access Center

- Set up devices

These 14 options are a great starting point for getting your new operating system up and running, Instead of having to search for commonly run tasks, you can access a good number of them here. These features are all detailed at various points of this book.

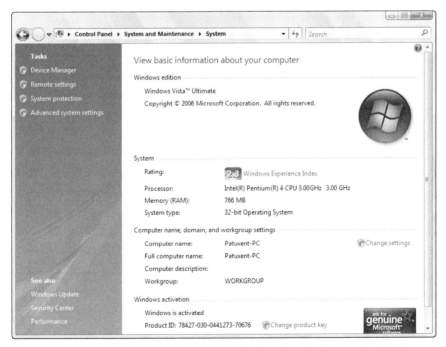

Figure 4.2. The Welcome Center displays additional information via the More Details link.

Keeping it real

One can imagine the folks in the marketing department at Microsoft getting together with the development folks, thinking of ways to make buying and activating your operating system something cool and fun to do. After much reflection, Genuine Microsoft is born (logo shown in Figure 4.3).

The imaginary backroom scenario aside, the Genuine Microsoft Software concept is very much real. In our case, it is Genuine Windows. The idea behind it is to see the tangible benefits of activating and validating your copy of Windows Vista (or any other Microsoft software).

For years, Microsoft has used a Certificate of Authority (COA) that represents genuine Microsoft software. Be careful, this is not a user license! This simply means that the software on your computer is true and legitimate and not off the streets.

Using genuine software is extremely important, especially when we're talking about operating systems. As a consumer, you want to know that your software is a genuine product issued by Microsoft. Using genuine products comes with certain guarantees and assurances (not to mention product support) that pirated or bogus software cannot.

To make sure your copy of Windows Vista is genuine, you can validate it. Microsoft creates a match between your computer's hardware profile and your license key (what you used to activate the software). Besides the obvious ethical and legal reasons for not using illegal software, there is an incentive to validating your copy of Windows Vista. If you fail to do so within the required time frame, features will stop working one by one until you either validate your operating system or until everything is disabled.

Figure 4.3. The Microsoft Genuine logo.

Beneath these options are seven other icons bundled under the Offers from Microsoft heading. These are links that open Internet Explorer and take you to various Windows Live components. These include

- Windows Live Toolbar
- Windows Live Mail Desktop
- Windows Live Messenger
- Windows Live OneCare
- Windows Marketplace

You can also find out more about the Windows Live program, as well as sign up for technical support. Unlike previous versions of Windows, Vista doesn't include a messenger by default (MSN Messenger no longer exists — it is now Windows Live Messenger). You can use the Welcome Center to download the new version.

Simply clicking any of these 21 icons displays informational text at the top of the Welcome Center. If you aren't sure about the purpose of any of these features, these are good overviews of what they do and how they can improve your Vista experience (see Figure 4.4).

Figure 4.4. Not sure about Windows Vista Demos? Click the icon to find out more.

Finally, as mentioned at the beginning of the chapter, you can decide whether or not the Welcome Center should appear every time you start your computer by selecting the appropriate box (see Figure 4.5). Should you decide not to see this screen every time your computer starts (by leaving the check box empty), you can manually open this window from the Control Panel. We like to keep the Welcome Center activated; we find it to be a nice central location for a number of the features that we use most. Given Windows's propensity to launch quickly, we didn't feel that its presence slowed down our experience in any way.

☑ Run at startup (Welcome Center can be found in Control Panel, System and Maintenance)

Figure 4.5. You can decide whether or not to display the Welcome Center at startup.

Introducing the Aero experience

Aero is the code name for the Windows Vista revamped graphical interface. The acronym stands for *Authentic, Energetic, Reflective,* and *Open,* and it is the premium Windows Vista experience. Considerably more dynamic than the Luna desktop of Windows XP, the refreshed Aero really puts an emphasis on graphics and greatly improves your overall experience as a user (see Figure 4.6). However, don't be disappointed or surprised if you can't experience it (and don't be embarrassed if you don't recognize the difference if you've never seen Luna). The requirements for experiencing Windows Vista Aero are pretty stringent; for more information on that, refer to Chapter 2. Overall, the Aero experience is a very cool enhancement to the Windows Vista operating system, however, there is a price to pay for going Aero as we discuss later in this section. Whether or not it is worth the technological firepower depends on how you use your computer and how badly you want to have a "pretty" interface.

Why is it so special? Windows Vista Basic is simply a decent environment that makes the user experience more enjoyable. Aero is remarkable because it goes well beyond the scope of the Basic environment and

Inside Scoop

Windows Vista will not display anything mentioning Windows Vista Basic in the Control Panel if your computer is not fully compatible with its requirements.

scales to your computer's capabilities. In other words, if your computer is fully Vista Premium, you can take full advantage of the Aero environment. If your video card is kind of weak, some features (for example, the transparent buttons) might be sacrificed. Of course, if your graphics card is simply not up to par, you won't be seeing anything in Aero; instead, you'll see the Windows Vista Basic environment.

Aero is a traditional theme in that it captures the essence of Windows, but it goes far beyond that. It goes a step further by offering a transparent, airy, see-through effect, just like glass! Want an example? Easy — just take a look at your Recycle Bin! It's completely transparent, as though it is floating on your screen. If you were to change your background, the recycle bin would remain transparent as if you were looking through glass, all while the background changes colors seamlessly and on-the-fly. Sticking with our recycle bin motif, notice that files in the Recycle Bin now appear as scrunched up balls of paper! As you can see, it remains transparent while carrying out its duties as a trash receptacle. Why would you want this transparency? Well, it allows you to better visualize folder content. It's also easy to customize it, including color and saturation levels.

Figure 4.6. The Windows Vista Aero desktop.

Aero is much more than a souped-up Recycle Bin; Microsoft didn't spend R&D money on making a jazzier trash bin. Aero features a much more intuitive navigation and improved toolbars and taskbar (see Figure 4.7). Also notice that Microsoft has increased visual clues (such as mouse-over text); for example, if you move your mouse over a taskbar icon or a feature, you see descriptive text explaining its purpose. Transparent dialog boxes and buttons and neon or plasmalike progress bars are all a new part of the Windows Vista Aero environment.

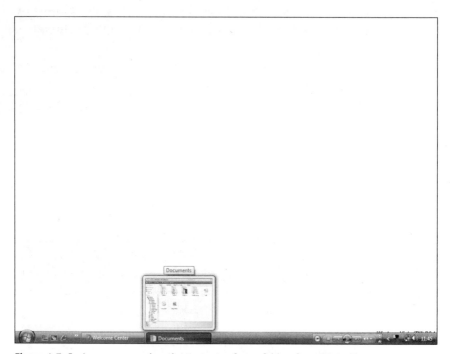

Figure 4.7. In Aero, you can view the contents of your folders from the taskbar.

Windows Vista uses the new Desktop Window Manager (DWM) to enable the Aero environment, assuming you have the proper video card to run Aero. Instead of drawing directly to your screen, applications draw on off-screen buffers that are in turn processed by the DWM and then displayed. By using the DWM, the details in the next paragraph are now made possible.

Take a look at the primary aspects of Aero. There are some pretty neat new features that enhance the Vista experience — if you are Aero compliant. Don't expect to see any of these if you are not Aero ready!

Aero versus Vista Basic

In all the excitement over the new features, it's easy to become confused or mix the two expressions.

The Aero experience is the full, transparent environment that Microsoft created for use with Windows Vista. Unlike any other environment precedent, parts of the window are transparent (yes, you can see right through them!). The dialog boxes also behave differently from what you are used to — they open in an expanding manner. In other words, they start off on the small side and grow gradually larger. The standard buttons at the top right of the window also glow if you hover your mouse over them. These buttons are also transparent, and give dialog boxes a ghostly effect.

The Vista Basic experience, on the other hand, is also nice, but not as exciting. The buttons and dialog boxes are not transparent; they have the setting as defined for the current theme. The Vista Basic environment is far less graphic-intensive than its souped-up brother. If your current configuration does not satisfy Aero requirements, you can use the Classic style that imitates the Windows 2000 user interface.

- **Dynamic windows.** A somewhat spooky feature, a minimized window "animates" to a specific part of your screen; in theory, this makes it easier to find when you maximize it. Instead of simply re-appearing like in Windows XP, the minimized window in Aero pops out at you.

- **Live taskbar thumbnails.** If you're Aero compliant, a live thumbnail snapshot of your taskbar icon appears (shown in Figure 4.7). This is similar to the Live Icons that we discuss in Chapter 6.

- **Windows Flip.** This is an improved version of the Alt+Tab feature of the past. Windows Flip shows you a live thumbnail of your available windows over a transparent background, as opposed to showing boring icons (shown in Figure 4.8).

- **Windows Flip 3D.** Using Start+Alt+Tab, open windows are displayed as a 3D stack (shown in Figure 4.9). You can flip through the open windows using arrow keys or the scroll wheel of your mouse. You can also use the display buttons next to the Start button on the task bar.

Figure 4.8. Toggling open applications now has a more visual bent.

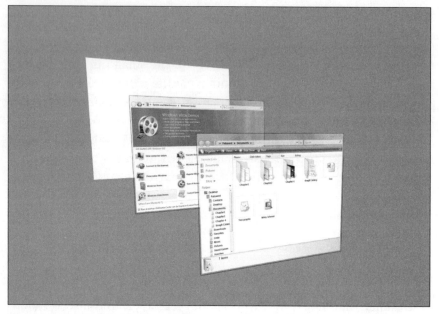

Figure 4.9. The Windows Flip 3D display is a very cool way to display your open windows.

There are two levels of Aero graphics (down from the originally planned three levels) in Windows Vista: Windows Vista Aero and Windows Vista Basic. The point of having two levels is to not exclude users who have a weaker graphics card. The Aero environment requires a bit of muscle in order to truly take advantage of the full Windows Vista experience. You want to make sure your video card can support Direct X 9.0 and is Vista Premium, though the onboard video memory is equally important!

As you can see, the entire Aero experience is much more the sum of its parts rather than a single item.

How does Aero affect Vista?

Who can benefit from the Aero theme in Windows Vista? If you are a professional user, or rather one who uses Windows either in a corporate setting or in a small office/home office (SOHO), you'd be hard pressed to find a manager who would red light or approve Windows Vista or its graphics requirements simply based on this environment. The video requirements alone would make most purchasing managers shy away from going Aero.

Nevertheless, the improved graphics and icons are very helpful. In fact, the entire user experience with this environment is simplified for users. Everything is so intuitive that it could possibly translate into fewer calls to technical support. Microsoft has stressed that the new Aero environment is the most efficient and intuitive front-end to date. Based on our experience over the past several months trying Windows Vista, we have to agree. We started off in Vista Basic before upgrading video cards to enjoy the Aero features. It is certainly much more enjoyable using the enhanced graphics.

Picking the right graphics card

As we mention in Chapter 2, the graphics card is the biggest roadblock to using Windows Premium. The key to running Aero isn't so much your processor speed or memory, but your graphics card. Although most recent computers, even budget computers, have the firepower to run Windows Vista, the video cards are often lacking.

The problem with video requirements is that they require a high-end video card, which is rarely inexpensive. If you are running a budget computer, you most likely will not have the proper video adapter on your motherboard, which could require a new motherboard or a new computer, not to mention a new graphics card!

If you are a gamer, then you will most likely have a sufficiently strong video card. Nevertheless, please consult Appendix A for a list of currently supported video cards for Windows Vista Aero.

Inside Scoop

Developers use theme values instead of hard-code colors in Aero (these are stored in comctl32.dll). The pixels also use a greater dpi (dots per inch), giving them a crisper effect.

Aero is a big bonus to users still working with a small monitor. By being able to resize folders, users may find their experience more enjoyable — no one likes having to use ill-sized folders or icons.

If you have the computer firepower, by all means, take advantage of the Windows Vista Aero or Basic themes. The improved graphics, cleaner-looking icons, and graphic representations help you adjust to Windows Vista and can also be a lot of fun to play with as you make your way around the new operating system.

Aero and the Vista interface

Aero also represents a major shift in Microsoft aesthetics. Since the days of Windows 98, Microsoft used a standard named Wizard 97 for managing design and layout for Microsoft products. Wizard 97 is now replaced by Aero Wizards, a design standard that is in line with the current Aero environment standards.

There are a number of changes in the Aero Wizards (see Figure 4.10), many of which you may notice; however, a few are a bit more subtle. For example:

- Wizards in Aero are resizable, as we mention earlier in this chapter. By comparison, in Windows XP, you could not change the size of a wizard window.

- Back buttons are no longer at the bottom of a window, next to the Next button. These are now located in the upper-left corner of wizard windows.

- Welcome screens in wizards are now a thing of the past; you'll notice that the first screen in a wizard is now an action page (it requires users to make a decision rather than just clicking Next to start the task).

- Options and contextual help is now represented as a hyperlink referred to as a "command link."

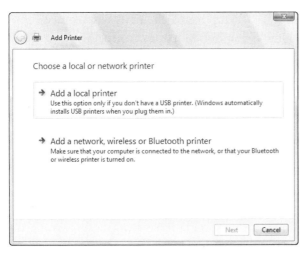

Figure 4.10. A sample wizard in Windows Vista running Aero.

Aero also changes the way you view things. The default font is Segoe UI, one of six new fonts introduced in Windows Vista. For readability purposes, Microsoft has increase the default font from 8 pt to 9 pt. Of course, you can change the default font and size using the Control Panel.

Back to the desktop basics

Before we get too deep into the Windows Vista desktop, we want to go over some important basics. In this section, we take an in-depth look at the Windows Vista desktop reviewing some of its new features, showing some of the new look, and discussing how you can maximize your efficiency with the new Windows Vista look and feel. After all, the desktop is most likely where you will have the most interaction.

As the old expression goes, "you don't get a second chance to make a first impression." This saying is just as true when meeting someone for the first time as it is for using a new operating system. Fortunately, Windows Vista does not disappoint. Windows Vista manages to mix the colorful aspects of Windows XP, but also integrates some of the more industrial feel of Windows 2000.

You can perform a number of graphical maneuvers from the Windows desktop. Doing this helps you create your own user experience by mixing and matching colors, icon styles, how dialog boxes appear, or themes in a way that best illustrate your own style and tastes. Being able to personalize Windows and its desktop is still one of its best features. You can change nearly everything, including wallpaper, icons, and resolution.

Time to launch and roll!

After you log in, Windows and the desktop loads and you notice a number of new occurrences that immediately remind you that this is not Windows XP anymore. For example, the new Windows Vista Welcome Center appears, acting as your initial host. (For more information on the Welcome Center, please refer to the beginning of this chapter.) Perhaps you noticed the new and improved icons on the desktop, which are larger and better indicative of what is in the file. Or, depending on your settings, perhaps it was the Windows Vista Sidebar running up and down the right side of the screen the way the Microsoft Office toolbar does. We're sure you noticed how fast Windows Vista loaded! This is a massive improvement over Windows XP, which seemed to take forever and a day to load all of the startup services and applications.

If you have a disc in your DVD-ROM, the AutoPlay window appears offering you a number of options. If you have already run Windows Vista and it closed with an error, a Windows dialog box appears at startup offering to diagnose and fix the problem. As you can see, even from startup, Windows Vista is busy analyzing and working to provide you with the most comfortable user experience possible. Of course, finding several dialog boxes and text balloons indicating problems is annoying.

Using the taskbar

Like its predecessor, Windows Vista continues to use a taskbar to facilitate your work environment, as shown in Figure 4.11. The basic tenants of the Windows taskbar are still the same, but a number of small differences mean easily recognizable cosmetic changes.

The first change you notice is that the ubiquitous Start menu button has been replaced by an orb featuring the Windows logo. If you mouse over the Windows logo with the Aero theme, it will glow. (We discuss the Windows menu later in this chapter.)

Another big change involves the Windows taskbar, which is now a transparent granite color in Aero; in Basic it is black. This color change gives Vista a cooler, more avant garde feel to it in our opinion. Open applications continue to appear as application icons, albeit transparent icons. The taskbar continues to include icons of important applications next to the Start menu as well as show desktop and Flip 3D buttons. These applications appear in the taskbar and in a submenu that you can access by clicking the double arrow icon. If you are using the Aero environment, you've already read about the changes, including live taskbar thumbnails.

The other changes to the Windows Vista taskbar involve the notification area on the right side of the taskbar. These individual changes are noted below.

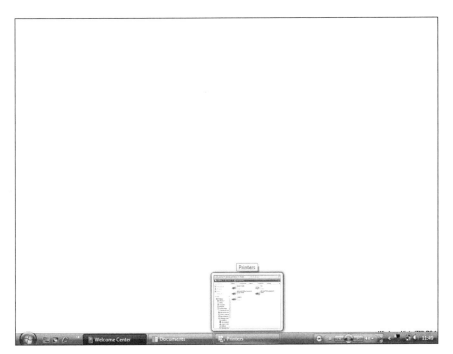

Figure 4.11. The Windows Vista taskbar.

Clock

The Clock feature is much more practical in Windows Vista (shown in Figure 4.12). Now more than a basic timepiece, you can now set up to two additional time zone locations in the Clock feature. After you set these additional time zones and name the clocks, you can see the set of clocks simply by performing a mouse-over on the notification bar or clicking the displayed time. The date also appears in the information box.

Figure 4.12. The greatly improved Clock can hold up to three different time zones.

Volume Control

The Volume Control dialog box has been refreshed to match the new, updated Windows Vista look and feel (shown in Figure 4.13). If you mouse over the icon, an updated information box appears with your current volume, expressed as a number (0–100; 0 being mute and 100 being full volume) along with the name of your audio device.

Figure 4.13. The Windows Vista Volume Control is modernized.

Network

The Network icon is partially new in Windows Vista. In Windows XP, the online computer is represented by an icon of two computers blinking, which indicates that a data transfer is in progress. In Windows Vista, if your computer is connected to the Internet, a small rectangle with a globe in the lower-right corner appears in the taskbar. If you mouse over this icon, the name of the server or Internet connection appears in the information box.

Inside Scoop

You can get rid of the Security Alerts icon from the notification area by opening the command prompt and typing HKCR\CLSID\{FD6905CE-952F-41F1-9A6F-135D9C6622CC}.

Windows Security Alerts

Windows Vista provides a real-time icon of the Windows Security Center; this icon changes color depending on the state of your system security. For example, if the icon is an orange color, this indicates that the Security Center requires your attention. The Windows Security Center now includes Windows Defender on board to watch for malicious spyware or ad tools. This program used to be available for download for Windows XP, only it was called Windows Spyware. More information on the application can be found in Chapter 7. For whatever reason, Microsoft decided to call the icon that opens the Windows Security Center the Windows Security Alerts icon.

Windows Sidebar

The Windows Sidebar looks like a monitor or television screen. There are two ways of working with this icon. Right-clicking it brings up the settings menu for the Sidebar. Double-clicking this icon makes the Sidebar disappear; double-clicking it again brings it back. This application is detailed later in this chapter.

Desktop resolution

Your desktop resolution is a combination of what modes your video adapter is able to display and which resolutions your monitor can display. Most new video adapters available on the market today can easily display 1600 (horizontal) x 1200 (vertical) resolution at 32-bit color. Older cards often do not have the power and memory to render all the computations needed at that rate. For information on supported resolutions for your video card, you can consult your user documentation or the manufacturer's Web site.

Monitors also vary and play a role in what resolutions to use from your video card. The older the monitor (or even if it is a newer LCD screen), the less likely it is to be able to render higher resolutions.

Inside Scoop

Even though Microsoft covers what kind of video adapter and graphics cards to buy for use with Windows Vista, the question of monitors never really arises. If you buy a computer with Windows Vista included, this won't be an issue. However, if you are upgrading or building your own system, you should strongly consider middle- to upper-range LCD monitors. If possible, avoid CRT (traditional) monitors. Be sure to verify the monitor's minimum and maximum resolutions before purchasing.

You can change your resolution easily: Right-click anywhere on the desktop and select Personalize — or go directly to the Control Panel and select Adjust screen resolution from the Personalization section.

The Display Settings window displays indicating your current video card, its current resolution, and current colors (see Figure 4.14). You can play around with the settings until you find one that you like. However, if you choose a resolution that is not supported, the screen will go black. Your monitor documentation undoubtedly lists supported resolutions. If you need to adjust settings for the graphics control, you can do this by clicking the Advanced Settings button.

Figure 4.14. The Display Settings window.

Windows Vista also uses a font-dithering algorithm first introduced in Windows XP called ClearType. Initially designed for laptops, it makes on-screen text more readable. Unlike in XP, Windows Vista turns this feature on by default. According to independent studies, ClearType can improve reading speed and comprehension by up to 5 percent. To maximize the benefits of ClearType, Vista introduces seven new fonts, as shown in Figure 4.15.

You can disable this feature, if desired, from the Appearance window under Personalization. Click Effects and make the necessary changes and click OK.

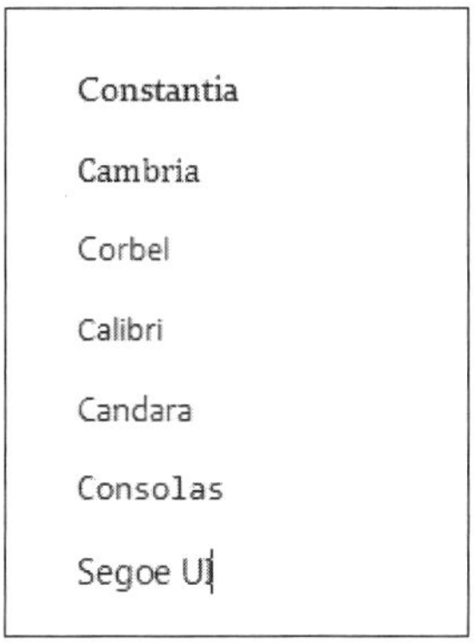

> Constantia
>
> Cambria
>
> Corbel
>
> Calibri
>
> Candara
>
> Consolas
>
> Segoe UI

Figure 4.15. The new fonts in Windows Vista.

Video cards, drivers, and management applications

Most new video cards come with comprehensive drivers and management programs that can adjust nearly every aspect of a card's performance. By the time Windows Vista is released, we suspect most major manufacturers will have Windows Vista drivers available. Frequently, these drivers install tabs in place of the standard Windows ones that change desktop resolution, color quality, and monitor refresh rates for you.

If you have one of these programs installed, you should use it to fiddle with your adapter's settings. Although you can still use the default Windows dialog boxes, you're better off playing the game the way video card manufacturers intended so that you can be assured that you are really setting the settings for your video card. Because the interfaces vary dramatically among adapters, an in-depth discussion of specifics is beyond this chapter. But here are a few tips on getting the best out of your card.

- Make sure your drivers and management applications are up-to-date. Even though the screamingly newest drivers may have bugs, any drivers that are more than a couple of weeks old are probably safe to use. And, as with many things in software, the older the hardware, the more likely the bugs have been pretty well squashed. In this case, the drivers for Windows Vista that are Vista ready and Aero compatible are quite new.

- Most video card help files and user guides are hopelessly obscure. Find an official or unofficial forum or message board for your video card, lurk there for a while, and learn from the mistakes of others.

- If you work in a profession such as graphics design or video editing, hang out on profession-specific forums. You will find a lot of advice about specific adapter settings for particular projects, including tweaks to make the card faster.

Desktop backgrounds and screen savers

If there's anything that people are usually familiar with in Windows, it's the desktop background and screen savers because they're easy to set up and people enjoy personalizing their Windows desktops.

Formerly known as wallpaper, Windows Vista has opted to use "desktop background" instead. That's not the only change! Backgrounds are better organized and of higher quality. In the Personalization menu of the Control Panel (Appearance and Personalization), choose Desktop Background. Backgrounds are divided into ten different categories in a drop-down menu; be mindful that it can take a few seconds for all the pictures to load (even with over 2GB of RAM). If you click on an image, it automatically appears in the background. If you decide to select another image, it will be replaced by the next image you click. If you decide not to add an image, the original desktop is restored. After you select a background, you can dictate how it is displayed: Fit to Screen, Tiled, or Centered. After you have set this parameter, click OK. You can also use the Browse button to select a different image. Some of the preloaded backgrounds are quite impressive, especially in Aero, where the colors really seem to come alive.

Setting a screen saver is just as easy! It's at the same root location as the desktop backgrounds, except that the last level is called Screen Saver (shown in Figure 4.16). This feature works pretty much just like it did in

Hint

If you'd like to use one of your own images as a desktop background, you should save it to Documents (the new name for My Documents) or even the same folder as the bundled images. Avoid saving it to an area where you may need to relocate it, for example, the desktop.

Windows XP. You can opt to display the logon screen when you resume activities once the screen saver is active and you resume your activity. The only noticeable difference is that the My Pictures Slideshow option no longer exists in Windows Vista's list of screen savers.

Figure 4.16. The Screen Saver window.

What has changed are the Power Options, which are still accessible from the Screen Saver window (Figure 4.16). Windows Vista now features power plans that help you to strike a balance between energy savings and performance. There are three plans:

■ Balanced

■ Power saver

■ High performance

If you are actively using your computer or laptop using an AC adapter, we would suggest that you use High performance. If you are away from your computer, or waiting on a long download, why not switch to Power saver? Each plan can be individually modified to set when the display should shut off and when the computer should hibernate. There are also a number of advanced settings. These settings, which include setting a wake-up password, sleep settings, and so on, are manually set in the Power Options window, shown in Figure 4.17, using the change plan settings link. You can always revert to the default plan settings by clicking the Restore default settings for this plan link in the Edit Plan Settings window.

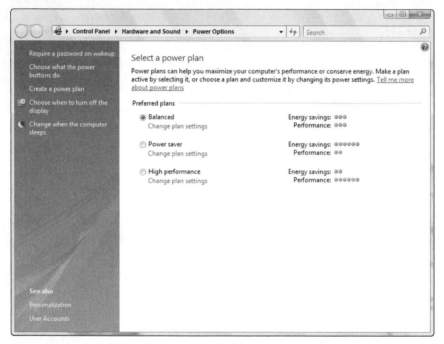

Figure 4.17. The Power Options window.

Working with themes

Themes are a central part of the last few releases of Windows. They affect almost every aspect of the desktop and, as a whole, the user experience. A good theme can make or break one's opinion, or at least enjoyment, of Windows. Don't believe us? Try using the Windows 3.11 color scheme and see how enjoyable that experience is, especially if you've grown accustomed to Aero!

Themes are readily available on the Internet for download; Microsoft even gives us three to get on our way. Most major motion pictures have a film-based theme available, and many fan sites create themes for just about any topic imaginable.

There are three themes (two real ones, to be honest): Windows Classic, Windows Vista, and My Current Theme (see Figure 4.18). Windows Classic has to be the ugliest theme ever created. We can't imagine any user would actually use this. Take a look and you may understand why. This is a throwback to early incarnations of Windows. Why Microsoft would choose to use this theme instead of developing a new "basic" theme is a mystery. We don't think many people are nostalgic for early 1990s Windows.

Figure 4.18. You can pick one of three themes or add your own.

The Windows Vista theme is the real deal, especially if you are equipped to run Aero. If you can take advantage of Vista, this theme is everything that you've read about in this chapter. Even if you can't quite take advantage of all the benefits of Aero, it's still a nice, modern theme

Watch Out!

You can run the Windows Vista theme even if you are not Aero capable. You still enjoy the benefits of the "new" theme and interface appearance, but without all the powered-up graphics.

with high-quality graphics and performance. All around, it can make for an enjoyable Vista experience.

The final theme, My Current Theme, is a bit of a cheat — it is activated any time you modify one of the other two themes. For example, if you change the default desktop background, your theme is now called My Current Theme.

When selecting a theme, you can preview it by using the minibrowser in the Theme Settings window. You can also save your customized My Current Theme settings by clicking the Save As button. You can also delete it or any other theme by clicking Delete. If you save a theme, it will be saved by default in the Documents folder. If you import a theme, this is one place to save it. The prebundled themes are found in the Windows ⇨ Resources ⇨ Themes folder. It's really up to you to decide where you want to save a theme. Some people aren't comfortable writing to the Windows directory; if that's the case, then by all means just use Documents. We personally prefer storing themes in a more discrete location, for example, C:\Themes, in order to prevent anyone (including ourselves) from inadvertently editing or deleting them from Documents.

At the end of the day, Microsoft doesn't leave much choice in terms of themes. You can't help but wish that you had another option or two. If you can run Aero, we recommend that you enjoy it. If you can't or aren't impressed with the Vista theme, we suggest that you download a theme that is more to your liking rather than trying to play around with the current themes, because tinkering around can be time consuming!

There are some big-name theme-management developers, such as WindowBlinds (www.stardock.com). Their creations are shareware and are relatively inexpensive, and the site has libraries of themes for you to browse. As Vista is arriving, it's a safe bet that they'll be selling Vista-oriented themes soon. We're not aware of one at the moment, but it's hard to believe that they won't create one for the Vista release. The SuperPacks traditionally include new themes, screen savers, games, and the odd add-on.

Inside Scoop

If you install a theme and it doesn't work, you must enable the Themes service. To do this, click Start and enter **services.msc** in the search box. Scroll down to the Themes entry, double-click it, set it to Automatic, click Start, and then click OK.

Themes, schemes, and skins

Microsoft uses the terms *themes* and *schemes* to mean different subsets of technology; unfortunately, most users probably don't make a distinction. In software development, anything that changes the look and feel of an application is called a skin. Many programs are "skinnable," such as Winamp, MSN Messenger, and even Windows Media Player.

Although you'd think the industry would keep the terms straight and use them consistently, that's not always the case. WindowBlinds uses skins with Windows, according to their Web site. Rather than worry about using the correct terminology, just recognize that they're all about the same thing — changing the interface so that it looks the way you want it to.

Icons

Icons are a vital part of Windows Vista. They are really worth 1,000 words. As mentioned earlier, and further discussed in Chapter 6, Windows Vista has created the notion of Live Icons. Icons come alive to offer true graphic representations of the files they symbolize; they're no longer simply a generic image file indicating a Microsoft Word file, they are scalable thumbnails.

If you're in a folder, you can easily resize the icons from the Views menu. There are four types of icons: small, medium, large, and extra large (Figure 4.19). Previously, you could set the icon size from the Display Properties window. In Windows Vista, you can locate the option in the menu bar of a given folder.

Perhaps you don't like the icon currently assigned to your file type? Open the Properties for the folder or file in question and go to the Customize tab. The Change icon button at the bottom allows you to pick

Watch Out!

If you decide to download any themes or icons on the Internet, be sure to run an antivirus check on the files before attempting to install them. These sites are easy prey for dodgy types to infiltrate and wreak havoc in the form of a virus.

from a decent list of icons. These icons are found in the shell32.dll system file on your computer. If you still aren't satisfied with your icons, you can download others from a number of Web sites.

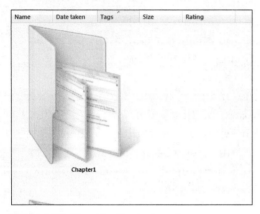

Figure 4.19. A sample of extra large icons.

Relearning the Start menu

The Start menu, evidently, is where it all starts. It's also where a large number of features, both visible and more discrete, have changed since the last version of Windows. The first noticeable change is that the green Start oval is gone and is replaced by an orb with a Windows logo in it (see Figure 4.20).

What you probably won't notice are the two primary reasons for the new Start menu look and feel. Microsoft wanted to make searching applications, Favorites, or e-mail easier than it has been in the past. The other is to make the All Programs menu easier to navigate.

This is where Microsoft hits a home run! If you click Start, a charcoal-colored menu appears. On the right, your account picture appears along with your account username. Below that are links to your documents, pictures, music, and games (there are also other features, such as a computer and network). Here's the best part — in the new Search box at the bottom of the Start menu, you can easily locate any application on the computer simply by typing a few letters of its name. As you enter the letter of an application, a list of appropriate applications appears and is reduced on the fly until you have the desired application. For example, if you typed "wor" in the Search box, you would find two applications: Microsoft Office Word (if installed) and WordPad. If there were any relevant Favorites or History entries, they too would appear. We've found this new method of searching particularly helpful when trying to locate Administrative Tools.

Figure 4.20. The Windows Vista Start menu.

The maneuvering of the Start menu also is different in Windows Vista. If you are familiar with Windows, you know that clicking Start and then All Programs results in a long list of applications and menus — often taking up most of your screen real estate trying to display the entire menu! You then see submenus, or if there are a lot of applications installed, you potentially miss an application at the bottom of the list because it was cut off. Microsoft responded to the many users who complained that the old way was too complicated. We agree with these users and really like what Microsoft did in Windows Vista. From now on, when you click All Programs, a tree-style menu and submenus appear on the left side of the Start menu. What was the Start menu and list of recently

Hint

Windows Vista is much more contextually-oriented than past versions of Windows. In Vista, if you mouse over an icon, a contextual menu appears with a description of the feature. If the icon is an application or file icon, it displays the path of the application or file.

used applications in Windows XP is now the sole location of Start menu application menus. If you click on a folder in the Start menu, it is replaced by the contents of the submenu, which expands. Clicking the submenu a second time collapses it and returns you to your starting point, which means that you maximize your screen real estate.

The menus and submenus in Windows Vista are much more responsive; clicking on an application icon is also considerably more responsive than in Windows XP, which always had an annoying delay. The interface is also considerably cleaner; you no longer have to potentially take up the entire screen expanding Start menu submenus (see Figure 4.21).

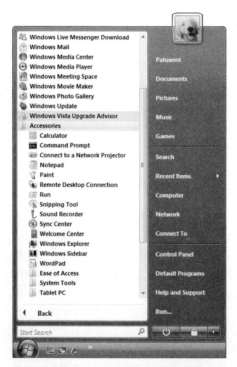

Figure 4.21. An expanded Start menu folder.

Inside Scoop

If you mouse over any of the shortcuts on the right side of the Start menu, the default picture located above the username will change depending on the current shortcut.

If you right-click any of the shortcuts (Start menu items) listed under the username in the Start menu, you'll notice that there are a number of options that can be set that are relevant to that particular feature. For example, if you right-click Pictures, you can add the content to the Windows Media Player list or even open it with Windows Media Player — all without having to actually open the folder.

If you'd rather have the pinned Start menu icons (shown in Figure 4.22), you can drag any of the text shortcuts to the left side of the Start menu and they'll appear at the top of the menu.

Figure 4.22. Pinned Start menu icons.

The final aspect of the Start menu is the improved set of buttons at the bottom right of the Start menu. The first button puts your computer into Sleep mode. Formerly called Stand By in Windows XP, this energy-saving feature shuts down your computer without turning it off. Pressing a key on the keyboard, or moving your mouse, wakes the computer. The second button locks your computer. Get in the habit of locking your computer, especially if you are at work or any other public or nonsecure location. If you have a password, you're required to enter it when you return to your session. If you do not have a password (and you should have one!), you can simply click on your user account from the Welcome screen (or switch users). The final button, which looks like a right arrow, is actually a fly-out menu and offers several options. You can

- Switch users
- Log off
- Lock the computer
- Restart
- Sleep
- Hibernate
- Shut down

The Sleep versus Hibernate issue is bizarre. According to Vista help, Sleep was created to combine Stand By and Hibernate. However, Vista keeps Hibernate (which saves your work) as well as Sleep.

Start menu properties

Like in Windows XP, you can unleash the power of the Windows Start menu by right-clicking the Start button and choosing Properties (shown in Figure 4.23). This includes yet another Search box, as well as the other Properties tabs. Although the content is primarily the same, the layout has changed significantly from Windows XP.

Inside Scoop

Though it looks like the Run command is no longer available in Windows Vista, it still is! In the Start menu properties, click Customize and select the Run command from near the bottom of the list. Once you apply your change, it appears in the Start menu.

Figure 4.23. The Start menu properties.

There are now four tabs, instead of two. They are

■ **Taskbar.** The Taskbar tab lets you set the appearance of the taskbar or set preferences unique to the taskbar. These are similar to Windows XP.

■ **Start Menu.** You can choose between the Start menu and the Classic Start menu, as well as choose privacy settings. You can also indicate whether or not you want recently opened files or programs to appear. If you choose the Classic Start menu, a Configure... button appears next to the Classic Start menu radio button; this window allows you to set parameters and preferences for the Start menu. If you really are not into the new Start menu navigation and want to go back to the multiple menus that take up most of your screen, use the Classic Start menu option (shown in Figure 4.24).

■ **Notification Area.** The Notification Area tab lets you determine how icons and system icons are handled. This is the equivalent of the Customize Notifications window in the Windows XP Taskbar tab. You can set whether or not to display inactive icons and which icons to show (Clock, Volume, Network, and Power — if applicable). You can use the Customize button to set how individual icons should appear (or not).

▪ **Toolbars.** This tab lets you determine which toolbars to add to the taskbar. These include the Address, Windows Media Player, Links, Tablet PC Input Panel, Desktop, and Quick Launch toolbars.

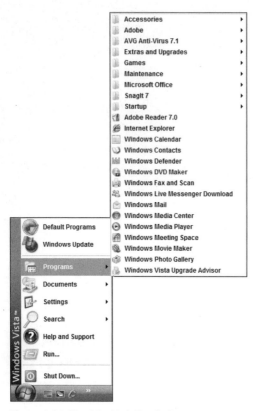

Figure 4.24. The (shudder) Classic Start menu.

Personally, we much prefer the new Start menu to the Classic Start menu. However, if you long for the Windows 2000 days, the Classic Start menu is available. There are no real advantages or disadvantages in this case; it's purely a question of personal preference. We much prefer the Start menu navigation so we use the new Start menu. Though it is considerably different from the old way of doing things, we found that the new Start menu was very easy to warm up to and didn't really find ourselves missing the old way. Remember, no one way is the right way! If you find that you tire of one Start menu, you can always change it!

Introducing the Windows Sidebar

Microsoft is unleashing the unwieldy Windows Sidebar with Vista (shown in Figure 4.25). As users who always have too many windows open on their screens, we can't possibly imagine running a wide sidebar that eats up about two inches of the screen. However, we have to admit that as we tested the Sidebar for this book, some of the gadgets are pretty neat. We believe that Microsoft got their inspiration for this from the sidebar that Microsoft Office used to have. Most likely, it was created as a place to use their gadgets (which we will discuss later in this chapter).

Figure 4.25. The Windows Sidebar.

By default, Windows Vista loads with the Sidebar. This is literally a bar that appears on the side of your screen. At the moment, we are using the Sidebar to get a better understanding of how it works. Our Sidebar configuration contains the following items: a picture viewer that allows us to view reduced size images from our photo gallery, a clock, and an RSS reader that is available in Internet Explorer 7.

You can add gadgets (the official, yet generic, term for the three items listed above) by clicking the plus (+) sign at the top of the Sidebar. An applet appears with four screens of gadgets (13 in total) that you can add by double-clicking the icon, by right-clicking it and selecting Add, or by dragging and dropping to the Sidebar (see Figure 4.26). If you click on a gadget, a brief description appears at the bottom of the applet. You can find more gadgets online by clicking on the so-named link in the applet. There is even a search feature that works just like the Search box in the Start menu. You can search all available gadgets, recently installed gadgets, or Microsoft Corporation. The Search box in the Add Gadgets window seems to work like the other Search features in Windows Vista, where you can simply type a letter or a combination of letters and the corresponding gadget is displayed.

Figure 4.26. The Add Gadget window.

If you right-click on an area of the Sidebar not occupied by a gadget, you can perform a number of tasks. These include bringing the gadgets to the front, adding gadgets, hiding the Sidebar, and setting properties. These properties include whether or not the Sidebar should always appear on top of other windows, whether it should start when Windows loads, which side of the screen it is on, and on which monitor it should appear (if you have multiple monitors). You can also View Gadgets, which displays a list of currently installed gadgets. You can also remove them from the View Gadget window. Finally, you can also exit the Sidebar from this menu.

If you right-click on any of the gadgets, a number of common features appear. These are adding gadgets, bringing gadgets to the front, removing or moving gadgets, detaching the gadget from the Sidebar, and setting the opacity. You can make a gadget virtually transparent by setting the opacity level to 20 percent. Some, but not all, gadgets have a Settings property on the right-click menu. The Settings menu changes depending on the gadget. You can also use the icons to the right of each gadget, which let you close, open, or move the gadget.

Overall, while it is a fairly interesting feature, it simply uses too much screen real estate for our liking. This is a feature that looks like it is enjoying its 15 minutes of fame, especially since rivals at Google have released a similar feature to give Microsoft a run for their money. Many users may still enjoy this feature, especially with the real-time stock ticker, the RSS feed gadget, and other downloadable gadgets.

Using taskbars and toolbars

Now that we've talked a bit about the taskbar and system tray, let's take a closer look at how you can make these two essential items work for you. Most of us aren't using large screens, so it's important to maximize your screen real estate and make every bit count.

Taming the taskbar

By default, the Windows taskbar appears horizontally at the bottom of the screen. It's safe to say that a very, very large majority of users probably never move the position of the taskbar, let alone know that they can! To do this, right-click on an empty area of the taskbar and make sure that Lock the Taskbar is not checked. Simply drag (from an unused area) and drop the taskbar as you please (see Figure 4.27). Keep in mind that the taskbar can only be on a border — either at the left or right of the screen or at the top or bottom. If you opt for the sides, this can help you reduce button crunch, which occurs when the bar is in the default position and you have a large number of open windows. When this happens, it's hard or impossible to tell what you are looking at. Though you cannot alter the length of the taskbar, you can make it as wide or narrow as desired.

Figure 4.27. The taskbar can also appear vertically.

Another valuable aid is to replace desktop icons with Quick Launch buttons. These are a series of one-click buttons that appear to the immediate right of the Start menu. These are frequently used applications that can be launched quickly and easily.

After you have your Quick Launch menu set to your liking, you can make room on your desktop by deleting any icons that are now available in this taskbar. If you are really interested in saving screen real estate, you

Hint

You can drag any file, folder, or application to the Quick Launch portion of the taskbar and customize your Quick Launch toolbar.

can always select auto-hide from the Taskbar properties, which you can access by right-clicking the taskbar and selecting Properties.

Customizing toolbars

Like Windows XP, Windows Vista features a number of toolbars for you to use. When first activated, they appear on the existing toolbar; you can drag them on to your desktop, creating separate windows. If necessary, you may need to increase the size of the taskbar. These toolbars include Address, Windows Media Player, Links, Tablet PC Input Panel, Desktop, and Quick Launch. There is also a New toolbar button that allows you to create a new toolbar based on an existing folder.

Here is a close look at these toolbars:

- **Address.** This is the most practical toolbar of the six offered. Using this toolbar, you can type or paste in a URL. The default browser launches and navigates to your URL.

- **Windows Media Player.** This one is a real mystery, given that there is a Quick Launch button (which Microsoft assumes we wanted) a few inches down the screen. There is no true added value to this toolbar.

- **Links.** This toolbar displays your Links folder from your list of Favorites — for Internet Explorer. This isn't very helpful if you don't put your links in folders other than Links; it's also not very helpful if you're using Firefox.

- **Tablet PC Input Panel.** This is a practical toolbar for Tablet PC users. It allows you to write notes, among other things.

- **Desktop.** This is another odd choice. It features a number of buttons that could be as easily reached another way, and more conveniently!

- **Quick Launch.** This is another useful toolbar. Quick Launch allows you to add any program, document, or URL for easy access.

Inside Scoop

For some reason, Microsoft keeps assuming that it knows what we want, and what we want are multiple ways of accessing Windows Media Player and Outlook. If you feel that you can reach them without Microsoft's help, simply delete them!

You can use drag and drop in the taskbar to reorder the toolbars. Of course, if you decide you that you want to remove a toolbar, simply right-click and go back to the toolbar and click Close toolbar or deselect the name of the toolbar from the list of toolbars (shown in Figure 4.28).

Figure 4.28. The taskbar can display various toolbars.

All systems are go: The notification area

The notification area is found at the far right end of the taskbar; it is also known as the system tray as this is where many system-related icons appear. Officially, Microsoft refers to this space as the notification area because when something goes wrong, this is where you find out. We've found the notification area to be slightly annoying at times because it tries to be too helpful. For example, when you log on, you are bombarded by a number of pop-up screens offering help in figuring out why the computer didn't shut down properly. Nine times out of ten, it has been about something insignificant. It offers more unsolicited advice than a mother-in-law!

This area has another purpose besides annoying users; many applications store icons here. These icons let you quickly access or set preferences for applications. Many of them are loaded by applets at startup, while others wait here when minimized instead of using up valuable taskbar space.

Perhaps you find that too many icons are in the notification area for your liking. You can reduce their presence by right-clicking on the

Inside Scoop

A backup icon appears in the notification area the first time you run Windows Vista.

Hack

If you are comfortable with tweaking Windows settings, there is a way to get rid of the notification area. From the Start menu Search box, type **gpedit.msc** and browse to User Configuration ⇨ Administrative Template ⇨ Start Menu and Taskbar. Change the policy in the Hide the notification area to Enabled and reboot.

notification area and selecting Properties. Don't click on any icons. Try to find an empty area, though difficult; you can also right-click the clock to get to the Properties menu. This displays the Taskbar and Start Menu Properties (which you can also reach by right-clicking the Start button and clicking Properties). There are two groups of icons you can set: (standard) icons and system icons (shown in Figure 4.29). For icons, you can opt to hide inactive icons. If you click Customize..., you can manually set the behavior of current and past items. You can hide the icon, show it, or hide it when inactive. If you hide icons, they are replaced by a left-facing arrow; if you click it, these icons reappear. You can hide them again by clicking the arrow (now right facing) again. For system icons, you can select ones to show from a list of four. By default, all are checked (except Power, which is dimmed).

Two other ways to reduce the number of icons are to tell applications not to use the notification area (when minimizing or simply running), and to reduce the number of applets that load at startup. Some options, like media players, give you the option of minimizing to the taskbar or the notification area. Some, like Windows Live Messenger, don't give you any option; for these applications, you must use the latter option.

Figure 4.29. The notification area lets you manage icons and system icons.

Creating shortcuts

There's no change in how shortcuts work in Windows Vista, so let's just have a quick recap. If you are trying to create a shortcut for a file or folder, right-click and click Create Shortcut. A dialog box appears indicating that you cannot create a shortcut in that location and offers to place it on the desktop. Go for it. A folder icon appears on the desktop with an arrow, indicating that it is a shortcut. If you'd like to rename the icon, simply right-click the shortcut icon and type in a new name.

If you are trying to create a shortcut for an application, you have two options. By right-clicking the application icon, you can either create a shortcut (by clicking the so-named menu), or you can select the Pin to Start Menu option. If you choose the latter, the application shortcut will appear in the upper-left part of the Start menu. However, it will not appear on the desktop. You must also select Create Shortcut in order for it to appear there.

We like to maintain a clean, orderly desktop, so we either avoid shortcuts or only pin applications to the Start menu. However, shortcuts are a great way to access often-used files and folders. They can be a real time-saver, too!

Using the Windows Help system

Microsoft drastically changed their Help system in Windows Vista. Unfortunately, at the time of writing, the system is not complete, but we can still give you a good idea of how it works. The Vista online help focuses more on accomplishing tasks rather than the principles of how things work. Microsoft has also taken the wise step of regularly updating its Help contents.

What prompted Microsoft to revamp its online help system? We don't know. However, experience shows that Microsoft's documentation is primarily limited to their online help systems plus knowledge base or technical articles on their Web site. This new online help system certainly offers a wider variety of support options for solving any problems, notably in part to Vista's ability to search support on the Internet.

The new online help has a completely different layout and color scheme (see Figure 4.30). Unlike the Windows XP help, Vista offers a more interactive Help system. For starters, the icons work in Windows Vista. The Find an answer section has six icons representing different areas of Help. Each one features section-appropriate help topics or information on Windows Vista. This streamlined interface lets the online help breathe easier, thereby making the user feel less attacked. The online help and support in Windows XP had too much small text on the opening page; as a user, we often felt overwhelmed and not really interested in using it.

Figure 4.30. The Windows Vista online help is a vast improvement.

Windows Vista help also features a search feature where you can ask a question or type in a keyword. Like XP, you can continue to use Remote Assistance, which allows you to get help from a friend, or post to Windows communities. Another new feature is that you can now contact Microsoft Customer Support, as well as access other support options. These other support options include the knowledge base, Windows communities, or even Microsoft support phone numbers!

Icons across the top allow you to return to the help starting point, print online help topics, browse the help (which is similar to past versions), or expand your search. The Options menu allows you to set text size and use options similar to the aforementioned icons. The Settings menu lets you decide whether or not to include Windows Assistance Online. This feature allows you to have the latest help files and updates if you're connected to the Internet.

The help is fairly informative, but it should be even better once completed. Even better, it's considerably more responsive and loads much faster than Windows XP help. Documentation hasn't always been Microsoft's strong point, that's why these books exist. But we think that the revamped online help system is good. The potential turnoff is that it contains much more text than previous Windows help systems. Finding a quick detail by skimming may not be possible now.

Working with Ease of Access

Microsoft made great strides in improving accessibility so that all users can enjoy Windows Vista. To that end, Vista introduces the Ease of Access Center. The Ease of Access Center is available in two different locations:

■ The Control Panel, under Ease of Access

■ The logon screen, represented by a round, blue icon in the bottom-left corner of the screen

To be fair, these buttons aren't exactly the same — the Control Panel option is great for setting accessibility options, while the logon screen lets you determine which accessibility features to enable (see Figure 4.31).

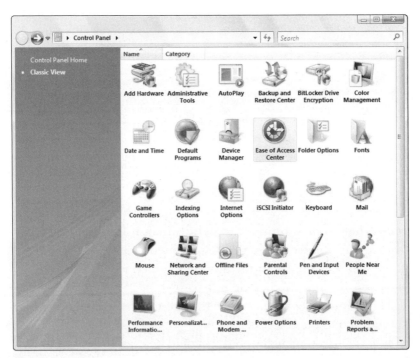

Figure 4.31. You can enable accessibility features from the logon screen or the Control Panel.

CHAPTER 4 ■ MANAGING THE WINDOWS DESKTOP   131

In the Ease of Access window on the logon screen, you can enable the following features:

- **Narrator.** This feature lets you hear text on your screen; it is read using a machine-reader.

- **Magnifier.** This feature magnifies the size of on-screen objects.

- **High Contrast.** This feature displays greater contrast in displayed colors.

- **On-Screen Keyboard.** This feature displays a mini-keyboard on your screen so that you can use your mouse to "type" by selecting letters as opposed to typing.

- **Sticky keys.** This feature lets you use keyboard shortcuts one key at a time.

- **Filter keys.** This feature lets you ignore additional keystrokes if you press a key multiple times.

Any of these features can be activated simply by selecting their respective check box and clicking Apply and then OK. On the other hand, if you select Ease of Access from the Control Panel, you can immediately let Windows suggest settings or manually optimize the visual display. If you click Ease of Access, you can access the Ease of Access Center to set Speech Recognition options.

The Ease of Access Center in the Control Panel has considerably more options than its counterpart on the logon screen (shown in Figure 4.32). It provides quick access to frequently used tools, which are the Magnifier, Narrator, On-Screen Keyboard, and High Contrast. If you select one of these tools (just click one), a second window appears for you to set up the feature (shown in Figure 4.33).

If you are new to working with accessibility tools, Vista is very helpful in this regard. You can use the Get recommendations to make your computer easier to use link for advice on going about setting up your computer. Of course, you can also move down to the Explore all settings area of the Ease of Access Center. This lets you set specific settings for a number of accessibility features. What we like about this section is that Microsoft has taken a very direct approach to helping you set up your system. Instead of beating around the bush or using confusing terminology, Microsoft uses true descriptions of the features so that users can easily and directly access the desired feature. For example, the Make the keyboard easier to use feature does just that.

Figure 4.32. The Ease of Access Center from the Control Panel.

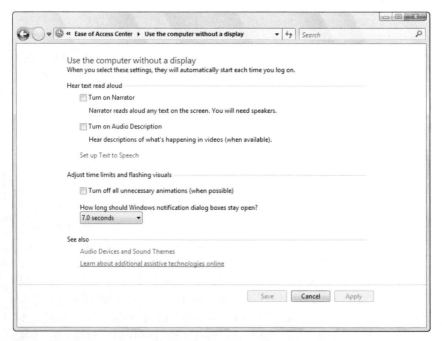

Figure 4.33. The Ease of Access Center is easy to use and easy to set up.

The Ease of Access Center also lets you change administrative settings so that all settings are applied to the logon desktop. If you go back to the Control Panel, you can also set up the Speech Recognition tool (shown in Figure 4.34).

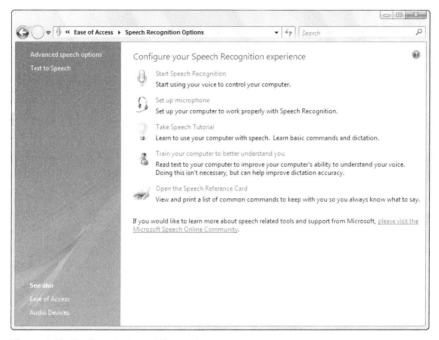

Figure 4.34. The Speech Recognition tool.

The Speech Recognition tool lets you set up a number of properties for your computer to work with Speech Recognition. This feature lets you use your voice to control your computer and act as your vocal mouse and keyboard. We recommend reading the Speech Tutorial, which is available from this page, before using this feature. You can also train your computer to better work with your voice. Microsoft also provides a link to the Microsoft Speech Online Community, which is a nice resource for finding out more about speech tools and getting feature support.

You can also set Text to Speech properties for controlling the type of voice, its speed, as well as setting more advanced options, such as audio output devices. You can also set up Speech Recognition profiles (see Figure 4.35) so that your computer can recognize a different voice or noise environment. For example, you can have a profile for when you are working at home, and perhaps another for when you are at the office.

Figure 4.35. Speech Recognition profiles help you organize your voice accessibility options.

Working with gadgets

As we discuss earlier, Windows Vista now features fully integrateable gadgets. Gadgets are small applications that provide information or services, and are designed to enhance the user experience. They can deliver information such as business data, current weather conditions, radio streams, RSS feeds, slide shows, or even traffic maps!

Three types of gadgets are available:

- **Desktop gadgets:** These gadgets can be run from the Windows desktop or the Windows Sidebar.

- **Web gadgets:** These gadgets run on Web sites, such as Live.com or Start.com.

- **Windows SideShow gadgets:** These gadgets run on auxiliary displays, for example, on mobile phones, using Windows SideShow.

Gadgets are created using dynamic HTML or .NET and are relatively easy to create (if you know these languages). The choice of programming languages is most likely why these gadgets are popular among programmers. The Web site www.microsoftgadgets.com features up-to-date information on Microsoft gadgets as well as gadget downloads.

Is it Live(.com)?

Microsoft came up with an interesting way of bundling services — put them online and integrate them. With that idea in mind, Microsoft launched the Live.com Web site in November 2005.

At the moment, Live.com is still in Beta, but eventually it will integrate services such as Hotmail, MSN Messenger, and antivirus software. Microsoft also plans on making Windows Live and Office Live available through this Web site; this is free software that is available online. Literally, you could go to the Web site and use a browser-based version of Microsoft Word for free to write a letter. This Web site can also take advantage of gadgets, using them in your customized Live.com to enhance your experience. It reminds us of a new Web presence for Microsoft, as if they're trying to make us forgive and forget the whole Passport fiasco!

In its current incarnation, it looks like a cross between a blog and Microsoft SharePoint (see Figure 4.36). Live.com is also the default Web site when you open Internet Explorer 7.

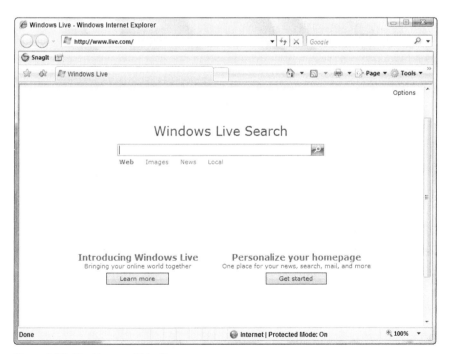

Figure 4.36. The Live.com Web site.

Tweaking your Vista experience

Even though Windows Vista is barely out the door, that hasn't stopped third-party software developers from coming up with a number of new tweak applications designed for use with Windows Vista.

Tweak tools are designed to help you customize your Windows interface (and overall experience) by "customizing" Vista in ways not easily accessible or made readily available by Microsoft (see Figure 4.37). There's nothing wrong in doing this; in fact, Microsoft released their own TweakUI tool with Windows XP's PowerToys.

Of course, not every aspect of Windows Vista can be tweaked. Some of the items that can be tweaked include

- User Account Protection

- Internet Explorer 7 Search engines

- DWM

- Bootloader information

Some of the early tweak applications already on the market include TweakVista (www.tweakvista.com/tweakvistautility/) and VistaBootPRO (www.vistabootpro.org/). Remember that these are third-party applications that are not guaranteed by Microsoft and should be used at their own risk.

Figure 4.37. TweakVista lets you make a number of interface updates without the hassle of trying to getting lost in Vista.

Using Windows Update

The Windows Update feature has been redesigned to be faster and more discreet, and to let you choose the best time to reboot your machine. This feature is particularly nice as the constant reminder in Windows XP always annoyed us.

What else is new in Windows Update? First, the feature is a lot more convenient. For starters, Windows Update is now run from a window in Windows Vista and not from a Web browser, which was the case in Windows XP. If you are used to using Windows XP, you know that you could only automatically download and install High Priority updates. Recommended updates had to be manually downloaded and installed. In Vista, you can decide to manage both High Priority and recommended updates (shown in Figure 4.38).

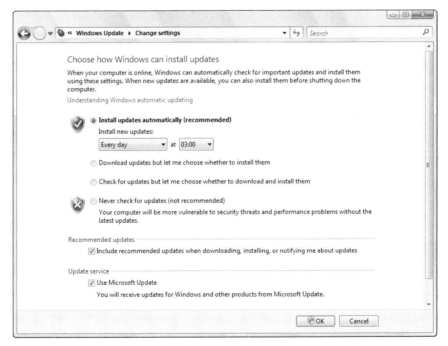

Figure 4.38. The Windows Update window lets you configure how your system is updated.

Vista is much more discrete in terms of updating your system. Previously, the download and install screen often took control of your desktop and you had to wait until it was finished. In Vista, downloads and updates occur in the background. Vista also gives you flexibility in terms of having to reboot your computer. If a download affects a file or application that you are using, Vista saves your work and then restarts the application.

From the Windows Update menu in the Security section of the Control Panel, you can update with the click of a button. This page indicates the last time you checked for updates as well as the content of the last update. This page also indicates whether or not you are using Automatic Updates. To set this last option, open the Change settings window from the left side of the screen. The Change settings window lets you determine how you want updates installed. You can either install updates automatically (in which case you can decide when and how often), download updates without automatic installation, check for updates without downloading them, or never check for updates. The final option allows you to decide whether or not Windows Update should include recommended updates or simply manage High Priority updates.

From the Windows Update window, you can also perform other tasks, such as:

- Force a check update
- Change Windows Update settings
- View update history
- Restore hidden updates
- View FAQs in the online help

The Extras page is an interesting page, as it tells you about additional programs, content, and services available for your edition of Windows Vista (see Figure 4.39). For example, these include applications and online publications to help improve your Vista experience. When you perform a Windows update, you will notice that the main screen performs two simultaneous updates: Windows updates and Windows Extras.

Depending on your comfort level with Microsoft updating your computer, the automatic update feature can be quite convenient. It's very easy to forget to update your computer, an oversight which can prove dangerous due to virus and spyware concerns.

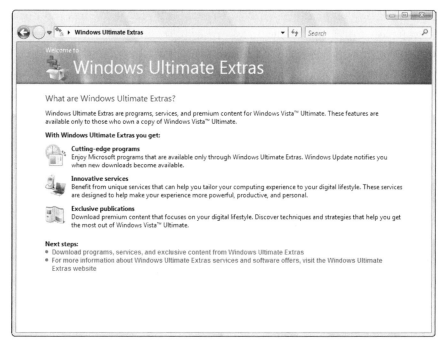

Figure 4.39. Windows Ultimate Extras can help improve your Ultimate edition performance.

Add, move, or change Windows components

The Change or remove a program feature hasn't evolved in terms of capabilities, though the interface certainly is different as is the name. This feature is now referred to as the Uninstall or change a program window. The jury is still out on the changes.

Here's what we like: Applications are presented in a clear, easy to follow format. At the bottom of the Uninstall or change a program window, the number of installed programs, as well as the total file size for these programs, is displayed (see Figure 4.40).

Windows XP conveniently allows you to add features (formerly called components) from the same window where you could uninstall software. This is no longer the case in Vista. Now, if you wish to work with Windows components, you must access the Programs section of the Control Panel. In the Installed Programs section, click Turn Windows features on or off. Notice that Windows doesn't talk about adding or removing (or even installing or uninstalling) components; the term is now "turning on or off." The Windows Features window (shown in Figure 4.41) lets you turn a feature on or off simply by clicking the desired feature. If the feature has a plus (+) sign in front of it, that means it can be expanded. If you select an expandable check box, all options are selected. If you only want to pick certain features from an expandable box, expand it and manually pick your desired feature.

Figure 4.40. Windows Vista lets you know how many applications you have installed.

Figure 4.41. The Windows Features window lets you choose which Windows features to keep.

If you simply want to modify an installed application, you must click the Installed Programs or Uninstall a program link. They lead to the same thing. This feature, unlike in Windows XP, now looks like a standard Windows Vista folder, including Organize and Views menus (see Figure 4.42). Click the desired program, and the toolbar changes depending on your options. You may be able to remove, repair, or change a program.

Unlike previous versions, in Vista, you can view installed updates in a separate window, buy programs online from Windows Marketplace, view purchased software, or turn Windows features on/off. This last feature is one that may confuse readers. Because it's rather discreet, many users might not recognize that this is where you actually add/remove Windows components (shown in Figure 4.43)!

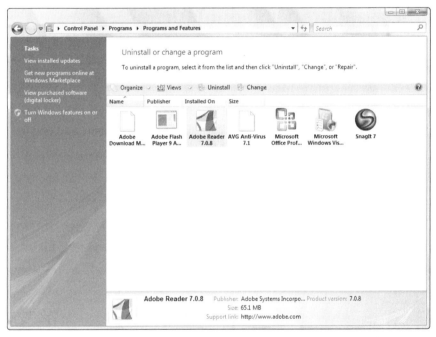

Figure 4.42. The Uninstall or Change a Program Window program window toolbar changes when you click an application.

Figure 4.43. You can still add or remove Windows components.

Manage applications with Task Manager

The Task Manager is still the same old boy it's always been. In fact, the only changes we've noticed since Windows XP are the loss of icon sizing options in the View menu and the suppression of the Shut Down menu.

The Task Manager (shown in Figure 4.44) provides a gold mine of information about the current state or health of Windows. More often than not, you can use Task Manager to shut down a program that crashes (it no longer responds).

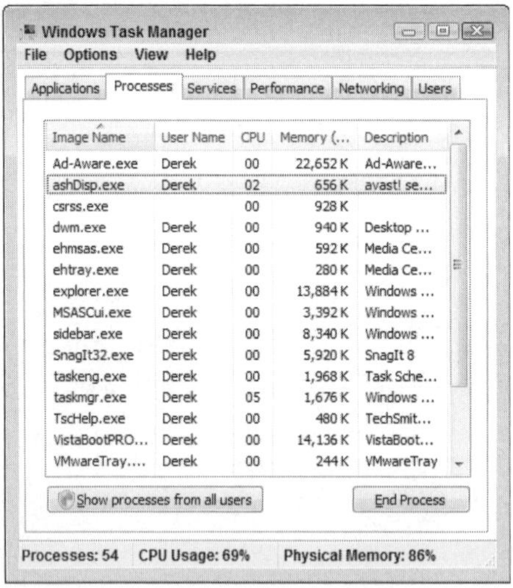

Figure 4.44. Task Manager, Vista style.

There are three ways of launching Task Manager. You can

- Right-click the taskbar and select Task Manager.
- Use the Ctrl+Shift+Esc key combination.
- Use the Ctrl+Alt+Delete key combination and select Task Manager.

Click the Applications tab and you see a list of all running applications on your system and each application's status. If the program has crashed and has stopped responding, Task Manager displays "Not Responding" next to the application name. Click the unresponsive application in Task Manager and click End Task. Sometimes the application closes immediately; sometimes a system notification appears indicating that "This program is not responding." Click End Now or wait for Windows to get fed up and close it for you. Sometimes, you may do both and the application won't close. Wait it out or reboot if this happens.

On occasion, it's not an application that goes haywire, but a system process. This often happens with poorly written device drivers or services related to hardware that are running around, listening for a response, but not smart enough to figure out that the hardware isn't responding. When this happens, the CPU usage (found in the Performance tab) usually rockets up to 100 percent. Click the Processes tab (see Figure 4.45) and find the process that is consuming all or most of the CPU cycles. Click the process and then click End Process; most of the time, this is sufficient to put down the misbehaving process.

Figure 4.45. The Processes tab lets you find out what is using all your system resources.

There are times, however, when the process won't be or can't be killed. Unlike UNIX-based systems, there is no way to log on as root and have ultimate control over what happens. Windows protects some processes even if you think they should be ended. A third-party program called Process Explorer is very effective for ending these processes and also provides far greater detail on your processes. For current compatibility, go to the Process Explorer Web site at www.sysinternals.com.

Backwards compatibility

Windows Vista has certainly made an effort in terms of guaranteeing compatibility between Windows and third-party applications. In fact, at the time of writing, Microsoft has already tested over 800 applications with Vista. They've also taken a few other steps to assure the highest level of compatibility:

- The Program Compatibility Assistant makes basic compatibility changes for Vista.

- The Application Compatibility Toolkit (ACT) 5 is designed to help you make sure your environment and applications are compatible with Vista, applying fixes for applications that are not Vista ready.

- The Application Compatibility Exchange Web site provides results from software makers and customers. These testing results are designed to help compatibility testing.

The Program Compatibility Assistant finds an appropriate compatibility mode for applications that were designed to run on earlier versions of Windows. For example, if you decided to use an XP application on Vista, the assistant detects this operating system difference and automatically prepares it to run on Vista without further action required by the user.

That's not to say it's perfect. For example, if you try to install software designed for Windows XP, it may act like it installed properly. Afterwards, a dialog box appears telling you that it has to intervene because of compatibility issues and then "fixes" the problem.

Unfortunately, these programs mentioned earlier are not available at the time of writing, so we've not been able to test them and see how effective they are. We have noticed the Compatibility Mode when using Microsoft Office 2007 on Vista and saving documents in Windows 2003 format.

A few more words about the Control Panel

We've made innumerable references to the Control Panel in Windows Vista, but we've not really discussed it in great detail (see Figure 4.46). The Control Panel can be thought of as the glue that ties Windows Vista together. This is your central location for handling pretty much any configuration or setting in the operating system.

Figure 4.46. The Control Panel in Vista picks up where XP left off.

Vista's Control Panel picks up where it left off in Windows XP; both use the Category View. The advantage of the Category View is that each category is logically arranged; in that respect it's much better than Windows XP. If you recall, XP offered categories, but no quick links to access commonly used tasks for that category. In Vista, there are a number of quick links. Using this view is also cleaner than using the familiar Classic View, which just lists a seemingly never-ending list of icons. If you're familiar with the Control Panel in Windows XP, you'll notice that the categories are similar but not the same.

If you use the Classic View, you'll notice the beefed up Control Panel (see Figure 4.47). In fact, the number of icons passes from 28 icons in

Windows XP to 49 icons in Windows Vista (or more if you are using a laptop). The number of available tasks for each Category or section is also significantly more important.

Figure 4.47. The Classic View has more icons than ever.

Although this book does not go into every new task or feature in the Windows Control Panel, the following list covers some of the most important additions:

▪ AutoPlay (this lets you change default settings for reading CDs and DVDs)

▪ BitLocker Drive Encryption (this lets you configure the new BitLocker Driver Encryption feature)

▪ Color Management (this lets you determine how graphics and displays should appear)

▪ iSCSI Initiator (this lets you connect to remote iSCSI targets and to apply settings to connections)

▪ Offline Files (this lets you set how offline files should be managed when you are off the network)

- Problem Reports and Solutions (this lets you check online for solutions to system malfunctions and other errors)

- Sync Center (this lets you manage synchronization between your computer and other devices)

- Windows CardSpace (this lets you manage stored logins and passwords for Web sites)

- Windows Defender (this lets you directly access the new Windows Defender application)

- Windows Sidebar (this lets you configure the new Windows Sidebar application)

- Windows SideShow (this lets you configure the new Windows SideShow application)

As you adapt to Windows Vista, you will gradually discover and learn all these new additions to the Control Panel and their possibilities. While it's true that some tasks can be difficult to find on occasion, it's overall a much better experience for the user.

Judgment day

Windows Vista has a greatly improved desktop experience that should please many users. While it certainly won't please everyone, and it's far from being a perfect operating system, we feel that Microsoft has greatly improved the product. Naysayers will posit that Aero simply looks too much like Mac OS X and its Aqua environment. It's hard to deny the similarities, from the transparency to the icon attributes.

While we find the various warnings and access request dialog boxes tiresome at best, intrusive at worst, we find Vista to be an overall positive experience. Who will get the most benefit out of the Windows Vista desktop?

Users who:

- Require efficiency or wish to be more productive

- Previously had trouble locating applications

- Have a graphic card that supports Windows Vista Aero

- Always felt earlier Windows versions loaded applications too slowly.

Who won't benefit much from the Windows Vista desktop?

Users who:

- Are Vista Capable, but not Premium
- Are not impressed with graphic enhancements
- Use Vista in their office and aren't using Aero

Just the facts

- Nearly every facet of the Windows basic look and feel can be configured.
- Additional wallpapers, themes, and icons can be added to further customize Windows.
- Windows gadgets and Sidebars can be used together to enhance the user experience
- The Windows Vista online help system is more responsive, more informative, and easier to use.
- The Ease of Access Center is the central location for setting up accessibility features.
- Windows Vista makes every effort to guarantee compatibility with software (even those designed for previous versions of Windows).

Manage the Vista Enviroment

PART II

GET THE SCOOP ON...
Adding users ▪ Modifying accounts ▪ Group membership ▪
Fast user switching ▪ Custom Management Consoles ▪
Taskpad views ▪ Group policies

Managing Users

L ike in Windows XP, users are a very important part of Windows Vista. You can think of a user as an account — a unique identifier created just for you that provides you with certain rights and restrictions while using Windows Vista.

There are three types of accounts in Windows Vista: Administrator, Standard user, and Guest. Figure 5.1 shows the User Accounts window. If you are familiar with Windows XP, then you will have no problems understanding account types in Windows Vista: Each account has the same roles; however, the Limited user in XP is now Standard user in Vista.

In this chapter, we cover the need for users and how they are used in Windows Vista. If you are a computer owner who is responsible for its upkeep, or have children who should not have full administrator rights, then this chapter is of particular interest. We will also disclose important new features such as the User Account Control (UAC).

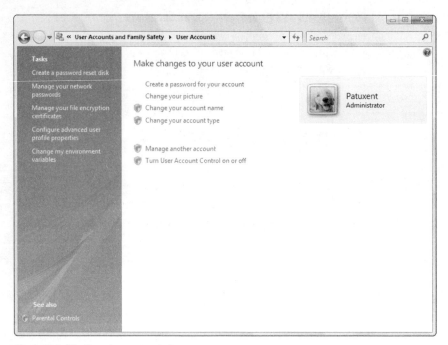

Figure 5.1. The User Accounts window.

The case for users

Maintaining separate user accounts for different users is a good idea on several levels. First, if you are the administrator for a particular computer, you will want to know who is using your machine. For security reasons, you may opt to disable a guest account and require all users to login using a custom created user account that is set according to the user's particular needs. If you are using a work computer, you'll want to make sure that you (along with an IT person) have administrator rights so that you can manage your computer; by the same token, you would want a colleague to have guest or standard user rights for security purposes.

Not every user has the same needs. For example, you may have a piece of software installed that only the system administrator needs to use. You can make that application only available to a particular user or just the administrator (or installer). Perhaps one of your children is a gamer. You may want to limit access to the game so as not to risk erasing or corrupting the game. Hiding applications is not a foolproof method:

The application is still installed to your disk, making it possible for others to access it. Although the icon might not be available, it can still be manually launched.

Privacy is another issue to consider. Perhaps you, as administrator, have a number of personal or work documents or shortcuts to system tools on your desktop and do not wish for these files to be accessible by other users. By creating a separate user account for others, you have guaranteed privacy of your desktop. Even though you can share applications with other users, they cannot access your files.

Speaking of files, did we mention that each user gets a Documents folder (see Figure 5.2)? This guarantees the privacy of your documents; there is no worry of another user accidentally erasing your documents, provided that they are stored here. Administrators, even if you eventually delete a user account, you can opt to not delete that user's Documents folder.

Figure 5.2. The Documents window.

 Watch Out!
The My Documents folder (as well as My Pictures, My Music, and so on) drops the My in Windows Vista. They are now simply referred to as Documents, Music, Pictures, and so on.

Inside Scoop

In the past, the My folders were found within the My Documents folder. These folders are now independent; each one is a separate folder found in the user directory per user account.

Another advantage of having separate user accounts is that each user can set options for folders, desktop settings, or Internet Explorer settings that are unique for their user account.

Depending on your setup, creating user accounts can be either simple or potentially confusing. If you are a home user, setting up a user account is as easy as clicking a button in the Control Panel and working with a wizard. On the other hand, if you are a professional user who is using Windows Vista over an office network and working over a domain, you must create a domain user account and not a local user account (like you would for home use). If you are using a workgroup, you must create the same user account on any computer that you will be using.

You should also determine what kind of account type you want. When you installed Windows Vista, you created an initial account for your computer. By default, this account was given Administrator status. You may want to create a second account for yourself, or perhaps for a friend or relative. In this case, we advise that you give these users Standard user access. Standard user accounts have many of the same privileges as the Administrator; however, any changes made are not system-wide. This prevents unauthorized users who do not or should not have Administrator access from doing things they should not, such as changing passwords.

Add an account

Adding an account is a mandatory step when installing Windows Vista; adding additional accounts, however, is optional yet highly recommended for the reasons discussed previously.

Watch Out!

Make sure that you are logged in as an Administrator before attempting to add a new account. Standard users are unable to perform this function.

The first step to creating a new user account for Windows Vista is to access the Control Panel. The best way to get there is to access it from the Start menu on the right-hand column. Otherwise, you can go to System Tools in the Accessories menu (also starting from the Start menu). After you open Control Panel, double-click User Accounts and Family Safety (see Figure 5.3).

Figure 5.3. The User Accounts and Family Safety window in the Control Panel.

The Shield icon

As you may have noticed, a number of options in the Control Panel are preceded by a multicolored shield (Figure 5.4). The purpose of the shield is unclear, and the lack of any key also adds to the confusion.

The icon looks similar to the Windows Defender application icon, but this is not its purpose. Any option preceded by this icon simply means that it requires the user's permission to use the program in question. You can either allow or cancel this request (which appears in a dialog box).

(continued)

(continued)

This feature is obviously a response to those who have long since criticized Microsoft of being weak on security. Unfortunately, it is a bit reactionary; we've lost count of how many times we have had to click and approve an action before getting something accomplished. This is part of the new User Account Control.

However, there is a workaround for disabling this omnipresent warning dialog box:

1. From the Search box in the Start menu, type **gpedit.msc**.

2. In the console, go to Computer Configuration ⇨ Windows Settings ⇨ Security Settings ⇨ Local Policies ⇨ Security Options.

3. Change User Account Control: Run all users including Administrators as standard users to Disable.

4. Change User Account Control: Behavior of the elevation prompt to No Prompt.

The User Accounts menu looks very similar to its counterpart in Windows XP; the primary difference is that the Vista menu is cleaner in its design. The window is broken into two primary regions; the left side of the window offers additional, but related, options. These options are detailed a little later in this chapter. The right side of the window contains the options relevant to User Accounts.

If you are going to add a new account, you must first click the Manage another account link.

Figure 5.4. One of the many occurrences of the ubiquitous security shield.

After you have given Windows Vista permission to access this window, click on the Create a new account option in the Manage Accounts page (see Figure 5.5). If you are unfamiliar with the concept of a user account, a help link will be available explaining the three types of user accounts.

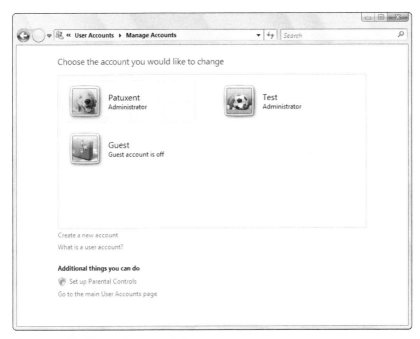

Figure 5.5. The Manage Accounts window.

If you opted to create a new account, the Create New Account window appears. Windows asks you to name the account (see Figure 5.6). Pick something that clearly indicates that either this account is yours or it belongs to a specific user. Remember that whatever name you give here will be visible to anyone who tries to log on to this computer.

After you name the account, you must decide whether or not this user account should have standard or administrator access. This page also features a help link designed to help you decide which type of account to use. Overall, the Administrator and Standard user accounts have many similar features and functions; the primary difference is that the Standard user cannot make system-wide changes. We would recommend setting most other accounts (other than your own) to Standard user. Too many Administrators can increase the chances of your computer being modified.

Inside Scoop

Of all the new changes in Windows Vista, one thing that has not changed is the maximum number of characters for account names. You are still limited to 20 characters, including special characters, such as accents.

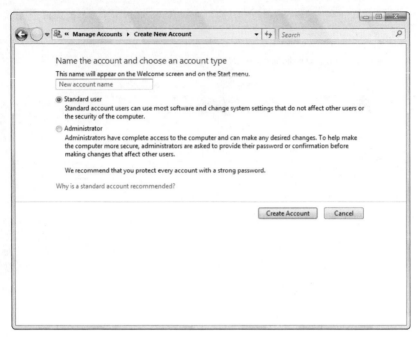

Figure 5.6. Naming the account is the first step to creating an account.

After you have created your account, you are taken back to the Manage Accounts window that now contains your new account and displays its name, default picture, and account type (see Figure 5.7). You can always go back and add as many accounts with varying account types as desired.

Like in Windows XP, you need to work with Group accounts in order to have full access over Standard user accounts. We discuss this feature later in the chapter.

Hack
Remember the third account type, Guest? Well, it is still an option! You cannot create a guest account, it already is created. However, you can activate or disable it (it is inactive by default). Simply click on the Guest account to start the quick activation procedure.

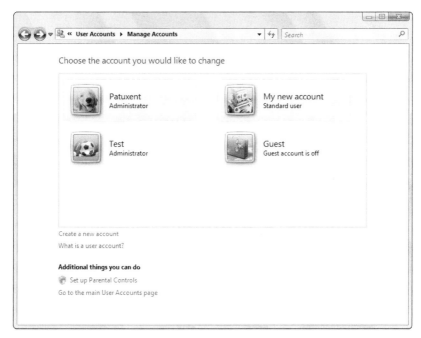

Figure 5.7. The Manage Accounts window with new account.

Modify user accounts

Now that you have created your account, you may want to go back and make changes to it. Perhaps you decided to give a trustworthy user Administrator access or you wanted to modify an account name or picture.

From the Control Panel, which is still accessible as detailed above, you should reopen the User Accounts window to make any necessary edits. Of course, just like when you create a new account, you must also have Administrator access when modifying user accounts. From the User Accounts window, click Manage another account from your account's task list so that you can select which account you wish to update.

The account parameters that you can modify depend on the user account type (see Figure 5.8). If you are modifying an Administrator account, you can modify the following:

■ Account name

■ Account password (create or modify)

■ Picture

Watch Out!
The User Accounts page lets you enable or disable the User Account Control (UAC) feature; it is not available from the Manage Accounts window.

- Account type
- Parental Controls

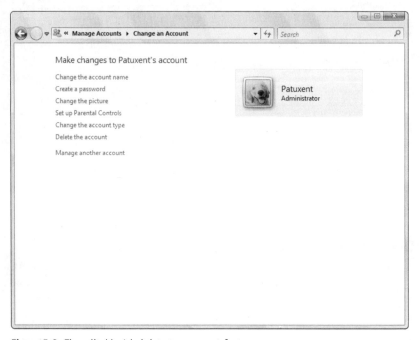

Figure 5.8. The editable Administrator account features.

If you have another Administrator account on your computer, you can use the Delete the account option. However, if you have only one Administrator account, this option does not appear. This is the minor difference between the two type of accounts in terms of change management.

If you attempt to modify a Standard user account, you can modify the following (see Figure 5.9):

- Account name
- Account password (create or modify)
- Picture

■ Parental Controls

■ Account type

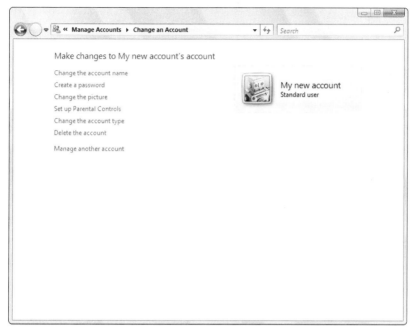

Figure 5.9. The editable Standard user account features.

Both Administrator and Standard user accounts let you set Parental Control settings. You can also set Parental Controls from the User Accounts page; it is available as a link at the bottom left pane of the window. This pane also features a number of more advanced tasks that you might be likely to use as a Windows administrator (see Figure 5.10). These include the following:

■ Create a password reset disk

■ Manage network passwords

■ Manage file encryption certificates

■ Configure advanced user profile properties

■ Change environment variables

Tasks

Create a password reset disk

Manage your network passwords

Manage your file encryption certificates

Configure advanced user profile properties

Change my environment variables

See also

Parental Controls

Figure 5.10. The available tasks for an administrator.

Changing your account name

Changing your account name is as simple as clicking a link in either the User Accounts or Change an Account window. Simply do the following:

1. Click the Change the account name link.

2. Type the new name of your account.

   Remember that you can only use up to 20 characters!

3. Click Change Name.

The new name appears on the Welcome screen and in the Start menu. This option is available for both Administrator and Standard user accounts (see Figure 5.11).

Create a password for your account

If you decide to password protect your account, or another account, this is the place to do it (see Figure 5.12). Whether you are creating a password for the first time, or changing an existing password, it makes no difference. In this window, you start from scratch.

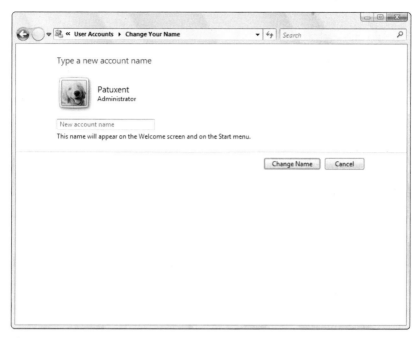

Figure 5.11. The Change Your Name window.

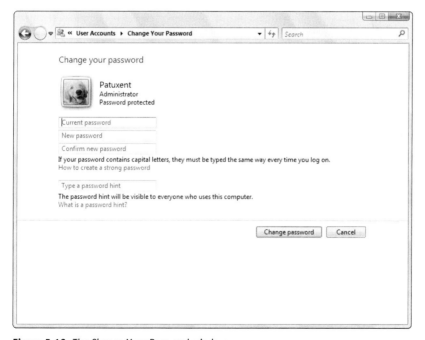

Figure 5.12. The Change Your Password window.

Watch Out!
Any EFS-encrypted files, passwords, or personal certificates are lost when you create a new password. To avoid this, create a password reset floppy disk from the User Accounts window.

1. Click Create password from the Change an Account window (or create a password for your account in User Accounts).

2. Enter a new password.

3. Confirm the new password by typing it again.

4. Type a password hint.

   Remember that your password hint is visible to anyone using your computer.

5. Click Create password.

After the new password is created, you automatically return to the Account management page. This page will have slightly changed because a new menu option is available: Remove the password. If you select this option, you remove the password currently set for the account. This does not require you to re-enter the password for validation. However, you will need to enter your password if you decide to remove it from your account.

If you have trouble thinking of a good password, you can check out the local help file entitled How to create a strong password found on this

---

Losing your password

If you are using Windows over a network, the number of incorrect password attempts before your account is locked depends on how your system administrator configured your Windows server. For home users, this feature is disabled by default. However, it can be set to prevent password hacking.

If you forget your password as a limited access account, you can use the Forgotten Password Wizard or ask the administrator to remove or reset your password. Administrators should use the Forgotten Password Wizard to reset their password. We discuss the use of the Forgotten Password Wizard later in this chapter.

page. Creating a reasonably secure password is essential; while no password is 100 percent safe, you can take steps to make your password as secure as is reasonably possible. For example, use at least eight characters in your password using a mix of uppercase, lowercase, numbers, or symbols. It is said that no part of your password should be a real word, but let's be realistic: If you have a bad memory, use a word, a part of a word, or a number that you can recall but isn't easily attributed to you. For example, it is not a good idea to use your children's names or a pet name. A password must be something that only you would think of — perhaps a first love, your favorite poet, or your lottery numbers. Passwords are case-sensitive, so do remember where you put those upper- and lower-case letters!

Changing your picture

One of the easier changes to make, Windows Vista lets you change the randomly assigned image that was associated with your account when it was created. This image appears on the Welcome screen. Click Change your picture from the Account management window (see Figure 5.13).

Figure 5.13. The Change Your Picture window.

Windows Vista offers 12 preinstalled pictures that you can use. Of course, you can browse for any other pictures on your machine that are in BMP, DIB, RLE, GIF, JPG, or PNG format. Simply click the icon and then click the Change Picture button. You can also click the "Browse for more pictures" link and select your desired picture. Once you select the image, you will return to the Edit Account page with your new picture displayed under the account name.

Changing the account type

Windows Vista also allows you the option of changing your account from a Standard user account to an Administrator account (see Figure 5.14) or vice versa. Click Change the account type in the User Accounts window. You are asked to select an account type, just like when you created the account. Accounts can be changed to Standard user or to Administrator accounts as many times as desired; the access privileges are instantaneous. Any administrator account can be deleted, on the condition that there is another administrator account on the machine. If you have a single administrator account, you cannot delete it.

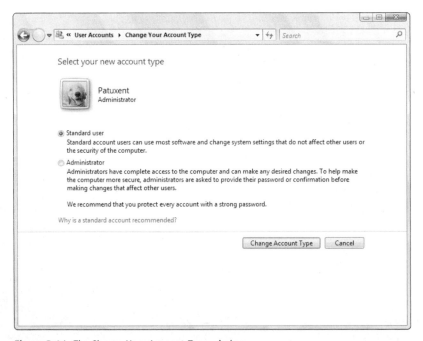

Figure 5.14. The Change Your Account Type window.

Watch Out!

You can downgrade from an Administrator to a Standard user account, but remember that you must have at least one Administrator account on your computer at all times!

Deleting the account

Administrators can easily delete any account by selecting the Delete the account option from the User Accounts window. When you select this option, you can either keep or delete the corresponding account files (see Figure 5.15). If you keep the files, Windows Vista will store the deleted account's Documents folder and desktop in a folder that has the same name as the deleted account to the administrator's desktop. Standard users, however, can only delete their own account.

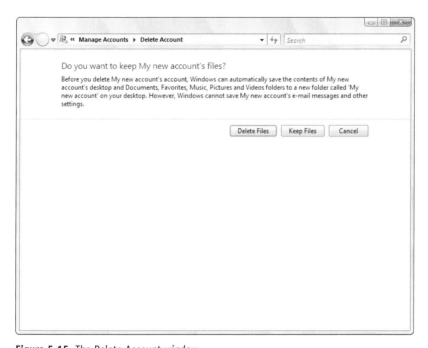

Figure 5.15. The Delete Account window.

Watch out!

Despite Windows Vista's generously saving Documents and the desktop for the deleted user account, it is unable to save other vital information such as e-mails, Internet Explorer bookmarks, or system settings.

When you decide whether to keep or delete the files, Windows XP asks you to confirm the deletion before going forward. Unfortunately, Windows Vista does not provide a gentle reminder that once the account is gone, it's gone (unless you have a backup). Like the other options, after you execute this command, you return automatically to the User Accounts window.

Working with Parental Controls

Windows Vista offers what we deem a new feature, called Parental Controls, though in previous versions of Windows, you could set your Internet Explorer settings to prevent children from going where they shouldn't. Of course, the Parental Controls offered with Vista go far beyond the IE customization (see Figure 5.16) and offer parents (or computer administrators) total control of what other people see and do on the computer.

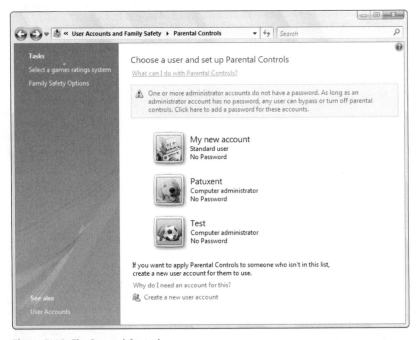

Figure 5.16. The Parental Controls page.

Watch Out!

Windows Vista does not allow you to set Parental Controls for any Administrator accounts. If you try to set controls on an Administrator account, Vista asks you to change the account type to Standard user.

The security surrounding Parental Controls and who can set them is somewhat strange. If you don't have any passwords set for your accounts, any user can get around these controls or even turn them off. Vista gives you two opportunities or warnings that you should really set passwords for an administrator account before setting Parental Controls. We agree that the Administrator should always be password protected; otherwise it sort of defeats the purpose of being an Administrator! We are somewhat surprised that Vista lets Standard users or non-password protected accounts have access to a feature that has such far-reaching effects. In Figure 5.16, you will need to acknowledge that you do not have a password for the account, do not wish to have one, and recognize the potential risks before you can continue. Alternatively, you can always set a password from this screen.

If you are editing a Standard user account, you can set a password from the Edit Account page. You can also access the Parental Controls from the Control Panel.

Start to take control!

When you open the Parental Controls page, you can select one of your available accounts, illustrated by the picture you chose earlier in this chapter. Remember, you need to have Administrator access to set these — at least for accounts other than your own.

The setup page appears when you select your account; this is where you set all the Parental Control parameters, including turning them on or off (see Figure 5.17).

By default, Parental Controls settings are off. As a result, all other setting options on this page are dimmed with the exception of Activity Reports. The Activity Reports contain up-to-date information on a wide array of activity criteria. The reports are broken into two themes: account activities and general system. The report names or headers are pretty self-explanatory (see Figure 5.18).

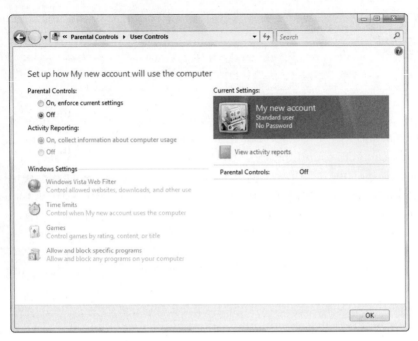

Figure 5.17. The Parental Controls setup page.

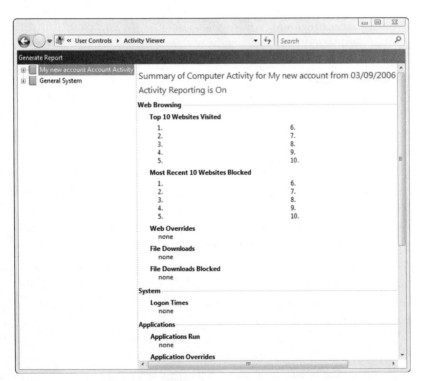

Figure 5.18. The Activity Reporting page.

After you enable the Parental Controls, you can then decide whether or not to turn on the Activity Reports. By default, Activity Reports are turned off and data is not collected. Getting down to the nitty gritty, it's time to set your computer up with Parental Controls! Microsoft really lets the Administrator assume the role of Big Brother using the Parental Controls; it certainly does its job. For parents who worry about their children's online activities, Vista will put their minds at ease. Of course, the amount of security you truly need depends on the user and their personal situation.

Windows Vista Web Filter

The Windows Vista Web Filter option lets you block certain Web content that may be inappropriate for some users (see Figure 5.19). You can also manually allow or block specific Web sites. There are four different levels of Web restriction levels, including a custom level. There are also a number of categories of potentially inappropriate subject matter that you can block; this includes hate speech, bomb making, pornography, and Web mail.

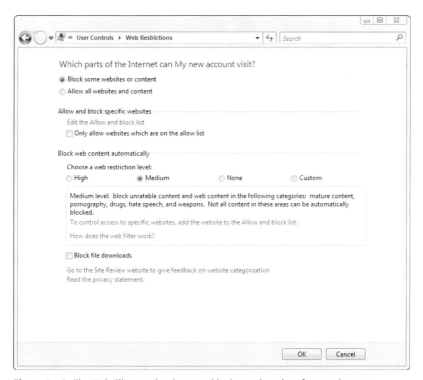

Figure 5.19. The Web Filter option lets you block naughty sites from prying eyes.

If a Web site cannot be rated, you may opt to automatically block the site. The Web Restrictions page also lets you block downloads. There are several onboard help topics on the Web Restrictions page.

Time limits

The Time limits option lets you mark off certain hours where a user can use the computer (see Figure 5.20). By dragging and clicking, you can select blocks of time where the computer is blocked to the user. By default, the computer is always available to the user. Users receive a 10-minute and a 1-minute warning that their session is about to expire. When it expires, the session is suspended and the login screen appears; the session remains active so that no activities or data are lost.

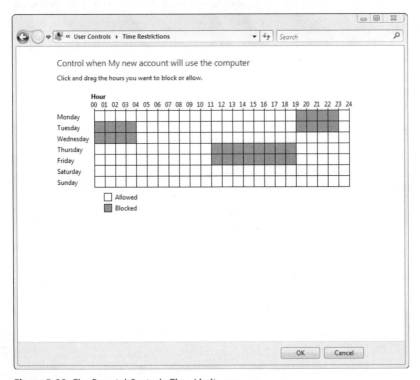

Figure 5.20. The Parental Controls Time Limits page.

Games

The Games option lets you set whether or not the user can access and play games on the computer. By default, all games are accessible to users.

However, you can set controls that forbid access to games depending on their content and ratings (see Figure 5.21). You can also set a maximum game rating that is allowed. Like with the Web restrictions, you can also manually allow or block games. Back on the main Parental Controls page, you can use the Select a games ratings system link to access a list of international ratings systems. These ratings systems seem to be primarily American and European rating organizations.

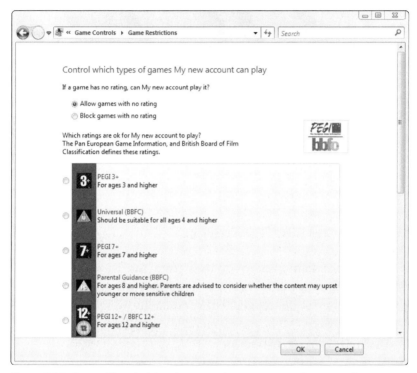

Figure 5.21. Games, like television shows, can have age-appropriateness ratings.

Block specific programs

This option lets you prevent users from accessing a specific application (see Figure 5.22). By default, the user can access all applications on the computer. However, by enabling this feature, you can select an application to block (such as a personal finance program, for example). When selected, it appears in the window.

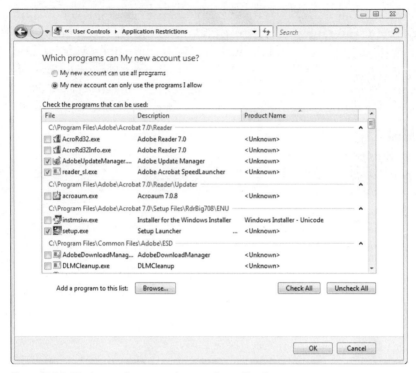

Figure 5.22. Block users from accessing certain applications.

You can also set family safety options from the Parental Controls page. Rather, it's just an option and not options; this feature simply lets you set the frequency of the report activity availability reminder.

Other Administrator options

If you are logged in as the Administrator, there are three other options available to you in the User Accounts page.

Create a password reset disk

This feature is just another name for the Forgotten Password Wizard; you may remember this feature from Windows XP. Its use in Windows Vista is completely identical (see Figure 5.23). Let's review for those who are new to Windows.

Figure 5.23. The Forgotten Password Wizard with Vista face-lift.

This feature offers Administrator and Standard user accounts to retrieve passwords (beyond the F8 reboot workaround) from a disk. External drives are preferable as they can be salvaged if your computer crashes. This disk, when saved to an external source, should be kept alongside your boot disk or rescue disk.

The Forgotten Password Wizard provides two bits of good advice in the opening window:

- This disk only needs to be created once regardless of how many times you change your password.

- Anyone can access this disk once created; it can be used to reset your password. In other words, be very careful where you leave it!

The next screen of the wizard asks you to insert a blank, formatted disk into drive A. Please refer to your computer for specific drive letters (the drive letter can change depending on your configuration). The next screen asks you to enter the password; simply enter it and click New. The wizard will then create the necessary files and copies to your drive.

Watch Out!

Before you start using the Forgotten Password Wizard, make sure you have some sort of external device, like a floppy drive or a USB drive, to which you can write. This is necessary in order to use this feature.

Inside Scoop

If you don't feel like using Microsoft's Forgotten Password Wizard, you can also keep an encrypted password table (simply a Microsoft Word document) and store it on a CD or a USB flash drive.

There are two unusual things about this wizard: first is its preventive nature, secondly is its very existence — the wizard helps you prepare for eventual password loss, however, it will not help you retrieve a lost password.

Manage your network passwords

The Stored User Names and Passwords window is not new to Windows. What is new in Windows Vista is the Backup/Restore feature in this window (see Figure 5.24).

Stored User Names and Passwords

Where did you save the backup file?

If you saved the backup file on removable media, insert it before entering the location.

Backup file location: [   ]   [Browse...]

Before you click Next:
If you have added, changed, or removed any logon credentials since your last backup, those changes will be overwritten.

[Next]   [Cancel]

Figure 5.24. The Backup feature.

You can add a Web site, server, or network location and store the relevant username/password for the target. This feature is helpful because you can store login credentials for often used sites or network locations, which saves you the hassle of always having to type everything in. On the other hand, you have the worry of leaving yourself vulnerable if anyone else uses your account and happens upon any of your stored locations.

Watch Out!

Any changes made to the login credentials (for example, adding, removing, or editing) since the last backup performed will be overwritten.

Unlike in Windows XP, you do not need to log into the Passport Web site to modify properties. You can simply click Properties and make the necessary updates. The Properties window also lets you change the domain password, if applicable.

Another difference, as stated earlier, is the Backup and Restore features. If you use the Backup feature, you are asked to select a location to store your login credentials. You can pick the file location using the browse button. Once you name and save your file, the following screen asks you to use the Ctrl+Alt+Delete combination to continue the backup. Vista then asks you to enter and then confirm a password to protect the backup file.

If you use the Restore feature, Vista asks you to select the login credential file that you saved earlier.

After you select the file, you can move on to the next screen where you once again use the Ctrl+Alt+Delete combination and then enter your password to restore the backup.

Manage your file encryption certificates

The Encrypting File System (EFS) feature is available in the more advanced editions of Windows Vista. We discuss the benefits of file encryption later in this book; however, suffice it to say that with the increasing dangers of identity theft and other online criminal activities, file encryption is something that you will want to seriously consider for sensitive data files. Users who are coming from Windows XP Professional or Windows 2003 (or 2000) will likely remember this feature.

Windows now uses EFS to store files to your hard drive in encrypted format. The principles of EFS are quite simple: By selecting EFS, files are

Watch Out!

You cannot open encrypted files without the proper decryption key.

encrypted when you save and close them and automatically decrypted when you re-open them. EFS is helpful, especially if you have multiple users sharing a computer and one user wants to make sure that certain data isn't available to other users.

To use this feature, you must first have an encryption certificate and a valid decryption key on your computer or another media. Obtaining or renewing certificates is discussed in greater detail in Chapter 7.

If you do not have a file encryption certificate, you can create one (see Figure 5.25). If you do have one, the certificate details appear in the feature. Vista allows you to create a self-signed certificate either on your computer or a smart card. You must then select a location for the certificate and, if desired, set a password for it. You can also wait until the next time you log on to set a password. If you're curious as to what the certificate does exactly, you can view it and the list of uses appears.

Figure 5.25. The file encryption certificate.

A hierarchical menu appears for you to select which directories are associated with the key — in other words, which directories are encrypted and updated. Be careful though, the more directories that you include means the longer it will take for your update and encryption to complete.

File Encryption Certificates

File Encryption Certificates are the centerpiece of encryption. These "documents" act as a passport that confirms a user's identity or even assures the safety of a Web site. These certificates are generated by special companies referred to as Certification Authorities.

You'll need to have a valid file encryption certificate in order to use EFS. It's also good to have for when you are navigating a secure Web site. Certificates are provided automatically, but it is possible that you may be able to manually obtain one. For example, if you wish to secure your e-mail communications, you would need to apply for such a certificate from a Certification Authority such as Thawte, VeriSign, or Computer Associates.

If you are using Vista Home (Basic or Premium), you won't be able to use EFS, but all is not lost! You can use the Cipher application (type Cipher.exe at your command prompt) to decrypt files or back up EFS certificates or keys. In order to use the Cipher application, you'll need to have the encryption key or certificate.

There are a number of third-party applications that can perform similar functions. However, there are some advantages to using EFS for file encryption, notably the fact that EFS is fully integrated with Windows' file system.

Configure advanced user profile properties

You can directly access your user profiles and toggle between local profiles and roaming profiles. This is almost the same window as the User Profiles window available in the Advanced System Properties (the Copy To option is not available here).

There isn't a lot of actual configuration that you can do from this window; you can simply change profile type. Beyond that, your only other options are to validate or cancel the operation.

Change my environment variables

Like the User Profiles window, this is the same Environment Variables window that you can find in the Advanced System Properties window. Environment Variables should be modified with the greatest care;

deleting or erroneously modifying a variable or its value can have disastrous effects on your computer, such as making it inoperable!

Environment variables also let you set variables for both your user account and system-wide variables. Proceed with caution; specifically, only if your system or application documentation tells you.

Change group membership

Changing group membership for a user account can only be done if you are logged on as an Administrator. In fact, your computer must be logged on to a domain and you must be logged on as a computer administrator and have the necessary network permissions to perform this task. Please see your network administrator should you have any questions about your access level. You cannot perform this procedure without the necessary permission.

Home users most likely do not need to worry about domains; in fact, office users probably don't need to concern themselves too much with them either. With respect to Windows, domains are a group of computers that are managed by a server. They contain user and group accounts as well as security policies.

Group accounts are similar to local user accounts, except that they are used to assign rights to a group of users instead of a single user. This makes life much easier for administrators, because they can add groups of users to a single category and apply similar properties across the board.

To change group membership for a user account, you work with the User Accounts window from the Control Panel. If you are working on a domain, you will find a User tab at the top of the User Accounts window. Click the name of the desired user account under the Users for this computer menu and click Properties. Select the new group for the user and click OK.

Windows offers nine default groups from which to choose:

- **Administrators.** Administrators have full access to the machine.
- **Backup Operators.** This group can override security settings only in order to back up or restore files.
- **Guests.** This group is similar to the Users group; the Guest account has additional restrictions.

- **Network Configuration Operators.** This group can have limited administrator rights in order to manage network configurations.

- **Power Users.** This group has many of the same rights as the administrators, but still has certain restrictions.

- **Remote Desktop Users.** This group can log on to the domain remotely.

- **Users.** This group can run certified applications, but not legacy applications (unlike Power Users). They cannot make system-wide changes.

- **Debugger Users.** This group can debug processes locally and remotely, if necessary.

- **HelpServicesGroup.** Group for Help and Support service center.

You can also add new groups in the Computer Management window. Keep in mind that this section does not apply to you if you are not on a domain.

Configure fast user switching

Windows Vista kept another cool feature from the XP days — the Switch user feature. This feature lets you toggle between user accounts on your computer without having to completely shut down your current session. By toggling users, you can safely switch to another account without fear of losing data.

The Switch user feature puts one account on hold while you log into a different account. This is practical, for example, if you are working on a document for work and another family member needs to use the computer to quickly e-mail a file from their Documents folder.

To toggle accounts, simply log off from the Start menu and select Switch User. Windows Vista displays the welcome screen and lets you select any available user account. After you are finished with the second account, go back to the Start menu and log off. Be sure not to shut down

Inside Scoop

Shut down any applications that use a lot of system resources before switching user accounts. The performance of the second account is very much affected by the resources used by the primary session.

the computer; should you do this, Windows reminds you that another user account is currently logged in and that you may lose any unsaved data.

Use the Run as administrator command to switch users

Windows Vista provides a special command that allows you to use an application with a different user account or permissions than what is currently set in your active Windows session. In other words, you can open an application as a user other than yourself. This command is both Windows-based (accessible from the Windows Vista interface) and command-line based (accessed from the command prompt or Run menu). This command was formerly called Run as in Windows XP; it is now Run as Administrator. This change may be confusing to users who are used to the Windows XP nomenclature; however, this change seems logical. Why would an administrator want to run an application as a Standard user?

You do not need to be an administrator to access or use the Run as feature. You can use it if you want to create a desktop shortcut for another user account, for example. It can also be helpful if you are an administrator logged on to a more restrictive account and want to perform some tasks that are not authorized using your account, but you do not want to log off.

Use Run as Administrator from the interface

If you are working within the Windows Vista interface, you can access the Run as Administrator command from any application icon or shortcut found in Windows Explorer, the Start menu, or Computer. However, the way this works is completely different from what you may be used to from Windows XP.

First of all, the Run as Administrator command only appears in menus of Windows-bundled applications and features (applications that are factory included with Windows Vista, for example, Windows Media Player or WordPad). The command lets you open the application with Administrator privileges. This amended command, on the other hand, does not appear for installed applications, such as Microsoft Office.

You can also switch users through the Properties command if you right-click the application icon (for both installed and onboard applications). By clicking on the Advanced button, you may be able to check the Run with different credentials option. This lets you run an application using a different user account or to continue accessing the application using your current account. If you activate it and right-click the application icon, the Run as Administrator command appears in bold. If you wish to go back to the status quo (and not Run as Administrator), you must go back through the Advanced menu and deselect the option. The Run as Administrator command reappears in normal font size.

If you are a Standard user, and you run an application as an Administrator, you do exactly as discussed above. The User Account Control window appears indicating that you must enter an administrator password and then click OK. Once you do this, you can access the application as an Administrator.

Use Run as Administrator from the command line

The command-line version of the Run as command is slightly more complicated than from the interface and contextual menus. You can access the command prompt where you will call the command in several ways:

■ From the Start menu, enter **cmd** in the search box at the bottom of the Start menu and click OK.

■ Also from the Start menu, you can click All Programs, Accessories, and then Command Prompt.

■ You can also access the command by creating a shortcut on the desktop and then typing **cmd** in the Create Shortcut dialog box.

The "runas" command accepts a number of parameters, or settings, which are shown below. For information on each of these parameters, please see the Windows XP Help and Support Center or simply type "runas" at the command prompt and press Return, and the definition for each parameter will appear.

Watch Out!

Another big difference between the command-line and interface commands is that the command-line command is runas while the interface command is Run as. Using Run as at the command prompt will return an error.

The proper syntax for the runas command is

```
RUNAS [ [/noprofile | /profile] [/env] [/netonly]
]/smartcard [/user:<UserName>] program
```

Some examples that Windows offers of the "runas" command syntax are as follows:

- `runas /noprofile /user:mymachine\administrator cmd`: No profile will be loaded, the user's environment will be used, and it will open the .cmd file.

- `runas /profile /env /user:mydomain\admin "mmc %windir%\system32\dsa.msc"`: The user's profile will be loaded using the current environment; the user will open the .msc file.

- `runas /env /user:user@domain.microsoft.com "notepad \"my file.txt\""`: The current environment will be used; the user will open the designated file with Notepad.

Create custom management consoles

Windows Vista uses consoles that list administrative tools, folders, Web pages, and other items to manage your Windows experience (see Figure 5.26). The console is the framework that holds these items together. Admittedly, consoles are something that the average user probably won't use. Consoles haven't changed very much in this new version of Windows, beyond the addition of a third panel, called Actions, which offers all the opportunities that the Action menu does.

You can create your own Microsoft Management Console (MMC) to monitor hardware, software applications, or networking devices on your system (see Figure 5.27). MMC creation is done by adding wizards, snap-ins, tasks, documentation, and so on. You can also view and use a number of preconfigured consoles in the Administrative Tools menu in the Control Panel. This menu includes familiar consoles, such as Computer Management and Data Sources (ODBC).

The MMC is easily accessible from the search bar in the Start menu. Simply type **mmc** and click OK. You can also add extensions, such as /**a** (to open in author mode), /**32** (to open in 32-bit mode), or /**64** (to open in 64-bit mode, however, this requires a 64-bit processor). A blank Console Root window appears inside the Console box, unless you added a path after **mmc** at the command line, in which case the desired existing console will appear.

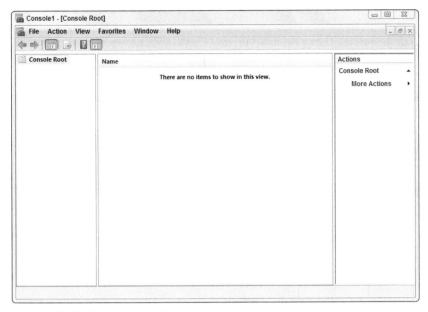

Figure 5.26. The blank Console window.

Figure 5.27. The Computer Management console.

Watch Out!

You should only use author mode when you need to create or update a console. Otherwise, use one of the three user modes — full access; limited access, multiple windows; or limited access, single window.

The Console Root window is now split into three parts: the console tree, the Details pane, and the Actions pane. The console tree, which shows the available components in your console, is the left pane of the window. The middle pane, the details pane, lists any information relating to the selected component in the console tree, for example, the name. The third pane, the Actions pane, provides all the options available in the Action menu of the console toolbar for the selected component.

There are two different ways of viewing the consoles, either in user mode or author mode. You view preconfigured consoles in user mode. Author mode is the mode required for editing or creating new consoles. These modes can be selected in the File ⇨ Options menu of the Console menu while in a new/nonbundled console.

Create a new console

Now that the Console window is up and running, it's time to get started on the console. Creating the console shell is the first step in creating a custom MMC. Before we begin, verify in the Options menu that you are set to author mode. You can potentially create a console that monitors computer management, IP security, and local users and groups. To do so, follow these steps:

1. From the File menu, use the Add/Remove Snap-in command to add or remove snap-ins (click Add to add a snap-in; click on an installed snap-in and click Remove to remove a snap-in); we'll be working in the Standalone tab. If you are adding a snap-in to your console, this dialog box lets you select from 24 snap-ins provided by Microsoft. For more information on your snap-in, simply click it and a brief description will appear at the bottom of the dialog box.

2. When you select a snap-in and validate your selection, either it will appear in the Add or Remove Snap-ins dialog box or a wizard will appear requiring you to configure the snap-in before it is added.

3. If you are removing a snap-in from the list, simply select the snap-in and click Remove. Some snap-ins, as we will discuss later, require

extra configuration; for example, you may need to select a machine, or set an ActiveX control.

Snap-ins are nothing more than tools or components that are designed to monitor or achieve a certain task and are stored in your console. There is no need to be confused by their presence because of the unusual name afforded them by Microsoft. There are two types of snap-ins:

■ The first is the snap-in that we saw in the list of 82 snap-ins back in the dialog box; these are called "standalones."

■ The second kind of snap-in is called an extension; this is a sub-snap-in that can only be added to an existing snap-in to enhance its functions.

The Add or Remove Snap-ins window is cleaner in Vista than in XP. Instead of having a two-tab window, your available snap-ins appear immediately. Once you select a snap-in, you must first configure it before it appears in the Selected snap-ins panel. In order to work with extensions, click on the snap-in from the list of Selected snap-ins and then click Edit Extensions.

If you click on the extension name, a brief description appears at the bottom of the dialog box (see Figure 5.28). If your snap-in has more than one extension available, there is a check box that allows you to select them all.

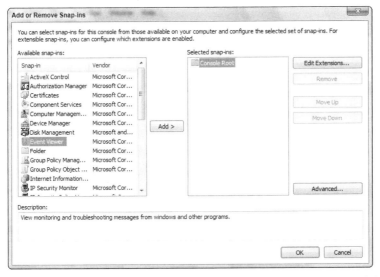

Figure 5.28. A description of the selected snap-in is displayed at the bottom of the window.

Watch Out!

Not every snap-in has an extension! If the Extensions tab is dimmed, that means that none of your snap-ins have extensions.

After you've validated your selection, your console should look just like one of the preconfigured consoles that you're used to seeing! The snap-ins appear under the Console Root in the console tree, and the relevant information for your snap-in appears in the details pane. Remember, you must click the snap-in in the console tree in order for it to appear in the details pane. By default, the Console Root is selected and the names of all the installed snap-ins appear in the details pane.

Simply save the console in the File menu and your new MCC will appear alongside the other preconfigured consoles provided by Microsoft.

Use your console

Now that you've created the console, it's time to put it to work for you. Consoles aren't an overly complex component in Windows Vista, but many people simply won't use them. At best, the average user may use one of the preconfigured Microsoft Management Consoles to troubleshoot a problem. Referring to the console we created in Figure 5.29, if you decide that you want to create or edit a user, you can do so by opening your console in the MMC, and then right-clicking the appropriate snap-in (Local Users and Groups). You can create a new user or right-click on an existing user that appears in the Details pane, and establish settings, for example, that prevent users from changing their passwords. Or you can disable or lock an account.

Snap-ins can be used or configured from the Console dialog box. To do this, in the console tree, click the name of the desired snap-in.

As you click the snap-in, you'll notice the details pane change. There are two other more subtle changes in the Action and View menus, although you may not notice those right away. These are the associated actions and commands in these menus that change.

The Action menu lets you perform any associated actions for a snap-in from a single toolbar menu. You can also achieve this by right-clicking the snap-in name in the console tree. The View menu, quite simply, lets you select how you wish to view the snap-in. Some View menus are more robust than others; for "Device Manager on local computer," you can select to view Devices or Resources by type of connection while other snap-ins may only allow you to select large or small icons.

If there is a particular snap-in that you find you use more than others, the Microsoft Management Console allows you to store favorites in the same way you would save a Web site as a favorite in Internet Explorer. You can even create Favorite folders to better organize your snap-ins.

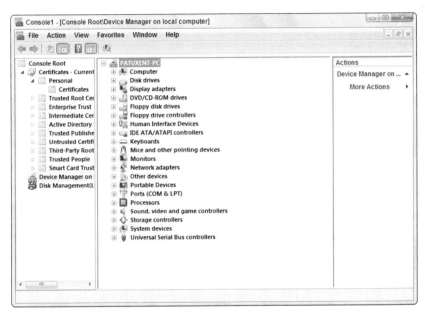

Figure 5.29. A customized console.

Create Taskpad views

The Microsoft Management Console also features Taskpad views; this hasn't changed either since Windows XP, so let's review their purpose. These views appear in the details pane of a console and feature shortcuts to other commands. Like many other procedures in Windows Vista, this too is facilitated through the use of a wizard.

The New Taskpad View Wizard (see Figure 5.30) is a rare commonality in the MMC Action menu (it is actually available for all snap-ins); you can find it by clicking the New Taskpad View menu item under the

Action menu. Select the snap-in to be changed (for example, the IP Security snap-in that we'll quickly add for these purposes).

Figure 5.30. The New Taskpad View Wizard.

The New Taskpad View Wizard starts off like most wizards. It provides a quick overview of what the wizard will achieve and what it will do for you. Make sure you click on the desired snap-in in the console tree before you launch the New Taskpad View Wizard.

The first screen in the wizard walks you through the Taskpad display, or style. In other words, you set up how the details pane will appear for a selected snap-in. The wizard provides three different styles for you to choose from: Vertical list, Horizontal list, and No list. If you're confused on which one to use, each style tells where it is most applicable if you select it. A sample picture appears real-time next to the style options. You can also opt to hide the Standard tab, which is a list of controls.

You may also choose between displaying task descriptions as text (they will appear below the task names) or as an InfoTip, where they will appear in a pop-up window. Finally, this screen lets you decide if you want the list size set to small, medium, or large. This is simply a question of

Watch Out!

Make sure you click on the desired snap-in in the console tree before you launch the New Taskpad View Wizard. The wizard takes into account the selected snap-in, so if it's not the one you want, you'll have to cancel and start over.

how large you want the details pane to be. By default, medium is selected (see Figure 5.31).

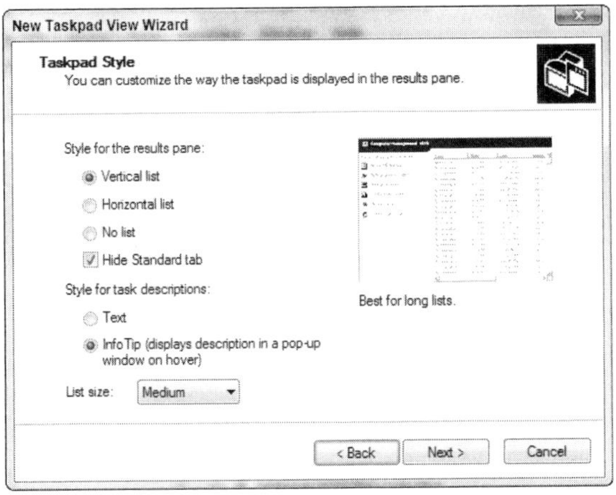

Figure 5.31. Taskpad style options.

The next wizard page lets you decide where to apply the new Taskpad view.

You can either apply the Taskpad view to the currently selected item or you can apply it to all occurrences of the item. In other words, if you have two instances of the Disk Defragmenter snap-in, you can apply the new Taskpad view to both instances (as well as make this view the default display for both instances of the snap-in).

The next screen of the wizard allows you to give a name to the new Taskpad view. By default, it takes the name of the selected snap-in. You can also add a brief description of the Taskpad view if you like.

The final step is to validate your work by clicking Finish.

Your new Taskpad view appears (see Figure 5.32). You have the option of adding new tasks to your new Taskpad view by selecting the New Task Wizard. The New Task Wizard allows you to create a task for the Taskpad you created earlier. You can launch the New Task Wizard immediately after you complete the New Taskpad View Wizard. After you launch it, you can select the type of command you will use:

- **Menu command.** Run commands from a menu.

- **Shell command.** Run scripts, launch a program, or open a Web page.

- **Navigation.** Navigate to a view chosen from your Favorites.

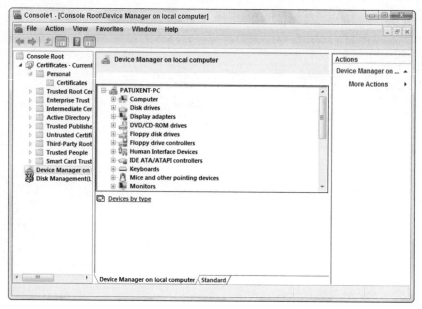

Figure 5.32. The new Taskpad view.

Create group policies

There are a number of places where you would create or use group policies. These include your local machine, another computer on your network, a Web site, a domain, or an organizational unit (such as, accounting, documentation, and so on). Group policies let you control the user environment. Examples of group policies include managing wallpapers, scripts, security settings, or software deployment.

Group policies are essentially group policy settings set using the Group Policy Objects snap-in from the Microsoft Management Console. These are stored locally on your machine; however, if you are working over a domain, the Group Policy is stored at the domain level (in addition to your local group policy). In previous versions of Windows (notably Windows 2000), this was primarily designed for use with Active Directory or a network. However, Windows Vista shows that it is also great for use for stand-alone machines because you can completely control your machine's environment without having to be on a network.

You can view the current Group Policy on your machine in the following directory: C:\WINDOWS\system32\GroupPolicy. The Group Policy

Watch Out!

Group Policies and the Group Policy Object Editor snap-in are only available with Windows Vista Business. This section does not apply to Home users.

folder is an invisible folder, so make sure you are able to view the contents. If you cannot see them, open Computer ⇨ Tools ⇨ Folder Options and click Hidden files and folders in the View tab and select Show hidden files and folders.

The contents of this folder may differ depending on the policies set, but there are a minimum of four items in the folder:

- **Adm folder.** This folder contains .adm files (Administrative template files) used for the group policy as well as the admfiles.ini configuration file.

- **User folder.** This folder contains a list of registry settings and Logon/Logoff scripts (if any were created).

- **Machine folder.** This folder contains a list of registry settings and a Scripts folder containing Startup/Shutdown scripts (if any were created).

- **Gpt.ini file.** This file details any extension modification settings.

You can view a Group Policy locally on your machine. To do this, you'll want to access the Microsoft Management Console (MMC) window we discuss earlier in this chapter. Working with either a console you created or a brand-new console, add a Group Policy Object Editor snap-in from the Add Standalone Snap-In menu.

When you select the Group Policy Object Editor, the Group Policy Wizard appears in a separate window. These objects are stored in the Active Directory or locally.

The wizard gives you the opportunity to select a Group Policy Object on your machine or on another machine on the domain. If you opt to browse the objects on another machine, the wizard lets you pick the type

Hack

If you are looking to access the existing group policy, type **gpedit.msc** at the command window, or in Start menu search box.

of objects as well as the location. There is a set of advanced options that looks similar to your standard Find menu.

After you finish the Group Policy Wizard, go back to the Add or Remove Snap-ins dialog box, and click the Extensions tab. Extensions are used to extend the functionality of the snap-in. The Group Policy Object Editor snap-in features a number of available extensions. When you validate your selections, the Console dialog box appears again.

Determine Group Policy settings

Now that you know a little bit about Group Policy, you can work with actual settings. For example, you may want to add or remove a user or change security settings. However, it's extremely important to note that any changes made to Group Policy settings could have profound effects on your system and how it performs or behaves.

You can use either the console you created in the MMC discussed earlier or use the gpedit.msc file to make changes to your Group Policy settings locally.

Using the console tree (see Figure 5.33), you can expand and collapse the various menus. When you find the desired policy to change, click it in the details pane. A detailed overview of the policy appears on the left side of the details pane (see Figure 5.34).

Double-clicking the setting in the details pane opens settings elements in the Extended tab of the pane on the right. Click on a name and then click the link to its immediate left to configure it. Right below the link you will find a brief definition of what the setting is.

Once you click the link, you can configure the settings according to your needs. Once you've finished, be sure to click Apply, and then click OK in order to make sure that everything has registered!

Watch Out!

Before you modify any Group Policy settings, make sure you have a recent backup of your machine as well as a bootable disk handy. Changes to Group Policy settings can make your system unstable or even crash it.

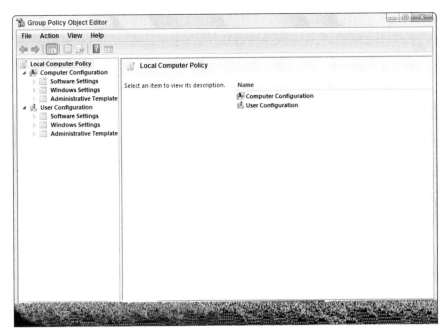

Figure 5.33. The Group Policy window.

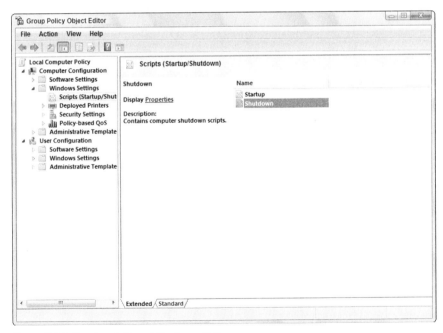

Figure 5.34. The description of the Group Policy.

Watch Out!

You may have noticed that the MMC or the Group Policy console had both Computer Configuration and User Configuration. Please note that the Computer Configuration setting always takes precedence over the User Configuration setting. By default, these settings have the same setting for both configurations.

Just the facts

- Windows Vista features three types of user accounts: Administrator, Standard user, and Guest. Each account has varying levels of access and rights.

- Using the Switch User feature, you can quickly toggle between multiple user accounts without having to shut down your session or having to log off.

- Switch users when launching an application from a particular account using the Run as command.

- Create customized consoles using the Microsoft Management Console to analyze and stay on top of your machine's activities.

- Create Group Policies to manage and control your user environment.

GET THE SCOOP ON...
Changing folder views ▪ Customizing folders ▪ Search
folders ▪ Adding files to Start menu ▪ File compression ▪
Windows BitLocker ▪ Encryption ▪ Sharing files and
folders ▪ Working with the Recycle Bin

Managing Files and Folders

Windows Vista has made a lot of progress, or at least a lot of changes, to the user experience by changing how folders are viewed. In some ways, the folks in Redmond made navigating folders and their contents a more integral part of how we use Windows. But that's not the only change in Vista. With identity theft on the rise, people are becoming increasingly concerned about protecting the data on their computers, and with good reason! Microsoft has responded to these uncertain times, albeit a bit late, with an improved feature that allows file and folder encryption, as well as a way of locking down your hard drive in the event it is physically stolen.

Windows Explorer is still very much alive and well in Windows Vista, though it is integrated with other folders, notably Documents. This is another example of how Microsoft has made navigation a lot easier by merging frequently used features with Windows basics, such as folders.

In this chapter, we take a look at how Microsoft made navigation easier for you in Windows Vista, as well as review some of the still-valuable features carried over from Windows XP. Of course, we also take a look at how file encryption can benefit you and why you should take advantage of this feature or some sort of encryption package.

Chapter 6

Watch Out!

Microsoft dropped the "My" from the Documents, Pictures, Music, and so on, folders for Windows Vista. This book refers to all of these folders by their new name.

Change folder views

Open a folder — any folder — and if you're a first-time Vista user, then you're bound to be blown away. The first thing you notice is that folders look nothing like the ugly old yellow things that you've grown accustomed to over the years in Windows. Folders in Windows are now actually informative, displaying a wide array of helpful information that wasn't as easily accessible in previous versions of Windows. The Documents folder (see Figure 6.1) is a perfect representation of folders in Windows Vista.

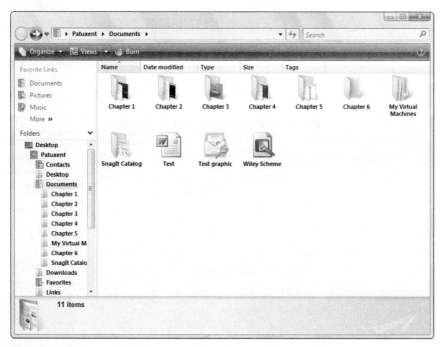

Figure 6.1. The Documents folder shows off the new look folder.

Would you like to supersize that?

Here's a perfect example of where Microsoft got something so right, that it merits a special notice. A major complaint among many Windows users in the past was that icons and their labels were too small to read. Microsoft rectifies this longtime lapse of judgment by offering four different icon sizes: small, medium, large, and extra large (see Figure 6.2).

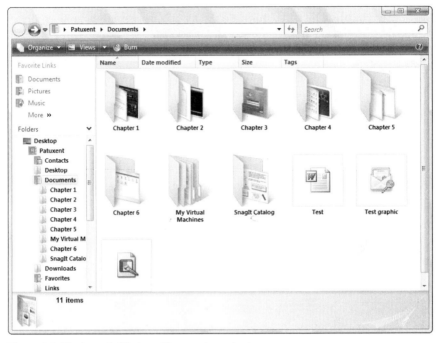

Figure 6.2. The icons in Windows Vista can be resized.

Although the icon is magnified, the label is not. But we still consider it a major improvement over past Windows versions. When you click on an icon, important file information is displayed at the bottom of the folder. The new Live Icons feature more than makes up for the small label text. No, they're not living and breathing icons (though in a way they really are); icons in Vista folders now display a "live" snapshot of the actual document it represents and not just a generic symbol. For example, a thumbnail of the actual file and not just a boring Word icon displays (see Figure 6.3).

Windows Vista doesn't offer much in the way of view types: in fact, there are only four view types: Icons, List, Details, and Tiles.

Icons display a graphic representation of your file or application. As mentioned earlier, they can display in one of four sizes. The List display displays your icons very much like small icons. It is also similar to the

Details display type; the only difference is that Details provides pertinent information, such as the date the file was last modified, the file type, and its size.

Thumbnails do not make the cut, though they can be made to appear without implicitly selecting them. For example, thumbnails are replaced with a new feature called Live Icons which we describe earlier. If you select the Details view, the filename, date modified, type, and size are still displayed like they were in Windows XP. If you look at the bottom of the folder, the same information, as well as any other available information, is displayed.

If you opt for the Tiles display, the folder or filename and type appear along with the appropriate icon for the type. Tiles display a medium-sized icon along with the filename, file type, and size. If you mouse over a tiled file, you can also find information such as the date it was last modified and information specific to the file type (picture dimensions for graphics, and number of pages for Word documents, for example). Like in Details view, relevant information of the clicked icon is displayed at the bottom of the folder.

Figure 6.3. Live Icons give a true view of your file.

Working with Properties

The Properties command, which is evoked by right-clicking a file, application, or folder, hasn't changed significantly in Windows Vista, but it is worth being reacquainted. Most users never think to use the Properties options, but they can be very helpful.

File properties in Windows Vista change depending on whether or not the file is a file, application, or folder. If you open the properties of, for example, a WordPad file, you notice four different tabs:

- **General tab.** This tab is exactly the same as in Windows XP. It features information such as file type, location, size, size on disk, number of files, creation date, and attributes. You can also set advanced attributes from this tab.

- **Security tab.** Allows you to set permissions for user accounts on the machine. This tab will likely be familiar to many users. The Advanced button provides additional security features that are discussed later in this book.

- **The Details tab.** Contains relevant information about the selected file or folder.

- **Previous Versions tab.** Lets you roll back to a previously installed version of your file, if applicable. To use Previous Versions, you must first create a restore point for your file.

If you are viewing the properties of an application, then your options are slightly different: General, Shortcut, Compatibility, Security, Details, and Previous Versions. Most of these are very similar to the options available in Windows XP. Folders display the General, Sharing, Security, and Previous Versions tabs. These are similar to the Windows XP options. We do find the Properties menu to be somewhat confusing; it seems that every file type has a distinct layout. For example, some Properties menus do not have Security or Detail tabs, and we're not exactly sure why.

Inside Scoop

Did you happen to notice that title bars and borders in Windows Vista are considerably larger in Aero? This pleasant weight gain makes it easier for you to resize windows.

The anatomy of the folder

So many options are available when it comes to working with folders that it starts to become overkill. Take a closer look at Windows Vista folders.

As you can tell from your first look at Windows Vista folders, everything has been streamlined into a united interface. The address bar at the top now features a hierarchical breakdown of where you are in relation to your hard drive. By clicking on any of the arrows in the address bar, you can go to another frequently used area, such as Pictures, Videos, Favorites, Music, and so on. By clicking on the arrow next to the folder icon, you can go to the desktop, Computer, and Recycle Bin (see Figure 6.4). By the way, the Pictures, Video, and Music folders are no longer found directly inside the Documents folder; they are now completely separate entities found within the user directory.

Figure 6.4. The address bar provides easy navigation.

The address bar also has another new feature — try right-clicking it. From the hierarchical listing, you can copy the address (either as a path or a text name) or even edit it. If you choose to edit the address, the address changes to show the path and not the text name (Documents). If you right-click on the path, there are a number of settings including an option to read from right-to-left, as well as Unicode settings. If you are working primarily with ASCII characters, you most likely won't be using these features.

The ubiquitous Search box is also present in Windows Vista folders. This Search feature works exactly the same as the Search feature in the Start menu. To facilitate navigation of Windows Vista, the left side of the screen features a list of favorite links. These links include documents, pictures, music, recently changed items, and searches. You can remove any of these links by right-clicking the link and selecting Remove Link. The main panel features relevant information about a file if you clicked

Watch Out!

As stated earlier, Microsoft has dropped the "My" from their folders in Windows Vista.

Inside Scoop

By double-clicking on the address bar, you can view the path of the current folder. For example, C:\User\Bob\Documents. Double-clicking it again returns the hierarchical menu.

one. This information is also displayed across the bottom of the folder. Do not mistake the Searches link for a standard Search feature; this link really points to the Search Folders feature. We discuss this new feature later in the chapter.

If you are viewing the search results or contents of a folder, you can do a lot from the column headers. These column headers are greatly improved in Vista, even if this feature is easy to miss. Beyond the usual way of viewing sorts, you can use the Stack View option (which organizes data by stacks based on content values) and the Group by View option (which displays content by groups based on content values). If you click on an arrow on the right side of the column header, you can set sort parameters.

If you right-click a column header and click More from the menu, you can access the Choose Details window (see Figure 6.5). You can choose which details should be displayed. This includes the default column headers plus an impressive amount of other details. You can also set the column width in this menu.

Figure 6.5. The Choose Details window with extensive details.

Inside Scoop

You can access the Internet without launching your browser by entering a valid Web address, or URL, in the address bar.

The most intriguing part of folders in Windows Vista is the menu bar, located just below the address bar. This menu bar features seven buttons that are shown in Figure 6.6.

Figure 6.6. The Documents menu bar.

Organize

The Organize menu is similar to the Tools menu in Windows XP. From the Organize menu, you can create new folders, use the usual editing features, and set folder options. You can also set and remove properties for a folder item. The folder options are pretty identical to those in Windows XP. The only difference is that the File Types and Offline Files tabs are out and the Search pane (which features options, not search capabilities) is in. If you make changes to a folder, these changes are carried over to all other folders for that user account.

What a pane!

The Layout menu in the Organize menu lets you decide how the folder should appear. If you select Classic Menus, a standard menu bar appears across the top. If you find yourself missing the standard File, Edit, and View menus in Windows XP, this layout will take you down memory lane. If you right-click the menu bar in Classic Menus, you can opt to display a Links menu or to lock the toolbars. By selecting Links, you can open a Web browser and add a Web site to your list of links.

Watch Out!

The Tools menu, which is displayed using the Classic Menus option, features Network Drive mapping and synching options that are not available in the Organize folder options menu.

The Search pane features a lot of confusing options. First, this pane is completely independent of the Search bar at the top of the folder. It's also somewhat disingenuous at first glance. If you select the Search pane, a toolbar appears that lets you sort folder content by Documents, Picture, Music, All, or Other. The interesting thing here is the actual Search feature and not the sort. Using the Search pane, you can perform a search using a number of criteria. These include file type, filters, date, size, and location. The problem with this search tool, while powerful, is that it is very easy to actually find out where this feature is. The Search toolbar has an arrow next to an Advanced Search label; click the arrow to access this Search feature (see Figure 6.7).

Figure 6.7. The Search pane can be difficult to maneuver.

The Preview pane is the information bar that appears across the bottom of the folder. This pane works wonderfully in tandem with the Details pane, because it packs a one-two punch of information about your file. This is helpful because it means that you no longer have to right-click a file and select Properties to retrieve the same information now displayed here.

The Reading pane displays a preview of the file (when possible) to the right of the Details pane. This preview is particularly helpful for pictures or music files. If you're used to working with Microsoft Outlook, it's similar to the preview e-mail feature.

Hint

If you want to protect your folders and prevent them from being modified, right-click the Classic Menus menu bar and select Lock the Toolbars. Keep in mind that only that menu is locked; other menus can still be modified.

Finally, the Navigation pane features your favorite links as well as a rather hard to find Folders menu. If you click on the up arrow icon, you can see a list of your folders as it would appear in Windows Explorer.

Views

The Views menu lets you set how icons are displayed — this includes size (small, medium, large, and extra large) as well as display type. In Windows Vista, you can also choose between Details view and Tiles view. For more information, please refer to the "Change folder views" section earlier in this chapter.

The other buttons

It's hard to tell you what to expect for the remaining menus simply because Windows is too smart. Well, not exactly, but one big improvement in Windows Vista is its ability to change menu appearance based on your actions. For example, if you are in the Documents folder, you have these options: Share, Burn, and Previous versions. If you are in Pictures, you have the same options plus a Slide Show option. If you are in the Music folder, you have the original three options plus Play all. If you are in the Searches folder or navigating your hard drive, you have an Open option to launch either the search or the application.

Previous versions

Windows Vista lets you roll back to an earlier version of a file using the Previous Versions tab of the Properties files. Activated by default, this lets you abandon changes to a file that, for example, a colleague may have inadvertently modified.

Although an interesting file, it's not as automatically helpful as it may sound. A user might reasonably assume that this feature automatically saves a copy of your many files every time you click Save. This isn't quite the case. Rather, when you create a restore point using the Back Up Files Wizard, you save specific files whose previous versions are stored as a shadow copy. The record of those shadow copies is displayed in that file's Previous Versions tab of its Properties.

While this feature may be helpful, it is possible that it could be a security risk, notably in cases where people believed that they deleted a file or in the workplace. Common sense and discretion should always be exercised; if you believe that this feature may be a security risk for you or your company, you can disable it in the System Protection tab in the System Properties (Control Panel).

Searches folder

You may remember the discreet Search option in the Favorite Links section of your folders. The Vista search tool is better known as the Searches folder. This folder contains 11 preconfigured searches (see Figure 6.8); you can also create and save your own. For example, let's say that you are looking for a document written by Farquhar contains the word "corporate." Your search is saved as "Author Farquhar/Keyword Corporate." In the future, you can go to "Author Farquhar/Keyword Corporate" and perform a search where the results are returned instantaneously and on-the-fly, regardless of where the files are found on your computer. This feature is helpful for oft-repeated search criteria; no more waiting for Windows to make its way through the hard drives, external drive, and USB drive just to find a handful of files! The only real negative about this feature is the potential for confusion when users expect to use it to perform customized searches.

Figure 6.8. Vista provides preconfigured searches in the new Searches folder for faster results.

Windows Explorer and Vista

Windows Vista still uses Windows Explorer — you can still find it in the Accessories menu of the Start menu. However, Windows Explorer's role hasn't evolved so much as it has become a more integrated feature. In Windows Vista, the hierarchical display is a little more discreet; it appears tucked underneath the Folders section (see Figure 6.9).

Figure 6.9. The decidedly discreet Windows Explorer.

Adding files and folders to the Start menu

The Start menu remains one of the easiest ways to track your files and folders. Although many people use the Documents folder to store important files or documents, you can do it just as easily from the Start menu (plus, it's quicker to navigate!).

If the Start menu is your location of choice for storing important information, don't forget that the actual document is still stored someplace on your machine. The file that appears in the Start menu is simply a shortcut. In other words, it points to the actual location of the file. It is just like many of the other icons found in the Start menu or on the desktop.

Inside Scoop

You can make the classic Windows toolbar appear temporarily in Windows Explorer by pressing the Alt key. To facilitate navigation, the meat and potatoes of Windows folders (Music, Contacts, Documents, Favorites, and Pictures) are now displayed with teal/green icons. For some reason, Windows decided to display Videos as a yellow folder.

Watch Out!

If you move a file or folder from Documents or Picture, you move the team instead of copying it. To copy it, hold the Ctrl key while you drag it to the proper folder.

So, what's the point of doing this when the file is still located in, for example, the Documents folder? For one, if the file is frequently used, it is a lot easier to click once in the Start menu and open it as opposed to potentially navigating several levels down in a folder.

To move a file or folder to the Start menu, all you need to do is open the folder of the desired file or locate the folder and drag and drop it onto the Start menu icon. Now, this is where you have a choice; be sure not to let go of the file while you decide. You can either:

- Drag the file or folder onto the Start menu and release; the file or folder automatically appears in the "Pin up" area. This is the area at the top left of the Start menu when it is opened.

- Drag the file or folder onto the Start menu and wait until it opens automatically. You can then drop the desired file or folder anywhere in the Start menu; this includes the "Pin up" area, the folders of other applications.

If you add a shortcut to the Start menu, be careful to which file you point. Use the Search function to manually locate the appropriate file instead of guessing. Some files or folders, for example, Microsoft Word, do not have obvious file locations. In my example, Word is winword.exe and not word.exe.

Shortcuts can be a real timesaver if used judiciously. By placing shortcuts in the Start menu instead of on the desktop, you can maintain a neatly organized computer.

Redirecting the Documents folder

The Documents folder is traditionally found on the same drive as the operating system. It is nicely stored in the Users directory for easy navigation.

Hint

Store any file/folder shortcuts in the Start menu and not on the desktop. If you install them on the desktop, you run the risk of accidentally deleting an important shortcut.

Watch Out!

You cannot use the Properties window for the Documents folder in the Favorite Links area. For some reason, though it points to the same directory, it doesn't include the Location tab in the Documents folder in the Preview pane.

Of course, you may decide that you would rather have your documents stored in another directory or perhaps another drive (internal or external). You may consider redirecting the Documents folder to another disk drive for hardware or security reasons; for example, your secondary hard drive has 50GB free and your operating system drive may have only 5GB available.

To change the location of your hard drive, you must open the Documents Properties window in the Preview pane of the Documents folder (see Figure 6.10).

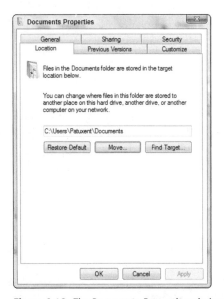

Figure 6.10. The Documents Properties window.

You now are faced with two choices: do you want to move the current Documents folder to another location or do you want to change the folder where your documents are stored (effective immediately). If you opt for the latter, the folders currently in your default Documents location remain in their initial location; any subsequent additions are added to the new location that you just set. In the Documents Properties window, you can select a new location from the Location tab; simply click the Find Target button or the Move button to change locations. When you have made your choice, you can change your mind and restore the default location, or you can apply your changes and click OK.

Create compressed files and folders

File compression is an important, yet often unnoticed, part of Windows. Windows Vista is no different. Of course, in this modern age of broadband Internet connections and virtually unlimited hard drive space, the urgency of file compression isn't what it once was. Though it seems like forever, it wasn't that long ago where we still used a 56k modem (at best!) and a phone line to get online. You can only imagine, or remember, how difficult sending files could be! File compression was created for this very reason; to crush a file down to its lowest possible size. This would reduce transmission time, and, by extension, lower the communication costs incurred by spending long periods of time tying up your phone line.

File compression was also a very important feature at one time due to the cost of hard drives and their limited sizes. This was the era where 3.5" floppy drives (or even 5.25") were the norm; long before even Zip disks were the talk of the town.

Software packages such as WinZip, PKZip and WinRAR helped home users create manageable file sizes and bundles to reduce space and increase convenience. Though it may seem that these applications are long-since obsolete, they are still as important and valid as ever! Why would you want to compress files today? There are a number of reasons; for example, file compression is still convenient for grouping a set of files so that they can be sent over e-mail. On a related note, file compression can reduce a file or folder to an appropriate size. Not all mail servers accept large file attachments; by compressing your files, it may mean the difference between a valid and illegal file transfer. Also, it's not because you have a lot of free space that you should waste it! The seemingly superfluous disk space available today may be gone tomorrow if you decide to install another operating system or a large application suite.

Microsoft, being the type of company that doesn't like to be outdone, now bundles their own compression software. This tool, though fairly bland, is still an effective way to reduce file size as well as to compress folders.

Squeezing the myth out of compression

Compression uses mathematical algorithms to reduce file sizes. There are several mechanisms that are used; one of the most common is through the use of tokens or small symbols that represent larger quantities of information. For example, if you use the phrase "Unofficial Guide to Windows XP" many times in a single page, a compression algorithm would replace that phrase with, for example, a two-letter token. This reduces file size, and the more tokens that can be used, the smaller the file.

Some file types are more amenable to compression than others. Picture files such as TIFF or BMP files that contain digital descriptors for each pixel compress nicely; a big stretch of blue sky, like Windows XP used to use by default, can be crunched down to a fraction of the size. A single token can be used to describe large chunks of data. JPG files, on the other hand, cannot be compressed because the JPG standard already uses compression to create the file. There is little additional benefit to running a file through a compression algorithm multiple times.

The Windows compression algorithm mechanism is decent, but it's not intended to be a replacement for full-featured applications like PKWare's PKZip or WinZip Computing's WinZip. In Windows, support for file compression is used more for compatibility than as a full-fledged power tool. If you move files across the Internet frequently, you should invest in one of those applications for your industrial-strength compression needs.

Turn on folder compression

Honestly, do you really need to keep the folder compression feature? This is a perfect example of Microsoft's "pack rat" tendencies or its inexplicable desire to remain "old school." In this modern age, where a "small" hard drive is 40GB and DVDs can hold 4.7GB of data, do you really need to compress folders to gain space?

The folder compression feature is designed to reduce the amount of space a folder takes up on your hard drive. If you opt to use this feature, Windows will compress the files in the background, slightly reducing computer performance.

Watch Out!

If your computer is just barely meeting Windows Vista CPU requirements, you should avoid compressing folders as this procedure eats up a decent amount of system resources.

If we haven't scared you off from this feature, please allow us to show you how to use it:

1. Simply select any folder that you wish to compress and open the Properties window by right-clicking the folder.

2. Click the Advanced button on the General tab and then select the Compress contents to save disk space attribute.

3. Click OK.

One small complaint here — users cannot be blamed for erroneously thinking that they might be able to select both the compression and the subsequent encryption option. If you select one and then try to select the other, it changes your selection. It would be clearer for users to see the other option grayed out when one attribute is selected.

Once you validate your change, Vista will ask you to confirm your changes. You can opt to apply the change just to that particular fold or extend it to its subfolder and files. If you decompress afterwards, a similar dialog box appears asking you to confirm decompression.

You can take it a step further by compressing an entire disk (see Figure 6.11). From Computer, click the desired drive and right-click to open Properties. The General tab opens and lets you select Compress this drive to save disk space. This procedure may take a while depending on the content of the drive.

If you're familiar with Windows XP, you may remember that you could also compress files using the Disk Cleanup program. For one reason or another, Microsoft removed this option from Windows Vista. The only way to compress your files is through the Advanced button as illustrated earlier.

Inside Scoop

If you have to change the location of a compressed folder, be careful! To maintain its compression attribute, you must copy the folder to its new location. If you simply move it, it reverts to its original compression.

Figure 6.11. The General tab of Documents Properties is the starting point for folder compression.

Create compressed archives

Compressed archives are a file that contains compressed files; you may have heard the expression "Zip file." It is simply a folder whose contents have been compressed, or "zipped," and stored in a single file. Compressed files are very practical for moving groups of files between computers or media; they are also often used in installation programs.

Compressed archives display as a folder icon with a filename appearing in blue (see Figure 6.12). By double-clicking the archive, the folder is automatically decompressed.

Creating a new archive is a very simple, straightforward process. From an open folder, right-click the file or folder you wish to compress and click Send To, and then select Compressed (zipped) Folder. The folder or file reappears in the same location as the source file(s) as a Zip file;

Watch Out!

Although Windows compresses and decompresses files and folders automatically, it doesn't do it for files within compressed archives. This means that applications cannot see those files unless you extract them from the archive first. Click File and then Save As to save an editable uncompressed copy onto your hard drive.

the icon appears according to your chosen compression software. For example, if you use WinRAR, the compressed file or folder appears with the WinRAR compressed file icon.

Remember that you can either copy a file into the archive (which keeps an uncompressed version on your hard drive) or move the file by holding down the Shift key and dragging it onto the archive. This removes the local copy from the hard drive.

There is an easy way to move the entire contents of a folder into a compressed archive. Select the desired files (or use Ctrl+A) and then right-click and click Send To before selecting Compressed (zipped) Folder. The archive is automatically named based on the first object in the archive.

Figure 6.12. The Documents folder with a compressed archive file.

Cab it!

You may have noticed another type of compressed file called "cab" files (short for "cabinet"). Their icons look literally like file cabinets. These are used by Setup when installing applications. Unlike compressed archives, you cannot add files to an existing cabinet file or make new ones. We strongly advise you not to delete or move them — simply know they are there, what they are, and then leave them be.

Encrypt files and folders

Encrypting files is a good way to keep other users out of your business; more specifically, it prevents other users from viewing or changing files. Although you can set permissions to prevent access to the Documents folder, this is an extra level of protection that is considerably safer.

Why would you want to encrypt files? Unfortunately, with cyber crimes on the rise, taking the proper steps to protect yourself and your data is now a necessity and not just something for us worrywarts. Many people keep important information on their computers, such as bank records, passwords and PIN numbers, and credit card information. By the same token, many people also tend to think that identity theft can't happen to them and take little to no precautions for protecting their data or computers from online attacks. Nowhere is the need more important for proper preventive measures than on a laptop — should your laptop be lost or stolen, wouldn't you want to at least know that your data is protected?

Let's talk about some of the old encryption tools Windows puts at your disposal. There are some pretty big improvement in Windows Vista, but let's review some of the old school technology and its rules.

Encryption keys are part of your Windows credentials. When you open or close an encrypted file, Windows checks to see if you can read the file. In other words, people who do not have permission to see a particular file will not be able to see it. Encryption and decryption methods change depending on what you are doing.

- If you move or copy an unencrypted file into an encrypted folder, Windows automatically encrypts the file.
- If you move or copy an encrypted file from an encrypted folder to an unencrypted folder, the file remains encrypted.

To encrypt a file or folder, right-click the file or folder you wish to encrypt, and do the following:

1. Click Properties and then make sure you are on the General tab.

2. Click Advanced again from the General tab, just like you did to compress a file.

3. Click Encrypt contents to secure data, and then click OK.

   When you click Apply, an Encryption Warning dialog box appears reminding you that you are encrypting a file in an unencrypted folder. You have the option of encrypting only the file or the file and its parent folder.

4. Once you decide (you may also opt to always encrypt just the file); click OK and encryption is applied.

Once you complete this task, a notification dialog box appears at the bottom of the screen telling you that you should back up your file encryption key. This is a very important step to take; should you lose a key or should it become unusable, you'll need this backup, otherwise you won't be seeing your encrypted files again!

The Encrypting File System window gives you three options: Back up now, Back up later, or Never back up (see Figure 6.13):

Figure 6.13. The Encrypting File System window.

We recommend, along with Microsoft, that you choose Back up now. We highly discourage the last option of never backing up. This is a quick and easy process; why tempt fate?

1. Click Back up now (recommended).

   The Certificate Export Wizard appears

2. Click Next.

3. Select the desired file format for your certificate and click Next.

   If you aren't sure which format to use, Vista provides suitable information with a direct link to the online help from this page.

4. Type and confirm a password for your key in the same screen and
   click Next.

5. Enter a filename for the file and click Next.

6. Click Finish.

   A dialog box lets you know if the procedure was successful or not
   (Figure 6.14).

Figure 6.14. The wizard will let you know if the export is successful.

You can share this file with other users without having to give them
the password or decrypting all files and folders. In the Advanced
Attributes page, you'll notice that there is now a Details button that
appears next to the encryption option. Click it and the current user
access window appears. As you can see, you are the only user currently
authorized to access this file. Click Add and then select one of the users
from the list. If desired, you can view their certificate by clicking the

Watch Out!

If you want to view your encrypted files or folders from a different computer on your network, you must store your certificate file to a floppy or USB drive, and use it to decrypt your files.

so-named button. For more information on digital certificates, please refer to Chapter 7.

Advances in Vista

Microsoft has certainly gone to great lengths to dispel their image of being lax on security. Some of these changes, which are discussed in greater detail in Chapter 7, include the Windows Rights Management Services (RMS) client for enterprise deployments, an improved Encrypting File System (EFS) mechanism, and control over device driver installation. However, in terms of encryption, the new kid on the block is BitLocker™.

Introducing Windows BitLocker™

This is a nice new addition to Windows Vista, but it's very typical of how Microsoft operates. They have a tendency to take inspiration from other applications and then make a version (sometimes better, sometimes worse) of their own. Let's just be blunt: If you want true encryption protection, go with PGP (www.pgp.com). They've been doing encryption, and doing it well, for almost two decades.

Of course, if you do not need the heavy-duty protection of PGP, or don't feel like spending beyond the cost of Windows Vista, BitLocker is still a viable option. This encryption program literally encrypts your entire hard drive; should your computer (especially laptop) be lost or stolen, you can rest assured that your data is secure — even if the hard drive is used on another computer.

How does it work? BitLocker encrypts your entire hard drive, including system files, and stores your key to a USB key. Ideally, it would use a chip called the Trusted Platform Module (TPM) — if available. However, this is a microchip that is only available in newer computers that are security-oriented.

The advantage here is that your hard drive is quite safe; you can rest assured that it won't be compromised. However, as much of a pain trying to crack it is for a thief, it's almost as much of a pain for authorized users

The early days of PGP encryption

The much-touted PGP is the brainchild of Phil Zimmerman, a long time privacy activist. The whole idea behind the program was to allow safe communications on BBS (Bulletin Board Systems) and to protect files and folders (just like Microsoft).

The first version appeared in 1991and was completely free; in fact, the source code was made widely available on Usenet and eventually the Internet. As you can imagine, it wasn't long before PGP was being used outside the United States — for home use, but also by dissidents in less-than-democratic countries.

The resulted in a criminal investigation of Zimmerman in 1993 for allegedly exporting munitions without a license. At the time, 40-bit encryption was the strongest allowed by law; anything beyond that qualified as munitions. PGP, on the other hand, has never used less than 128-bit encryption. Fortunately for him, the investigation went nowhere.

In 1996, PGP went commercial and was eventually bought by NAI. Zimmerman worked with NAI on PGP for a short period of time before quitting. NAI eventually went under and sold off PGP assets. From the ashes rose the Phoenix, and PGP Corporation was born.

to access an encrypted drive. For example, if you stored your key on a USB flash drive, you must insert it every time you boot your computer. This flash drive must be kept away from the computer because if a user of nefarious intent happens upon the computer and the flash drive with the key, he can easily decrypt the drive. This is why the TPM security chip is preferable; it has anti-tampering protection.

To start BitLocker, open the Security menu from the Control Panel (Figure 6.15).

Watch Out!

Besides a USB flash drive and TPM technology, there are a few other requirements that must be met before using BitLocker. You must have at least two partitions on your hard drive (the active partition remains unencrypted so you can start your computer) and have a TPM/USB-compatible BIOS.

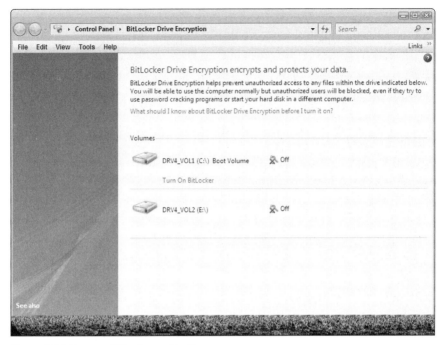

Figure 6.15. The new BitLocker application.

1. Click on BitLocker Drive Encryption; a list of available drives is displayed indicating which drives or partitions are eligible for encryption.

2. Click the Turn On BitLocker link to start the wizard. The wizard automatically detects if you have TPM on board. If not, you are asked to save a startup key on a USB drive.

3. A list of available USB flash drives appears; click Save.

4. You must now create a recovery password; you can either save it to your USB flash drive, save it to a folder, show it, or print it. It is preferable to store it to USB for security reasons.

The next step is the actual encryption. This process could take a fair amount of time depending on the amount of information to encrypt. You can pause the procedure by clicking the Drive Encryption icon at the bottom of your desktop. Should your computer reboot or you need to turn it off, you can easily resume encryption once you are back online.

- To turn off or decrypt BitLocker, go back to the BitLocker Drive Encryption page and click Turn off BitLocker for this drive.
- You can decrypt the drive by clicking Decrypt the drive.
- If you click Disable BitLocker, you can temporarily suspend the application.

Enable file sharing

It's hardly worth mentioning that Windows Vista maintains file sharing capabilities. A staple of Windows, sharing information is the whole reason networks even exist!

There are several different ways of sharing files in Windows Vista. The most common and easiest way is to share files from your computer by using either a standard folder or the Public folder. To share a folder, do the following:

1. If you are sharing a standard folder, simply click on the desired folder to share and click Properties.

2. The Properties window for that folder opens. Go to the Sharing tab; notice that the folder icon appears with the folder name and text "Not shared." The Network Path entry box is empty.

3. First, click Advanced Sharing. Though it may seem logical to click Share, the Advanced Sharing window lets you establish file sharing (see Figure 6.16).

Figure 6.16. The Advanced Sharing window lets you set up your folder sharing.

4. Click the Share this folder check box. The name of the folder appears in the Share name box. From this window, you can limit the number of users logged on at the same time. You can also add comments pertaining to the shared folder in the so-named box. If you click Permissions, you can set the permissions for users accessing the folder. By default, it is read-only. We would advise leaving this status as is.

5. By clicking Add, you can add objects, such as users or groups, if available. Back in the Sharing window, you can set how the shared contents appear to offline users. For example, you can opt to not make files or programs in the shared folder available offline. You can also make all files and programs available offline or make only select files and programs available offline.

6. Once you are ready, validate any open dialog boxes, and return to the Properties page. The folder icon now is set to Shared and the network path appears, pointing to your computer and the shared folder.

7. If you click the Share... folder, you can either change permissions or stop sharing. If you opt to change permissions, you can choose with whom you will share and set their appropriate permissions level. You can also create a new user, which takes you to the User Accounts screen.

You can also stop sharing from this folder simply by clicking the so-named option. However, don't be alarmed if your folder still indicates that it is shared. If you close and re-open the folder, it will change to the correct setting.

Working with the Public folder

Windows Vista now features a Public folder, which is just that. Finding it can be a bit tricky. In the Documents folder, click the Folders menu and scroll down to the bottom and click Public. By default, access to this

Watch Out!

Don't forget that if another user accesses the Public folder, it is as if they are working on a folder on their own computer. They can add, delete, or edit freely.

folder is disabled. However, when enabled, this folder is visible to anyone who is on your network (see Figure 6.17).

If you turn on file sharing for this folder (see the next section for how to do that), every file will be visible to anyone with a user account and password. Unfortunately, you cannot pick and choose file or application access in the Public folder for a given user, nor can you grant or deny access on an individual basis. In other words, it's an all or nothing situation — either everyone or no one can access the Public folder.

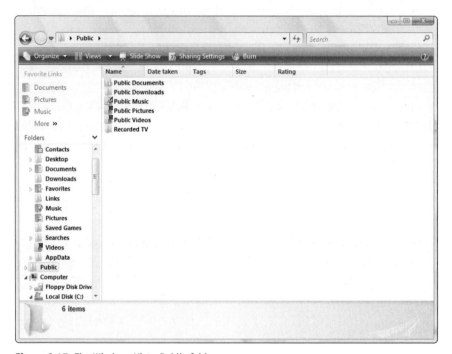

Figure 6.17. The Windows Vista Public folder.

Which one should I use?

There are a number of criteria that may help you influence how you share files. You may want to share a folder if any of the following apply:

- You do not wish to move items to the Public folder and prefer keeping them in their original location.

- You wish to set permissions on an individual level and not a network-wide level.

- You are trying to make a large number of media files (oven voluminous in size) available but do not wish to have them copied in another location, thereby wasting disk space.

On the other hand, the Public folder is a valid option for a number of scenarios:

- You don't want to bother making multiple folders available and would prefer to share all files from a central location.

- You require quick access to all shared files.

- You want to be sure that your shared files are separate from personal files that should not be shared.

- You prefer setting network-wide permissions.

Using the Network and Sharing Center

The Network and Sharing Center replaces the Network File and Printer Sharing features, which is the key to the aforementioned file sharing options. This is accessible from the Control Panel and controls file sharing settings, particularly for the Public folder (see Figure 6.18). Ironically, this is a very important element of the operating system, yet finding it is like looking for a needle in a haystack. In the Control Panel, click Network and Internet and then Network and Sharing Center.

To be honest, we're not sure why Microsoft decided to discard the Network File and Printer Sharing feature. This new creation combines both network and sharing preferences and status. We'll concentrate on the Sharing and Discovery aspect of this window; the Network details are discussed in ample detail in Chapter 9.

The Sharing and Discovery section of the Network and Sharing Center is very clean; it's a simple list of your basic options and a status indicator. This list covers:

- Network discovery
- File sharing
- Public folder sharing
- Printer sharing
- Password protected sharing
- Media sharing

Hint

Make sure you have set your Windows Firewall settings (or any other firewall you are using) to allow network browsing.

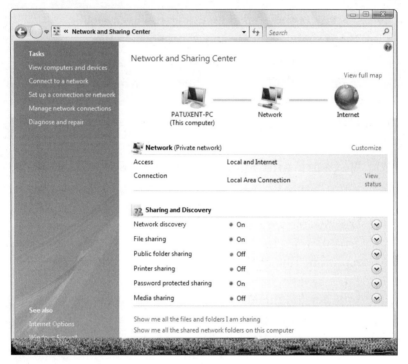

Figure 6.18. The Network and Sharing Center window.

You can find out specifics for each of these by clicking either the status indicator or the arrow icon at the right of each list item; the items mentioned in the following paragraphs are illustrated in Figure 6.19.

Network discovery is the state whereby your computer can see other computers on the network and these computers see you. This is discussed in greater detail in Chapter 9; however, you can turn this feature on from the Sharing and Discovery section. The Network Discovery section also lets you rename your computer using the System Properties window. By default, it is set to Custom.

File sharing poses a simple question: Do you want shared files and printers to be made available to other people on the network? By default, it is disabled, but you can easily change that; just remember to click Apply before you go on to the next section. If you don't click Apply, your changes are not taken into account!

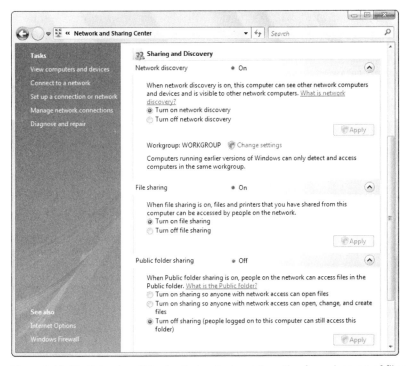

Figure 6.19. The Network and Sharing Center displays information for each aspect of file sharing.

Public folder sharing is similar to the File sharing option, only this refers specifically to your Public folder and its contents. You can opt to let anyone with network access open your files or let anyone with network access read, write, and create files. Of course, you can leave it at its default setting, which is to not share the Public folder. The Apply rule in the previous paragraph also applies here. If you are working on a collaborative effort with a trusted user, you may consider write (Co-owner) access; otherwise, it would be safer to grant read-only (Reader) access by default.

Printer sharing, which is turned off by default, lets you share your printers with any user with network access. Once again, be sure to click Apply if you change the default setting.

The Password protected sharing section probably should have been number one or two on this list. This feature dictates whether users accessing your shared files and printers need to have a user account and password on your computer. By default, this is enabled. We recommend keeping it on, otherwise anyone can access your shared files. One would reasonably expect that you set this feature before you determine what parts of your computer will be made available to other users. It's perfectly normal to want to know who is accessing your computer and what they're doing.

Media sharing lets you share music, pictures, and videos from your computer with other uses. This is turned off by default, but can be easily changed by clicking Change. This feature is detailed later in Chapter 8 that discusses the Windows Media Player.

Other ways of sharing files

There are other ways to share files with users; in fact, it's highly likely that you use these options quite frequently without realizing it! Each of these options offers varying levels of reliability or security. These options include

- **E-mail.** This is a quick, easy option if you are trying to share a small number of files; particularly if they are not large.

- **External drives.** This includes external hard drives, CD/DVDs, flash cards, and USB thumb drives. These are quick and convenient solutions for transporting files one time as opposed to requiring them to be available for a longer period of time.

- **Temporary network.** Also called an Ad Hoc network, you can create a computer-to-computer network between two computers on the same network. This is discussed further in Chapter 9.

- **Windows Live Messenger.** Like e-mail, this is a quick, convenient option for trading a limited number of small files on-the-fly.

- **Windows Collaboration.** Windows Vista offers a new collaboration tool for sharing documents and programs. This is also discussed further in Chapter 9. Another worthwhile option is Microsoft's Groove, which is available with Microsoft Office 2007.

There are other options available to you as well, such as Web-based file sharing applications or Web sites that offer file and photo sharing (some may be fee-based). However, this should inspire a number of file sharing options.

Watch Out!

If you opt to skip the Recycle Bin, remember that you will not be able to try and perform a file recovery operation.

Managing the Recycle Bin

The Recycle Bin, as we noted in *The Unofficial Guide to Windows XP*, is where old files go to die. Most people use it without thinking a whole lot about it, but you can do a number of small things to make it work more efficiently for you! The Recycle Bin is a little different in Windows Vista, which just proves that even the folks in Redmond were thinking about improving it! Indeed, it even takes advantage of the Aero theme with its transparent background.

If you right-click it and click Properties, the Recycle Bin Properties window appears (see Figure 6.20). It displays your account and your Public folder, indicating how much space is currently available (in the past, it displayed hard drives). You can set a maximum size, which is 4617MB by default — but be careful! This means the largest file size allowed in the Recycle Bin and not the capacity of the Recycle Bin. You can also option to remove files when you delete them and not go to the Recycle Bin.

Figure 6.20. The Recycle Bin Properties window.

The other option is whether or not to display the delete confirmation dialog box. If you disable it, deleted files go directly to the Recycle Bin instead of asking you if you're sure. We recommend leaving this option selected as a safety measure. It's quite a hassle to retrieve a deleted file, so the dialog box reminding us that we're about to delete our corporate earnings report is quite alright with us!

A (very) few words about Indexing Service

The Indexing Service was first introduced to the desktop in Windows 2000 Professional. Originally part of the Windows NT 4.0 Option Pack, Indexing Service was designed to provide content indexing services primarily for Internet Information Server, but also for early versions of Microsoft's Commerce Server products. As disk sizes grew and information expanded rapidly, putting indexing services on the desktop sounded like a great idea and so the service has been available on desktops ever since.

In the Properties menu for your hard drive(s), you can select a check box allowing you to index the drive for faster searching. If you opt to use this feature, be aware that it could take a long time to perform. If you plan on using it, we recommended doing it right before you go to sleep; it should be ready when you get up.

Just the facts

- Desktop folders can be enhanced with performance and cosmetic changes.
- File compression saves space; file encryption protects data.
- You can't use both compression and encryption on files.
- Microsoft BitLocker™ can help reduce the dangers of a lost or stolen hard drive.
- File and folder sharing, either traditionally or using the Public folder, can be easily set up.

Managing Security

For the Vista release, innovation was sacrificed in the name of a safer, more secure product. Microsoft hits the target in some areas and misses in others. However, no matter what your opinion is of Microsoft, it's obvious that Redmond gave it the old college try and is interested in (re)gaining your trust. Clearly, security was priority number one at Microsoft when they were planning the Vista release. A virtual lightning rod for security experts and the anti-Microsoft crowd, it's fair to say that many of the complaints about Windows security are warranted.

As a computer user, security has to be on your mind when you surf. There's no escaping the Internet, it has permeated most, if not all, of Western culture and is as natural as a coffee break at the office. However, dangers lurk on the Web — phishing, virus attacks, spam, and identity theft, to name a few. To combat the risks, you must take necessary precautions to make sure you have the safest online experience possible. Remember, it only takes one virus to wreak havoc on your computer; it takes much longer to clean up the mess of a virus than it does to download the file that brought it. Although it's true that you can never be 100 percent safe, you can lessen the likelihood of virus infection and being the victim of any other attack.

This chapter helps you understand what's out there and how Windows Vista can help you prepare for it, including some of the new security features in this release.

Making Windows safe

Microsoft really tries to make security a top priority for Windows Vista. They did this by working on five areas: platform security, access security, malware protection, a safer Internet Explorer, and data protection. Each of these issues, with the exception of platform security, is discussed later in this chapter. First, Microsoft developed a Security Development Lifecycle (SDL), which is a process whereby all software is built from scratch. By doing this, Microsoft hopes to reduce security risks. What does the SDL mean to users? It means that you can rest assured that your operating system went through a battery of tests to measure design and coding to make sure that it can be used safely. This involves extensive review and testing — both of the code and against Windows XP vulnerabilities. Fortunately, Microsoft took good notes during the security panic back in 2003. As a result of this experience, as well as working with security experts, Microsoft finally saw the light and tried to correct past errors. Relatively new, Vista is the first operating system to use this new development plan.

Microsoft also worked to minimize the risk of being attacked through system services. A number of well-known worms and their subsequent attacks made mincemeat of Microsoft's earlier security gaps. Worms are similar to viruses, in that their intent is to damage or destroy computers. These are actually little programs that self-replicate, continually propagating until it brings a system down. To combat this, Microsoft designed system services to work in a limited environment — by using the least amount of account privileges and limiting activities to a single machine or network. These services are called restricted services.

Finally, Windows altered how it handles buffer overruns. A *buffer overrun*, also known as a buffer overflow, is when a process tries to store data in an area beyond the limits or boundaries of the computer's memory buffer. To protect computers from worms or viruses taking advantage of these occurrences, Vista terminates a program if it suspects that buffer tampering occurs. By terminating the program, damage is limited.

Working with the Security Center

The Windows Security Center is a relatively new addition to the Windows family. It first appeared in Windows XP Service Pack 2 and is probably that operating system's most important upgrade. The Windows Security

Center is designed to be the central location for handling all security-related matters, as well as managing any third-party security applications that you may opt to install.

Easy Hacking 101:
The short history of Windows security

As glad as most of us are to have the Security Center, it wasn't met with much enthusiasm. In fact, a good number of users considered it to be a day late and a dollar short. As we mentioned in the introduction to this chapter, Microsoft doesn't have a stellar track record when it comes to security issues. In fact, if you use Automatic Update, you know that Microsoft frequently wants you to download and install security updates. These include hot fixes and security patches, not to mention Windows Office updates that helped shore up the security gaps present in most Windows installations. However, we must be realistic. Windows controls over 90 percent of the desktop market share, so Windows is the default target. Most hackers haven't found it worthwhile to write viruses for RedHat.

Why exactly does Microsoft come under so much fire for their security? For starters, Microsoft is guilty of acting reactively and not proactively. In other words, security updates only came well after your computer was made vulnerable. How was it made vulnerable? In the past, Microsoft left a number of potentially dangerous services turned on (enabled) by default instead of making them disabled. As a result, once you got your computer online and started surfing the Internet, worms and viruses had a field day wreaking their havoc. The Microsoft response was to not open attachments from people you don't know. Nice, except that viruses were smart enough to infiltrate address books and send e-mails from people that you knew. Why wouldn't you trust a file attachment from your best friend? Additionally, it's highly plausible that in a professional setting, you may receive many e-mails with attachments from people that you do not know, making this well-intended advice somewhat ill-advised.

As Microsoft floundered, third-party software vendors rubbed their hands in glee. Antivirus, privacy, and spyware software popped up and did well for themselves. Firewalls and routers hit the market to help people make up for Microsoft's deficiencies. Finally, it seemed, Microsoft had enough.

During the Windows XP development period, Microsoft stopped all development so that every line of code was reviewed for security and design flaws. The result was monthly security updates and Windows XP Service Pack 2. As Vista rolled forward, Microsoft put even more effort into security.

The Windows Security Center

Let's jump right in and take a look at the Windows Security Center (see Figure 7.1). Don't be too hopeful — it doesn't do as much as it reports. In other words, it doesn't actually perform any security measures, it simply reports status and lets you know how your machine is doing.

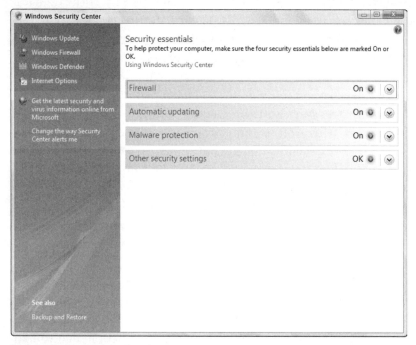

Figure 7.1. The Windows Security Center.

When you open the Windows Security Center, the Security essentials page appears. This page contains four main areas of Windows Security: Firewall, Automatic updating, Malware protection, and Other security settings. Each one is surrounded by either a red or green box and has a matching status button; it is either red or green, like a traffic light. This section is largely informative; you cannot set preferences, nor can you

Watch Out!

Windows OneCare is currently in the works for Windows Vista; currently, it is still only available for Windows XP. For up-to-date information on the availability of Windows Live OneCare, click the link in the Offers from Microsoft section of the Welcome Center.

enable or disable any of them! Each of the four sections simply indicates your current level of protection as well as a link to the relevant help file.

As you most likely know all too well, Microsoft surprisingly hasn't introduced a serious antivirus application until now (odd, given its penchant for getting hit), though it's ironic that you have to pay extra for it. They did, however, offer Microsoft Anti-Virus (from Central Point, later Symantec). If you do not have a recognizable antivirus program, you can select one using Find a program. Of course, you could always give Microsoft's new security bundle (including the aforementioned antivirus program) a try — Windows Live OneCare. It is comparable in price to its competitors.

On the left side of the Windows Security Center screen, you have some legitimate options. These include Windows Update, Windows Firewall, Windows Defender, and Internet Options. You can also click on a link (Internet connection required) that provides the latest in security updates. This window also lets you set whether or not you want to be notified when your computer is at risk. Note that these links do not let you set preferences for these applications, but rather take you to the applications directly.

Checking your six

Besides the tips and information provided in this chapter, there are a number of things you can do to help reduce your chances of being hit by a virus or spyware. These are low-cost, easy to implement ideas.

- First, when surfing, make sure you turn off pop-ups. If you are using Internet Explorer 7, this is an integrated feature. Otherwise, most third-party toolbars, such as Google or Yahoo!, feature a way to disable pop-ups. Pop-up menus are largely responsible for spyware. In addition to disabling pop-ups, you can also set your security settings to medium. We discuss more of these suggestions in Chapter 10.

- Pay closer attention to your passwords. For example, change them regularly. Pick passwords that are not easily identifiable. It's important to think of passwords that you will remember, but be careful not to pick ones that you'll forget.

- When using e-mail, try using encryption programs for sensitive data. PGP (www.pgp.com) is an affordable and secure solution to sending encrypted data. Speaking of e-mail, here are two pieces of advice: Limit the availability of your e-mail address, and pay attention to the content of your e-mail.

- The more you broadcast your e-mail address, the more likely you are to receive spam. Try using free e-mail accounts, like Hotmail (www.hotmail.com) or Gmail (www.gmail.com) for mailing lists or for advertisements. Set up spam filters to prevent the overabundance of unwanted spam. When you do receive spam, avoid clicking the "unsubscribe" links that are required by law. These do not unsubscribe you; rather, they validate your address and you can be sure that you'll be seeing even more spam in the future.

- It's important to check the contents of your e-mail; attachments can easily be "disguised" to resemble normal files. However, check out the attachment's extension (the three letters to the right of the period in the filename); if it looks unusual, it's most likely a virus. Also, phishing is a relatively recent problem that has besieged Internet users. This is when e-mail is disguised with a link that is meant to "verify" information or lure you to a site and then hits you with shareware or viruses, not to mention worse possibilities. For example, some phishing sites ask you to verify bank information or other personal data. Once entered, this data is stored on a remote server and can lead to identity theft.

Windows Vista Firewall

If you've ever worked in a company with an IT department, you're probably familiar with the term firewall. A firewall is a virtual barrier that stands between your machine or network and the outside world. Most companies use firewalls as a first line of security. Firewalls protect your system or network by keeping out malware or unauthorized users before they reach your computer or network.

Watch Out!

The term malware is a rather generic term that refers to software that is designed to cause harm. This includes viruses, worms, spyware, and adware.

A firewall isn't just a tool for professional use. Every user, even at home, should hide behind a firewall. When incoming data reaches the firewall, it checks the data packets against a VIP list; if it checks out and is authorized, the firewall lets it through. Otherwise, the data is refused and discarded. This type of protection is absolutely essential, especially if you are a laptop user. Think of all the places you might connect your laptop for Internet access, especially with the dawn of Wi-Fi! Malware only needs to hit once to be lethal, don't adapt the "it won't happen to me" attitude.

Microsoft has offered a bundled firewall since Windows XP Service Pack 2. In Vista, you can easily access it from the Windows Security Center by clicking on the link on the left side of the page. Although firewall is enabled by default, you should set your preferences quickly. In Vista, Microsoft decided to make a true firewall by featuring bidirectional filtering, but they also make you work for it.

Bidirectional means that the firewall monitors both incoming and outgoing data. However, a number of corporate clients didn't want outgoing filtering because of the difficulties that it would cause with local IT security design and policies. So, by default, the firewall only monitors incoming data. If you want to use the more advanced firewall (see Figure 7.2), you'll have to hunt for it.

Configuring Windows Firewall

Windows Firewall is a basic, but decent, firewall. Your average user should find it sufficient for their needs. Many people opt to use it in conjunction with other security measures. For example, we use the Windows

Inside Scoop

The standard firewall does not offer bidirectional support. To use this feature, you must use the Windows Firewall with Advanced Security. Type **firewall** in the Start menu Search box and select this option. Be careful not to select Windows Firewall instead.

firewall with Norton protection, Defender, and Lavasoft spyware detection, as well as a few other applications to protect our computers and their content when online.

The quickest three ways to open Windows Firewall are

■ Double-click Windows Firewall from the Control Panel.

■ Click Windows Firewall from the Windows Security Center.

■ Type **firewall** in the Start menu search box.

When you open the firewall, click Turn Windows Firewall on or off. In the Windows Firewall Settings window, you see three tabs (see Figure 7.3): General, Exceptions, and Advanced. In the Advanced tab, you have two simple options: On and Off. If you opt to leave it enabled, you may also decide to block all programs. This is a good idea if you are working in a public place; however, if you are at home, you can probably just leave it unchecked. This option, formerly called Don't allow exceptions, blocks all incoming traffic, regardless of any exceptions.

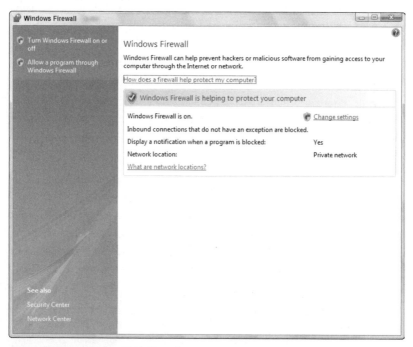

Figure 7.2. The Windows Vista Firewall.

Watch Out!

Windows Firewall may be set to Off, even if you are covered. These check boxes are a bit unreliable.

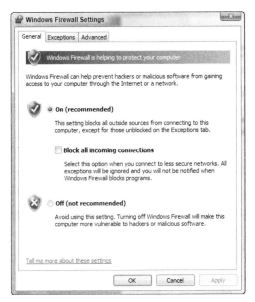

Figure 7.3. The Windows Vista Firewall tabs.

Exceptions tab

If you click on the Exceptions tab (see Figure 7.4), you'll see a long list of services or programs. You can manually check items that you want to unblock. When you connect to the Internet for the first time (and subsequently for each Internet connection source), you are asked to designate the network as Public or Private. (See Chapter 9 for more information.) The Exceptions tab indicates whether you are working on a public or private network. Just remember that if you opt to block all programs, this list is overridden and everything is blocked. For example, if you block Windows Live Messenger, you can send messages until dawn; however, no one will hear you.

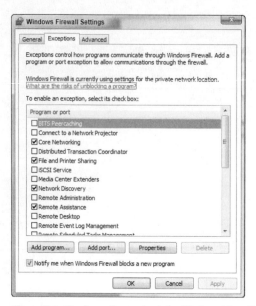

Figure 7.4. The Exceptions tab of the Windows Vista Firewall.

Exceptions are important because it's important to be safe, but not treat your computer like a prison. Individually deciding on the status of each program helps you strike a good balance between necessity and security. By checking the option at the bottom of the page, you can tell Vista to let you know when a program is blocked. This tab also lets you add individual applications that are on your computer by clicking the so-named button. By default, only Windows-bundled applications, such as games, are included. However, you can easily browse to other applications. You can also set block/unblock programs from other computers by changing the scope. A button in the Add a program window allows you to set the scope of your settings: any computer, only the network (subnet), or custom lists (by entering IP addresses or subnets). The Add port button lets you open a port through Windows Firewall. For example, if you wanted to use an SSH port to access a shell, you tell it to open port 22. Applications with outgoing data use a port to send and receive data, including applications such as telnet, ftp, or even MSN Messenger. This feature also allows you to change the scope as mentioned earlier. The final option on this tab is the Properties button, which simply displays the purpose of a program from the list if you click it. Please note that not all programs have a property.

Watch Out!

Be sure to only have one firewall on your machine, or at least only a single active firewall. Using more than one firewall will just confuse Windows and the old gal won't know who to believe. The result is that nothing may be blocked and you're back to square one.

Advanced tab

The Advanced tab (see Figure 7.5) has quite a few different options. For starters, you can decide which of your internet connections should be protected by the firewall in the Network connection settings. It's as simple as checking the box of the connection to protect. You used to be able to set logging and ICMP options from this screen; now, there is a link that is supposed to bring you to these options. The logging options are limited: logging either successful connections or dropped packages. Nevertheless, you can select the location of your log file as well as its maximum size.

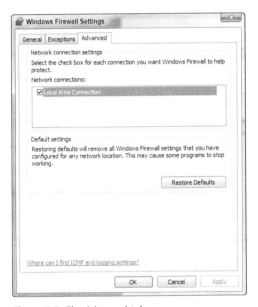

Figure 7.5. The Advanced tab.

This Internet Control Message Protocol lets you set settings. The settings let you dictate how, or if, a computer on a network can share important status information. By default, Vista only allows incoming echo

Watch Out!

Restoring default settings may cause some applications to stop working. Be careful and audit your settings before deciding to use this feature.

requests. You can select any of the available options you deem necessary. Most users probably won't use this feature very much. We recommend against touching them unless you know their purpose. You can also restore default settings.

If you do block applications and then try to use them, for example, if you block all incoming connections but work with an instant messenger, a dialog box appears and offers you three different options:

- **Keep blocking.** No exception is created.

- **Unblock.** An exception is created and it is enabled, allowing traffic through to your machine.

- **Ask me later.** Creates an exception in the list, but does not enable it, so the connection is blocked for now.

Today's lesson: Buy a hardware firewall. Now.

A hardware firewall is a device whose job is dedicated to network connectivity and packet inspection. Because it is such a narrowly focused device, there is a very small "attack surface" and it is difficult to compromise. Many residential and SPHP routers or gateways come with firewall capabilities built in. This gives you a much more flexible and configurable solution than putting two network cards into your computer and then using the computer as a gateway. With a hardware firewall, you can protect other Internet devices, such as a TiVo or Xbox without having to turn on your computer every time. On the other hand, using only a software firewall leaves you open to danger. If compromised, it is possible for your entire computer to be open for business to the bad guys. Even if you are using Windows Firewall to protect your direct connection, you should invest in a hardware and software firewall for every computer on the network. Security is improved with layers; every added layer means less chance of vulnerability.

Inside Scoop

Perhaps you're having a stroke of bad luck and cannot connect to an application, despite having created an exception? Open up hardware firewall ports; some firewalls will do this for outbound traffic, but require you to do it for inbound traffic. Check your router instructions for more information.

These changes take immediate effect, so if you grant an application access, it will begin communication with your computer.

Test your firewall

Setting up your Windows Firewall is easy, but don't take my word for it! Nor should you assume that everything is a-okay and in working order; testing your firewall is just as important as properly configuring it. Your computer may have over 65,000 ports open at any given time, so you want to make sure that any hacker or other disingenuous entity can't reach them.

If you do this from behind a corporate firewall, you'll probably get a visit (unpleasant) from IT staff. If you're performing this on a home network, you shouldn't worry.

Firewall test services basically "sniff" the available ports on your computer, looking for any potentially vulnerable areas. At the minimum, these tools scan frequently used services and protocols (which are more likely to be hacked anyway). When finished, the tool usually generates a log for you to analyze the results.

Several firewall test sites are available; a quick Web search can yield a number of results. If you prefer to stick with Microsoft's proprietary software, you can download the Microsoft Baseline Security Analyzer (`www.microsoft.com/technet/security/tools/mbsa2/default.mspx`). This tool helps you detect security misconfigurations; you can run it from either the graphical interface or from a command line.

Watch Out!

If you are trying to test your firewall at the office, be sure to consult your system administrator, as your company's firewall may consider these tests as attacks. It's better to let your administrator perform such tests. If you are administrating your SOHO (Small or Home Office) network, realize that any signaled attacks may really just be the firewall test.

Hack

To show all open ports plus the process ID of which application opened the port, open a command prompt and type **/a /o**. Most open ports are harmless or required, but you should check this list occasionally for mystery entries.

If you'd prefer the independence of a third-party tool, you can choose from a number of options. The following is a non-exhaustive list of some of the testers currently available:

- SecurityMetrics Firewall Test Services (`www.securitymetrics.com/portscan.adp`)

- Audit My PC (`www.auditmypc.com/`)

- Symantec Security Check (`http://security.symantec.com/sscv6/home.asp?langid=ie&venid=sym&plfid=23&pkj=IYEQJPUVGCWETOMGMCY`)

- HackerWhacker (`http://hackerwhacker.com/`)

Personally, we find the SecurityMetrics site to be quite effective. It, like a large number of firewall testers, is free. Of course, the important thing here is that you test your firewall and that the results show that you have a safe network environment!

Logging activity

Logging firewall activity is a key component of a complete security system on your computer. It's important to log and verify activity stored in the log because Windows doesn't tell you when an attack is blocked. In the firewall setup window, you can stipulate where to save the firewall activity log, as well as its maximum size. We recommend leaving the default settings for file size, but you may want to store the log file in a more accessible location on your hard drive.

If you are so inclined, you can audit this data by importing the log file into Excel. Doing so allows you to fully view and analyze your information, which makes decision-making regarding security strategies a little easier. If you are working behind a corporate firewall and notice unusual activity or patterns, let your IT department know so that they can take care of any problems.

Working with the Advanced Firewall

If you're going to stick with Microsoft's firewalls, we highly recommend that you use the Windows Firewall with Advanced Security. You can access this by typing **firewall** in the Start menu Search box. Though the names look similar, Windows Firewall with Advanced Security and Windows Firewall are not at all the same product.

The Advanced Security firewall is a true firewall (see Figure 7.6). It monitors incoming and outgoing data for true protection. This is a major improvement over the standard Windows Firewall in Vista that only monitors incoming data.

The firewall is displayed through the Microsoft Management Console (MMC). When you launch it, the firewall gives you a quick status overview of how your system is being protected. The overview gives you high-level information concerning your Domain Profile, Private Profile, and your Public Profile. Each profile allows you to see whether or not inbound and outbound connections that do not match a rule are allowed. By default, all inbound connections not matching a rule are blocked, while all outbound connections are allowed.

Figure 7.6. The Advanced Security firewall has even more options than the default firewall.

Windows Firewall properties

In the overview section, there is a link that lets you set firewall properties. This opens up a window that has four different tabs (see Figure 7.7):

- Domain Profile
- Private Profile
- Public Profile
- IPsec Settings

Figure 7.7. You can set parameters for three different profiles: domain, private, public.

The first three tabs are identical in form; you can turn the firewall on or off and set whether or not to allow or block inbound and outbound connections. You can customize the firewall so that users are notified when programs are blocked from receiving inbound connections. There are also settings for using unicast responses and rule merging; however, it is unlikely that most home users would use these. Finally, you can also customize log settings for each profile. This includes log location, size limit, and whether or not to log dropped packets or successful connections.

The settings in the above paragraph can be set for Domain profiles (when your computer is connected to a corporate domain), Private profile (when your computer is connected to a private network), or Public profile (when your computer is connected to a public network).

The fourth tab, which lets you set IPsec settings, lets you customize IPsec defaults as well as exemptions. IPsec is a set of protocols that are used to protect network traffic (data) through the use of digital certificates with keys and security services.

The defaults can be changed for key exchange, data protection, and authentication methods. This window also provides a link to relevant online help so that you can make the best decision for your firewall. This tab also lets you exempt the Internet Control Message Protocol (ICMP) from IPsec requirements. ICMP enables computers on a same network to share status and error information.

Once you've set your firewall properties, it's time to move on to the Getting Started section of the firewall. You first need to create rules for your firewall to follow with respect to your connections. Click Connection Security Rules to get started (see Figure 7.8).

Figure 7.8. The Connection Security Rules page lets you dictate how your firewall works.

Connection Security Rules

The Connection Security Rules are similar in layout to an MMC snap-in. To create a new rule:

1. Click New Rule from the Actions pane.

2. Select the desired Rule Type and click Next.

3. Set authentication requirements and click Next.

4. Select the authentication method and click Next.

5. Select which profile(s) to which the rule will apply and click Next.

6. Name your rule and add a short description if desired.

> The new rule appears in the Connection Security Rules. You can filter your list of rules, refresh the list, or export it from the Actions pane. If you click on a rule, it appears under Actions and you can disable or delete the rule or edit its properties.

To get back to the firewall home, click Windows Firewall with Advanced Security from the pane on the left.

The previous steps also apply if you click the Inbound Rules and Outbound Rules links. The Monitoring setting lets you find out more about your current policy settings and other security information for your active connections.

Back on the firewall home page, you can also export your settings as a policy using the Export Policy... option in the Actions pane. You can also import a saved policy.

The Advanced Security firewall is a significantly better firewall than the basic firewall that Windows also makes available. Quite frankly, one wonders why they would include both; it makes much more sense to include this advanced edition. Users will most likely find it easy to use, especially more computer savvy users, but they may also find that there's a lot of reading to do. The Windows Vista interface is quite verbose in some areas, this being a notable example.

Getting ready for Windows Live OneCare

Windows Live OneCare is a fee-based security solution that bundles anti-malware software, performance enhancers, backup and restore, as well as an improved firewall.

Windows Live OneCare has gone through a number of changes since its inception. Currently only available for Windows XP at the time of writing, a Vista version is intended to be available by the time Vista launches. Initially designed to ship as an antivirus program alongside Windows Vista, it was redesigned to work through MSN and then as part of the Windows Live program.

Windows Live OneCare doesn't include Windows Defender, though the anti-spyware integrates perfectly into the Windows Live OneCare application — you simply have to download Windows Defender separately. So, what exactly does Windows Live OneCare give you that Vista does not? First, it features a robust anti-malware section that links to the antivirus program and Window's automatic update settings. Like most antivirus program software, the Microsoft version can monitor your system as well as do a full system scan of all your files. Virus definitions are regularly updated and can be downloaded automatically or manually.

You can also use Windows Live OneCare to fine-tune your computer's performance. It features a couple of throwbacks from Vista: disk defragmenter and backup and restore. Although the backup and restore is good, we personally prefer Norton's Speed Disk to Windows' disk defragmenter. The virus scan (file scan) is available in the Performance Plus section, as well as a feature that removes unnecessary files. Windows Live OneCare also features a tool called Tune-up, which does a full system check and maintenance, including a full system virus scan.

Reasonably priced for a one-year subscription for up to three computers, Windows Live OneCare provides regular security updates. Many people might complain about having to pay so much money for security software on top of the cost of the Windows Vista upgrade, but this price is quite reasonable compared to competitors. For example, we have used Norton SystemWorks for a number of years; while it offered a number of invaluable security tools, it doesn't come with a firewall. The price was also higher than the Windows Live OneCare offer. Another attractive advantage over competitors is that it offers user support by e-mail, phone, or even chat.

The final verdict: If the Vista version is on par with the current Windows XP release, this seems like a good investment of a modest sum of money each year. If you opt not to go with Microsoft's offering, you can look to competitors to release a competitive version soon or put together a home security solution piecemeal.

Windows Vista Defender

Windows Defender (see Figure 7.9) is an anti-spyware tool that Microsoft released in early 2006 for use with Windows XP and Vista beta versions. You can download the latest version of Defender at `www.microsoft.com/athome/security/spyware/software/default.mspx`. It is available in both 32 and 64 bit.

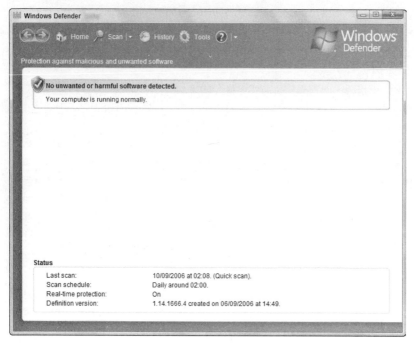

Figure 7.9. Windows Defender interface is easy to navigate and understand.

What is spyware?

Spyware is a relatively recent "phenomenon" that isn't as cute as it sounds. It is a malicious (not as bad as a virus) software that can seek and collect personal information or change the way your computer behaves. The beauty of spyware is that it does these types of things without requesting permission or otherwise notifying you.

Many people think of adware when the think of spyware; these are advertisements that pop up at random moments advertising some product or service.

Though pop-ups may seem annoying, kind of like a fly, they can be problematic. Recurring pop-ups can crash your system, or simply prove to be embarrassing due to their content. Regardless, it's important that you regularly check for spyware.

Avoiding spyware

There are some easy steps you can take to reduce your risk of being infested with spyware.

First, do not install any questionable software or software from dubious sources. For example, file-sharing software (eMule, eDonkey — we're looking in your direction) is a hotbed for spyware, pop-ups, and other nasty malware.

As cute as they are, downloading cutesy icons, screen savers, and toolbars from weird Web sites can be a bad decision. Stay clear of these.

Also, don't install cracked or hacked software. In addition to being illegal, it's also a great way to subject yourself to a malware attack.

Windows Defender helps protect your computer by guarding against pop-up menus created by spyware and other applications. Spyware can cause annoying behavior (such as the aforementioned pop-ups — even if your browser is closed!), cause slow computer performance, or even add new cosmetics, such as toolbars, to your browser.

Windows Defender can help rid your computer of these little pains in the backside; don't worry, everyone gets these every now and then, especially the more you surf the Internet. Windows Defender detects and then removes known spyware. You can manually launch a scan or even program a system scan according to when is best for you. If any spyware is found, Windows Defender lets you choose how to handle it. Windows Defender also provides around-the-clock protection by continually monitoring your computer; it notes any system changes that usually mean that spyware is attacking. To help stay on top of the latest spyware definitions, you can receive regular spyware definition updates using Windows Update.

We are currently using Windows Defender for both Windows XP Professional and Vista Ultimate. We really don't have any complaints about this application; it gets the job done! However, we also use a second anti-spyware program, called Ad-Aware by Lavasoft (www.lavasoft.de/software/adaware/). Another good choice is Spybot S&D (www.safer-networking.org/). Why do we use multiple anti-spyware programs? We often find that one application finds spyware that the other doesn't, due to differing spyware definitions. These programs are rather light in terms of necessary disk space and memory requirements, so we recommend using two packages to be on the safe side, especially if you do a lot of surfing.

User account protection

Windows Vista introduces the User Account Control (UAC) feature (see Figure 7.10), which is designed to make your computer more accessible for Standard users. As we discuss in Chapter 4, each and every user account can be tailored to a customized level of access. For example, you can decide which applications, games, or even Web sites each user account can access. Even as an Administrator, you may happen upon a program that has Standard user permissions, but requires administrator level access. Windows Vista asks you to provide the administrator password and, once validated, lets you go to town! The actual User Account Control feature works hand in hand with the User Accounts window.

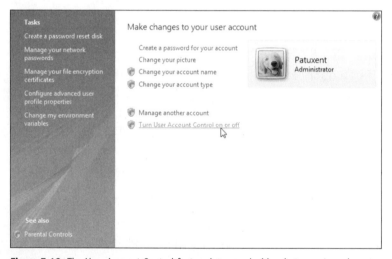

Figure 7.10. The User Account Control feature lets you decide what users can do on your computer.

The point of the UAC is to prevent other users from making changes to your computer without your authorization. The administrator can literally control just about every aspect of the Vista experience for the standard user accounts. With that in mind, creating specific childproof user accounts makes perfect sense. By taking advantage of the User Account

Control, you can help reduce the risk of being infected by malware. The administrator is essentially a prison warden, able to grant privileges or go to total lockdown, which prevents any unauthorized installation or configuration changes.

The UAC lets you set programs and tasks with standard user access. Any tasks that are defined as administrator tasks are limited to administrator accounts. When an administrator application is launched, Vista first asks the user if they approve of the status change via the Admin Approval Mode. Though it sounds serious, it's more of a notice that you're not dealing with low-level standard user material! Of course, if you are using a Standard user account, you will be prompted to provide an administrator password or permission before you can continue.

Authentication

Windows Vista gives more power to companies and software shops to handle authentication. Microsoft finally recognized how predictable short passwords can be — many people still tend to use really obvious passwords — and how hard long passwords can be to remember.

In Windows Vista, you may opt to use biometrics or token-based authentication. These technologies are not germane to this book; however, do know that you do have this option!

Credentials management

Handling all that data, user account or hardware related, can be some tough business! If you're the type of user that's always on the go, you'll appreciate Vista's Digital Identity Management Service (DIMS) as well as a certificate enrollment process. If you're really on board, you can even use smart card technology, including a PIN reset tool! SOHO users can keep a backup of all this data in the Stored User Names and Passwords feature.

Cryptography services

At the behest of a number of companies and governments, Microsoft really got their act together and offered Crypto Next Generation (CNG) services. Who knew that Fortune 500 companies or governments didn't want to be open to e-theft? The CNG helps fight this risk; it allows the addition of new algorithms that you can use in SSL/TLS as well as IPsec.

Using the UAC

You can configure the UAC through the Local Security Policy window. To access it:

1. Type **secpol.msc** in the Start menu Search box.

2. The console appears. Expand the Local Policies menu in the left pane of the window.

3. Expand Security Options at the next level of the hierarchical menu in the same window.

4. Scroll down to the bottom of the policy list.

5. Select any of the User Account Control policies and double-click it.

6. Set the new policy settings and click OK.

You can turn the UAC on, if it isn't already, from the Other security settings section of the Windows Security Center. If it is already on, you cannot turn it off from here. However, you can turn it on or off from the User Accounts page in the Control Panel (see Figure 7.11).

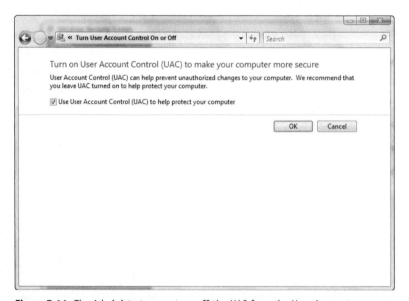

Figure 7.11. The Administrator can turn off the UAC from the User Accounts page.

Adding antivirus protection

Windows Vista still does not contain an integrated (or at least free) antivirus application. However, there is an option: Windows Live OneCare.

Bright Idea

If you decide to scan your system for viruses, why not scan for spyware too? This will help provide the best conditions possible for your computer.

As mentioned earlier in this chapter, OneCare is set to be released for Windows Vista around the same time the operating system is released.

Like many of its competitors, OneCare's antivirus application allows you to both monitor your system for attacks, as well as perform a full system scan. Through Automatic Update, you can manually or automatically download regular virus definition updates.

If you'd prefer to go with a more trusted, third-party source, you certainly have a number of options. We've been using the antivirus software bundled with Norton SystemWorks for a number of years and it has gotten the job done. Our complaints don't really go beyond the price tag compared to the OneCare subscription, and that it can be slow at times. One advantage of some third-party software is that some of them, for example, Norton, allow you to simultaneously scan for both viruses and malware.

If you bought a new computer, you may have a trial antivirus application to test drive. Because most antivirus programs offer the same protections and features, it's hard to say if one is better than the other. McAfee, Norton, Microsoft — all of these will get the job done. Decide which one you feel comfortable with and regularly update and scan your system.

Of course, everything depends on what is currently available for Windows Vista. At the moment, there are several antivirus programs that you can use with Windows Vista:

- Avast! Antivirus (www.avast.com/eng/avast-antivirus-and-windows-vista.html)
- Grisoft (www.grisoft.com/doc/1)
- PC-Cillin (www.trendbeta.com/index.php?get=80)

Windows Security Center and antivirus software

At the beginning of this chapter, we discuss the Windows Security Center and the "placeholder" for antivirus software. If you do not currently have any antivirus software installed, the title appears in a red box with a red light (see Figure 7.12); this indicates that your antivirus software is either not installed or it is disabled.

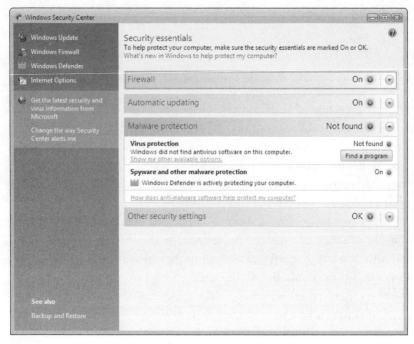

Figure 7.12. The Windows Security Center displaying a placeholder for antivirus application.

After you install antivirus software, Windows Security Center should turn green (see Figure 7.13). At launch, Vista looks for an antivirus program; if it does not find your application, you can always manually locate it from the Windows Security Center by clicking the so-named button.

Updating your operating system

Just like many people spend time working in their garden or caring for their car, it's also important that you care for your computer and the Vista operating system. Similarly, the folks at Microsoft frequently release product updates; these include security patches, product updates, or even driver updates. The easiest way to do this is through the Windows Updates feature available in Windows Vista (see Figure 7.14).

Watch Out!

Unless you install antivirus software, a red shield will appear in the notification bar indicating that Windows Security Center requires your attention. What it really means is that an essential Vista security component is either missing or disabled.

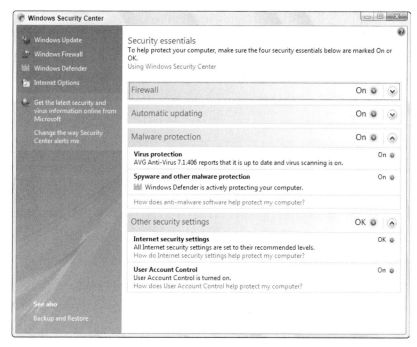

Figure 7.13. The Windows Security Center with installed antivirus software.

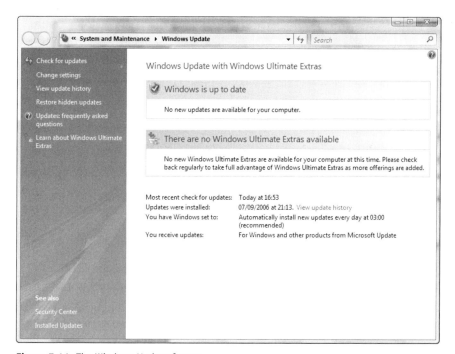

Figure 7.14. The Windows Update feature.

As we mentioned earlier in this chapter, you can access Windows Updates: from the Windows Security Center. Microsoft gives you three choices; do nothing and pass on updates altogether (not recommended), manually install updates, or automatically download/install updates (see Figure 7.15). Vista downloads any updates from the Windows Update Web site, which is an independent Web site.

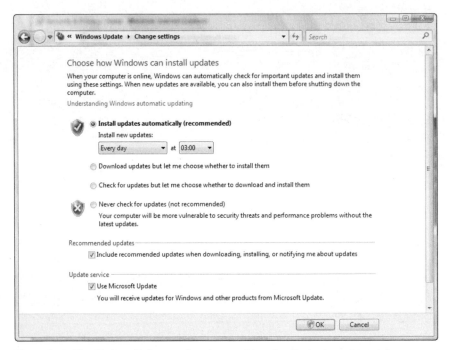

Figure 7.15. The Windows Update settings let you determine the best way to update your computer.

Configuring Windows Update settings

Using this feature is the easiest way of making sure your computer is up-to-date with the latest fixes. Vista downloads any updates for you. What happens next is up to you. You have four options for automatic updates configuration:

■ **Install updates automatically.** This is the fully automated option that automatically downloads updates for you and proceeds to install the updates. If you are comfortable with Microsoft deciding when and what to install on your computer, there's no harm in this feature.

- **Download updates but let me choose whether to install them.** An option similar to the previous one, except that it doesn't install the files; rather, this decision is up to you. Vista lets you choose which updates to download and when to install updates. Fortunately, once an update is downloaded, Vista lets you decide when it should contact you. After you install an update, Vista asks you if you want to reboot your computer (if necessary) or to postpone it.

- **Check for updates but let me choose whether to download and install them.** This choice is good if you are in the middle of an important project. Downloading and updating your computer can be a major drain on your system. Personally, we recommend either this or the previous option. We believe that it's important to verify and personally approve anything installed on your computer — even an update!

- **Never check for updates (not recommended).** Windows Vista never updates your computer for you; you'll have to manually update in order to receive the latest patches, and so on.

Of course, you can also turn off Windows Updates (not recommended). Unlike Windows XP, Vista lets you determine if automatic updates should include both high-priority updates and optional software updates or just the former. Optional updates frequently involve third-party hardware or software, which should raise a potential red flag. We recommend only taking high-priority updates into account. For optional updates, check them frequently and make sure you have the necessary resources to update them.

What exactly is a high-priority update? This includes critical updates, security updates, service packs, and update rollups that should be installed once made available. The optional updates, as mentioned above, provide noncritical fixes for both Windows and third-party applications. These are optional and should be updated only after you have installed all high-priority updates.

Watch Out!

The Windows Update Web site used an ActiveX control that must be installed before Internet Explorer can use this feature. Relax, it's okay. As a rule, be wary of any site wanting to install ActiveX controls, but this is fine. Right-click the Information bar and then click Install ActiveX control.

Inside Scoop

Microsoft is pretty reactive when it comes to providing updates. If you hear about a new virus or security gap, you can be sure Microsoft will be releasing something within a few days. In the past, the second Tuesday of each month meant a new high-priority update release.

Removing updates

Sometimes necessity forces you to remove any updates; for example, some security fixes in the past have actually made computers less stable than before update installation. This isn't often the case, but it's impor-tant to recognize that it does happen, and that you shouldn't feel bad about having to roll back an update or fix.

There are two steps to doing this. First, from the Windows Update Web site, you can review your update history from the Review your update history link. This displays a list of past installations downloaded from this Web site; this includes the name of the fix and Knowledge Base (KB) number that details the fix. This information is twofold. First, you can consult Microsoft's support site (http://support.microsoft.com) and look up the KB number. And then you can use the name of the fix to remove it from the Add or remove a program window (see Figure 7.16).

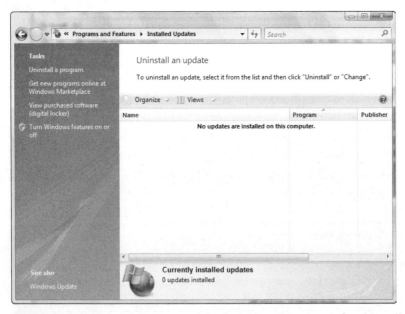

Figure 7.16. The Add or remove a program window keeps any updates separate for other applications.

Watch Out!

If you are also running Microsoft Office on your machine, keep in mind that the Windows Update doesn't provide updates for the Office suite. To update Microsoft Office, you can access the Update Office Web site from any Office application.

Using the Windows Software Update Service

If you have just a few computers to manage, the Automatic Update service works fine, especially over a shared DSL or broadband connection. However, if you're talking about 25 computers that need to be updated, doing so will strain a network connection if all the computers are downloading the same fixes at the same time.

To take care of this concern, Microsoft developed the Windows Software Update Service (WSUS). This service lets you download updates to a company server, and network computers would receive them from this server. In short, updates and fixes are downloaded just once and IP departments can test the code (to make sure it works with the company IT infrastructure) and then schedule a time for the updates to be rolled out across the company.

If you have a significant number of computers to update, take a look at the WSUS Web site. You can find out more at `www.microsoft.com/windowsserversystem/updateservices/downloads/WSUS.mspx`.

Other Vista security features

We'd be remiss if we didn't at least mention some of the other new security features in Windows Vista. Of course, a number of these are "behind the scenes" and not applications that users can enable to make their Vista experience safer. In fact, there are simply new services built in to Windows Vista that make it an overall safer operating system.

Windows Service Hardening

Microsoft developed a new hardware initiative called Windows Service Hardening. The name is strange, admittedly, but it works well in tandem with the Windows Firewall (especially the version available with the

Windows Live OneCare service). Here's basically how it works: Service Hardening is a set of network rules that help your computer — in conjunction with Windows Firewall — prevent important Windows services (for example, Remote Procedure Call) from being used inappropriately in the Windows registry, your network, or the file system. This prevents the unauthorized modification of system settings. In the case of our Remote Procedure Call, Service Hardening prevents it from making changes to the registry or randomly replacing system files.

Network Access Protection (NAP)

It's time for your nap! Bad jokes aside, system administrators or IT staff will appreciate the new NAP feature. To help combat ever-prevalent network attacks (which are malicious 99.9999 percent of the time, if not 100), NAP lets you enforce access requirements for your company server. These requirements are "health" related — in other words, is the computer requesting access in good shape. You can set requirements that demand current antivirus software, up-to-date definitions, and recent system scans. When a computer tries to log on to your network, NAP scans the requirements and compares it to the information on the client machine. If the client machine is not "healthy" (does not meet requirements), it's not getting on. You can think of the NAP as one mean bouncer at a trendy New York club.

Integrated IPsec/firewall management

Windows Vista now offers a one-stop location for handling your firewall and Internet Protocol Security (IPsec). You can do both from the new Windows Firewall with Advanced Security feature. By combining both functions, security settings are easier to find. The WFAS feature is useful for handling security needs, such as bidirectional traffic filtering or handling settings for the IPsec server or domain isolation.

Analyze Windows security

Earlier in the chapter, we mention the Microsoft Baseline Security Analyzer 2.0 (MBSA). Although Windows Vista is a complex system, it is still easily vulnerable to outside attacks. Hackers and malware authors often enjoy attacking Microsoft due to its popularity, its omnipresence, and the fact that Windows is synonymous with computers in general. Many of the attacks are due in part to misconfigurations of your Windows system.

Inside Scoop

Microsoft offers two different versions of the MBSA; for Windows Vista, use the latest version of the tool.

One of the first steps Microsoft took to dispel the reputation of being bad with security, not to mention of being a company with openness issues for its technology, was to create the "genuine Microsoft Windows" program. This program validates your copy of Windows and it also checks your system's security.

The MBSA is a quick download that is available at `www.microsoft.com/technet/security/tools/mbsa2/default.mspx`; this tool is easy to use and helps small and medium businesses determine their security state in accordance with Microsoft security recommendations, and offers specific remediation guidance. It allows you to improve your security management process (see Figure 7.17) to detect common security misconfigurations and missed security updates on your systems.

Figure 7.17. The MBSA tool is a valuable friend when looking for security issues.

One nice aspect of the MBSA is that it doesn't have to be installed on every computer; it can remotely scan computers in your network or in your domain for security vulnerabilities. If you administer any size network, this is a good way to find out if any of your computers at home or in a small office have any potential holes in them.

Apply security templates

Now that you have a report on the potential shortcomings of your computer's settings, you can choose to apply a template to your computer and change the settings to the ones recommended for your desired security level. You can also choose to edit the imported template's settings so that they match your company's policies. For example, the maximum password age of 42 days may be too few; you can double-click the setting, change it to 90 days, and then rerun the analysis if you want.

To apply the template to your computer, open the Microsoft Management Console.

1. Add the Security Configuration and Analysis (SCA) snap-in from the File - Add/Remove Snap-in menu.

2. Right-click the Security Configuration and Analysis snap-in.

3. Click Open Database (see Figure 7.18).

4. An open file window appears. Enter a name for the database; even if this seems counterintuitive, it is the right step.

5. Choose a configuration file to import.

6. Click Configure Computer Now.

7. Type or browse to a location for the error log and then click OK. The SCA snap-in applies all the template settings to your computer. Some of the settings may not take effect until the next time you log out and back on again.

 Watch Out!

If you made any changes to the template, you should export the changes to a new template instead of overwriting the old one. Right-click the SCA snap-in and select Export Template.

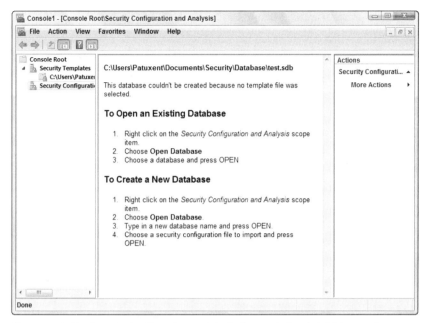

Figure 7.18. The Security Configuration and Analysis snap-in has helpful instructions once you install it.

Install and manage digital certificates

Digital certificates figure prominently in Windows Vista. However, it probably won't affect your day-to-day Windows activities. In fact, you may never notice them until they are set to expire, in which case Vista will remind you of this fact.

If you're not familiar with certificates, they are used for three primary reasons:

▪ To identify a person

▪ To identify a service

▪ To encrypt files

Certificates act as a public key to perform the above tasks. Most common certificates adhere to the X.509v3 certificate standard and are provided for you automatically. Of course, there are a few cases where you're on your own. For example, if you want to use a digital signature for protecting your e-mail, or you want to protect your Web site, you need to obtain these certificates. The cost varies depending on the provider; Thawte (www.thawte.com/) and VeriSign (www.verisign.com) are two of the most well known certificate providers. Their respective Web sites provide information on their various services and cost schemes.

Using the Certificate Manager

Windows Vista features a centralized location where you can manage your certificates; it is called, oddly enough, Certificate Manager (see Figure 7.19). You can open it by typing **certmgr.msc** in the Start menu search box. The Certificate Manager provides an organized list of the certificates found on your machine (in the Certificates - Current User location).

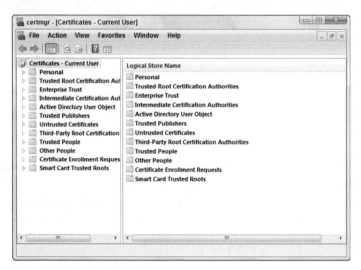

Figure 7.19. The Certificate Manager.

When you click on a certificate, the right panel displays several bits of important information regarding the certificate. This includes the following:

- Certificate subject (you)
- Certificate issuer
- Expiration date of the certificate
- Purpose of the certificate
- Friendly name
- Status
- Certificate template

Bright Idea

If you want to search for a certificate instead of sorting through folders, right-click a category in the left pane and click Find Certificates.

If you double-click a certificate, the Certificate window appears (see Figure 7.20). This window features information that is similar to that listed in the right pane. It mentions the purpose of the certificate (in a wordier fashion), the issuer/subject, the validity, and any issuer statement (if any).

Figure 7.20. The Certificate window of the Certificate Manager.

If you want more information on your certificate, you can click the Details tab in the Certificate window (see Figure 7.21). This tab lists extensive information on your certificate, including version details and algorithm information. The Certification Path tab displays the certificate and confirms that it is authentic and reliable. For a number of certificates, you can click multiple certificates and then click View Certificate to view a copy of them.

Managing certificate properties

Like most elements in Windows, you can access file properties simply by clicking Edit Properties (see Figure 7.22). You can also access it from the Details tab mentioned above. This Properties page lets you set a friendly name and description for your certificate. (Although the certificate may have some outstanding qualities, friendly name doesn't mean anything other than a common name for it.) You can assign a name to your certificate; if you're not sure that you'll remember the correlation between your friendly name and its purpose, you can always add a description!

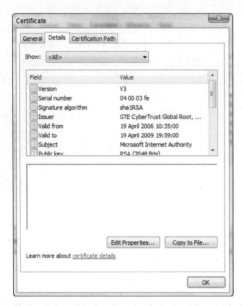

Figure 7.21. The Details tab of the Certificate window.

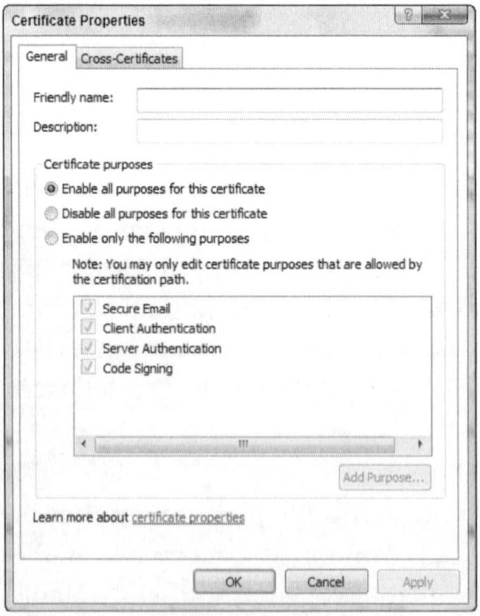

Figure 7.22. The Properties window for a certificate.

You can also manage certificate purposes for the certificate. You have three choices:

- Enable all purposes
- Disable all purposes
- Enable only specific purposes

Only if you choose the third option can you select/deselect a purpose. Some certificates let you edit purposes or add additional purposes. Most home users probably won't view certificates; but unless you have reason not to, you can probably leave the default settings.

The Cross-Certificates tab (Figure 7.23) lets you add a download URL for your certificate. Cross-Certificates can be used both in an intranet and extranet setting. They are designed to create trust between two separate certificate hierarchies. You can also use them to define namespaces of certificates in one hierarchy and if Cross-Certificates can be used in the second hierarchy.

Figure 7.23. The Cross-Certificates tab of the Certificates Properties window.

The procedures in the following sections can be performed by either an Administrator or a Standard user.

Requesting a new certificate

If you need a new certificate, you can get the ball rolling by right-clicking the Personal folder, selecting All Tasks, and then going to the Advanced Operations menu and selecting Create custom request. This is a rather odd name for this feature, because it helps you to request a new certificate, rather than a custom request (see Figure 7.24).

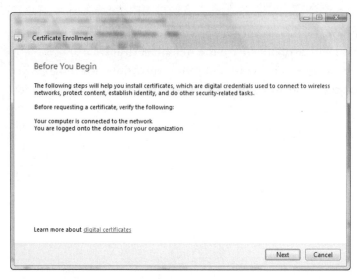

Figure 7.24. The Certificate Enrollment Wizard.

To request a new certificate:

1. Click Create Custom Request. The Certificate Enrollment Wizard appears. In order for you to use this wizard, you must have an internet connection and be logged on to your domain. Click Next.

2. The next screen allows you to select a template or choose from either the CNG or Legacy keys (neither of which are templates). You can also select a request format. Click Next.

3. Click Next on the Certificate Information screen to accept your selection, or click Details to customize your request. If you do the latter, you can create a friendly name/certificate, set a subject name for the certificate from the drop-down list, set various extensions, or set information related to the public key.

4. You can save a copy of your request in Base64 or binary format. This should be saved to your hard drive or, preferably, a flash drive.

5. When complete, click Finish. Keep in mind that you cannot request a certificate for a service!

Renewing a certificate

A relatively straightforward process, renewing a certificate is also done from the Certificate Manager. Since most certificates have a decent life-span, you shouldn't expect to have to do this too often!

1. Click on the certificate to renew in the Certificate Manager.

2. In the Action menu, select either the Renew certificate with new key option or the Renew certificate with same key option.

3. Follow the instructions in the wizard to renew your certificate.

Importing a certificate

You can use the Certificate Manager and its wizard to import a certificate (Figure 7.25). However, be very careful about importing certificates. Only import certificates that you are certain are from a reliable source. Importing a hacked certificate could spell big trouble for your system or network if imported. Here's how to import a certificate:

Figure 7.25. The Certificate Import Wizard.

1. Right-click in the right pane and select Import from the All Tasks menu and Click Next.

2. Click the Browse button to select the desired certificate to import and then click Next.

   If requested, enter the password for the certificate. There are also three other options on this page: enable strong key encryption, make the certificate exportable, and include extended properties.

3. Select the certificate store where the certificate will be added. By default, it is added to Personal. However, you can select a different store, or let Vista decide based on the certificate information.

4. Click Next.

5. Click Finish.

Exporting a certificate

You may want to export a certificate for use on another computer. This is also a good way to back up your certificate file. As you might have guessed, this is done from the Certificate Manager and its wizard (Figure 7.26). Follow these steps to export a certificate:

Figure 7.26. The Certificate Export Wizard.

1. From the Certificate Manager, right-click on the certificate to export and click Export. The Certificate Export Wizard appears.

   The wizard asks you if you want to export the private key along with the certificate (which is a public key). If you decide to do this, you'll need to enter a password a little later. If you are performing a backup, do not export the private key.

2. Depending on your answer in Step 1, the wizard will let you select your format. For information on the types of formats, there is a help link at the bottom of the Export File Format page. If you are exporting the file for use on a machine running Windows, you should use the PKCS #7 format (if available). Otherwise, try to use DER Encoded Binary (especially if this is a backup) or Base64 Encoded.

3. If you opted to export the private key as well, enter a password and then verify it.

4. Specify the name of the file you wish to export using the Browse button. By default, it is saved in the Documents folder for the user.

5. Click Finish to close the wizard and then close the confirmation box that appears.

Change Data Execution Prevention settings

The Data Execution Prevention (DEP) feature works exactly the same in Windows Vista as in Windows XP. If you didn't read *The Unofficial Guide to Windows XP*, we'll cover DEP again here.

DEP is a technology designed to stop exploitation of buffer overrun hacks. Most home users probably never think about such scenarios, but it is important to understand. A buffer overrun occurs when a specific piece of code is flawed and a malicious software program deliberately stuffs more data into the buffer than it can handle. Rather than just toss away the extra code, most applications will attempt to run the additional code. A cleverly crafted piece of malware knows exactly how much data it takes to overrun the buffer, and the executable code begins immediately after that point in memory.

DEP attempts to stop this by locking memory and marking it as not executable. Should data overrun a buffer, unless it overruns into an area specifically marked as executable by a program, the excess code will not run. The program may still crash, but at least it won't spawn something nasty that takes over your computer as it dies.

As you might have guessed, there is a catch to using DEP. There are two components to DEP: software code that Windows Vista monitors and manages, and hardware support in your computer's CPU. The latter is only found in the newer 64-bit processors that contain the necessary checks to prevent code from being executed after a buffer overrun.

The software portion can be run on any computer that has Windows Vista installed. By default, only essential programs and services have DEP enabled. While, in theory, it would be nice for all applications to have DEP coverage, the reality is that some applications — such as Java applications or software that doesn't mark generated code with execute permission — have compatibility issues with DEP.

Fortunately, DEP does not take an all-or-nothing approach. You can set DEP to apply for all applications, and then place specific applications in an exception list, essentially opting out of the DEP protections in case of compatibility issues.

To view and configure DEP:

1. Right-click Computer from the Start menu and open Properties.

2. Click Advanced system settings. The system Properties window appears.

3. Click the Advanced tab.

4. Select Settings in the Performance section.

5. Click Data Execution Prevention (see Figure 7.27).

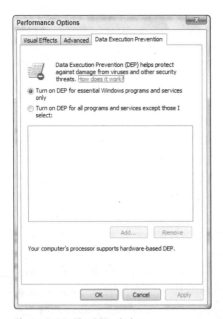

Figure 7.27. The DEP window.

Hack

You can configure DEP at boot time, instead of switching it off in Windows. Edit the boot.ini file with execution option "/NoExecute-OptIn" (system binaries only), OptOut (all binaries, process exception list), AlwaysOn (all binaries, no exceptions), or AlwaysOff (DEP fully disabled).

If your processor does not have hardware DEP support, you will see a notice to this effect at the bottom of the dialog box. You can still use software DEP, and by default software DEP is enabled for "essential Windows programs and services only." A casual search at MSDN does not reveal what this list entails, so you just have to take Microsoft's word for it that they really know best how to protect you.

You can choose the Turn on DEP for all programs and services except those I will select option, and hopefully gain more protection from buffer overrun. However, the Help and Security Center reports problems with some Windows programs. If you enable the global setting, you should watch to see which programs inexplicably crash, and then add them to the exceptions list. Unless, of course, you expect that the program has been hacked and is crashing because of a buffer overrun exploit.

Our best advice is that if you notice system slowdown with DEP enabled, turn it off.

If you have more interest in how DEP works, you can read a technical, but detailed, discussion of DEP at http://support.microsoft.com/default.aspx?scid=kb;en-us;875352. Note that this discussion involved Windows XP, but the detail is still relevant for Windows Vista.

Audit computer and security events

As one of the main pillars of security, auditing is perhaps the least known and overlooked. When a system crashes, most people reboot, hoping the problem is then sorted. However, did you know that Windows can be configured to audit just about anything that happens on its watch? This includes security issues and performance. This gives you some idea of what went wrong, and in the case of audit events, it provides a warning that unauthorized activity is afoot.

Auditing can be done for many things, but the two most connected to security are auditing access policies and auditing file usage. To audit access policies, you need to change some settings to the local computer's policies. This can be done using the Local Security Policy (see Figure 7.28) snap-in for standalone or workgroup computers, or using the Group Policy Editor for computers attached to a domain.

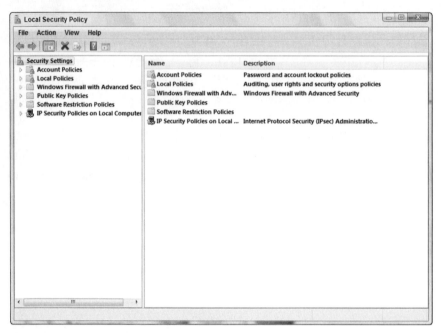

Figure 7.28. The Local Security Policy snap-in.

Determine effective group policies

If you are running Windows Vista over a domain, the administrator can apply policies at various levels. These include domain, unit, computer, use, and your local computer. The problem with policies and having so many different levels is that the user can easily become confused, not to mention that it is not uncommon for policies to be in conflict, or indeed contradictory!

Fortunately, Microsoft recognized how unpleasant going through all of the policies can be, so they gave us an MMC snap-in to help things out. The Resultant Set of Policy snap-in (Figure 7.29) provides a more extensive look at which policies are being applied and where they came from.

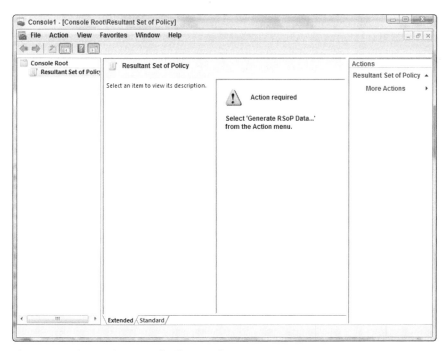

Figure 7.29. The Resultant Set of Policy snap-in.

To install it, simply

1. Open **mmc** from the Start menu search box.

2. Use the Add/Remove Snap-in menu to add this snap-in.

    After it is installed, right-click the snap-in and select Generate RSoP data. The Resultant Set of Policy Wizard (see Figure 7.30) appears.

3. Click Next and then select Logging mode and click Next again.

4. Select This computer and then click Next.

5. Select Current user and then click Next.

6. Review the selection summary before clicking Next.

7. Click Finished at the end of the wizard.

The only real downside to this tool is that you must reload the snap-in each time you want to use it. It's also unfortunate that there is no way to print any of the policy descriptions for future reference.

Figure 7.30. The Resultant Set of Policy Wizard.

Audit access policies

To audit access policies on the local computer, click Start, type Run, type **secpol.msc**, and then press Enter.

You can also launch the snap-in by clicking Start ⇨ Administrative Tools ⇨ Local Security Polices ⇨ Audit Policy (see Figure 7.31).

Each policy has three settings: Audit Success, Audit Failure, and No Auditing (no check boxes selected). Recommended settings are:

- **Audit account logon events:** Failure
- **Audit account management:** Failure
- **Audit directory service access:** Failure
- **Audit logon events:** Failure
- **Audit object access:** Failure
- **Audit policy change:** Success, Failure
- **Audit privilege use:** No auditing
- **Audit process tracking:** No auditing
- **Audit system events:** Failure

After you set these audits, you must log out and back in again to put them into effect.

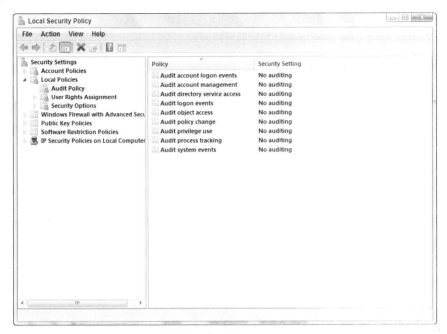

Figure 7.31. The Local Security Policy's Audit Policy.

Audit file access

File access is recommended only for particular files and not for entire folders or (!) entire drives. If you attempt to audit all events of all files, you will not only fill up your log file (and overwrite earlier entries when the log "rolls over" to the beginning), but you will quickly get bored digging through pages of information in search of one single event.

If you want to audit file permission, there is only one rule to remember: You must use NTFS file sharing rather than simple file sharing. You can turn on permission auditing by following these steps:

1. Right-click the file and then click Properties.

2. Click the Security tab and then click Advanced (see Figure 7.32, which shows result of doing so).

3. Click the Auditing tab, click Add, type in the name of the group or user you wish to audit (only one object at a time please!), and then click Check Names. If the object exists, the group or user will appear with an underscore.

4. Click OK.

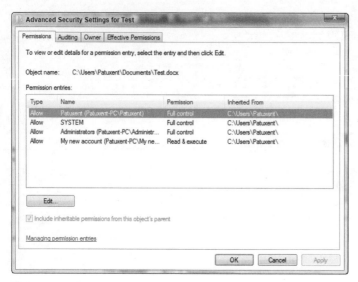

Figure 7.32. The Security tab with Advanced properties.

The permissions can be audited for successful use or failed use. For example, you may have set your accounting program's database file to full permission for yourself and denied permission to everyone else. You may want to audit failed read, write, execute, and delete permissions on the file. While it's conceivable that some of the other permissions may be attempted, you don't need to carry the paranoia too far, unless your company's policies regarding sensitive information require it. In that case, it's most likely that audits have been applied at a group policy level anyway. But it's always nice to know that you can audit so many things that you'll know when the file so much as sneezes without your permission.

Review the Security log

The toughest part about auditing isn't enabling auditing, but poring over the event log in search of failed events or other indications of misbehavior occurring on your computers.

The tool used to view security-related events is, not surprisingly, the Event Viewer. To open the Event Viewer, click Start, Administrative Tools, and then Event Viewer. You can use either an Event Viewer filter to show only the types of events you want to review, or you can use the Find command to look for specific event IDs that may have been logged to the Security log file (see Figure 7.33). Some common access audit event IDs to look for are

- **Event ID 529:** Unknown username or bad password
- **Event ID 530:** Log on time restriction violation
- **Event ID 531:** Account disabled
- **Event ID 532:** Account expired
- **Event ID 535:** Password expired
- **Event ID 539:** Logon Failure: Account locked out
- **Event ID 627:** NT AUTHORITY\ANONYMOUS is trying to change a password
- **Event ID 644:** User account locked out

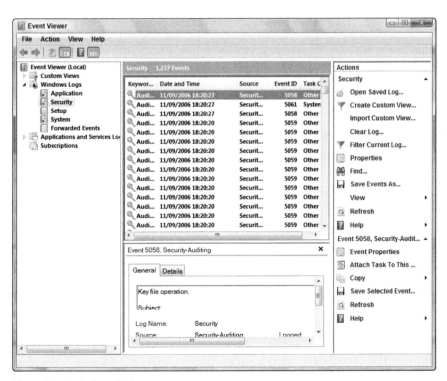

Figure 7.33. The Security log.

Auditing at home

If you are not on a corporate network and have otherwise protected yourself with a firewall, antivirus, and anti-spyware programs, setting up auditing sounds extreme. Who could possibly want to gain access to your system?

If you have sensitive information on your computer (bank data, work files, book chapters), or even valuable information (such as family photos), you really can't afford to take a risk.

Unfortunately, many people seem to adopt the "it could never happen to me" attitude and then are angry when it finally does happen.

The audit feature can be a valuable friend, like a family dog, that looks out for you and tells all (it does its job, and does it well). If you leave your computer on extensively, think about checking the logs to see if any unauthorized logon attempts occurred.

The truth about Windows Mail

Where do we begin with this one? Windows Vista brings you Windows Mail with little or no fanfare. A wolf disguised as a sheep is still a wolf — and Windows Mail is still a bad bet. What's in a name? Yes, you may have noticed that Outlook Express is now a thing of the past — in name only. It was re-baptized as Windows Mail (see Figure 7.34).

Originally, we planned on primarily discussing how to secure Windows Mail. However, we'd be remiss if we did that. Mail, or Outlook Express II, represents one of Microsoft's darkest hours, and we highly recommend against using it. True, it has a new phishing and anti-spam filter — but who doesn't? That's not a sufficient enough reason to use it.

If Outlook 2007 is not something you are willing or able to consider, there are a number of other options out there that we find to be much better (and more feature rich).

For starters, why not Thunderbird? The Firefox e-mail client is easy to use, priced nicely (read: free), and contains some nice features. Besides the anti-phishing and junk mail features, it also features advanced security features and RSS feeds. It's yours for the taking at www.mozilla.com/thunderbird/.

Figure 7.34. The "brand-new" Windows Mail.

We're long-time fans and users of Qualcomm's Eudora. This is a paid e-mail client, but it easily manages multiple accounts, features a rather nice e-mail editor, and also features security features. The price is a bit high, but we really enjoy how comfortable it is. You can use an ad-based version for free — it has all of the features of the paid version; you simply have to endure ads in the interface. You can find out more at www.eudora.com.

If you're the type of user that is always on the go, perhaps Microsoft Live Mail or Web-based e-mail services, such as Google's Gmail (http://gmail.google.com/), may be to your liking. Security is well under control for these services; Web mail used to be known as a hotbed for malware activity. The major concern with these is any personal concerns you may have with privacy policies.

Watch Out!

Though Google's Gmail is free, you need an invitation to join. By implementing such a practice, Google is trying to prevent any bots or other unauthorized users from compromising their system. You can also obtain an account through an SMS to your mobile phone.

If you absolutely must use Windows Mail, there are a number of things you can do to assure a better level of security. First, you can work directly with your Internet Service Provider (ISP) and enable their anti-spam feature. We'd be very surprised if your ISP or Web host service didn't have some sort of way of blocking spam or dubious e-mails before they reach your mail service.

From Windows Mail, you can block a sender (see Figure 7.35). Spammers are increasingly clever; they quickly find ways to "work around" local security settings. Should a piece of spam hit your mail box, you can still block the sender or its domain and silence both forever. Doing this should still be considered an extra step to increasing security. First and foremost, work with your ISP/Web host to set up spam filters.

You can also make your Windows Mail safer by blocking attachments. Although this option may not be possible for many users, let us offer an alternative: Don't open attachments from unknown senders.

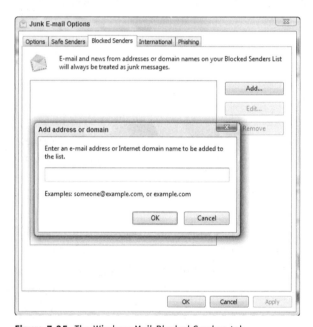

Figure 7.35. The Windows Mail Blocked Senders tab.

Secure Internet Explorer

Windows Vista offers increased security features in Internet Explorer 7 (see Figure 7.36). These include a new Protected Mode, which is tantamount to a browser lockdown. These features are aptly detailed in Chapter 10. Let's continue the conversation there!

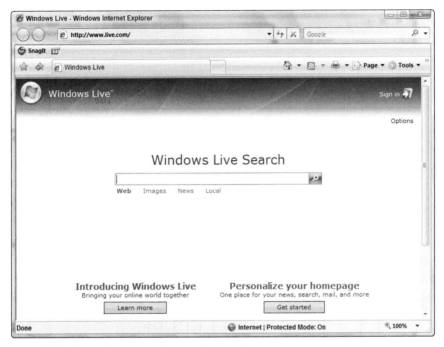

Figure 7.36. The much improved Internet Explorer 7.

Just the facts

- Windows Vista, based on Windows NT code, is considerably safer than previous versions of Windows operating systems.

- Windows Live OneCare is Microsoft's foray into helping solve problems it helped create.

- The Windows Firewall with Advanced Security is a good "free" firewall that offers bidirectional monitoring.

- Windows Vista has a number of viable, third-party antivirus applications currently available.

- Securing your e-mail is as important as securing the whole of your computer.

Mastering Multimedia with Windows Vista

Chapter 8

For home users, the multimedia features of an operating system such as Windows Vista account for a large part of the use they give to their computer. So, how does Vista shape up? Could the most recent edition of Windows Media Player finally be the one to give Apple and its iTunes a run for their money? Is the latest incarnation of Windows Media Center the tool that is going to power the digital entertainment system that will soon be at the heart of every home? Will we still be able to upload photos from our old digital cameras — and what will we be able to do with them once we have? This chapter looks at just a few of the ways in which you can work with sound, photos, and video in Windows Vista.

Introducing Windows Media Player 11

Let's not be coy. Windows Media Player (WMP) 11 is a big, big improvement on previous versions of Microsoft's digital media player — and much of that is down to the interface. Microsoft seems to have recognized the need for WMP to have a simpler, more visual front-end that in many ways is more akin to Apple's iTunes. Fortunately, they have managed to produce just such an interface — and not by dumbing it down, as many feared they might, but by smartening it up.

Perhaps the most significant impact on the interface comes in the shape of the reconstructed menu buttons that appear at the top of the screen when Windows Media Player is running (see Figure 8.1). Limited to just five main choices, each of these buttons opens up a series of submenus that provide access to a whole host of useful options. Under the Rip submenu, for example, you'll find options to specify the output format or adjust the bit rate, and under Library you can create playlists or decide which types of media are displayed. That's not all the menu buttons let you do, of course, and we'll look at each of them in more detail in the following sections.

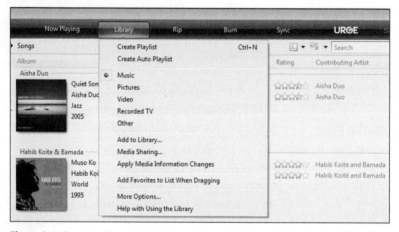

Figure 8.1. Revamped menu buttons provide access to a whole host of useful options.

Incidentally, although this new interface is a great step forward, it's worth pointing out that you also have the option of working with the classic menus that may be more familiar to you from previous versions of Windows Media Player, should you find the new interface a little hard to get used to at first. To do so, simply click the Layout Options button (see Figure 8.2) and then select Show Classic Menus.

Figure 8.2. The Layout Options button lets you customize the interface.

The playback controls that appear at the bottom of the screen (see Figure 8.3) are larger and more inviting, and they include shuffle and repeat options. Their appearance also mimics the controls in the Photo

Bright Idea

If you find that you are missing some album art, you can replace it yourself with any image from your clipboard by right-clicking the album in question, then clicking Paste Album Art.

Gallery viewer, helping ensure a visual coherence that gives a real sense of how the different multimedia components in Vista form part of a whole. The interface also helpfully features backward and forward navigation buttons, which you'll find in the upper-left corner of the screen, to make sure you never get lost.

Figure 8.3. The playback controls are large and inviting.

Overall, Windows Media Player has become far more visually impressive — or, to put it more bluntly, less boring to look at. The plain text display of previous versions of WMP has been replaced by thumbnails for your photos, screenshots for your video files, and album covers for your music. As well as simply looking nicer (which in itself is no small improvement), this also makes it much easier to find and manage your files.

Another feature that gives the player an extra touch of personality is the use of album art. Windows Media Player can track down album art images and ID3-tag info (title, artist, album, track number, or other information about the track) that it uses to update your library automatically in the background.

Getting started with Windows Media Player

You can choose from a number of ways to start using Windows Media Player. For example, if you want to listen to an audio CD, simply insert it into your CD-ROM drive and wait for it to load. If you haven't already set Windows Media Player as your default player, a screen appears proposing a number of suggested actions (see Figure 8.4). Select the option to play the CD; if you are certain that this will always be your response to this window, select the Always do this for audio CDs check box. If you change your mind later, you can always edit this setting in Start ⇨ Default Programs ⇨ Change AutoPlay settings.

Figure 8.4. The AutoPlay dialog box.

Once Windows Media Player is running, you can select any media files (CD, mp3, and a wide array of Windows files — video, TV show, picture, or audio) using the standard Open file dialog box (Ctrl+O). You can select these files either individually or using your standard Ctrl+A (select all) or Ctrl (multiple selection) shortcuts.

You also have the option of playing a CD that is in your CD-ROM drive by clicking the Now Playing button, as you can see in Figure 8.5.

Figure 8.5. Play audio CDs in your CD-ROM drive.

Watch Out!

Depending on the quality of your CD-ROM drive and the type of CD you are attempting to play (standard music CD, CD-RW, or DVD-RW), Windows Vista may take a little bit of time to load the CD. Don't be surprised by this; it's perfectly normal.

Inside Scoop

To minimize CD lag (the time required for Windows Media Player to read your CD), consider ripping the CD to audio files for use with the player. We discuss how to do so in "Rip CDs," later in this chapter.

Finally, you can play any items directly from your digital library. You'll find out more about how your library helps you organize your digital media collection in "Manage your digital library," later in this chapter.

Now playing

When your musical selection starts playing, you notice the following:

- The Now Playing tab is the selected tab by default.

- The Visualization screen takes up most of the Windows Media Player interface. Depending on your settings, it may display the Album Art associated with the music you are playing, or a psychedelic pattern that doesn't serve any real purpose other than to look good.

- The album title and its track listing (the title of each song and its length in minutes) appear on the right side of the screen, underneath a thumbnail of the album cover. When you roll your mouse over it, the size reduces to display the Album Name, Artist, and Genre, along with a button to buy the track from an online store if you have an active Internet connection. It has to be said, however, that the advantage of being offered the chance to buy a track you clearly already possess was not immediately apparent to us.

Of course, you can now just sit back and enjoy the music. But the fun doesn't stop there. The Now Playing split button provides you with a number of options for customizing how Windows Media Player handles your media, both how it looks and how it sounds.

One particularly interesting addition to Windows Media Player 11 is the introduction of Enhancements. Enhancements are a range of tools that enable you to determine how your media is played. Enhancements include a Graphic Equalizer (see Figure 8.6), Play Speed Settings to let you speed up or slow down tracks, and Video Settings where you can set the hue, saturation, brightness, and contrast of your video output. We found the Crossfading and Auto Volume Leveling Enhancement to be particularly useful when listening to playlists that contain tracks from a range of difference sources; not all tracks are recorded at the same volume level, and this Enhancement lets you minimize the aural shock of passing from a quiet track to a loud one.

Figure 8.6. Enhancements such as the Graphic Equalizer let you customize how your media is played.

As mentioned previously, Windows Media Player comes with a number of Visualizations, which are display patterns, organized by category, that react to an audio signal as if they're "dancing to the beat" of your musical selection. One change in Windows Media Player 11 is that these dancing visualizations can now be replaced by Album Art instead, which may appeal to those who found the previous offerings a little too psychedelic for their taste.

Whichever option you select, your chosen visualization is displayed in the main Now Playing area. You can select your desired Visualization in two ways:

- By clicking the Now Playing split button and selecting the Visualizations submenu.

- By right-clicking the Now Playing submenu.

Visualizations are separated into different categories or collections (see Figure 8.7). From the Now Playing split button, you can download additional Visualizations by clicking Download Visualizations, and you can set certain parameters for some of your existing visualizations by clicking Options.

Inside Scoop

The Web site www.wmplugins.com is an excellent resource for downloading visualizations, effects, codecs, and other tools for customizing your Windows Media Player experience. At the time of writing, it did not contain any resources specific to Windows Media Player 11, but many of the resources available there work with WMP11 as well.

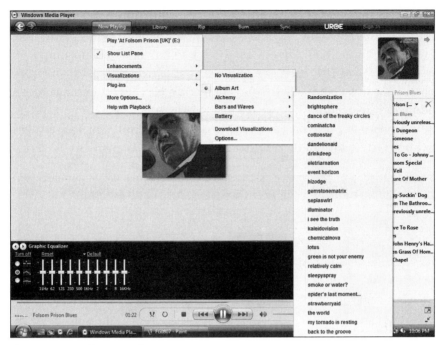

Figure 8.7. Visualization options.

Manage your digital library

Windows Media Player 11 recognizes the fact that your digital library may have grown slightly from the days when it consisted of nothing more than a handful of mp3 files, photos from your most recent vacation, a few family snapshots, and one or two "humorous" video clips that some friends may have sent you via e-mail. Today's digital media libraries are made up of thousands of different elements; fortunately, Windows Media Player 11 provides the tools that enable you to find exactly what you're looking for at any given time.

You can now specify the type of media you want to display in your library, rather than having all your media appear at once as was the case in previous versions of Windows Media Player. Click the Library button and then make your choice between Music, Pictures, Video, Recorded TV, or the all-encompassing Other (for any media that do not fall under these first four headings). By default, the media displayed by Windows Media Player is Music.

You can then sort your media under a range of different headings; in the case of Music, these include Artist, Album, Songs, Genre, Year, and Rating (see Figure 8.8). How likely you are to wake up one morning and say, "I really feel like listening to some songs from 1997!" is open to debate, but this ability to sort your media is a very useful enhancement and takes into account that we each organize our digital content differently. To choose how you want your media to be displayed, simply click the appropriate sort method under Library in the List pane on the left.

Figure 8.8. Sort the digital media in your library.

The search tool is another impressive new feature that simplifies the task of finding a particular media file. Type a search item in the search box (even just part of a word) and you see the results of your search immediately, even before you press Enter. If you are at the root level of your library, the results are broken down by Artist, Album, or Song (if you are looking for music); if you are already in one of the subcategories, the specific results that meet your criteria are displayed (see Figure 8.9). Search results appear quickly, even with very large libraries.

Figure 8.9. The search tool makes it easier to find items in your library.

Create playlists

What's the difference between a library and a playlist? They do sound somewhat similar. The library is an actual database that stores information concerning your media files on your computer or network. The playlist, on the other hand, is literally a list that you can create (or have created automatically) of various media files that you would like to listen to or watch. You use the library to create a playlist, as follows:

1. Click the Library split button, then select Create Playlist. This creates a new, empty playlist in the Info pane.

2. Drag tracks or even whole albums from your library to your playlist (see Figure 8.10).

3. Move the items in your playlist around either by dragging an item to where you want it to go or by right-clicking the item then selecting Move Up or Move Down.

4. When you've finished adding tracks, click the Save Playlist button and give your playlist a name. It's that simple.

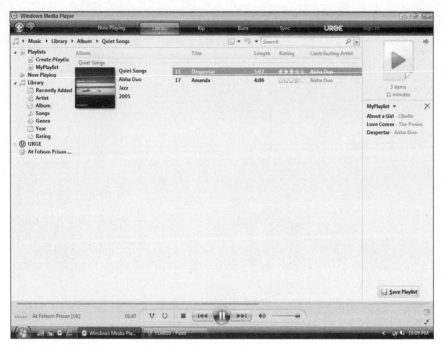

Figure 8.10. Drag items from the library into your playlist.

If you like to be surprised (and who doesn't from time to time), you can also have Windows Media Player create playlists for you, based on certain criteria that you define beforehand. To create an Auto Playlist, click the Library split button, then select Create Auto Playlist. The New Auto Playlist Wizard opens (see Figure 8.11). In this wizard, you define a series of filters that decide what items get added to the playlist; as well as standard options such as Album Artist, Genre, or My Rating, these also include more exotic choices such as how often you've played the item at a certain time of day, or Mood. You can mix different media types (for example, music and video) and you can also apply certain restrictions, such as the total number of items, the total duration, or the total size. This could be useful for preparing a playlist to sync with your portable music player if you don't want to go to the trouble of choosing which tracks to include for yourself.

Figure 8.11. The New Auto Playlist Wizard lets you define criteria based on which Windows Media Player will automatically update your playlist.

Rip CDs

One nice feature in Windows Media Player is its ability to copy content from a CD to your computer's hard disk. This process is known as ripping. You should know from the outset that not all CDs can be ripped. If your disc uses next-generation anti-piracy technology, as is becoming more and more common, you will not be able to rip the disc.

To start the ripping process, simply click the Rip button in the top menu bar. If you have a valid audio CD in your CD-ROM drive, each individual track of the album appears along with relevant information such as the title of each track, the length, and the artist (see Figure 8.12).

By default, all tracks are selected for ripping. You can customize the information that appears for each track by clicking the Layout Options button and then clicking Choose Columns. Information you can display includes Title, Album, Artist, Genre, and Release Year. Rip Status (which is a mandatory column) is blank but changes to Ripping, Pending, or Ripped to library after you start the process by clicking Start Rip.

After your CD is ripped, the resulting WMA files will appear in your Music folder under the name of the group; the files are stored under the name of the album title. In the event that the music database couldn't find information on your artist or CD, the files will appear under Unknown Artist or Unknown Album.

Figure 8.12. Rip CDs to your computer's hard disk.

The Rip split button also lets you define some of the details regarding how your tracks are ripped, including output file format and bit rate. When you decide which bit rate to choose, remember that the higher the rate, the higher the quality — and, obviously, the higher the file size in MB. If you are ripping an album for use on your computer or on a portable device with a large storage space, ripping at the highest rate possible is best. For older devices where storage space is more limited, you might want to consider using the default rate of 128 Kbps. In any case, you should really avoid ripping at any rate below 128 Kbps unless absolutely necessary, because the resulting loss of sound quality can be particularly noticeable.

It's important that you look through the Rip Music tab of the Options dialog box (see Figure 8.13). Click the Rip split button, and then More Options to open it. The options available include typical settings, such as where you want your files to be ripped to and the naming convention to use for your files when ripping music.

On this tab, you can also choose whether you want to copy protect the music you rip; if you do, the ripped files are protected and media usage

A word about formats

Windows Media Player lets you select from a range of output formats — so which one should you choose? The difference between Windows Media Audio, Windows Media Audio Pro, Windows Media Audio (Variable Bit Rate), and Windows Media Audio Lossless may not be immediately apparent. MP3 files can be used on a wider range of devices (including iPods), although there is some debate about whether MP3 or WMA files provide better quality.

To find out more about the different formats offered, click the Rip split button ⇨ More Options ⇨ Compare formats online to be taken to a page on the Windows Media Web site that provides more information.

rights are required to play, burn, or sync them. If you're a home user, you'll probably have no need for this option because there's every chance that you'll want to be able to use your ripped files on more than one computer.

Figure 8.13. The Rip Music tab of the Options dialog box.

CD ripping and piracy

Ripping CDs is convenient, and there certainly are valid reasons for doing so, but it is something that is becoming increasingly difficult to do within the context of current legislation.

Driven by fears of piracy, more and more music publishers are using next-generation copyright systems that either limit or outright prevent ripping CDs to individual audio files. In some cases, you may believe you successfully ripped a CD, but once you listen to it on your computer or other device, you realize that you don't have a ripped audio track at all, but rather white noise.

Burn CDs

Not surprisingly, Windows Media Player also lets you burn CDs, not just rip them. This can be practical for making backups of valued CDs or imports that are hard to replace. Needless to say, it should not be used for illegal copying.

To start burning CDs in Windows Media Player, simply click the Burn tab in the top menu bar. You will be asked to insert a writable disc in your CD-ROM drive if you have not already done so.

You then simply drag and drop individual tracks, or even whole albums, into the burn list that appears on the right-hand side of the screen (see Figure 8.14), until you fill up the whole disc. A good example of the more visual nature of Windows Media Player 11 can be seen in the way it displays a gauge showing how much room you have remaining on the disc you are about to burn, which can prove very useful in squeezing as much music as possible onto your CD.

You can sort the tracks manually (by dragging and dropping them where you want them to go) or by clicking Burn List, then Sort, and then deciding whether you wish to sort your tracks by title, album artist, release date, rating or filename. You can also generate a random list by clicking Shuffle List Now.

On the Burn tab of the Options dialog box (see Figure 8.15), you can specify settings for burning audio and data discs. Options include burn speed (it's best to select a mid-level speed — not the fastest, which can cause errors, nor the slowest, because the artist whose work you're burning to CD will have released a new album by the time you're done) and whether to apply volume leveling across tracks on the CD when combining tracks from different sources.

Figure 8.14. The Burn list.

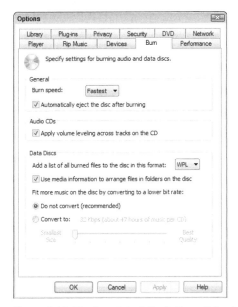

Figure 8.15. The Burn tab of the Options dialog box.

Burn baby burn

There are a number of decent shareware programs out there that can do the same things as the Windows Media Player burn feature, and then some. A quick Google search will yield a number of fine examples.

If you're more comfortable with buying software, try the highly rated Nero. This program is the real deal, although it is intended for advanced users.

After you have sorted your files and tweaked your settings, click the Start Burn button to get the process underway. The length of time it takes to burn your CD will depend on the size of the disc and the settings you have chosen.

Sync with other devices

Windows Media Player also lets you sync some of the contents of your digital library with other devices, including portable music players.

The first time you connect your device to your PC, Windows Media Player automatically selects the best sync method for your device: automatic or manual.

- If your device has a storage capacity of more than 4 gigabytes and your entire library is less than this size, Windows Media Player automatically syncs every single item in your library, and then updates it whenever you connect your device to your PC again in the future.

- If your device has a storage capacity of less than 4 gigabytes, or if your entire library can't fit on the device, Windows Media Player selects manual sync instead. This means that you decide for yourself which files or playlists you want to sync to your device, and that you have to delete files manually.

Regardless of what Windows Media Player first suggests, you can switch between automatic and manual sync at any time. To do so:

1. Click the Sync split button, select your device, and then click Set Up Sync.

2. Check or uncheck the Sync this device automatically check box, as appropriate.

Additionally, even if you opt for having your device sync automatically, you are not obliged to sync your entire library every time you connect your device. You can also choose only to sync specific playlists, which will then be copied onto your device whenever you connect it to your computer.

To choose what syncs automatically, do the following:

1. Click the Sync split button, select your device, and then click Set Up Sync.

2. In the list of Available Playlists, select the playlists you want to sync and then click Add (see Figure 8.16).

3. To remove a playlist, click it in the list of Playlists to Sync, and then click Remove.

4. To arrange the order in which your playlists appear, move them up and down using the arrows. Note that if your device fills up before the sync is complete, those files and playlists that are towards the bottom of the list will not sync. To let Windows Media Player decide what to sync instead of doing so yourself, click Shuffle what syncs; with this option, whenever you connect your device, all of the files it contains are removed and replaced by new playlists and files.

5. Click Finish when you're done.

Figure 8.16. Select which playlists to sync automatically to your portable music player.

Windows Vista N

In order to meet the requirements of an antitrust ruling in the European Union, Microsoft has also been required to release Windows Vista N editions that do not include Windows Media Player and other media-related functionality for the European market.

This does not mean that European residents cannot enjoy Windows Media Player, of course. It just means that Europeans will have to download the player themselves. If you're in this situation, you can find Windows Media Player on the Windows Media Web site at www.microsoft.com/windows/windowsmedia.

Interestingly, Windows Media Player 11 supports reverse synchronization. In other words, if you connect a device that contains media files that are not already present on your PC, these files are automatically copied over from the portable device to the PC.

Using the Windows Media Center

Windows Media Center is the tool that Microsoft hopes will be at the heart of every digital home entertainment system in the years to come. In Microsoft's vision of the future, we will manage all our television, music, video, and picture content directly from Windows Media Center on a PC running Windows Vista (or some subsequent version of Windows), and we will then either listen to or view this content on the PC itself, or stream it to a specialist device.

Before you even think about using Media Center to watch the latest episode of your favorite nighttime drama, you need to consider how you're going to set up the whole system. Basically, there are three ways of playing back content from Windows Media Center:

- You can watch or listen to the content on your computer. This is fine for occasional use in an office or bedroom, but not so good for a home theater setup because you are obviously limited by the quality of your monitor and speakers.

- You can connect your PC directly to your television set. Although doing this improves output quality (which is nonetheless still dependent on your video card), unfortunately, you'll be left with a noisy computer whirring away in your living room.

■ You can connect a Media Center Extender to your television set and stream content over a wired or wireless network. In this case, you can store the PC somewhere less prominent while you watch TV in the living room. At the time of writing, the only extender option currently available for Windows Vista is an Xbox 360.

Navigate the Media Center interface

Opinions are divided on the Media Center interface in Windows Vista — which is a polite way of saying that many people find it incredibly annoying. Still, whenever you get extremely frustrated at having to scroll through yet another interminable list of menus, up pops a cool piece of poster art for the DVD you're about to watch that makes you think that maybe life isn't so bad after all.

However, before judging its interface too harshly, it's important to bear in mind the context in which Media Center is used. Yes, it can be difficult to get used to the idea of scrolling horizontally through the different menus and submenus (and sub-submenus!), but let's not forget that Media Center is designed to be driven by a remote control, not a mouse. And while the list of options may often be too long to fit on your computer monitor, it does look pretty good on a widescreen TV, which is more its natural environment.

The Media Center start menu (see Figure 8.17) initially contains five separate options: Pictures + Videos, Music, TV + Movies, Online Media, and Tasks. Let's dive right in and look at what each one does.

Touch up your photos

The Touch up feature (which you access when viewing a picture by right-clicking the picture, then selecting Picture Details, and then Touch Up — see Figure 8.18) lets you improve your photos by removing red eye, adjusting the contrast, or cropping the image. While Touch Up is unlikely to put many fuller-featured image-editing suites out of business, it is a useful addition for making some on-the-spot, last-minute improvements to your photos.

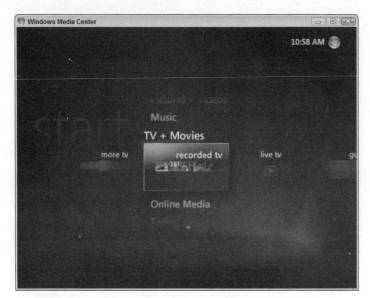

Figure 8.17. The Windows Media Center start menu.

Pictures + Videos

From the Pictures + Videos menu, you can work with the contents of your picture and video libraries, either individually or as part of a slide show.

The options in the Pictures + Videos menu (where each element is inexplicably written in lowercase) are as follows:

- **picture library.** Lets you view any of the photos stored in your Pictures folder (and wherever else you told Windows Media Center to look for digital images). You can browse through your photo collection by folders, tags, or date taken. You even have the chance to perform minor edits to your pictures.

- **play all.** Displays all of the photos stored in your Pictures folder, as a full-screen slide show.

- **video library.** Lets you watch any TV shows you may have recorded, or videos stored in your Videos folder (and, again, wherever else you told Windows Media Center to look for videos).

Inside Scoop

Windows Media Center watches your Music, Pictures, and Videos folders for media files. If you store your media elsewhere, you can add other folders to watch under Tasks ⇨ Settings ⇨ Library Setup.

Figure 8.18. Touch up your digital images directly in Media Center.

Music

The Music menu provides access to your music library, which it shares with Windows Media Player. The options available in this menu are as follows:

■ **music library.** Lets you browse through your music collection by albums, artists, genres, songs, playlists, composers, years, and album artists. A range of submenus lets you do pretty much everything you would expect — playing individual tracks, creating lists of music to be played (called queues), and burning music to CD — and there are often several ways of carrying out the same task. Too many, in our opinion.

■ **play all.** As the name suggests, this plays all the tracks in your collection. You can "shuffle" the queue in order to make its content appear in a random order.

■ **radio.** Allows you to listen to digital radio stations.

■ **search.** Use the search tool to find specific tracks in your music library. When you operate this tool using your remote control, it can be a little difficult to get used to typing text on the virtual numbered keypad, where multiple key presses are required for certain letters, like on a cell phone.

TV + Movies

From the TV + Movies menu, you can watch live TV or shows that you recorded earlier and stored on your hard drive, play DVDs from your DVD drive, or consult programming schedules in the TV guide.

These are definitely some of Windows Media Center's most interesting features, at least in terms of Microsoft's vision of placing this piece of software at the heart of every home's digital entertainment system. But whether or not Media Center is going to replace your TiVo or other digital video recorder (DVR) will, it seems to us, depend more on the quality of your hardware than on the software itself. The functionality is certainly there — whether your graphics card is up to the job is another question entirely.

The TV + Movies menu contains the following options:

- **recorded tv.** As well as letting you watch TV shows that you've already recorded, this is also the place where you manage your recording schedules, either by setting up new programs to record or viewing the list of recordings already scheduled.

- **live tv.** Watch what's on now. The pause function (which lets you take a break from a show, for instance to answer the phone, then restart exactly where you left off), while it may be common to most DVR products, was a particularly useful discovery for us.

- **guide.** Browse through a 14-day program listing for each of the television channels available to you.

- **play dvd.** Play DVDs from your DVD drive.

- **search.** Search through the TV guide to find specific programs. Where this differs from the program listing, which is simply a schedule, is that here you can search by title, keyword, or category.

As your collection of recorded TV shows grows and space on your hard drive becomes an issue, one feature that could come in handy is the Keep Until option, which lets you specify how long movie files should be stored. To change this setting, click the movie in your movie library, click

---

Inside Scoop

Use the Keep Until option to manage how much space TV programs and other videos take up on your hard drive.

Keep Until, and then choose whether to keep the file until you need the space, keep it until a specific date, keep it until you watch it, or keep it until you decide to delete it manually.

Online Media

The Online Media menu is one of the more intriguing features of Windows Media Center. From here, you can access a range of music, videos, and other content and applications from third-party media partners including Fox Sports, MTV, and AOL.

In theory, taking advantage of the fact that your PC is connected to the Internet to allow you to purchase and download content over the Web is what takes Media Center beyond being merely a glorified DVR and music player. In practice, we found these services hard to get working, not least because each one seems to have a different interface, and these interfaces are not always particularly user-friendly. While we love this idea, we would like Microsoft to impose some kind of standard user interface rules to help make the service easier to get to grips with.

The different options available in the Online Media menu are as follows:

- **program library.** Provides you with quick access to the different media providers you subscribe to and the content you have downloaded.

- **what's new.** Lets you view a collection of the latest content providers, grouped under the headings Showcase, TV & Movies, Music & Radio, News & Sports, Games, and Lifestyle.

- **browse categories.** Enables you to search through a more complete list of all content providers, again grouped under the headings listed in the previous bullet.

Tasks

The Tasks menu lets you burn CDs/DVDs, sync your PC to a portable media player or a digital camera, shut down your computer, or add a media extender. The different options available in the Tasks menu are as follows:

- **shutdown.** Opens a new menu where you can close Media Center, log off as the current user, shut down or restart your PC, or put your PC to sleep.

- **burn cd/dvd.** Lets you record music, pictures, or video to writeable media.

- **sync.** Enables you to transfer content between Media Center and a portable device (such as an mp3 player) or a digital camera.

- **add extender.** Opens up a wizard for adding a Media Center Extender that enables you to stream content from your PC directly to your television set.

- **media only.** Keeps Windows Media Center displayed in full-screen mode, with the minimize and close buttons hidden.

- **settings.** Lets you define a range of general settings for how Media Center should handle TV, pictures, music, and DVDs, how to work with extenders, and how to set up your libraries.

Sharing media

With Windows Media Player and Windows Vista, you can now share the contents of your digital media library across your home network — not only with other PCs running Windows Vista, but also with other net-worked digital media players, such as an Xbox 360, which you can then hook up to your TV or home stereo system to play music or watch videos in comfort, even in those rooms of your house where you don't have a computer.

If you want to share your library in this way, you must first tell Windows Media Player that you want to make your library available to other devices on your network. To turn on library sharing in Windows Media Player, do the following:

1. Click the Library split button and then click Library Sharing.

2. In the Library Sharing dialog box, select the Share my library check box.

If the option to share your library is grayed out, Windows Media thinks you are either connected to a public network or to no network at all. In the interests of security, sharing is turned off unless you are on a private (home) network. However, you can override this setting by clicking the Networking button in the Library Sharing dialog box and changing your network connections manually.

The next step is to connect your digital media player or other computer to your home network. You can connect to a wired network using

Watch Out!

Take care not to grant all devices on your network access to your library unless you are sure the network is secure. This is particularly important if you have a laptop and you often connect to different networks.

an Ethernet cable, or you can use a wireless network adapter to connect to a wireless network. Note that if the other device you want to share your library with is a computer, it must also be running Windows Vista.

Deciding who to share with

When you decide to share your media, you need to authorize which devices on your network can access your library. You have the choice between manually deciding which specific computers and devices can access your library, or automatically granting access to all devices on your network. The former obviously requires more work, since you will be prompted to allow access whenever a new device or computer tries to access your library, but the second can prove to be a real security risk unless you are sure that you are connected to a secure network. If you have a laptop, for instance, you may inadvertently find yourself sharing your media library with everyone across the wireless network at your local coffee shop.

To specify whether or not you want to allow access to all and sundry, click the Library split button, and then click Library Sharing. Click Settings in the Library Sharing dialog box, and then check or uncheck the Add new devices and computers automatically check box. Regardless of which option you choose here, you can always allow or deny access to specific devices in the Available devices box in the Library Sharing dialog box.

Deciding what to share

By default, Windows Media Player automatically shares all the music and picture files in your library with all the devices and computers you have authorized. If this is not what you want, you can change the settings to share other Media types such as video as well, or only share media with a particular Parental rating or Star rating.

To define which content you share by default, do the following:

1. Click the Library split button and then click Library Sharing.

2. Click the Settings button. The Library Sharing - Default Settings dialog box appears.

3. In the Media types area, check the different types of media you want to share (for example, only Music, or Music and Video).

4. In the Star ratings area, select the options and check boxes beside the ratings you want to share. You could choose, for instance, to only share content that you have rated with five stars.

5. In the Parental ratings area, select the options and check boxes beside the ratings you want to share. For instance, you may only wish to share video content with a PG rating.

You can also decide to customize the media you share with each specific device, so that, for instance, you may share videos with one device on your network, but not any of the others. To do so:

1. Click the Library split button and then click Library Sharing.

2. In the Available devices box, select the device for which you want to customize access to your library, and then click Customize. The Library Sharing - Customize dialog box appears.

3. Deselect the Use default settings check box.

4. In the Media types area, check the different types of media you want to share with this device.

5. In the Star ratings area, select the options and check boxes beside the ratings you want to share with this device.

6. In the Parental ratings area, select the options and check boxes beside the ratings you want to share with this device.

7. If you want to customize access for more than one device or computer, repeat Steps 2 through 6 for each device.

Playing your content on another device or computer

After you have configured your library to allow access to other devices or computers, you are ready to use these other devices to select which content to play.

With a networked digital media player, such as an Xbox 360, you will need to use the device's remote control to find the computer that is sharing your content and then browse for the content that you want to play. For full details about how to do so, consult the documentation that came with your device.

If you want to play shared content on another computer that is running Windows Vista, do the following:

1. Start Windows Media Player on the other computer.

2. Click the Library split button, and then click Library Sharing.

3. Check the Find other media libraries check box and then click OK. You only need to do this once; afterwards, you will always see any other libraries that others have elected to share with you.

4. Click the Library button, and in the Navigation pane, click the name of the remote library you want to connect to. When you are connected, you can then play any items in this remote library just as you would if they were in your local library.

Using URGE

With URGE, the new digital music service from MTV Networks, it would seem that Windows Media Player 11 has finally got its own version of the Apple Music Store (see Figure 8.19). Whether this service, which is deeply integrated into WMP11, proves compelling enough to win a sizeable slice of the online digital music market from Apple remains to be seen. Certainly, having the MTV brand behind it can't fail to help.

Where URGE differs from iTunes is in its focus on subscription services. While you can buy individual tracks or albums through URGE as well, the emphasis is very much on encouraging you to pay a set fee every month for "unlimited" access to the millions of songs in the URGE catalog. And that sounds great — millions of songs is a lot of music, after all — were it not for one thing: Digital Rights Management, or DRM.

PlaysForSure

Before you buy music from a service like URGE, you should check that the tracks you buy are going to work on your portable music player. Fortunately, Microsoft runs the PlaysForSure program, dedicated to the validation of devices and online stores to ensure their compatibility with Microsoft's software and formats. You can find out more about the program by visiting the PlaysForSure Web site at www.playsforsure.com.

Figure 8.19. URGE, the digital music service from MTV Networks, is deeply integrated in Windows Media Player.

Like most digital music services, iTunes included, URGE places serious restrictions on what you can do with the music you download. URGE offers three membership plans, each with different usage rights:

▪ **URGE All Access.** You can download an unlimited number of tracks that you can play back only on your PC. You also get access to playlists and radio stations, along with news, features, interviews, and blogs.

▪ **URGE All Access To Go.** You have the features of URGE All Access, and you can also transfer the music to which you subscribe to up to two compatible portable music players.

▪ **URGE By The Track.** As the name suggests, this plan allows you to buy individual tracks by simply right-clicking the track name and clicking Buy. Only tracks that you have bought outright in this way can be burned to CD. All the other music you download can only be listened to on your PC or your portable music player. Think of this as the difference between renting and buying the tracks you download.

This is not a tirade against DRM; far from it. But it is important when signing up for a service like URGE to be aware of exactly what you can do with the content you download. If you're happy only being able to play tracks on your PC, that's fine.

Work with cameras

Until Windows Vista, amateur photographers who wanted to get the most out of their digital cameras were pretty much forced to use the proprietary or third-party software recommended by the camera manufacturer. The options and features for digital cameras that were built in to previous versions of Windows, while they did exist, were fairly low-key and easy to miss. With Vista, all of that has changed.

Import photos from your digital camera

For starters, you no longer need to use specific software to get the photos off your camera and on to your PC. When we first plugged in a digital camera, Vista immediately recognized the device and installed the relevant drivers without even asking me for the CD — a first in our collective experiences! — then presented me with a choice between browsing through the files with Windows Explorer or, best of all, having Vista import photos for us (see Figure 8.20).

While these enhancements may not prove to be the death knell for all third-party photo management tools, writers of such software must be at least a little worried to see that a tool for managing and editing your digital photos now comes fully integrated in Vista. And users who are willing to sacrifice a few more advanced options that they rarely (if ever) use for the simplicity of working with an interface they are familiar with may well have reason to rejoice.

Figure 8.20. Windows Vista can import your digital photos directly from your camera.

Hack

If your camera is not plug-and-play compatible, you may have to do things the hard way and add the device using the Device Manager. See Chapter 13 for more about the Device Manager. For more information on installing your device, please consult the documentation that came with it.

Tag and you shall find

Before importing the photos from your camera, Vista gives you the choice of adding tags to your pictures. Search is a big part of the Vista experience, and tags make it easier for you to find pictures once your photo collections start to grow. Tags are a way of attaching additional information to each photo such as who is in it, where it was taken, and what you were doing at the time. Be aware that you can only add a single tag when importing; don't try to separate numerous tags using commas or quotes, as that won't work and will just leave you with one very long tag instead.

If you want to add more than one tag, which you probably will if you are to take full advantage of the value of tagging, then you will have to do so in Photo Gallery after all your photos have been imported.

To add a tag in Photo Gallery:

1. Click the picture you want to add a tag to.

2. Click Add Tags in the Info pane on the right.

3. Type your new tag and then press Enter.

One useful feature when it comes to adding tags to your photos is the ability to reuse existing tags by dragging. Simply select the picture to which you want to apply the tag, and then drag it to the tag in the Navigation pane on the left and the tag will automatically be added. This also has the advantage of helping prevent you from creating slightly different tags for the same type of picture, which would otherwise make it more difficult to find all the relevant pictures in a single search.

Bright Idea

Tags have other uses beyond helping you find old photos more easily. You can also use them to leave temporary notes for yourself; you could use a tag like Email to identify the pictures of your child you want to send to her proud grandparents, for example, or Edit for those photos you want to work on later.

Photo Gallery

Windows Photo Gallery has replaced Windows Picture and Fax Viewer as the default tool for viewing photos and other images; and we have to say, this new tool leaves its predecessor very much in the shade. As well as being more visually impressive, Windows Photo Gallery also offers several more advanced options such as the possibility to touch up your digital images and to order copies of your photos from online printing services.

Photo Gallery functions in two modes: Gallery mode, where you can browse through all your images, and Viewer mode, where you can take a closer look at each individual item.

When you are using Photo Gallery in Gallery mode, your screen is divided into five main areas (see Figure 8.21).

Figure 8.21. Photo Gallery is a powerful new tool for viewing and managing your digital images.

- **The Navigation Tree.** Located on the left of the screen, use it to browse through the different folders where your digital image collection is stored.

- **The List View.** You can view thumbnails of your photos, and this view includes a search box just above it to help you find items containing a particular word or phrase.

- **The Info Pane.** Find out additional information about the image selected, including the filename, the date and time it was created, the file size and resolution, and a star rating and any tags that you have assigned.

- **The Navigation Bar.** This feature is located at the bottom of the screen (which maintains the same visual style as the playback controls in Windows Media Player); you can use it to move through your photo collection, rotate images, zoom in and out, and delete files.

Not to be left out, the toolbar at the top of the screen allows you to perform a series of tasks for managing your digital images. We look at these tasks in more detail in the following paragraphs.

Performing tasks from the Gallery toolbar

The Gallery contains a series of buttons that provide quick access to a range of digital image management tasks.

- **File.** Opens up a submenu where you can add additional folders to your gallery, import images from a camera or scanner, and carry out all the standard tasks for managing files such as deleting, renaming, and copying.

- **Fix.** Opens up a page where you can touch up your image (see Figure 8.22) by adjusting exposure, adjusting color, cropping the picture, fixing red eye, or even having Photo Gallery carry out the appropriate edits automatically (which is often a wise choice with digital images).

- **Info.** Displays or hides the info pane on the right-hand side of the screen.

- **Print.** Gives you the choice between printing out your image or ordering digital prints from an online printing service.

- **Create.** Lets you burn images and videos to a disc (DVD or data disc), or create a movie using Windows Movie Maker. (We discuss Windows Movie Maker 2 later in this chapter.)

- **E-mail.** Allows you to send an image by e-mail using your default e-mail client, and helpfully gives you the option of resizing it before you do so.

- **Open.** Opens your image in a new program (by default, Paint) to allow you to make more advanced edits than you can with the Fix button.

Figure 8.22. Touch up your images with the Fix option.

The Viewer mode is very similar; the main difference is that the navigation tree does not appear, leaving more screen space for the viewing pane that displays your image.

Creating a customized screen saver

If you want to have a customized screen saver on your machine that makes use of your own photos and images, Windows Vista lets you scroll through your pictures and take a literal stroll down memory lane.

Watch Out!

When you create a custom screen saver based on the photos in your gallery, Windows Vista will scroll through every single one of your photos. If you have any sensitive or non-work appropriate photos, you may wish to tag them as Private to ensure they don't appear.

To set up your screen saver, do the following:

1. Click Control Panel ⇨ Appearance and Personalization ⇨ Personalization ⇨ Screen Saver, and then select Photos from the drop-down list.

2. Click Settings. The Photos Screen Saver Settings dialog box appears.

3. You have the option of using all pictures and videos from the Photo Gallery, or specifying a location. If you choose to use all the pictures from your gallery, you can limit those which appear by indicating a specific tag, or only displaying those photos with a certain rating, or you can even elect not to show items with a certain tag (such as Private).

4. In this dialog box, you can also specify the theme to use as a background for your images, decide whether you wish to shuffle the content so that it appears randomly, and set the slide show speed.

5. Click Save when you're done.

Work with scanners

Another way of getting images onto your computer is of course to use a scanner. Scanners have come in many shapes and sizes and have added new features over the years; indeed, many of today's scanners now come combined with photocopiers, fax machines, and printers in what are called "all-in-ones."

Like its predecessors, Windows Vista uses the Intel standard, Plug and Play, which lets you install a device and lets the computer find and install the necessary drivers. This is still very much the case. To install your scanner, you may have to do nothing more than connect it to your computer, turn it on, and let Windows Vista install the appropriate driver.

If you have an older device, or if Windows Vista doesn't recognize your scanner for some other reason, you'll have to install its drivers yourself. To do so:

1. Start the Scanner and Camera Installation Wizard by clicking Start ⇨ Control Panel ⇨ Hardware and Sound ⇨ Scanners and Cameras.

2. You will be prompted to select your scanner from a list; if your device isn't listed, you will have to obtain the drivers on a CD or directly from the manufacturer's Web site. If this is the case, click Have disk when you are asked to choose your device.

3. If you can't see your scanner in the list, even after clicking Refresh, then click Add Device to start the wizard and follow the instructions on-screen.

After you have installed your scanner, you can view it in the Control Panel under Hardware and Sound ⇨ Scanners and Cameras.

After you have scanned a document, you can use the Windows Picture and Fax viewer to preview it. That said, it is often preferable to use the proprietary or third-party software that shipped with your scanner.

Create DVDs with DVD Maker

DVD Maker is a nifty new program in Windows Vista that lets you create DVDs featuring your videos and digital photos for playing back on your TV or any other device connected to a DVD player.

To work with DVD Maker, do the following:

1. Click Start ⇨ All Programs ⇨ Windows DVD Maker.

   When DVD Maker opens (provided you have a writeable DVD in your drive), you will immediately be invited to start adding pictures and videos to your DVD.

2. Click Add items, and then browse to find the pictures or videos you want to add. As you add new items, the interface displays a thumb-nail of each item, and the duration of the slide show (for pictures) or the video (see Figure 8.23).

You can define certain specific options for the DVD you are going to create by clicking Options (see Figure 8.24). These include deciding how your DVD is to be played back (should it start with the DVD menu, or play the video first), selecting the aspect ratio (4:3 or 16:9), and choosing the appropriate format (NTSC or PAL).

Figure 8.23. Add pictures and videos to a DVD with Windows DVD Maker.

Figure 8.24. DVD-Video options in Windows DVD Maker.

When you're done adding photos and videos, click the Next button to go to a new screen (see Figure 8.25). You can make a few last-minute tweaks before you burn your disc.

Figure 8.25. Burn DVDs containing your pictures and videos.

Like all DVDs, the DVD you are going to create will include a menu where viewers can choose whether to play the DVD all the way through or skip to a specific scene. To choose which style of menu you want to use for your DVD, simply click the appropriate thumbnail under Menu Styles on the right of the screen. At the time of writing, there were 20 different styles to choose from, and it would come as no surprise if more were made available for download at a later date.

You can also change the appearance of the text on your menu. To edit the DVD menu text, click the Menu text button. On the Change the DVD menu text page that opens (see Figure 8.26), you can specify both the text that is to appear and the font in which it is written.

Figure 8.26. Customize the menus for your DVDs.

You customize your menu still further by clicking Customize, which takes you to a page where you can define your own menu style, complete with foreground and background videos, an audio soundtrack, and the format of the buttons for selecting each scene on your DVD.

Finally, if you click Slide show, you can set up how you want the pictures in your slide shows to be played back: the length of time each image should be displayed, the transition from one picture to the next, and even which music should accompany your images.

When you're satisfied with the final result (don't forget to click Preview to check), click the Start Burn button to burn your masterpiece to DVD.

Work with video cameras

You can use digital video cameras with Windows Vista, specifically with Movie Maker 2, which we discuss in the next section. But before you use Windows Vista to create your next film, make sure that you have the necessary cables.

Watch Out!

As you add more and more peripheral devices, such as digital cameras, hand-helds, and video cameras, it's important to make sure that you have enough USB ports to get the job done. Most likely, you'll need to buy an adapter because most machines (especially laptops) only have three or four USB slots.

Digital video cameras tend to be FireWire (IEEE 1394) devices that require a special cable and adapter. Make sure that your machine supports this standard and make sure that you have the correct cable (there are several types of adapter pins at the ends of the cable — in other words, the ends can be of different sizes).

Edit video using Movie Maker 6

Windows Movie Maker (see Figure 8.27) is a "home studio" for assembling and editing movies that you can eventually share on CD/DVD or put online for download. Overall, this is a very solid application that is a lot cheaper (read: free) and easier than buying a professional software package. However, although it's not overly complicated, Movie Maker isn't a beginner's tool, and it can seem intimidating to the uninitiated. Microsoft realizes this and has put together a pretty extensive support system that includes newsgroups, documentation, and books on the product. For more information on the product, visit `www.microsoft.com/windowsxp/using/moviemaker/default.mspx`.

Before you make a movie

The first thing you'll need to do to make your Movie Maker 6 experience a positive one is to know your hardware and know some video basics. Take the time to read the documentation that came with your digital video camera. Knowing all of the features of your hardware can help you make better movies, which in turn will make using Movie Maker 6 easier. The better footage you have to begin with, the less editing you'll have to do later in Movie Maker 6.

Watch Out!

FireWire (IEEE 1394) cables don't come for free; make sure that your machine has an adapter and then see what kind of cable you need. Some cables have four or six pins; don't waste time having to run back to the store because you didn't properly verify the appropriate cable.

Figure 8.27. Windows Movie Maker is a powerful video editing suite.

Make a movie

Once you're ready to go, shoot your film!

When you're finished, hook up your video camera to your computer. Be sure to set your video camera to Play (not just turn it on); otherwise, the Movie Maker 2 software will not recognize the device when you begin to import your video.

Although most people will use Windows Movie Maker to edit footage from their digital video camera, you can import the raw material for your movie from other sources as well, including existing videos, pictures, and audio or music files in a range of different formats. Just click

Bright Idea

When you import footage from your digital video camera, you can do so in AVI or WMV format; if you choose WMV, you have the option of importing as a single file or as one file per scene. Otherwise, to cut a clip into smaller sections, press the Split button while your clip is playing and it will be cut in two at that point.

the appropriate item in the Tasks pane on the left, then browse to find the item you're looking for.

Whichever import method you choose, all the items appear in the central workspace, with the most recently imported item selected by default (see Figure 8.28).

Figure 8.28. The workspace in Movie Maker contains all the elements you are going to use in your movie together.

Work with the storyboard

Despite what we said earlier about Movie Maker not being a beginner's tool, putting together a movie is actually quite simple, and the storyboard is where it all happens (see Figure 8.29).

To make a really basic movie, all you have to do is drag the different pieces of imported media that you want to include and drop them into the storyboard. You can preview individual clips by clicking them in the storyboard or in your workspace, or you can view the entire movie by clicking the playback controls in the Preview pane (see Figure 8.30).

And that's all there is to it.

Figure 8.29. The storyboard in Movie Maker.

Figure 8.30. The Preview pane.

Except, of course, it isn't. We hate to be the ones to break it to all the budding Scorseses out there, but if you're going to go to all the trouble of making a movie — even a simple video clip to share with your family and friends — then you want to make it interesting enough for people to actually watch. Fortunately, Movie Maker is there to help you.

Effects and transitions

The Windows Vista version of Movie Maker comes with over 100 different effects and transitions to help bring your movies to life.

To add an effect to a scene in your movie, click Effects in the Tasks pane, then drag the effect of your choice onto the scene in the storyboard you want to apply it to. You can also right-click the scene in question; then click Effects to open the Add or Remove Effects dialog box (see Figure 8.31).

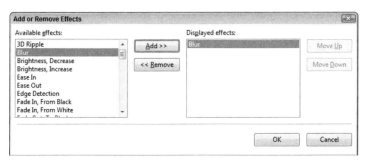

Figure 8.31. The Add or Remove Effects dialog box.

Transitions, which let you define the way your movie passes from one scene into another, are another useful way of making your movies seem more polished and professional. Again, you add transitions by clicking Transitions in the Tasks pane and then dragging the transition of your choice onto the storyboard; in this case, however, you drop the transition into the space between two scenes (see Figure 8.32).

Titles and credits

Of course, no movie would be complete without titles and credits. To create the titles that appear at the beginning of your movie and the credits that, logically, appear at the end, simply click Titles and credits in the Tasks pane. You then enter the appropriate text, choose from various animation options, and then edit the font and color to your liking. For titles, you have the option of having them appear before your selected clip, with a default background, or overlaying the text above the selected clip; credits always appear at the end.

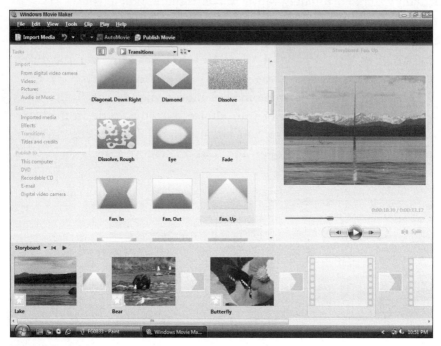

Figure 8.32. Adding smooth transitions between scenes help make your movies seem more polished.

Publish your movie

Putting together your movie is only half the fun. You want to share it with other people.

When it comes to publishing your movie, you have a range of options. You can simply generate a file that appears in the Videos folder on your computer (or any other location of your choice), you can burn it directly to DVD or CD (depending on its length), you can prepare it for sending by e-mail, or you can even reload it back on a digital video camera.

To publish your movie to one of these formats, simply click the appropriate choice in the Tasks pane and follow the instructions on-screen.

Just the facts

- Windows Media Player 11 could well be the tool to give iTunes a run for its money.

- Windows Media Center lets you access your digital libraries (music, photos, videos, and television shows) from your television set.

- Photo Gallery is an impressive new tool for viewing and managing photos and other digital images.

- Movie Maker allows you to put together your own movies and, in conjunction with DVD Maker, burn them to DVD for sharing with your friends.

Networking with Windows Vista

GET THE SCOOP ON...
Network Center ▪ Diagnostic tool ▪ Wireless connections ▪
LAN/Broadband connections ▪ Connection sharing ▪
Windows Meeting Space ▪ Windows Live Messenger ▪
Windows Mail

PART III

Networking and the Internet

Networking and Internet connectivity are still very much a central part of the Windows operating system. In fact, Microsoft has increased or better facilitated their networking options in Windows Vista. It appears that Microsoft's goal was to centralize connectivity features into a single location — the new Network Center.

In this broadband era, networking and connectivity capabilities are a crucial part of any operating system. As emerging technology becomes more available and less expensive, more users will opt to create home networks. Not so long ago, a home network was something that only a fellow geek could set up in his basement. Today, it's so common that most retail stores offer to set one up for you (for an nominal fee, of course) when you buy a new system from their store.

In this chapter, we discuss the basics of networking (including why you might want one if you've never considered it), the new Windows Vista Network Center and Sharing Center, and how Vista lets you connect to the Internet or other networks. We also discuss the many ways of connecting to the Internet and Microsoft's latest stab at a "free" e-mail client, Windows Mail.

This chapter really focuses on the basics; the information is pertinent to SOHO connections or single machines.

For more information on working with domains or Active Directory, see Chapter 12.

Home networking 101

Home networking can be a real benefit for SOHO users with multiple computers. Networking is really a great idea if you have a single desktop and need to make data available to laptop users. A home network is basically a shared Internet connection among users. In the past, you could use Microsoft's Internet Connection Sharing (ICS) features, but today, why bother? With the advent of Wi-Fi, "wired" networking is so 1990s! Wireless hardware has decreased dramatically in price, while the technology has continually improved.

There are a number of benefits to having a home network. First, it allows you to share a single printer for multiple computers. Instead of having to plug the printer into a different computer each time you wish to print, simply connect to the networked printer and go! This is particularly helpful if you have multiple printers spread across your house and do not wish to have long connection cables litter your floor. You may also want to be able to share files across your network. For example, you may want to share the contents of your Pictures folder with network users. With a home network, this is possible. It's also an easy way to "virtually" transfer files. For example, you may be working on a large file on your laptop. Instead of having to copy it to CD/DVD or a flash disk, put it in a shared network folder. You can now use it on your desktop computer without the need for external media.

No matter what your reason for switching to a home network, the technology behind it is the same. Networks are comprised of a number of "behind the scenes" components that work together to make your life a little easier. The following sections of this chapter help you make your way through the jargon that can often seem like a foreign language.

Getting physical

Back in the old days (circa 1980), a single computer didn't network. In fact, it did anything but. File transfer was in the form of a floppy disk. Eventually, technology evolved and prices dropped, making it easier for the business and then people like you and us to afford them with some pretty basic off-the-rack materials.

Jump forward to the present day, and you have to go out of your way to find a computer that isn't network-enabled, ready to serve (literally) in just a few mouse clicks. Today, most computers feature network cards; if you use a laptop, they virtually all (we don't say all, because someone, somewhere, probably has the lone laptop without network capabilities) feature wireless capabilities. Regardless, the most common types of connections are

- **Ethernet.** Ethernet connections physically link your computer to a network or router. The jack is like an oversized phone plug and has eight wires.

- **Wi-Fi.** The darling of the modern age in connectivity, this is the common term for 802.11 wireless protocols, including several flavors, such as a, b, and g. 802.11g has more or less become the standard, though some early wireless cards and certain hotspots still support only a or b.

- **Dialup.** Quickly becoming a blast from the past, this is a connection involving your computer, your modem, your phone cable, and your wall jack. The modem cable is your everyday phone cable, complete with four wires.

Are there other types of connections? Absolutely (ISDN, for starters). However, if you are a SOHO user, it is highly unlikely that you would use any other type of connection but these.

Now that you're (almost) connected, let's talk about how you actually form a network. You actually get "on" the network with the help of a router or hub. You plug your computer into a hub or router and it connects to your network. When you have two or more elements (computers, printers, and so on) plugged into a router or hub, then you have a Local Area Network (LAN). If you are a not a Wi-Fi user, it is likely that you are connected to a LAN using an RJ-45 (Ethernet) cable.

Getting on the Internet is, of course, a whole different plan of action. Think back to the hub or router that we discuss in the previous paragraph. You need to run that through a modem (DSL modem or cable modem) or a gateway. Modems and gateways are able to translate communications between the LAN and communication protocols.

Vista Network and Sharing Center

The Network Connection feature now goes by a new name (and layout) called Network and Sharing Center (see Figure 9.1). Like in Windows XP, this is where everything connectivity-related comes together. You can locate Network Center in Control Panel's Network and Internet menu, or by right-clicking the network icon in the notification area. In earlier iterations of Windows Vista, Microsoft had network management as a single entity called the Network Center. For some reason, they decided to tie it together with its file sharing management tool — and the Network and Sharing Center was born!

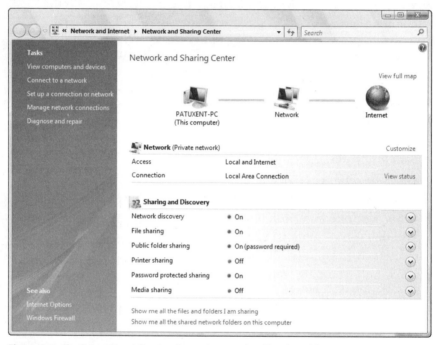

Figure 9.1. The Network and Sharing Center lets you handle a lot of features, perhaps even too many for one screen.

The Network and Sharing Center is particularly helpful for checking out your network status, pinpointing exactly where any "down" networks are, and then fixing the problem.

The Network and Sharing Center is divided into two sections: Network and Sharing and Discovery. The Sharing and Discovery section is detailed in Chapter 6. At the top of the page is a "map" of how your computer is connecting to the Internet. The connections are represented by a line that indicates your connection status. For example, if you are having connectivity issues, a yellow triangle with an exclamation point appears. If you connect without incident, a double green line appears. If you are unable to connect, a red X appears, meaning to drop it and go take the dog for a walk because you're not getting online at the moment.

The Network and Sharing Center gives you the option of viewing the full map through a link at the top of the page. We clicked on this link expecting a more robust or detailed network connection map. This link simply opens the Network Map page, which pretty much contains the same level of detail or information. Even the Tasks between the two pages are basically the same. The only real difference is that Network Map offers an online help link as a Task. We're not really sure why Microsoft did that because online help topics aren't really tasks.

Network

The Network section indicates the status (in text, not with an icon) of your connection (see Figure 9.2). Here is where you will find the name of your connection, the type of connection (Did you connect over wireless? Or is it a LAN connection?), as well as your current level of access. From this section, you can click View status to go directly to your connection properties. You can also customize your network connection through the Customize link next to the Network header.

Figure 9.2. The Network section lets you know how your connection is doing.

Bright Idea

Windows Vista displays the network location type next to the Network header.

The Customize link brings you to the Customize network settings screen. Windows Vista introduces the concept of a network category, which includes two or three different types: Public, Private, and Domain (see Figure 9.3).

- A Public category is designed for use when connecting to a public network. These include cybercafes, airports, or any other network connection that is public. This type of connection is more restrictive than a private connection category. For example, file sharing and network discovery features are disabled by default.

- The Private category is the opposite of Public. This category is intended for use at home or in a small office setting. This type of connection is more open; this includes file sharing, and the network discovery feature is enabled.

- The Domain category, as you might imagine, is designed for use when working in a domain, as in a corporate setting. A domain is a group of computers that are connected to a network with a shared database. Home users will rarely use domains; this is more for companies. The Domain option does not appear if you are not on a domain.

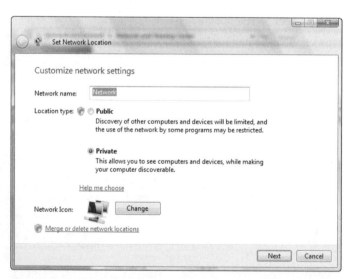

Figure 9.3. The Customize network settings page in the Network Center.

Watch Out!

Windows Vista isn't very consistent in terms of window labeling. For example, the Customize network settings window is referred to as Set Network Location at the top of the window. This is one of the most annoying aspects of Windows Vista in the later builds.

Vista lets you personalize your network connection from this window. You can rename your network in the Network name text box. By default, Microsoft uses the rather lame Network as the name of your connection. You can also change the location type; if you're not sure which type is right for you, a contextual help link is available.

This feature also lets you change your network icon (see Figure 9.3); Vista offers 12 icons for you to choose from. You can also use the Browse button to use other icons. The last option on the Customize network settings window is the Merge or delete network locations link. This feature is somewhat discrete; unlike the other page options, this one is relatively easy for users to miss because it appears under both an icon and a button. Clicking the link opens the Merge or Delete Network Locations window. If you have more than one network location, you can merge them into a single location or even delete one. Two important pieces of information here:

■ Managed network locations (such as your corporate network connection) cannot be merged.

■ Network locations currently in use cannot be deleted.

In easier terms, this means that if you are connected to a network via wireless connection, you can plug in to the network using an Ethernet cable and Windows Vista treats this as the same network. Therefore, you can switch connection methods without the fear of losing your connection and losing your current connection. Speaking of wireless connections, Windows Vista also supports what are currently the latest wireless security protocols, including WPA2.

Sharing and Discovery

We won't discuss the Sharing and Discovery section in great detail; this is done in Chapter 6. However, the first option in the list (Network discovery) seems like it might have been equally as effective in the Network part of the page.

Network discovery isn't so much a new concept as it is new terminology. If you choose to enable this feature, your computer can see other computers or devices (such as printers) on the network. This also means that your computer is visible to other computers on the network.

You can also change your Workgroup settings; this link simply opens your System Properties. From there, you can provide a brief description of your computer, join a domain or workgroup, or rename your computer. System Properties are detailed elsewhere in this book since this window is accessible in a number of ways.

If you decide to turn on Network Discovery, keep the following in mind. You essentially lose any claim to privacy as you open two-way communications between your computer and other computers. They can see your computer and access your files and folders and vice-versa. As you might expect, just the opposite is true if you turn it off. You cannot see other computers and files/folders and other computers cannot see you. Custom means that you have manually changed the setting for discovery and sharing in the Windows Firewall. Depending on what you've done in the firewall, you may or may not be able to see other computers or them you. Finally, discovery only means that while you can see other computers and other computers see you, neither of you have access to each other's files or folders.

Choosing the appropriate level of security depends mostly on your need for privacy/security balanced with the realities of how you use your computer. If you are a SOHO user working with a desktop PC, you could reasonably use Custom. Personally, we would avoid using Network Discovery unless you purposely wish to share files or folders with another computer. However, any other time, you may wish to use either of the aforementioned options. If you are working on a laptop, then all bets are off due to security concerns. We recommend leaving this feature off or at Custom. Again, if you are planning on letting another computer access your system, then you can switch it on, but it is never a good idea to leave your laptop open. This is tantamount to leaving the front door of your house unlocked and open while leaving for the weekend.

Tasks

The real interest in the Network and Sharing Center page is the information on it that you are likely to miss! There are several "secondary" action items on the left side of the screen that will certainly be of interest to most users. Understandably, user interface real estate is a scarce commodity and therefore isn't cheap; however, some of these options may be better suited on the central page and not relegated to a sidebar. These include

■ View computers and devices

■ Connect to a network

■ Set up a connection or network

■ Manage network connections

■ Diagnose and repair

View computers and devices

The View computers and devices (see Figure 9.4) option takes you to the Network page. The Network page displays a list of the various computers and devices on your network. To use this, you must have first turned on Network Discovery; if it is off, you can enable it from the Network page as well using the information toolbar. This toolbar appears if the feature is not on and reminds you that it must be enabled before you can see your network computers.

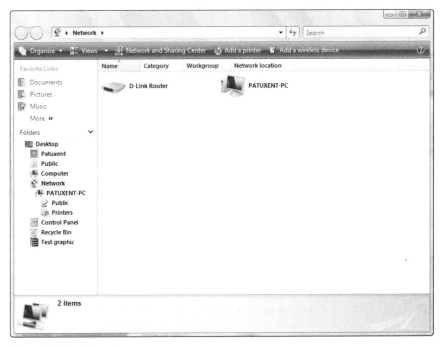

Figure 9.4. The Network page.

Connect to a network

The Connect to a network option (see Figure 9.5) is the equivalent of Windows XP's Network Connections window, though much better presented. In Vista, you can view any additional networks. If you're on a laptop and moving about, you can click the Refresh button to make sure you have the most up-to-date network information. This page also lets you go back to the Network and Sharing Center, diagnose your connection, or even set up a connection or network.

Figure 9.5. The Connect to a network page is a cleaner version of Network Connections.

Set up a connection or network

The Set up a connection or network window (see Figure 9.6) is similar to the New Connection Wizard in Windows XP. The menu options are basically the same, though Microsoft has updated their option names for Vista. Now you can

- Connect to the Internet
- Set up a Wireless router or access point
- Set up a dial-up connection
- Connect to a workplace

Admittedly, we've used very few of these options in either Windows Vista or XP. Most ISPs (Internet Service Providers) have some sort of proprietary installation that sets up your Internet connection for you, especially if you are dealing with broadband. Even if you are still using dialup, carriers such as People PC have an installation CD-ROM that configures Windows for you to use their service.

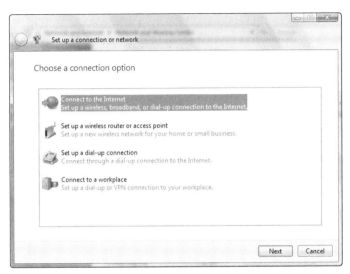

Figure 9.6. The Set up a connection or network window.

The last option lets you connect to your office — assuming they have and allow VPN access — in order for you to emulate your desktop environment on your home PC or laptop. This option is generally for larger companies with an IT infrastructure and not a SOHO user. We think that the title is somewhat misleading. An unsuspecting user may be led to believe that it is possible to create a VPN connection. Not quite — this option simply lets you enter the name of your company's VPN server and give it a name.

This option also lets you dictate whether or not to use a smart card, to let anyone else use that connection, and also whether or not to connect

Watch Out!

You may need to contact your system administrator at work in order to gain access to your VPN. Many companies require special permissions to access the VPN.

now or simply prepare the connection. One final note about this option; your company may require you to download a piece of additional software that has been specially configured to work with the corporate VPN. If this is the case, be sure to stick with corporate policy and use their desired VPN client. It's generally a good idea to keep your system administrators at work happy; one great way to do this is to respect their IT security policies.

VPN for President

VPN is one of the coolest things available when it comes to home computing. While many managers may not like it, because it pretty much negates any reason not to allow employees to work remotely, it also allows you to be much more efficient and productive in your tasks.

The VPN creates a virtual network or communication link between your desktop (home or other) or laptop and, for example, your office. Your local firewall protects your connection to the server, which in turn, provides the necessary physical security.

By using a VPN client (for example, Cisco Systems' VPN client), you can literally log onto your company network on your home PC or laptop. After you are connected, you can use the Remote Desktop Connection feature (discussed in Chapter 11) to literally connect to your office computer. Your screen displays a new window that is literally your work computer. You can access Outlook and network servers exactly like you would at the office.

Home users can sign up for VPN service for their SOHO computers for use with laptops or PCs when traveling. Unfortunately, this can be a somewhat cost prohibitive measure and so most SOHO users don't use VPN. There are some open source VPN clients currently available, though we haven't used them. These include OpenVPN (www.openvpn.net) and SSL-Explorer (www.sshtools.com/showSslExplorer.do). Since third-party software developers are still coming out with Vista-compatible applications, make sure that your computer meets all hardware requirements before buying or installing.

Bright Idea

No one knows your Internet connection better than your ISP, not even Windows Vista. If you have installation software for your Internet connection, then by all means use it. This software is designed to make your life easier and reduce the chance of human error and throwing a real monkey wrench into your Windows operating system.

The Connect to the Internet option lets you set up a high-speed (wireless or LAN) or dialup connection to the Internet. If you are currently connected to the Internet, the feature reminds you of this fact, but still lets you continue and add a new connection if desired. What is nice about this option is that it only displays options that your computer is equipped to handle. For example, when we tried to create a new connection, a broadband connection was our only option. However, there is a check box at the bottom of the Connect to the Internet page that allows you to view all available options, including those for which your computer is not set up (in our case, this was dialup). If you decide to set up a connection, Vista will ask for such information as your username, password, and dialup number (if applicable). Unfortunately, there is no way to enter this information for later use; once you enter it, you must click Connect in order for it to be stored.

The Set up a dial-up connection feature is self-evident. The feature is similar to the Connect to the Internet option as it lets you manually enter ISP information, such as dialup number, username, and password. You can also save your password and allow other users to use this connection to access your ISP. If you don't have a modem connected, Vista reminds you of this fact, but will still let you manually add a dialup connection.

The Connect to a workplace option is an amalgamation of the above features. You can connect to a corporate account or mainframe by using either your Internet connection (VPN) or by phone (dialup). Frankly, we're not convinced that this feature really merits its own option. After

Bright Idea

If you do not have account information for the Internet connection or dialup account, you can obtain this information from your Internet Service Provider (ISP).

all, these features can be set and used in other features within the Network Center.

The Network Center mentioned earlier also features Set up a network option. This is Microsoft's "out of the box" network option that is helpful for SOHO users looking to share Internet connections, files, or printers. This is clearly not intended for medium- to large- scale companies. It is designed to "link" or network several computers in a single location.

The Set up a network option feature uses a wizard that helps you quickly configure hardware and prepare your computer for file and printer sharing. Vista does a quick search to determine what kind of network hardware, if any, exists. If you are not physically connected to a router, Vista lets you configure wireless settings and save it to a USB flash drive that you must later transfer to the router (assuming it accepts USB connections.)

Add a wireless device

The Add a wireless device feature (see Figure 9.7) lets you add devices or computers that are detected on your network, but are not configured. You can do this from the Network window. Once you successfully add the device, it will appear among your list of network devices.

If the device that you would like to configure is not detected automatically, you can either add the device using a USB flash drive or do so manually.

Figure 9.7. The Add a wireless device window.

Managing network connections

The last link in Figure 9.1 takes you to on the Network and Sharing Center options on the left panel is the Manage network connections page (see Figure 9.8). This feature merits its own special header because it has several "cousins" that provide similar features. These include the Network Explorer as well as Network List (available in the See also section of Network and Sharing Center).

If you click Manage network connections, the window displays an ordered list of all the Internet connections on your computer, whether or not they are active. Like all folders in Windows Vista, you can sort these connections based on a number of criteria, including status, connectivity, and device name.

Likewise, the Network List (see Figure 9.9) lets you view existing networks. These too can be sorted based on a number of criteria, including status, name, type, and when last connected. Other features available in this window include renaming wireless connections, viewing properties and status of a network connection (the Personalize window in the Network Center), as well as removing the connection from your computer. Of course, you can also organize the folder layout and views.

Figure 9.8. The Network Connections page.

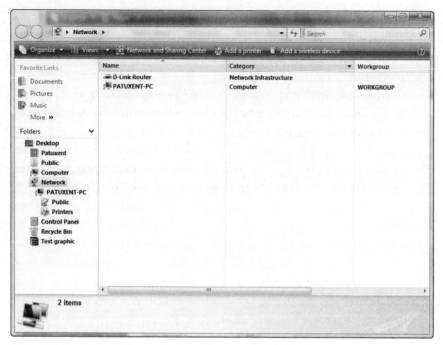

Figure 9.9. The Network List can be viewed in a more helpful fashion.

Windows Vista also contains Network Explorer, which is like Windows Explorer for networks. Like the two other similar options mentioned earlier, disconnected or unconfigured devices and networks appear in the Network Explorer.

All of these options make handling your network connections considerably easier, which is a big plus when you deal with multiple network connections. Trying to juggle a work connection, a home connection, as well as a wireless connection can be quite a chore!

Putting it all together

Windows Vista now features a helpful tool called the Network Map. This is a graphical representation of your network and how it all fits together. As networks become increasingly complex and numerous, they can become difficult to understand. Network Map illustrates the links between each network and connection. You can find the Network Map in the Control Panel.

Diagnose Internet Connection

The Diagnose and repair option has been very helpful to us in these early stages of Windows Vista pioneering. On occasion, it has been difficult to make the wireless connection work properly and this feature has tried to help in its own way. This feature opens the Windows Network Diagnostics window, which runs a number of behind-the-scenes tests (all you see is a progress bar) to sort out your Internet connection (see Figure 9.10). If Vista does find a problem, it attempts to fix it. In the event that it cannot or does not find a problem (and you maintain that one exists), you have the option of sending Microsoft a report. Though this is all very nice and well, you'd first have to have an active Internet connection in order for you to submit the report to Microsoft, wouldn't you? Perhaps they should provide a fax or phone support number in this window instead?

Figure 9.10. The Windows Vista Network Diagnostics window.

Windows Network Diagnostics

Windows Vista offers a new tool to help you figure out connection problems. In the past, you might find that everything was in order and working properly, but yet you still couldn't connect to the Internet. Or, even worse, you have an Internet connection, but yet you cannot connect to anything!

If you try to connect to a network (wired or wireless) and encounter difficulties, Windows Vista displays the Windows Network Diagnostics tool automatically. Otherwise, you can access the tool by right-clicking the Internet/network connection icon in the notification bar and selecting Diagnose.

The Windows Network Diagnostics window (see Figure 9.11) is only a semi-interactive tool. When it launches, your participation is limited to either letting it do its thing or to cancel it. We recommend not cancelling it, as this has caused other problems, namely Explorer crashes. The tool does a quick analysis of the problem (it usually lasts 30–60 seconds on our computers), and then offers a response. On occasion, no problem or diagnosis is found, and nothing happens. Other times it confirms your concerns and offers possible solutions (when available). This can be system related, in which case Vista can help you make the necessary changes to your computer. These errors can also be ISP related, in which case Vista leaves you high and dry.

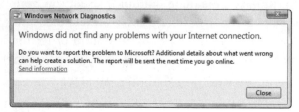

Figure 9.11. The Windows Network Diagnostics window.

Configuring broadband connections

No matter what you think of Microsoft, you have to admit that connecting to a server or network is pretty easy. In fact, you could almost qualify it as "automatic." If you install a new adapter to a desktop or need to configure a wireless adapter to your laptop, Windows does most of the grunt work and configures the basic necessities. If you just installed Windows, you set up your configuration during installation; if you used the Files and Settings Transfer Wizard, the necessary information was shuttled over to your new computer.

But it's not Microsoft that decides how to configure your network connection; rather it's your ISP! Most home users likely are assigned all the necessary network details by their ISP during logon. These details include IP address, subnet mask, default gateway, and a DNS server address. For more advanced users, depending on your needs, you may opt for a static IP address. In this case, you need to provide the following information:

■ **IP address.** The IP address is the unique address for every device on the Internet. Your address will look like 124.103.225.250, four sets of numbers separated by periods.

- **Subnet mask.** This number is used to subdivide address spaces. The most common subnet mask is 255.255.255.0, but use the one your ISP gives you.

- **Default gateway.** This is the point where your piece of the network puzzle connects to the Internet. If you don't have this address, your computers can talk to each other, but that's about it!

- **DNS server addresses.** These computers do nothing but translate people-friendly names like www.derektorres.net into computer-friendly IP addresses like 64.254.238.205. Without DNS servers, your Web browser can't find anything unless you know the exact IP address for a Web server.

Because of the potential for error in entering so many numbers, most ISPs prefer using dynamic addressing. Your computer's network adapter looks for a DHCP server and gets the necessary configuration information automatically. A DHCP server (Dynamic Host Configuration Protocol) makes networking easier for users because it uses a set of rules for devices to obtain IP addresses; if you don't have an IP address, you won't be surfing the Web! When you boot up your computer, it sends out a broadcast, seeking a DHCP server. Once it finds one, the DHCP server assigns the above information, and the rest, as they say, is history!

Configuring cable or DSL connections

If your computer connects directly to your ISP without a router between you and the modem, you can do the following:

1. Open the Network Connections page from the Control Panel.

2. Right-click the Local Area Connection and then click Properties. Depending on how you named the network or the number of local area connections, there may be a number after Local Area Connection.

3. Highlight Internet Protocol (TCP/IP) and click Properties (see Figure 9.12). Remember that Windows Vista supports TCP/IP versions 4 and 6.

Inside Scoop

If you want to access the Network Connections page even faster, type **ncpa.cpl** from the Start menu search box.

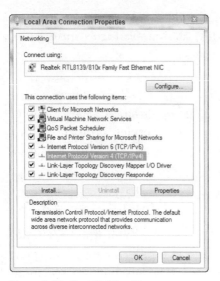

Figure 9.12. The TCP/IP settings.

If you are using dynamic IP addressing, then you can simply sit back and relax. You can leave the default options, which obtain the IP address and DNS server automatically. If you have these details, you can enter them in the appropriate location. If you are using a router or gateway on your home network, you can set it up so that its external or public interface uses the configuration information from your ISP. Each router or gateway has a separate configuration procedure, but they are usually quite easy to follow.

Working with wireless

If you've bought a laptop within the past couple of years, you are undoubtedly familiar with a little thing called Wi-Fi. The freedom of movement is hard to beat — especially with the number of free wireless providers that you can encounter in metropolitan areas. If you are a home user, it's hard to beat working from your sofa or bed without having troublesome wires following your every step.

Although it's true that you do not get the same speeds with wireless connections that you can if you use the traditional "wired" approach, it is a very convenient step forward in technology. For those who don't work with a laptop, you can still buy a wireless card for your desktop PC, but we prefer plugging in and exchanging mobile practicality (something that is lost on a desktop PC) for higher speeds. Beyond desktop computers, a number of peripherals (digital video recorders, gaming platforms, printers — just about anything) can be made "wireless."

Types of wireless protocols

Computers and technology are ever-changing; it's hard to stay on top of the latest and greatest. The same can be said for wireless protocols, which have greatly evolved over the past couple of years. The currently available, or most used, protocols are

- **802.11a.** This protocol was one of the earliest that was adopted for home and SOHO use. It transmits on the 5 GHz band, with a theoretical throughput of 54 Mbps (actual throughput closer to 20). The higher frequency means shorter available range.

- **802.11b.** This is another older protocol that transmits on the 2.4 GHz band rather than the 5 GHz band. Actual throughput is around 6 Mbps, though theoretically it can reach 11 Mbps. It has a longer range and is more popular than 802.11a.

- **802.11g.** This is the most common newer protocol that transmits on the 2.4 GHz band. It has a theoretical throughput of 54 Mbps and nearly 25 Mbps throughput in the real world. It is backwards-compatible with 802.11b.

Some wireless manufacturers have proprietary extensions to the above protocols that purport to give you higher speed boosts, but only if all your wireless equipment is from them (for example, Netgear's RangeMax). Almost all new adapters support b/g, though some support a/b/g. Another protocol on the horizon, but not yet finalized, is 802.11n, which may support real-world throughput of 100 Mbps and possibly a longer range than existing protocols. If you are looking to go wireless, make sure your access point and your wireless adapters support the same protocols. If you plan to be hanging out in cybercafes or coffeehouses working on the Great American Novel, look for a b/g or a/b/g adapter so you are practically guaranteed a connection.

Using wireless safely

Wireless networks have the major disadvantage of being less secure than wired connections. All it takes is someone with a wireless adapter in

---

The new cybertheft: Wireless connections

Not so long ago, cybercrime sounded like some sinister plot designed to throw the world into total chaos. Today, it has a whole new face, especially with the widespread use of wireless technology.

Recently, someone was successfully prosecuted for "poaching" someone else's wireless connection. While the details of the case were somewhat egregious (and hilarious), it does serve as a reminder that the law may consider the unauthorized use of someone else's access point unlawful.

Of course, there are some differences in intent — for example, if you live next door to the McDonald's that offers free Wi-Fi, it would be hard to imagine that you should go out of your way to avoid that particular access point. On the other hand, driving around the block with your laptop or camping out in someone's backyard just to get Wi-Fi access, well, that's another story.

Many Internet users believe in "sharing the wealth" and purposely leave the WEP key inactive so that others may surf for free. However, many users also believe in securing their Internet connection and not leaving their machines vulnerable. One rather popular phenomenon in recent times involves naming the SSID "Joe's Wi-Fi connection — contact to share" and enabling the WEP key. Interested parties could visit Joe and pay a portion of his ISP bill each month and, in return, could have his WEP key and use his connection.

---

range of your router and an unsecured access point to connect to your network and surf the Internet or even take a gander at what's on your network and computers.

Once your router or computer authorizes access, the other user is inside your network, simple as that. However, there are a number of things that you can do to secure your access point and network. You would be surprised by how many people do not think to use any of these options!

- **Use encryption.** Whether WEP or WPA, configure your access point to use it and configure all your wireless devices to use the same encryption method. It's far too easy to sniff packets transmitted without encryption. Use encryption!

- Turn off remote administration and use HTTPS. Unless you have a compelling reason for doing otherwise, you should always require a wired connection to your access point and use HTTPS for your administrative connections. There is rarely, if ever, any need to work on your access point from across the Internet, and especially not "in the clear."

- Use MAC filtering. If you have a small number of wireless devices, you can use MAC filtering in your access point so that only connections from those devices are allowed to connect. See Chapter 14 for information on using ipconfig to locate your adapter's MAC address.

- Turn off SSID broadcasts. You don't need to broadcast the Service Set Identifier (SSID) to the world; just configure your computers with the SSID and reduce your exposure.

Before installing wireless networking, do a realistic threat assessment of the area and people around your home or business. If you are in a single-family residency in the middle of nowhere, the chances of anyone hacking your network over your wireless access point are slim. Conversely, if you are in a high-rise or in the middle of a business park, the chances of someone "browsing" around in your network are significantly higher. Be smart about security and look at everything with a balanced eye to see what additional security measures may be needed.

Setting up wireless security

Wireless connections are configured basically in the same way as a regular network connection. Windows Vista automatically detects the hardware and sets up the basics. You can then edit the connection if you want to use a static IP address.

Windows Vista lets you set up a wireless network using the Set up a home or small business network (see Figure 9.13) feature, which is discussed earlier in this chapter. To create a wireless network, you will need the SSID name as well as the network security type and key (or passphrase). If you're not comfortable or relatively new to setting up wireless networks, this wizard is a safe bet.

 Inside Scoop

If you are just installing your router or are reconfiguring it, think of updating the firmware, which are drivers for your router. The manufacturer's Web site will have information on how to upgrade to the latest code.

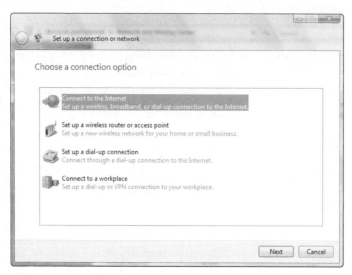

Figure 9.13. This window lets you take the first step to setting up a network.

Before you start working on your wireless adapters, you need to configure your wireless access point with the information detailed above. You will almost always be using a wireless infrastructure, rather than ad hoc, and the SSID can be anything you want as long as you change the default SSID from "default" or other obvious names like "Netgear" or "Linksys." Think of something original that you won't forget, and keep it short! Just remember that you are limited to 32 characters and spaces are not allowed (they are automatically replaced with underscore characters). If you use the Windows Vista Set Up a Network Wizard, the default SSID name is the name of your computer followed by an underscore and then "network." Once you decide on a SSID name, click Next.

The next page of the wizard allows you to choose your security type from one of four options: WPA-Personal, WPA2-Personal, WEP, and No Security. By default, Vista doesn't offer the selection of encryption types; you must click the Show advanced network security options link. Once you click the link, the four options appear in a drop-down menu (see Figure 9.14). Vista recommends (and we agree) that you should use the WPA2-Personal access, as it is more secure than the other connection types. However, make sure your hardware is relatively recent if you use this option because hardware made before 2001 is not compatible with this protocol. WEP should be avoided when possible, simply because it is not very strong. Basically, it can stop a subpar snooper from hacking your machine; however, if you have any sensitive data on your machine, you definitely want to go for WPA2.

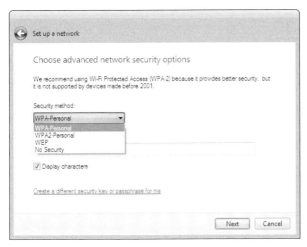

Figure 9.14. The encryption settings page.

Windows creates a random passphrase for you. If, for whatever reason, you do not like the generated password, you can click the Create a different security key or passphrase for me link, and a new one is generated on-the-fly. Of course, you can also create your own passphrase provided that it follows the rules and norms for the chosen protocol. For example, WPA accepts up to 1,024 characters in a passphrase. When you are satisfied with your encryption type and passphrase, click Next.

Now it's time for you to set file and printer sharing options (see Figure 9.15) for your wireless network.

Windows Vista offers four options:

■ **Do not allow file and printer sharing.** Full stop.

■ **Allow sharing with anyone with a user account and password for this computer.** This means that your Public folder and shared printers may be available to some users.

■ **Allow sharing with anyone on the same network as this computer.** This means that your Public folder and shared printers may be available to any users who happen upon them.

■ **Keep the custom settings I currently have.**

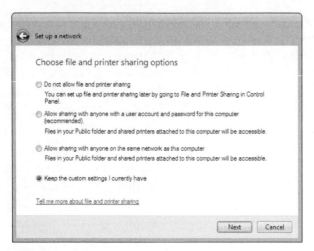

Figure 9.15. The file and printer sharing options.

Congratulations, you've successfully set up your wireless network at this point. A window displays with your SSID name and passphrase.

Connecting to a wireless network

After you have configured a wireless network, connecting to your network is automatic. In fact, Windows Vista puts this connection at the top of the list of available networks. If you want to manually connect to a wireless network connection, you can do so either using the Internet icon in the notification area (right-click and select Connect to) or through the Network Center by clicking Connect to from the left pane. Either option opens the Connect to a network window (see Figure 9.16).

The Connect to a network window displays available networks for one of three categories: All, Wireless, and Dial-up and VPN. You can sort and view the available networks for one of these categories using the drop-down menu at the top of the window. If the window is unable to find any available networks for a given category, you can click Try again to provoke the feature to take another look for available networks.

As we mention at the beginning of this section, Windows Vista places your home wireless network at the top of the pecking order. In other words, it will always try to connect to this wireless connection first. If it is unable to make a connection, Vista will go down the list of available networks until it is able to make a connection. You can change the order in which Vista looks for available networks by using the Wireless Networks page of the Control Panel. This option lets you reorder the connection priority of your networks. This window features the SSID being broadcast by an access point, information on its encryption type, and a visual indicator of signal strength. To modify this list, simply drag and drop your desired network connection to where you want it to appear in the list of networks (see Figure 9.17). This is a particularly helpful feature, for example, if you are working away from home (another office or a hotel while on vacation) and want to make sure that Windows Vista keeps on connecting to a particular network, and not your home network. To be honest, Vista is going to connect to the first available network. Even if your home network is the first priority, it is skipped if it is out of range. Unless you have multiple access points within range of your remote location, Windows Vista will most likely connect to your desired network (which you probably picked because it had the strongest connection).

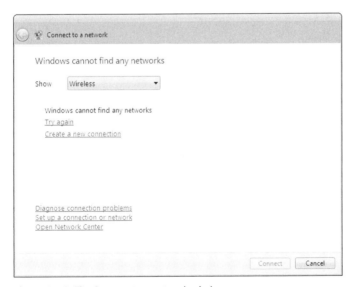

Figure 9.16. The Connect to a network window.

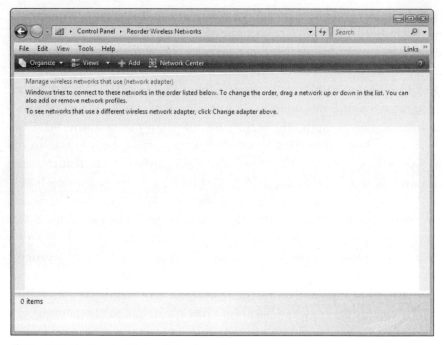

Figure 9.17. The Reorder Wireless Networks option.

Configuring Internet Connection Sharing

Internet Connection Sharing (or ICS) is just as important today in Windows Vista as it was when it first appeared in Windows 98 Second Edition (remember that one?). ICS was designed to be an inexpensive way for multiple computers to connect to the Internet without each machine having to have its own dialup connection. Of course, times have changed, and the prices of hardware and routers have dropped considerably since ICS came on the scene, so it's a safe assumption that ICS is used considerably less than it used to be. It can still be an effective tool for broadband users; if you are still using dialup, you won't want to have multiple users sharing a single 56k line as it will be painfully slow.

There are two ways to share Internet connections across several computers. One way is over a router; if you are a broadband user and have a wireless network set up, this is probably what you use. For example, you can share a single connection over multiple wireless users and several desktop users that are plugged in to the router.

The other option is ICS. To use ICS, you need a host computer (your computer) that has a live Internet connection. Your computer is then connected to a hub (which looks similar to a router) where other computers are plugged in and ready to accept the Internet connection.

To get started:

1. You must open Network Connections from the Control Panel. This page lists the current network connections for your computer.

2. Select the desired connection to share and open its Properties from the right-click menu (see Figure 9.18).

3. Go to the Sharing tab, and click the Allow other network users to connect through this computer's Internet connection check box. Yes, it's really that easy.

Figure 9.18. The Local Area Connection Prroperties let you determine connection sharing.

Once ICS is enabled, your computer's LAN connection is re-assigned a static IP address; any connections with other network computers must be re-established. However, before you can use ICS, you must make sure that each network computer is configured to obtain an IP address automatically. This is quite simple; open Network Connections as mentioned above and select Internet Protocol (TCP/IP) from the Properties and click Properties again. Click Obtain an IP address automatically and you're ready to go. Of course, be sure that you perform this task for every net-work computer!

There are some situations where you should not use ICS; for exam-ple, if you are using a domain controller, a DNS server, a gateway, or a DHCP server. If you are using VPN access on your host computer, net-work computers can also access your corporate VPN if you enable ICS on the VPN connection. However, if you do not turn on ICS for the VPN connection, your network computers will not be able to access the corpo-rate VPN.

The primary disadvantage to using the ICS option as opposed to a router is that the host computer must always be on and have a live Internet connection. If the host computer is turned off or loses its Internet con-nection, the entire network goes down and loses its Internet connection. We recommend the use of a router for several reasons; including cost, ease of setup, a permanent Internet connection, and the ability to sup-port wireless connections.

If you would like a more "assisted" way of setting up a shared Internet connection, you may want to use the Network Center to set up a home network. Windows Vista provides a Set Up a Network Wizard that walks you step by step through the network creation process. This feature is detailed earlier in this chapter.

Working with Windows Mail

Windows Mail is the "new and improved" version of Outlook Express. While we still recommend using other e-mail clients, such as Eudora or even Outlook, many people still use the out-of-the-box e-mail client pro-vided by Microsoft. Despite our dislike of this application, Microsoft has added some new features that make Windows Mail more like an e-mail client and not a dinosaur.

Microsoft's Outlook Express always suffered a bad reputation because of security flaws. We'll admit that it's not a bad e-mail client for basic needs — it serves its purpose — but up until now, it didn't offer very much in the way of security. As we inferred earlier, Windows Mail is the free e-mail client, compared to the somewhat costly Microsoft Outlook. All things considered, we still prefer Microsoft Outlook, especially the new 2007 version that we have been testing in recent months.

Before you begin using Windows Mail, make sure that you have a valid e-mail address and password from your ISP. Most ISPs these days offer detailed instructions on their support sites on how to set up an e-mail address with Windows Mail, rather than Outlook Express. Since Windows Vista is taking its first steps, most ISPs probably still have the old screenshots even though the information is the same; being the nice guys we are, we'll help you set it up in the following paragraphs.

Set up e-mail accounts

There are two ways to access Windows Mail:

- If you don't currently have another e-mail client installed, for example Outlook, you can click Start and then E-mail to open Windows Mail.

- If you wish to use Windows Mail, you can access it from the Start menu.

If you haven't set up an e-mail account, a wizard appears (see Figure 9.19) to help you set up the necessary information.

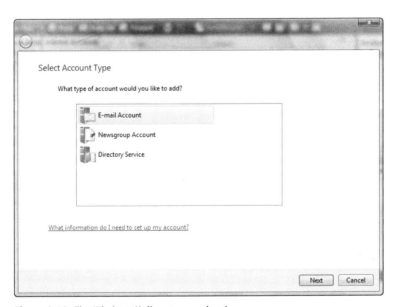

Figure 9.19. The Windows Mail new user wizard.

1. **Type** the name that you want to appear in the From section of your e-mail and then click Next.

2. **Type** your e-mail address that you will use with your ISP; often it is something along the lines of yourname@yourisp.com, but use the one that you've set up with them.

3. **Click** Next. The E-mail Server Names dialog box appears.

4. **Select** the type of incoming mail server from the drop-down list box and click Next (see Figure 9.20). In most cases, this will be a POP3 server. Type the incoming and outgoing mail server addresses in the appropriate boxes. Many times an ISP makes it easy by using the same name, such as mail.ispname.com. Use the addresses they give you.

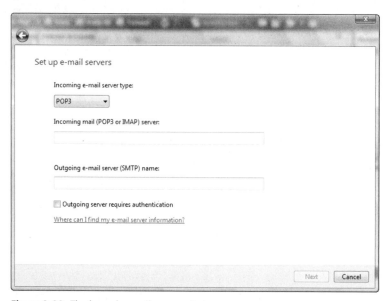

Figure 9.20. The incoming mail server window.

Inside Scoop

Most ISPs either provide multiple e-mail addresses or allow for it. Creating separate e-mail accounts for various family members is a good idea. Perhaps you have an account just for yourself, in which case you can create a separate account that you use for Web sites or services. This way, you can make sure only desired, personal e-mail arrives at your personal address.

5. The Internet Mail Logon dialog box appears. Type the account name you set up with your ISP and the password. You can select whether to remember your password or to have Windows Mail prompt you every time you connect to enter your password. Click Next.

6. To save the settings, click Finish, but first decide whether or not you want Windows Mail to check for e-mail now or not. Once that is taken care of, you're all set!

Using a P.O. Box for E-mail

There are a number of e-mail forwarding services available, including the inimitable www.pobox.com. Pobox is a wonderful service that allows you to receive e-mail at a pobox e-mail address that is then forwarded on to your personal e-mail address.

You may want to use a forwarding address if you are sending out resumes or need to protect your identity for any other reason. We like using this forwarding service because it has a very thorough spam trap. This allows us to give out an e-mail address without the sender having our personal e-mail address; pobox acts as a buffer between the sender and our ISP. If we receive spam, it's pobox.com that is noted and not our personal mail servers.

Another big reason to use this kind of service is the SMTP server services. If you travel considerably, you know the frustration of connecting to high-speed Internet access in your hotel room, only to discover that your ISP doesn't allow relaying e-mail and won't send any outgoing e-mail messages. This is especially annoying if you spent time while traveling preparing e-mails offline to send once you arrive at the hotel. Many ISPs don't allow relaying e-mail, which is sending e-mail from an e-mail address with a domain name different from the outgoing mail server; this is often how spam is sent.

Pobox.com allows you (for a fee) to send e-mail over their SMTP server using authentication (it allows relaying), thereby eliminating this problem. At the moment, full service (including relaying) costs $50 per year; this is well worth the cost, especially for those who travel.

Securing your Windows Mail experience

Windows Mail has joined Internet users in the twenty-first century by including some very nice, and much needed, security features to make this application considerably more secure. These new security features are all bundled under the Junk E-mail Options moniker. These options include:

Junk E-mail

In Windows Mail, you can now set Junk E-mail protection levels (see Figure 9.21). Windows Mail scans incoming messages, and if they are determined to be junk e-mail (spam), they are funneled off into a separate folder called, oddly enough, Junk E-mail. This tab lets you set the protection level: No Automatic Filtering, Low, High, and Safe List Only.

- If you select No Automatic Filtering, Windows Mail doesn't scan incoming e-mail; even blocked senders are allowed and go straight to your inbox.

- If you select Low, only obvious junk e-mail is moved to the folder.

- If you select High, most junk e-mail is caught and sent to the Junk E-mail folder. Unfortunately, regular e-mail can get caught up in this too, especially if your sender doesn't include a subject or it has an unusual message content or subject. If you select this option, you should check the Junk E-mail folder regularly to make sure you don't miss any important e-mails.

- The Safe List Only option only delivers e-mail from addresses or domains that you have stipulated as a safe e-mail address. Any other e-mail is sent directly to the Junk E-mail folder.

There is also an option that lets you permanently delete any e-mail marked as junk e-mail instead of forwarding it to the folder. Given the at-times overzealous nature of spam checkers, we recommend not using this feature. You never know when you may miss out on an important personal or business-related e-mail!

Safe Senders

The Safe Senders (see Figure 9.22) tab lists your e-mail address or domains that Windows Mail should consider safe; e-mail from these entries is never considered as junk mail. You can simply click Add to enter an e-mail address or domain. If you need to make any changes, click Edit. If you change your mind about an entry, you can always click it and then click Remove.

Figure 9.21. The Junk E-mail options.

Figure 9.22. The Safe Senders options.

This tab also allows you to add e-mail from people who are in your Windows Contacts. You can also opt to add anyone you e-mail to the Safe Senders tab.

Blocked Senders

The Blocked Senders (see Figure 9.23) list is the exact opposite of the Safe Senders list. Anyone or any domain added to this list is considered to be junk e-mail and is treated accordingly.

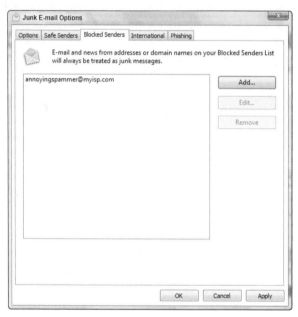

Figure 9.23. The Blocked Senders options.

E-mail from these entries is always considered as junk mail. You can simply click Add to enter an e-mail address or domain. If you need to make any changes, click Edit. If you change your mind about an entry, you can always click it and then click Remove.

International

The International tab (see Figure 9.24) has become a very good friend in recent months. Experience has taught us that spam knows no boundaries (geographically or content-wise); so Windows Mail has adopted a longtime Outlook feature that allows you to block e-mail from certain countries where spam is known to often originate. By clicking the Blocked

Identities: Who are you?

Windows Mail introduced identities many moons ago (circa Windows 95) because user accounts with separate access rights and security privileges weren't supported. This feature is no longer supported, however, Mail still assumes that some users may have them.

If you click Identities from the Windows Mail File menu, you can import an identity's e-mail into the appropriate user account. The Import Messages and Contacts Wizard helps you import identities, account information, and messages into the new and improved Windows Mail application.

Top-Level Domain List button, you can block e-mail coming from any country or region.

To be safe, there is also a Blocked Encodings List button that allows you to block e-mail that uses a certain encoding (alphabet type). For example, you may decide to block any Western European encoding, US ASCII, or Chinese.

Figure 9.24. The International options.

Both of these options allow you to manually select your options or to select all of them for ultimate security. Of course, if you select all for both of these options, you will likely have a very lonely inbox.

Phishing

Phishing has become a real problem in recent times. In a nutshell, phishing is the deceitful act of trying to sham Internet users into a trap whereby they reveal their identity, or worse, personal information that is never used for good. For example, one classic phishing example is an e-mail that comes from a "bank" asking you to verify your account information. The e-mail looks legitimate and the link on the page says that you're going to the right bank, but in reality you are transferred to another Web site where you may be asked to enter personal information. Once you do this and send it, it is sent not to the bank but to the phisher who now has access to your identity.

This tab (see Figure 9.25) lets you activate an anti-phishing measure whereby any potential phishing e-mails are sent to the Junk E-mail folder. You may also opt to remove any links from these e-mails.

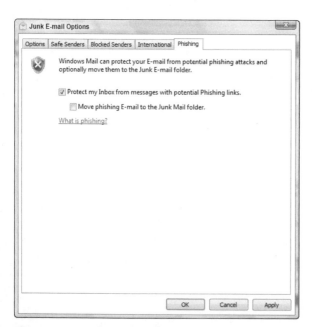

Figure 9.25. The Phishing options.

All of the options detailed previously are major improvements in the overall security of Windows Mail. If you are going to use e-mail, you must accept that no system is 100 percent safe from spam or phishing attempts. However, that doesn't mean that you shouldn't lessen your chances by taking the necessary steps.

Encrypting messages

Windows Mail now lets you send encrypted messages, if you are using a digital ID. However, in order to send an encrypted message, the recipient must also have a digital ID.

In the event that your recipient doesn't have a digital ID in your Windows Contacts, that person can send you a digitally signed e-mail. Windows Mail automatically saves any digital IDs from a digitally signed e-mail into Windows Contacts.

To encrypt an e-mail message, simply click Encrypt from the Tools menu of your e-mail message.

Using advanced features

Windows Mail doesn't have all the glitz and bright lights of Outlook or other e-mail clients, but it does have some features that most people probably don't use or know about.

Create distribution lists

Distribution lists are collections of e-mail addresses put into useful categories. Most people associate distribution lists with e-mail servers, such as Exchange, where the address book contains entries such as DevAll or LunchPals. When selecting addresses for the To: field, you can select a distribution list, and the e-mail will automatically go to all the members of the list.

You can create your own distribution lists in Windows Mail for quickly sending e-mail to numerous addresses. Click the Contacts button or choose Contacts... from the Tools menu. The Contacts window opens. Click New Contact Group.

Type a name for the group, such as Sailing Buddies or Goat Farmers. From here you can select group members from your contact list, create a new contact and then add the person to your group, or add a name and e-mail address without creating a new contact. When you are done, click OK.

E-mail paranoia: Return receipts and bcc

For the cover-your-assets crowd, Windows Mail provides return receipts and blind carbon copies (also known as bcc) to help you make your way through the dog-eat-dog corporate world. Windows Mail return receipts are automatically generated when the message is read by the recipient. This can be useful if you are under the gun to deliver a report and want to confirm whether it was received in time.

There are two ways to request read receipts. First, in an e-mail you are about to send, click Tools and then Request Read Receipt (see Figure 9.26). Your message will generate a receipt when it is read or marked as read, which is not necessarily the same thing. Some e-mail applications let you disable or ignore the sending of a receipt.

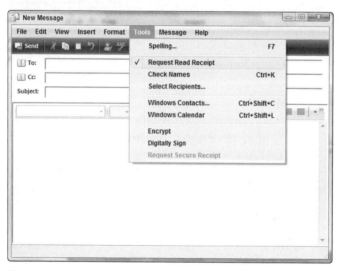

Figure 9.26. Request Read Receipt from a new e-mail message.

Second, you can configure Windows Mail to always generate a read receipt for all e-mail. In the main Windows Mail window, click Tools, Options, and then the Receipts tab. Select Request a read receipt for all sent messages. Whenever you create a new message, the Request Read Receipt option is checked, and you can uncheck it if you don't absolutely need a read receipt for that message.

You can also request a digitally secure receipt for any message that was digitally signed. Conversely, you can also send a secure receipt from this same menu if so desired. This type of receipt verifies that your message (digitally signed) was free of security errors and properly displayed on the recipients machine.

However, know that just because you request a security receipt doesn't mean that you're going to get one! On the Receipts tab, there are options that determine how Windows Mail will handle read receipt requests. It can always send a receipt, ask whether to send a receipt, or never send a receipt. The default is to notify when one is requested, and you can then decide whether to send a read receipt. Just remember that if you can request a read receipt, so can anyone else; and if you decide to toss all read receipts into a black hole, so can anyone else.

Bcc:, or blind carbon copy, is a third address field you can use with your messages. It is a way of sending a copy of the message without alerting the others in your To: and CC: fields. We use it regularly when sending out updates or humor e-mails to friends, many of whom don't know each other. More conspiratorial-minded individuals use the bcc: to notify the boss that things are afoot without letting the other recipient(s) know the boss is included as a recipient. No matter how you use it, it's there for you whenever you need it.

Create a new message. Click View and then click All Headers. The Bcc: line is available in your message, and will be there for all new messages. If you wish to take up less screen space, you can always add e-mail addresses to the Bcc: line using the Address Book icon (in your e-mail message), which has a button specifically for blind carbon copies.

Viewing e-mail headers

E-mail headers (see Figure 9.27) are a part of every message sent across the Internet. As each message passes through a mail server, it adds a few (okay, many) lines of information that identify the server, the time the message passed through it, and any specific message handling information. These lines are normally hidden from view, since most people really don't care how the e-mail message arrived, so long as it did arrive.

There are occasions when this information is needed, especially if there is mail delivery failure, or even worse, if spammers are at work. The mail headers are like footprints that can help track down where things went wrong.

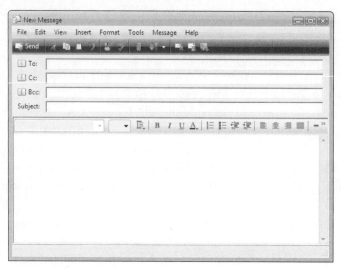

Figure 9.27. E-mail headers in action!

To view the message header, open the e-mail message. Click File, Properties, and then the Details tab. All the message header information is there in all its glory.

Manage e-mail with message rules

Many people view e-mail as *the* mission-critical application, both for conducting business and for personal communications. Over time, people quickly build up a steady stream of incoming e-mail: business documents, pictures from friends, electronic newsletters, and spam! While Windows Mail has some ability to handle spam, it's the other types of e-mail that can sometimes be disorganized and overwhelming.

Fortunately, Windows Mail (like most other e-mail clients) has the ability to automatically sort and organize your e-mail for you. This lets you determine what is important and what can be dealt with at a later time.

1. First, create folders for your e-mail in Windows Mail.

2. Right-click Local Folders and then click New Folder.

3. Type a name that is meaningful to you, such as project names or ones based on topics. You can create nested folders if you want, so that projects are broken down by milestones or subject matter. Then click OK.

4. Create some message rules to route your mail to the folders you just created.

5. Click Tools ⇨ Message Rules ⇨ Mail. The New Mail Rule dialog box appears (see Figure 9.28).

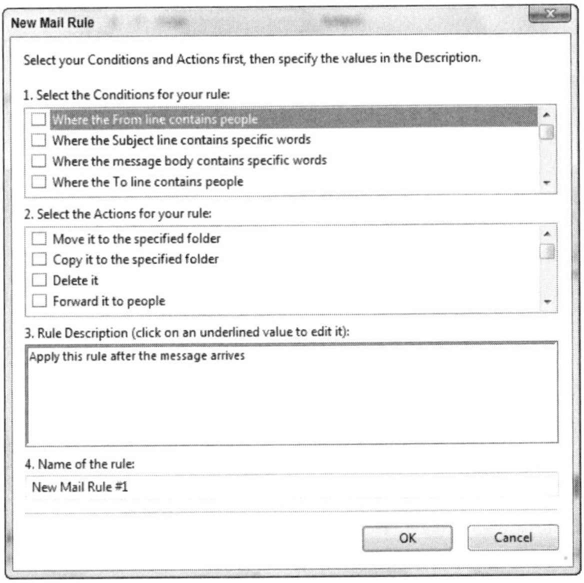

Figure 9.28. The New Mail Rule dialog box.

Scroll through the conditions list and select one or more conditions that you want to look for. Do the same thing for the actions that you want Windows Mail to take when the conditions are met. When you click a condition or an action, an underlined value appears in the Rule Description field. Click the value to bring up an additional dialog box where you can enter the information needed to process the rule. Fill in the conditions, click OK to return to the rule dialog box, and then click OK again. Your rule is added to the Message rules dialog box where you can modify or delete a rule, or change the order in which it is processed.

Set up and subscribe to newsgroups

Newsgroups are the vast, untamed wilderness, or as some might quip, the pale white underbelly of the Internet. There are two kinds of newsgroups: private ones that may be run by a business and are usually moderated

---

Effective rule making

Windows Mail doesn't have a very sophisticated rule-processing engine, certainly not one on the scale of Outlook. But, it is still effective for many people and can do most of what you want within its conditions and actions. Some tips for effective rule-making are

■ Keep rules simple. Don't try to create complex sets of conditions and actions within a single rule; use single conditions and actions within a rule. This is much easier to troubleshoot or edit later.

■ Use negative rules. You can create conditions that apply to messages that don't have specific words or people associated with them. This is simpler than creating rules with all possible words or people associated with them.

■ Create rules from e-mail. You can quickly create a rule from a message by selecting the message and then clicking Message, Create Rule From Message. This opens the New Mail Rule dialog box with Windows Mail's best guess as to what conditions and actions should be applied. You can then edit the rule to fine-tune its behavior.

■ Processing order matters. Rules are processed in the order listed. If mail isn't being processed the way you think it should, try changing the order of some of the rules.

(Microsoft has a number of newsgroups available) and public ones that are available through your ISP and may or may not be moderated.

Private ones tend to be topic-specific or product-specific, and the content is related to those products. The public ones are like a gargantuan public bulletin board with every conceivable topic available for browsing. This means that there is a lot of mature language and adult content available, so if you have concerns about children wandering onto newsgroups, you can arrange with your ISP not to allow newsgroup connections with your account.

Setting up a newsgroup connection is similar to creating an e-mail account (see Figure 9.29). Follow these steps:

1. Click Tools ➪ Accounts ➪ Add ➪ Newsgroup Account. Like when creating a new e-mail account, the wizard walks you through the process.

2. First, start by typing your name and then clicking Next.

3. Type your e-mail address and then click Next.

On the Internet News Server Name dialog box, type in the server address. Many ISPs configure this as news.ispname.com, but use the name you have been provided. There is also a check box to select whether your news server requires you to log on. If so, you will be taken to a dialog box similar to the one you used to log on with your account name. Click Next and then click Finish. When you are done, Windows Mail returns to the Internet accounts page, where the new newsgroup account appears. Windows Mail also asks if you want to download newsgroups for your new account. Depending on where you are located or how much time you have on your hands, you may not want to do this just now. Depending on how many newsgroups to which your ISP subscribes, plus your connection speed, this could take some time to complete.

To read newsgroup messages, you need to subscribe to a newsgroup. Right-click the account in the Windows Mail application and then click Newsgroups. The Newsgroups Subscriptions dialog box appears.

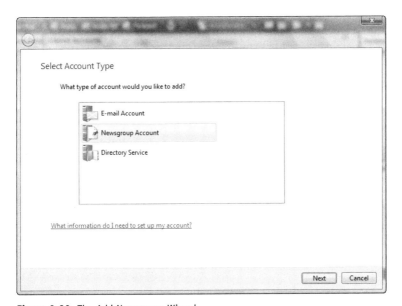

Figure 9.29. The Add Newsgroup Wizard.

The listing is a fully-expanded, hierarchical one; you can take time to scroll through the thousands of names in the list or you can type all or part of a word or phrase in the Display newsgroups which contain field. This will narrow down the newsgroup list to ones that match your filter. When you have found a newsgroup that sounds interesting, click the Subscribe button. An icon appears next to the newsgroup name, and the newsgroup appears on the Subscribed tab. When you are done subscribing to newsgroups, click OK.

By default, Windows Mail will synchronize new messages to the newsgroup, including both message headers and content. Unfortunately, the first time you subscribe to an account, it will download both the headers and the content of all new messages in a newsgroup. If the group has a lot of traffic, this could be a problem, especially over dialup or slow connections. Make sure the synchronization settings grab only the information you need. Click the Settings button and choose the option you want:

- Don't Synchronize
- All Messages
- New Messages Only
- Headers Only

The other setting you should know about controls the number of headers that are downloaded at one time. Click Tools, Options, and then the Read tab. In the News section, you can select to download only a certain number of headers at one time. By default, Windows Mail downloads only 300 headers; deselect this option to download all headers since the last time you synchronized the newsgroup. You can also mark all messages as read when exiting the newsgroup. By default, any newsgroup message you haven't read is left marked as unread, but if you are a casual newsgroup reader, you can select this box and all messages will be marked as read and eligible for cleanup.

At the end of the day, Windows Mail is one of several options available to users when looking for an e-mail client. During the beta period, it was

Bright Idea

In the interest of saving hard drive space, think of compacting and cleaning up your message base using the Clean Up Now option in the Maintenance tab of the Options page.

somewhat difficult finding a third-party e-mail client that worked smoothly on Vista. During our product testing, Windows Mail did hold its own. While it's still far from being a client that we would recommend over other applications, it has made great progress in its weakest area — security. If you are looking for a basic e-mail client with the minimum of bells and whistles, Windows Mail may be right for you. However, if you are a heavy-duty e-mail user, Windows Mail probably doesn't have the juice you need.

Using Windows Meeting Space

Yet another new feature in Windows Vista, Microsoft gives us Windows Meeting Space. Windows Meeting Space is a peer-to-peer tool that works over an ad hoc network that lets users transfer files, applications, or even a desktop with other Windows Meeting Space users. At first glance, we wondered why they didn't just include Groove 2007 as part of Windows Vista instead of making it an expensive addition to Microsoft Office 2007; these applications serve pretty much the same purpose.

Existential questions aside, Windows Meeting Space is a very good idea on paper, and it's about time that software companies recognized the importance and relevance of tools designed for geographically disparate professionals.

Getting Started with Windows Meeting Space

The first time you try to launch Windows Meeting Space, a dialog box (similar to the ones that appear when an error occurs) is displayed, asking you to enable file sharing and Windows Firewall exception. If you allow this, you'll be asked for your credentials and to sign up to People Near Me (see Figure 9.30). If you decline to enable file sharing, the window will close and you'll have to launch Windows Meeting Space again when you are willing to grant Microsoft its wish.

Your first step is to set up People Near Me. This is a tool used to designate other computers near you that can be used with Windows Meeting Space. You can set up a display name, opt to log in automatically when Windows starts, and whether or not to include a picture when sending invitations. Before you begin, you should (it's not required to move on to the next page, but we highly recommend it) read the privacy information and then click OK if you are fine with everything. You can also access People Near Me from the Control Panel.

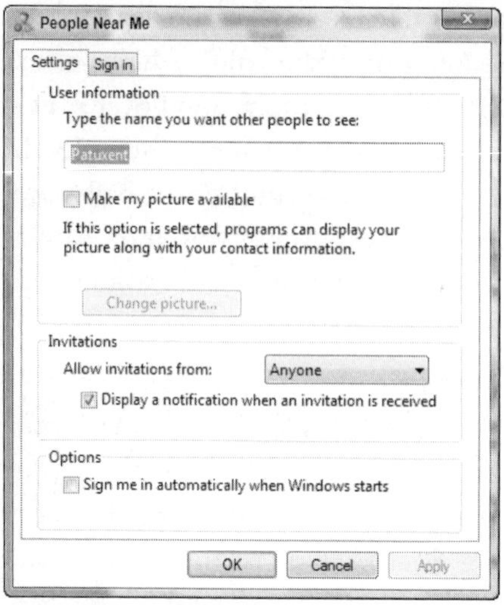

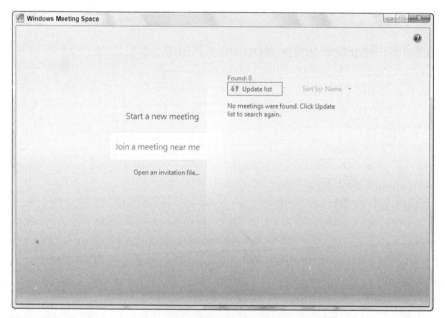

Figure 9.30. You're going to need to set up People Near Me to use Windows Meeting Space.

Windows Meeting Space appears with a list of sessions near you (see Figure 9.31). You can sort this list by a number of criteria; if no sessions are listed, you can always refresh the list or create a new session.

Figure 9.31. Sessions, if available, are displayed in Windows Meeting Space.

To start a new session, click the so-named title. By default, the name you designated in People Near Me appears with the local time. You must set a password in order for the logon button to appear. In the Options page, you can decide whether or not to allow People Near Me users to see the session. The network options in this page let you create a private ad hoc wireless network and to set your geographic location or connect to an existing wireless network. After you have set everything, you can click OK twice and Windows Meeting Space connects.

Windows Meeting Space is meant to remain a relatively private party. Up to ten users at a time can be connected, all of whom must be using Windows Vista. Previous versions of Windows are not supported.

Using Windows Meeting Space Safely

A large element of trust is needed when using peer-to-peer software. After all, you are letting another user access your computer and files. You have to be comfortable that this other user will not "break" anything on your machine, and that he or she also is up to date in terms of malware applications and definitions. As a safety net, you are always in control of your computer, applications, and files unless you temporarily give control to another user. To take back control, you can use the Control menu or the Windows key plus the Esc key.

To that end, you should only join sessions or invite users where you either know or trust the other users. Be sure to scan individual files or folders before opening them from another computer.

As another security precaution, all communications are encrypted, so that only authorized and authenticated session members can access these communications.

Goodbye Windows Messenger, hello Live Messenger

Internet chat is a virtual necessity in our world of convenience; you can think of it as a cross between a telephone and a typewriter. In fact, the chat application is one of the most popular applications available. Ironically, despite the fact that these are relatively small applications, they use different protocols, do not work well together, and have different strengths and features that appeal to different groups.

Don't let the name fool you. Chat programs aren't just for chatting! Almost every chat client on the market allows for Webcams and headsets for both video and audio capabilities. Up until Windows Vista, Microsoft included Windows Messenger (pretty much the same product as MSN Messenger, except that the former integrated with Microsoft Exchange). During the Beta 2 phase of Windows Vista, Microsoft released the replacement for both Windows Messenger and MSN Messenger: Windows Live Messenger. Windows Live Messenger users still tend to refer to it simply as "MSN" or "Messenger." Whatever you choose to call it, it still is part and parcel of the new Microsoft Windows Live service set. Though it still isn't included with Windows Vista, the Welcome Center provides a link for you to download the application.

Nice features in Windows Live Messenger

Windows Live Messenger lets users perform a number of features; in fact, you may just forget that you can actually use it to chat! Besides the obligatory chat feature, you can also use it to use video (Webcams), share folders, and make PC-to-phone calls, and it even integrates with Xbox 360!

The sharing folders feature is the new iteration of the "direct connect" feature in earlier versions of MSN Messenger. A shared folder for both users is created. If one user deletes a file, the other user is affected as well. The PC-to-phone feature lets you place phone calls to and from North America and Europe. At the time of writing (beta phase), the price was 2.3 cents per minute.

Overall, Windows Live Messenger is a good chat program. This marks the official "goodbye" to the whole Microsoft Passport, which is replaced by the Microsoft Live ID. Another nice feature is that you can set yourself to Appear Offline and still send messages (unlike previous versions of MSN Messenger).

Microsoft does come in for some criticism on this release because it is really geared only to PC — Macintosh and Linux users are pretty much left in the dark. However, because most of these users tend to be adverse to PC anyway, they most likely wouldn't use this chat application. Another frequent complaint is that Windows Live Messenger runs ads across the top of the application.

Set up the chat service

At the time of writing, Windows Live Messenger (see Figure 9.32) is not integrated with Windows Vista. In order to download it, you must go to its current Web site: `http://get.live.com/messenger/overview` or click on its link in the Welcome Center.

In order to use Windows Live Messenger, you must sign up for a Microsoft Live ID. The downside to the Live ID is that you must use your e-mail address as a login. If you would prefer not giving your e-mail address, you can go to `www.passport.com` and get a limited use ID instead. As we note earlier in this chapter, the Microsoft Passport is now a thing of the past, even if the basic principle of Microsoft Live ID is the same.

Figure 9.32. The new Windows Live Messenger.

Both of these applications connect to Windows Live Messenger as well as the other services. If you want to work with only one user interface but multiple chat services, either of these clients work well. In any case, switching to one of these applications is easier than convincing all of your friends to switch to your chat service of choice.

Chat with friends

In order to chat, you need to add contacts to Windows Live Messenger. Click Add a contact to start a wizard (see Figure 9.33). You can add a contact using an e-mail address or sign in name, or even search for the user. The search function is anemic, so don't bother; add people using e-mail or contact name. Click Next.

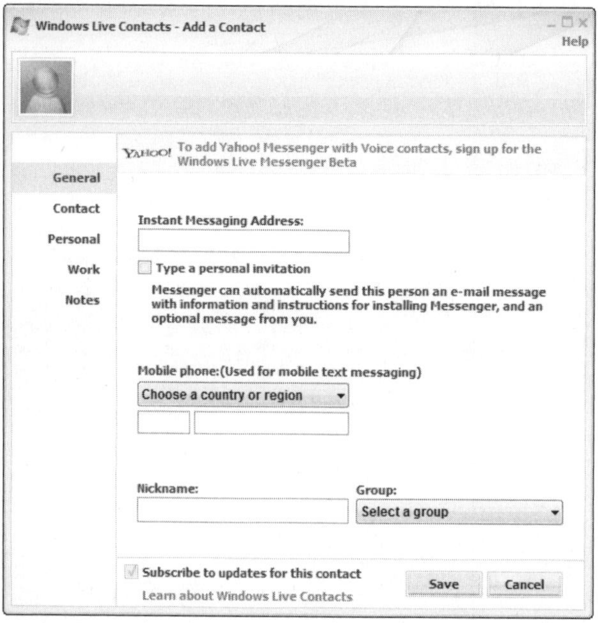

Figure 9.33. The Add a Contact Wizard.

Once you add a contact, their name appears in the Contact List, either as an online or offline contact (see Figure 9.34). You can create various categories and assign contacts to different groups. If your contact is online, you can double-click their name from the Contact List and start chatting. It's that simple!

Figure 9.34. The new Windows Live Messenger Contact List.

Universal Chat: Gaim and Trillian

Windows Live Messenger is not the only chat game in town. Other chat services are available such as Yahoo Chat, AIM (AOL Instant Messenger), and IRC (Internet Relay Chat). If you wanted to chat on those systems, you needed a wholly separate client for each chat provider — that is, until now.

Two popular multiservice chat clients are Gaim (gaim. sourceforget.net) and Trillian (www.ceruleanstudios.com). Both are free; Gaim is open-source and multiplatform, while

(continued)

(continued)

> Trillian is Windows only and offers a Pro version for a price. Gaim is quirky but offers straight-ahead chat on multiple services with no frills. Trillian has boatloads of eye candy, is skinnable, and prepares a spot of tea if you are polite.

The hidden gems of Windows Live Messenger

Windows Live Messenger started out as a quickie text utility, but it quickly matured into a multimedia communications application. You can do many things with Windows Live Messenger:

- If you have a sound card with a microphone jack, you can plug a headset into your sound card and have live audio chat sessions with other similarly-equipped Messenger friends. Start off by having a text chat session, and then click Start a Voice Conversation. If this is the first time you have run the voice chat, you will run through the Quick Tuning wizard to adjust audio levels.

- If you have a Webcam, you can have live video feeds between chat partners. Most Webcam software is integrated with Windows Live Messenger and will have its own tuning and picture adjustment software.

- File exchanges are available via a shared folder so that you can swap large files without worrying about e-mail server attachment limits. This is a great way to share large PowerPoint files or get program fixes from technical support.

- Application sharing lets you share Word, Excel, or any other Windows application with someone else. You can both edit and change the document in real time, or you can walk people through a new application you've written without having to package it up and distribute it to them.

Adieu, NetMeeting

One would be hard pressed to say that the writing wasn't on the wall. As of Windows XP, Microsoft started "hiding" NetMeeting and made finding it a bit of a scavenger hunt. It's now official: NetMeeting is dead, long live Windows Meeting Space.

In other words, this application no longer exists. It is replaced with Windows Meeting Space, which is discussed earlier in this chapter.

Just the facts

- Networking isn't complex, and there are many ways to get connected to the Internet.

- The Network and Sharing Center is your central point for Internet and network connectivity.

- Windows Meeting Space is the new kid in town when it comes to file and application sharing with a peer-to-peer network.

- E-mail can be best managed with a few message rules and a bit of common sense.

- Chat applications can do much more than just chat; they can enable multimedia conversations with others.

GET THE SCOOP ON...
What's new in Windows Internet Explorer 7 ■ Surfing in
Protected Mode ■ The Phishing Filter ■ Additional security
enhancements ■ Tabbed browsing ■ Using Web feed tools

Working with Windows Internet Explorer 7

With the growth in popularity of other Web browsers, in particular Mozilla Firefox, Microsoft has been forced to react if it wishes to retain its position as the producer of the world's most widely used browser. Windows Internet Explorer 7, the first major update of the software for half a decade, offers many new features, several of which are clearly inspired by Firefox.

Some of these changes are aesthetic, such as the new, less-cluttered interface that leaves more of your screen real estate for the Web page you are visiting; others are more fundamental, such as the explicit security measures that are a prominent part of Windows Internet Explorer 7.

There are issues, of course. Windows Internet Explorer still fails to implement Cascading Style Sheets (CSS) in a fully standards-compliant manner, and it remains to be seen whether the new security features will have any real effect other than to make users think they are surfing more safely. But Windows Internet Explorer 7 is still a major leap forward when you compare it to previous versions of the browser. After five years, it couldn't afford to be anything else.

Chapter 10

Inside Scoop

Windows Internet Explorer 7 is completely separate from the Windows shell, and no longer acts as a file browser. If you type a local file address in the Windows Internet Explorer address bar, it is opened using Windows Explorer. Conversely, if you type a Web site address in Windows Explorer, it is opened using Windows Internet Explorer.

What's new in Windows Internet Explorer 7

It has been such a long time in the making that you shouldn't be surprised to learn that Windows Internet Explorer 7 comes with many changes and improvements. Large amounts of the browser's underlying architecture have been completely reviewed and rebuilt, particularly in the areas of security and rendering.

The first major change concerns the name of the tool. It is now called Windows Internet Explorer, a rebranding that seems to emphasize its close integration with Windows Vista. This is despite the fact that, from a technical viewpoint, the browser is now a fully stand-alone application; it is no longer integrated with the Windows shell, which means that it cannot act as a file browser the way previous versions did.

Enhanced security

Security lies at the heart of Windows Internet Explorer. Microsoft doesn't exactly have the greatest reputation when it comes to security. A little ActiveX-related loophole here, a hastily-released patch there, and before you know it, people are accusing you of producing unsafe code.

Windows Internet Explorer 7 goes some of the way towards addressing this issue, not least from a public relations viewpoint. Some of the browser's important new security enhancements include

- **Protected Mode.** You can run the browser with greatly reduced privileges as a way of protecting your computer against attack.

- **The Phishing Filter.** Helps prevent you from falling victim to certain online scams.

- **ActiveX opt-in.** Allows you to decide which ActiveX controls you want to run — and, importantly, turns them off by default.

Additionally, changes have been made to the Secure Sockets Layer (SSL) and the Transport Layer Security (TLS) protocols to protect data that make the default settings more secure.

We will look at each of these topics in more detail in the following sections.

Display improvements

Another area where Microsoft has come in for serious criticism in the past concerns problems with the way Internet Explorer displays Web pages. Web developers have had to come up with a whole series of often complex hacks or workarounds to overcome these CSS bugs that would otherwise cause pages to display in an unexpected manner; of course, such bugs exist in other browsers as well, but to nowhere near the same extent as in Internet Explorer. Happily, Windows Internet Explorer 7 addresses the issue by tackling some of the major bugs, as well as making other important changes to how pages are displayed.

Some of these enhancements include

- A completely rewritten rendering engine to compete with the faster rendering engines of Opera and Mozilla Firefox.

- Improved support for CSS, Document Object Model (DOM), and HyperText Markup Language (HTML), which, while not quite the full standards compliance many have been demanding, does at least sort out some of the biggest bugs.

- Native support for transparent Portable Network Graphics (PNG) images.

- A zoom feature that lets you increase the size of an entire page (images as well as text) for easier viewing.

Surfing in Protected Mode

Windows Internet Explorer 7 introduces Protected Mode (see Figure 10.1). This innovative feature deals with some of the browser's previous and much-publicized security shortcomings while still ensuring that existing Web pages continue to work as intended. Protected Mode helps protect your computer from attack by running Windows Internet Explorer in isolation from the rest of the system and with greatly reduced privileges.

One of the principal security issues faced by both Windows Internet Explorer and other Web browsers such as Mozilla Firefox stems from the fact that browser plug-in mechanisms are exploitable. Mindful of all the compatibility issues that would be raised if it were to restrict what plug-ins can do, Microsoft has chosen to limit where plug-ins can operate instead. Windows Internet Explorer runs in a kind of sandbox; under the reduced privileges of Protected Mode, a malevolent plug-in can only reach a fraction of the data, files, and processes to which the user has access.

Protected Mode is based on several security features that are new to Windows Vista; two worth mentioning in this section are

- **User Account Protection (UAP).** This feature makes it easy to run without Administrator privileges and allows Windows to prevent malicious code from carrying out damaging actions.

- **Integrity levels.** Access to securable objects such as files and registry keys is now restricted depending on whether you are an administrator or a user with fewer rights.

These and other security features are described in more detail in Chapter 7.

In short, Protected Mode grants Windows Internet Explorer sufficient privileges to browse the Web, but withholds those privileges that could be exploited to silently install programs or modify system data. It does so by restricting write access to securable objects that have high integrity levels. When you run Windows Internet Explorer in Protected Mode, it is a low-integrity process, and low-integrity processes are only able to write to objects such as folders, files, and registry keys that also have a low integrity level.

In practice, this means that Windows Internet Explorer and its plug-ins, when running in Protected Mode, can only write to such locations as the temporary Internet file folder, the History folder, the Cookies folder, the Favorites folder, and the Windows temporary file folders. By preventing unauthorized access to sensitive areas of the system, Protected Mode greatly limits the damage that can be caused by a rogue process.

Hack

If you want to turn off Protected Mode, go to Tools on the tab bar, then click Internet Options. Under the Security tab, uncheck Enable Protected Mode. But remember, do so and you'll be opening yourself up to potential security risks!

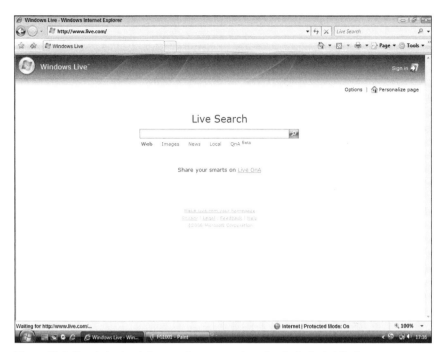

Figure 10.1. The status bar tells you when you are browsing in Protected Mode.

The Phishing Filter

Phishing is a technique used to trick people into revealing personal or financial information through communications that pretend to come from a trustworthy source. For example, you might receive an e-mail message that has been made up to look as if it was sent by your bank. When you click the link in the message, you are taken to a fake Web site where you are asked to provide sensitive information, such as your account number or password. This information can then be used to withdraw money from your bank account, or carry out other illegal actions.

The Phishing Filter is a new feature in Windows Internet Explorer that aims to help protect you from such scams. You can use it to do the following:

- Compare the address of every Web site you visit against a list of Web sites that Microsoft considers legitimate. The list is stored locally on your computer, which is good from a privacy point of view since no information about your browsing habits is sent to Microsoft, but it does mean that the information the file contains can never be fully up-to-date.

Bright Idea

For privacy reasons, you need to give your explicit consent to sending Microsoft a sample of addresses from Web sites you visit. If you choose not to enable Automatic Website Checking, you can still check suspicious Web sites on an individual basis by clicking Tools ⇨ Phishing Filter ⇨ Check This Website.

- Analyze the sites you visit to see if they present any of the character-istics common to phishing Web sites, which in practice will just mean the bad guys will need to get more creative, as they have been forced to do in the past to overcome anti-spam measures.

- Send Microsoft a random sample of addresses from Web sites you visit so that these may be checked against a frequently updated, cen-tralized list of reported phishing Web sites.

How well this all works in the real world remains to be seen. As we mentioned, the list stored locally on your computer is never going to be completely up-to-date, and even the frequently updated list is going to have trouble keeping up; reportedly, phishing sites only stay live for an average of 5.8 days.

To keep its list as up-to-date as possible, Microsoft wants your help. The Phishing Filter comes with a Report This Website option (Tools ⇨ Phishing Filter ⇨ Report This Website) that you can use to report a site you suspect of being involved in a phishing scam. If you do so, you are taken to a page on the Microsoft Web site where you are asked to confirm a few details about the site — the URL and language, basically — that will then allow Microsoft to carry out its own investiga-tions. This may be a good idea in theory; however, we have doubts about whether people who are tricked into visiting a phishing Web site will use this reporting feature in large enough numbers for it to be of any real use.

Watch Out!

Tools such as the Phishing Filter offer a certain degree of protection against scams, but they can also lull you into a false sense of security. No system is infallible, and the best protection of all is to use your common sense.

Additional security enhancements

Protected Mode and the Phishing filter are not the only security enhancements introduced in Windows Internet Explorer. Some other important changes are described in the following sections.

ActiveX opt-in

By default, the ActiveX opt-in feature blocks ActiveX controls unless you specifically allow them to be installed. When you visit a Web page that has a disabled ActiveX control, a message appears in the Information Bar inviting you to allow the control to run. ActiveX controls have been the source of many security breaches in the past, and it is good to see Microsoft is now erring on the side of caution by blocking them unless you say otherwise.

Not all ActiveX controls are disabled by default, however. Windows Internet Explorer 7 ships with a pre-approved list of common controls that have passed Microsoft's security test, and any ActiveX controls that you were already using in a previous version of Internet Explorer before upgrading to version 7 are also enabled by default. This compromise is practical — the risk that users who are forced to accept or deny dozens of different controls may end up doing so indiscriminately is very real.

Through the IE Security Settings panel, you can also choose to disable the ActiveX opt-in feature entirely, on a zone-by-zone basis: It is controlled by the setting Allow previously unused ActiveX controls to run without prompt. By default, this setting applies to controls used on the Internet and restricted sites zones but is disabled for the intranet and trusted sites zones.

HTTPS enhancements

HTTPS (which stands for HyperText Transfer Protocol Secure, and is the protocol used by Web servers and Web browsers to transfer data securely across the Internet) uses encryption to secure your Internet traffic and protect the integrity of your data. Several important changes have been made in how Windows Internet Explorer implements HTTPS; in particular, the default settings are now more secure and there is less of an onus on the user to make the "right" security decision.

HTTPS enhancements in Windows Internet Explorer 7 include the following:

- The default HTTPS protocol settings have been changed to disable the weaker SSLv2 protocol, which has known security weaknesses, and to enable the stronger TLSv1 protocol.

- Weak encryption ciphers (40-bit and 56-bit encryption) have been disabled, and stronger ciphers are enabled by default. SSL connections can only use 128-bit ciphers, and TLS connections can use 256-bit.

- Windows Internet Explorer 7 blocks navigation to HTTPS sites that present security certificates containing errors. Instead of showing a modal dialog box, as was the case in IE6, Windows Internet Explorer 7 displays an error page that explains the problem with the certificate. You can choose to ignore the warning and proceed anyway (unless the certificate was revoked), but if you do so, the Address bar turns red to remind you of the problem.

- When you view a page that mixes HTTPS and HTTP content, you are no longer faced with a modal dialog box asking you whether you want to continue. Rather, IE7 renders only the secure content by default and gives you the option of unblocking the non-secure content using the Information bar.

Increased protection against spoofing

Windows Internet Explorer's support for Internationalized Domain Names (IDN) leaves the browser more vulnerable to look-alike attacks (also known as homograph attacks), in which one domain pretends to be another by using a visually-similar domain name (such as www.examp1e.com instead of www.example.com — a numeral 1 instead of the letter l). Such spoofing is also possible within the ASCII character set, but supporting IDN extends the range of characters available to many thousands and increases the attack surface considerably.

Watch Out!
The importance of being "secure by default" cannot be overstated. Very few users have enough knowledge of security and its implications to be able to make these decisions themselves. Bear this in mind before you alter any security settings.

To protect against these attacks, Windows Internet Explorer imposes a series of restrictions on which scripts can be displayed in the Address bar, based on your language settings. If a domain name contains characters from outside your chosen languages, Windows Internet Explorer displays it in Punycode form. (Punycode is used to encode Unicode strings into the limited character set supported by the Domain Name System.) This may not be the prettiest solution, but names like `xn--bcher-kva.ch` (the Punycode version of `Bücher.ch`) do provide a highly visible clue when things are not what they may seem.

Domain names are also displayed in Punycode if they contain characters that are not part of any language, if they contain a mix of scripts that do not appear together within a single language, or if any of their constituent parts contain characters that appear only in languages other than your list of chosen languages.

If Windows Internet Explorer prevents a domain name from displaying in Unicode, an Information bar appears notifying you that the domain name contains characters that the browser is not configured to display. You can add additional languages to the list of those allowed using the IDN Information bar.

Address bar and Status bar

In Windows Internet Explorer 7, an Address bar and Status bar appear in all windows, including pop-ups. This helps to prevent malicious sites from disguising themselves as trusted sites.

The Address bar also features a color code to visually indicate the trustworthiness of a page. It turns red when you visit a page with an invalid security certificate, white if the site does not use any encryption, and green if the page uses a high security certificate.

Fixing unsafe security settings

Windows Internet Explorer 7 comes with a feature that checks at startup, or whenever a setting is changed, whether the current security settings are safe. If they are not, an Information bar appears at the top of the browser with Fix Settings for Me as the first menu option. Clicking this option restores all relevant settings to their secure default value.

Inside Scoop

Windows Internet Explorer 7 considers as unsafe any settings that would allow code to run on your computer without your consent. They are one ones marked "not secure" in the security zone settings.

Clearly, receiving constant reminders about your security settings has the potential to become a real pain, but that's the whole point. Using non-recommended security settings leaves the door wide open for spyware and other malicious programs. For that reason, while this feature can be controlled by an administrator using Group Policy, there is no way of turning it off from the user interface.

Tabbed browsing

Better late than never! With the latest edition of the Internet Explorer Web browser, Microsoft has finally caught on to the idea of tabbed browsing (see Figure 10.2), a concept initially made popular by its competitors Opera and Firefox.

Those of us who are fans of tabbed browsing believe it lets us stay more organized by viewing several different Web sites at once, all within the same window. Tabbed browsing eliminates the need to have a whole row of windows open in the taskbar with labels so small they are impossible to read.

Tabbed browsing may be nothing new, but there are some nice touches to the way it is implemented in Windows Internet Explorer 7. When you open a new tab, for instance, it opens an about:Tabs page with the address bar highlighted; as well as letting you quickly enter the address of the page you want to visit, this also deals with a common complaint from users of previous versions of Internet Explorer, which was that new windows always opened displaying a duplicate of the current page. The Quick Tabs feature (the tab with four little squares on it just below the Address bar), which displays a thumbnail preview of opened tabs, can also come in handy if you're like us and tend to browse with several tabs open at the same time.

Watch Out!

When you try to close the browser with more than one tab open, a warning appears asking whether you're sure you want to close several tabs at once. You can turn this warning off, but we like to leave it on; it's saved us both on more than one occasion.

Multiple home page tabs

One of the first features we loved about the latest incarnation of Internet Explorer is the option of assigning multiple home page tabs, rather than the standard about:blank or www.yahoo.com we all use.

Now you can specify several pages you want to load whenever you open the browser, simply by adding the URL for each of them on a separate line in the Home Page section under Tools ⇨ Internet Options ⇨ General. Choose the two or three pages you visit most often, and you may well be able to go for days without having to type a URL in the address bar.

Figure 10.2. Tabbed browsing in action.

Using Web feed tools

In recent years, it has become more and more common for Web site publishers to syndicate content from their sites through feeds. Typically

XML-based, feeds are special files that contain the most recent items from a site (such as news stories or blog posts), and they come in a range of formats. Users can subscribe to feeds from many different Web sites in an aggregator, which allows them to read all the new entries in a single location without having to visit each individual site to find out what's new.

RSS feeds? Web feeds? Atom?

Spend more than two minutes reading about feeds and the first thing you discover is that no one can agree what to call them. RSS feeds is a popular choice (and the one favored by Microsoft in most of its literature), but one which doesn't take into account that, for many feeds, the format used is Atom, not RSS. At the time of writing, the feeds-related features in Windows Internet Explorer support each of the following file formats: RSS 0.9x, RSS 1.0, RSS 2.0, Atom 0.3, and Atom 1.0. For this reason, we prefer to use the more inclusive term Web feeds throughout this section; from a reader's perspective, how each of the formats works is pretty much the same.

Subscribing to Web feeds

Windows Internet Explorer features a Web feeds button on the toolbar that lights up when Internet Explorer detects that the Web site you are visiting has one or more feeds available (see Figure 10.3). You can also configure Windows Internet Explorer to play a sound when a feed is found.

Subscribe to Web feeds by clicking the Web feeds button; if the site has more than one feed, click the arrow button to show a list of all the feeds available, then click the name of the feed to which you wish to subscribe. A formatted version of the feed is displayed directly in your browser, with a short explanation at the head of the page of what a feed is, followed by an invitation to subscribe to this feed. When you click + Subscribe to this feed, a dialog box opens asking you to confirm your subscription. Click the Subscribe button, the feed is added to your Favorites Center, and you can come back and view it whenever you like.

Viewing Web feeds

When Windows Internet Explorer 7 detects that the page you are visiting is really a Web feed, it formats and displays the feed directly in your browser. In previous versions of IE, the (not very useful) XML source code was displayed instead.

Figure 10.3. The Web feeds button.

The Favorites Center is where you manage all your stored links, including Web feeds. By default, Windows Internet Explorer stores Web feeds in a folder called Feeds. When you click a feed, it is displayed in your browser (see Figure 10.4).

A number of options exist for customizing how feeds appear:

- **Inline search.** Type a word in the search text box and your view displays only those items that contain this word.

- **Sorting.** Typically, you can sort the feed by date, title, and author, and some Web site publishers also customize their feeds to include more sorting fields.

- **Filtering.** If a feed includes categories, as is the case with many blogs, you can filter it to display just one category.

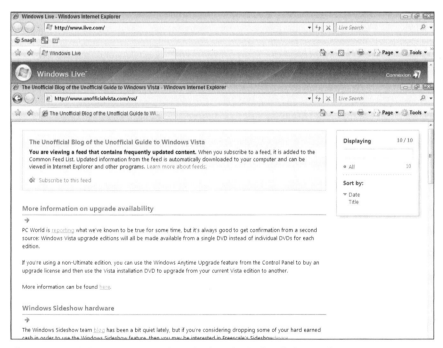

Figure 10.4. Windows Internet Explorer displays feeds directly in your browser.

Managing Web feeds

You manage each feed individually by selecting it in the list in your Favorites Center, right-clicking, and selecting Properties. You can then specify how often you want Windows Internet Explorer to check if new content is available, how many items you want to store in its archive for this feed, and whether or not you want to download enclosures (such as mp3 files if the feed in question is a podcast).

Searching in Windows Internet Explorer

Windows Internet Explorer now comes with an integrated search box built into the toolbar. In terms of usability, the new search box is a big improvement on previous versions of the Microsoft browser. In past editions, you could carry out a search by typing search terms in the Address bar, but this feature (which also still works in Windows Internet Explorer 7) was not immediately apparent to all users.

Now, in Windows Internet Explorer 7, searching is simple. Just type a couple of words in that little box in the top-right corner next to the address bar, click the magnifying glass, and away you go. Unsurprisingly, the search engine used is initially set as Windows Live Search, but fortunately you have the option of customizing the toolbar search by adding other search engines of your choice — even Google!

Adding new search providers

To extend the list of search providers available to you when you perform a search, click the arrow next to the magnifying glass by the search box, and then click Find More Providers. This takes you to a page on the Microsoft Web site containing a list of all available search providers (see Figure 10.5). Interestingly, this list is not limited to Web search engines such as MSN, Google, and Yahoo!, but also includes what Microsoft calls Topic Search sites, such as Amazon, eBay, and even Wal-Mart.

1. For each search provider you want to make available, click its name to add it to your browser. A dialog box appears asking you to confirm your selection.

2. Check the Make this my default search provider option if you want to do so, then click Add Provider to confirm your selection. You can add as many search providers as you like.

Hack

When searching from the built-in search box, type your search terms in the box, and then press Alt/Enter. This opens your search results in a new tab so you don't lose the page you are currently viewing.

3. When you're done adding new search providers, click the arrow by the search box and you will see a list of all the search providers you enabled, with your default search provider in bold.

4. Click the search provider you want to use for your current search (if you do not want to use the default), and you'll be good to go.

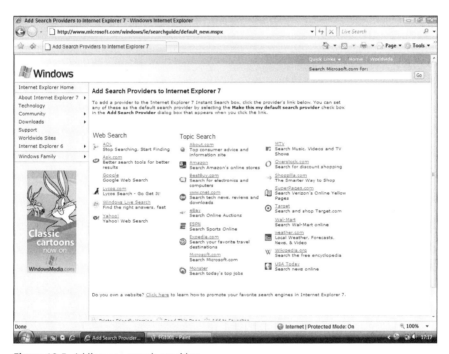

Figure 10.5. Adding new search providers.

Changing search defaults

When it comes to searching, we're a fickle bunch. Can you remember the days when all the cool kids were using AltaVista? The search provider you choose as your default today may not necessarily be the one you will be using most a few months from now, or you may simply need to

Watch Out!

If you click the Restore Defaults button when changing your search defaults, you are not asked to confirm your choice and there is no undo. This option removes all your search providers except Windows Live Search — and when they're gone, they're gone forever.

perform a few searches using a different provider for a particular task and not want to have to specify this other provider manually each time. Whatever the reason, it's not out of the question that you might want to change to a new default search provider after you have set up your initial list, or remove one or more search providers from your list.

To edit your search providers, do the following:

1. Click the arrow next to the magnifying glass by the search box.

2. Click Change Search Defaults.

3. In the dialog box that appears (see Figure 10.6), you have the option of setting one of your current search providers as your default, removing one or more search providers from your list, or restoring the default options. Click the button that corresponds to your choice, and then click OK when you're done.

Figure 10.6. Changing search defaults.

Just the facts

- Features such as Protected Mode, the Phishing filter, and the ActiveX opt-in prove that Microsoft is getting serious about security.

- Improvements in CSS, DOM, and HTML support have ironed out some of the idiosyncrasies that led to Web developers being forced to use "hacks" in order to have their pages display correctly in Internet Explorer, but full standards compliance is still some way off.

- Windows Internet Explorer 7 allows tabbed browsing, which has become standard on other Web browsers.

- Windows Internet Explorer 7 helps you discover RSS and Atom Web feeds and keep track of your favorite Web sites more easily.

- An integrated search box lets you perform searches directly from the toolbar using a customizable range of different search engines.

GET THE SCOOP ON...
Printers and faxes ▪ Configuring servers ▪ Web servers ▪
Remote desktop ▪ Remote assistance ▪ Sync

Working with Network Services

Windows Vista is meant to pick up where Windows XP left off in terms of being a good network citizen. One of the nice things about these two latest Windows releases is that you don't always need a server version to enjoy features often attributed to servers! Obviously, Windows Vista (nonserver) isn't a wise idea for hosting a large company; you can go pretty far in terms of meeting the needs of SOHO settings, though.

Some of these services include file and print services to Web and FTP servers. Windows Vista also includes a new Sync feature for you to coordinate your computer and devices. This chapter takes a look at some of these network technologies and turns your Windows Vista desktop into something a little more powerful!

Share and manage printers

You've probably deduced that the two big boys of networking are sharing printers and files. For a small company, these are often the only legitimate reasons that a network is necessary. As you can imagine, it's a lot more cost-effective to share a printer than to buy a printer for each individual computer. For example, you can share a photo printer, a laser printer, and a color printer with others on the network. While everyone can dream up reasons why they *need* a dedicated color laser printer, the printing technology built into the Windows family makes it easy to share, control, and manage shared printers on your network.

Install a printer

With all of the options — USB, Plug and Play, the Add Printer Wizard, and the device driver library on your hard drive — Windows Vista is able to get you up and running with all but the newest or oldest printers.

Printers come in two varieties: those that attach to the computer you are working on, and those located elsewhere on your network (stand-alone or attached to another computer). They are referred to as local and remote printers. The processes for connecting to them and setting them up are similar. If you upgraded to Vista from an earlier version of Windows, or if you had your printer connected during a clean install, most likely your printer is set up and configured already. If you need to add a new printer, you can follow the procedure detailed in the following paragraphs. To install a local printer, you must be logged on to an account with local administrator rights.

It is likely that your printer may come with a CD-ROM with all the necessary drivers (and documentation) plus any additional applications that may take advantage of your printer's features. If you run the CD's setup program, it will configure your printer for use with Windows Vista, which means that you'll never have to use the Add Printer Wizard!

1. Plug your USB, parallel, or serial cable into your computer. If Plug and Play detects your printer (which should almost always happen), it will install the necessary drivers automatically.

2. If not, open the Add Printer Wizard from the Hardware and Sound section of the Control Panel. The Add Printer Wizard starts and asks you if you want to install a printer to your computer or a network computer (see Figure 11.1). This wizard should only be used for non-USB printers; which are automatically installed.

Bright Idea

Ever thought about using a Bluetooth or wireless connection for your printer? It's possible in Windows Vista!

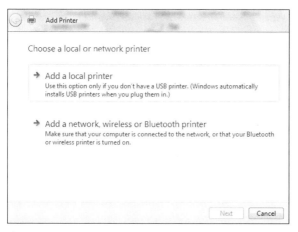

Figure 11.1. The Add Printer Wizard.

3. If you are looking to install a wireless or Bluetooth printer, you will want to select a network installation. If you are looking to install a printer on your computer, like in this example, click Next.

4. You can either select the port to use from the drop-down menu or create a new port. The drop-down list contains a number of ports, including LPT, COM, File, and ports used for third-party applications. Windows Vista recommends using LPT1. Otherwise, you can select another port or create one. You can create a local port or standard TCP/IP port among others.

5. Click Next and then select the manufacturer and model of your printer (see Figure 11.2). Of course, if your printer shipped with an installation CD, you should insert it now and click Have Disk. If the CD doesn't autorun, or Vista doesn't locate the necessary files, browse for the INF file on the disk.

6. Vista also includes a Windows Update button in this window (Install the printer driver). Don't be fooled by this button as it doesn't update Windows Vista like the usual Windows Update, but rather updates the list of manufacturers and printers compatible with Vista.

7. The Type a printer name dialog box lets you name your computer. By default, it is named after the manufacturer and model (for example, Aficio BP20 Series PCL 6). This page also lets you decide whether or not to make this new printer the default printer.

Figure 11.2. Select your printer manufacturer and model.

8. Windows Vista installs the printer after you click Next.

9. Click Finish to complete the installation or click Print a test page to do just that. You can use your printer without having to reboot your computer.

Psycho printer

Most print devices today have settings for print quality, paper size, printer trays, duplexing, and other whiz-bang features. You probably want to print your résumé on good paper at high dots per inch (DPI), your draft documents at low quality, and duplexed on the cheap paper.

With Windows, you can create different printers (Windows printing software plus appropriate device driver) that print to the same print device but with different settings. That way, when you print a document, and select the appropriate printer from the print dialog box, the printer you selected will automatically have the correct settings for paper, print quality, and paper tray already configured. You may feel that you're doing the impossible, but you're not; you're just leveraging the different facets of your printer's personality.

Setting up a network printer is basically done the same way.

1. After you start the Add Printer Wizard, you select the network printer option from the Local or Network Printer page and click Next. Vista looks for any available network and wireless printers. This search can take a few minutes depending on how your system is set up.

2. If you decide to skip this step, you can either click Stop and then Next or just click The Printer that I want isn't listed.

3. The Find a printer by name or TCP/IP address page lets you set the address of the printer. Vista lets you browse for a printer, select a network printer by name (via the Browse button), or connect to a printer at a specific IP address (see Figure 11.3). Use whichever option works best for you; once you have found your printer, click Next.

4. If you select the Browse for a printer or Connect to a printer at an IP address option, Vista takes you to the corresponding page for you to find the printer. From here, the dialog boxes are the same for a local printer. You can print a test page to confirm how your new printer works.

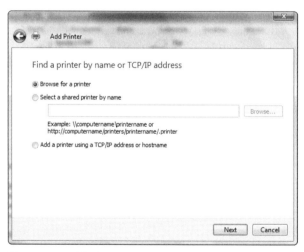

Figure 11.3. Add Printer screen.

Improving upon shared printers

If you decide to share a printer, there are features you can enable that may help others on your network with their printing and print jobs. Sharing a printer can be done simply by file sharing. Right-click the printer and click Sharing (you can also reach this tab from the Properties menu of the printer, but this is the long way). When you click the Change Sharing Options (this appears by default the first time you open the Sharing options), Vista asks you to confirm the step. Click Continue and the Change Sharing Options button disappears.

The wizard that appeared in Windows XP is gone; in Windows Vista, you simply decide whether or not to share the printer. If you share the printer, the name of the printer appears in the Share name text box (see Figure 11.4). The check box entitled Render print jobs on client computer is checked, as it should be. There is one last option to consider, which is whether or not to install additional drivers so if other users are using earlier versions of Windows, they do not have to find the print driver for the printer in order to use it. When you are ready, click OK and your printer will appear in Network, under your PC name.

Figure 11.4. Choose a simple name when sharing a printer.

If you click the Additional Drivers button, a dialog box appears with drivers for various processors. In Vista, Itanium and x64 processors are available if you are running 32-bit Windows Vista. The x86 (32-bit) is both selected and grayed out (see Figure 11.5).

Figure 11.5. The Additional Drivers window.

You can configure shared printers to use separator pages for print jobs. Open the Printers page, right-click the desired printer, and select Properties. Click the Advanced tab (see Figure 11.6).

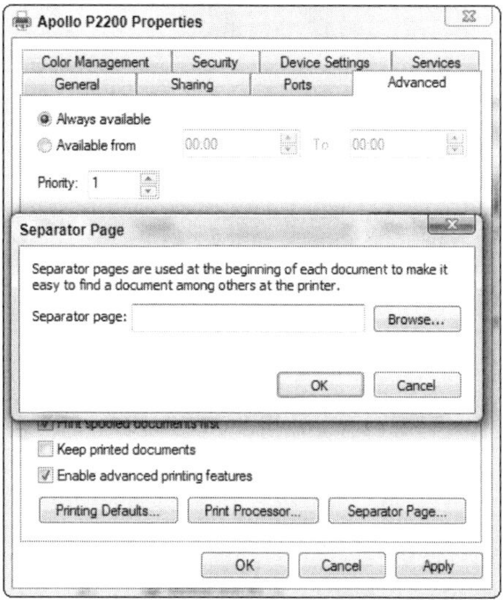

Figure 11.6. Use separator pages for tracking numerous print jobs.

Click the Separator Page button and then click the Browse button. The Windows\System32 page has four separator pages you can use (they may be difficult to find among the many folders on this page). These pages are

- pcl.sep uses Hewlett-Packard's Printer Control Language to print out a page with the username, print job number, date, and time.

- pscript.sep prints out the print job using PostScript but does not print out a separator page.

- sysprint.sep switches the printer to PostScript and then prints a separator page with the username, job number, date, and time.

- sysprtj.sep does the same, but uses Japanese fonts if they are available.

Select a separator page file and click Open. Click OK twice. Your print jobs will now use a separator page.

Networked versus shared printers

A printer directly attached to a network is a nice addition to a home or SOHO environment because it is always available, doesn't require a print server such as your computer, and can handle most normal-sized print jobs without too much effort. Each computer on the network manages its own print queue, so printing multiple print jobs is slower than with a dedicated print server.

A shared printer server is best for larger businesses or organizations. It provides greater print job management and more resources for creating and spooling print jobs. The computer acting as the print server doesn't need to be robust; any computer with a slower CPU is just dandy. The two major requirements for a decent print server are sufficient disk space to hold all the spooled print jobs and enough RAM to work with the largest print job.

Both a networked printer and one connected to a print server benefit by adding more RAM to the printer. When you purchase your printer, you should seriously consider adding more RAM than the default it ships with. You will be pleased by how fast your print jobs, especially graphics-intensive ones, fly through the printer.

Manage print jobs

In general, users manage their own print jobs. When a print job is sent to the printer, it is put into a print queue where it can be paused, restarted, or removed from the queue.

You can show the print queue (see Figure 11.7) by double-clicking the name of the printer from Printers or by double-clicking the printer icon in the lower-right notification area of your screen.

Figure 11.7. The print queue lists what jobs are printing, pending, or paused.

Documents in the queue can be managed by selecting a document (or using the Document menu), and then selecting one of the following menu items:

- **Pause a print job.** You can pause a print job that's in the queue by right-clicking it and then clicking Pause. If the job is already printing, Pause only stops the portion of the job that is still being spooled; if it's already in the printer's buffer, the printer will continue to print. When a job is paused, other jobs will move ahead of it in the queue automatically.

- **Resume a print job.** Right-click a paused print job and then click Resume. The remainder of the document in the spooler will be sent to the printer. If some of it has already been printed, you will need to collate the pages yourself.

- **Restart a print job.** If you have a paused printing and want to start the print job over from the beginning, right-click the print job and then click Restart.

- **Cancel a print job.** If a job has yet to print, this removes the print job from the queue altogether. Right-click the print job and then click Cancel. You can also select the print job and then press Delete. If the print job is already printing, any part of the job still in the spooler will be deleted while the remainder in the printer's buffer will continue to print.

Bright Idea

There are many ways to print in Windows Vista. You can print a document from the File ⇨ Print command or the Print icon in an application. You can also right-click the filename and select Print.

If you need to manage the entire queue, not just individual documents, click Printer and then click one of the following menu items:

- **Pause printing all print jobs.** You can also pause all print jobs by right-clicking the printer in the Printers window and then clicking Pause Printing. All print jobs in the queue are paused, though any print jobs in the printer's buffer will continue to print.

- **Cancel all print jobs.** You can also cancel all print jobs by right-clicking the printer icon in the Printers window and then clicking Cancel All Documents. Any print jobs in the printer's buffer will continue to print.

Print jobs can be reordered in the print queue by dragging them higher in the queue. This is handy if you discover you're running late for a meeting and need a particular printout now, not in ten minutes.

If you need to stop printing immediately, such as to clear an ongoing paper jam or replace a toner cartridge, you should take the printer offline at the printer's own control panel. This printer's status changes to offline and all print jobs become paused. However, if you manually turn off the printer at the source, any print jobs that were in progress will need to be restarted. Any information that had been spooled to the printer's buffer is lost when you shut off the printer.

While the printer is offline, you can still send print jobs to the printer queue and they will be held and spooled until the printer is back online. This is a handy trick to use if you are on the road with a laptop; set your printer to offline status, print as usual, then when you reconnect to your network, change the printer status to online and your print jobs will complete. This is much handier than keeping a list of documents you want to print out at a later date.

Advanced printer management techniques

Depending on your office situation, you may want to use some advanced printer management techniques. These let you define global settings such as providing notification for print job completion or error condi-tions, to setting user permissions and hours of use. These latter are con-venient if you don't want everyone printing to the expensive color laser printer for everyday print jobs.

Controlling global settings

You can control the global settings for all printers installed on a com-puter by right-clicking anywhere in the Printers window and selecting Server Properties (see Figure 11.8). The most useful of these are on the Advanced tab.

Figure 11.8. Print server properties can help you monitor and manage printers.

The first option available is the spool folder. By default, it is in the Windows]System32\spool\PRINTERS folder. You can move the folder to another hard drive in case the default drive is full or to improve print spooling performance. You can also set error logging options so that errors will appear in the System log for troubleshooting purposes.

If you want to be notified when a remote printer is having a bad day, select the Beep on errors of remote documents option. The next two options generate informational messages near the notification area.

Watch Out!

The Printer notifications for down level clients option that used to exist in Windows XP for the Alerter service no longer exist in Windows Vista.

There are advanced options you can set on a per-printer basis that give you greater control over who can use your printers, when they are available, and how they are managed. For example, you probably don't want everyone printing to the boss's printer and walking into her office at all hours to retrieve a print job. The downside is that these options aren't available in the more basic versions of Windows Vista because these types of features are more likely used in a domain-based setting.

Adding printer security

There are four permissions types available for each printer. To access them, right-click the printer and select the Security tab from the Properties menu. These permissions are

- **Print.** Users with this permission can print documents, control their own documents' properties, and pause, resume, restart, and cancel their own print jobs. By default, the Print permission is assigned to all members of the Everyone group.

- **Manage Printers.** This permission allows users to share printers, change printer properties, add, delete, or install new print drivers, change permissions for other users, and pause or cancel all print jobs. The user can pause and restart the printer, change spooler settings, share a printer, adjust printer permissions, and change printer properties. By default, members of the Administrators and Power Users groups have full access, which means that members of those groups have all three permission types assigned to them.

- **Manage Documents.** This option allows users to pause, restart, move, or remove all documents that are in the print queue. However, the user cannot send documents to the printer or control the printer status. By default, the Manage Documents permission is assigned to members of the Creator Owner group.

- **Special Permissions.** Special permissions allow you to set permissions for entries that you create.

If you want to set special permissions, you can:

1. Click Advanced from the Security tab of the printer Properties. This is accessible from the Printer menu in the Control Panel.

2. Click Add in the Permissions tab of the Advanced Security Settings window.

3. Enter the object name in the Select User or Group window that appears.

4. Click OK once you enter the object name.

5. Set printer permissions.

6. Click OK.

The procedure for setting advanced permissions is the same as setting permissions for files and folders. To set permissions for a specific printer:

1. Right-click the printer for which you want to set permissions.

2. Click Properties.

3. Click the Security tab (see Figure 11.9).

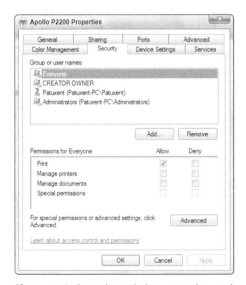

Figure 11.9. General permission categories can be set for individuals and groups.

4. On the Security tab, click Add and then select Object Types and select what you are looking for.

5. Then click Locations and select where to look. In the text box, type the name of the user or group you want to set permissions for, separating each name with a semicolon.

6. Click Check Names. Recognized names are underlined. Once all the names you want are in this box, click OK.

7. Click the Advanced button at the bottom of the Security tab. In the Permissions tab in the Permission entries area, select the desired user and click Edit (see Figure 11.10).

8. Click the Allow or Deny check box for each permission you want to allow or deny.

9. Click OK until you get back out to the Printers window. These changes take effect immediately.

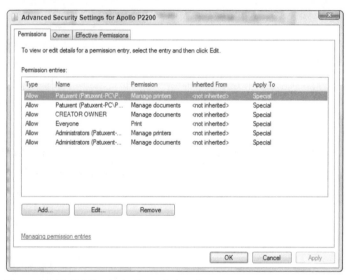

Figure 11.10. Set the desired permissions for a user.

The other management tool you can use for printers is setting the hours of use. This is considerably easier than setting permissions and may be the better way to manage printer use. To set the hours of use, right-click the printer, select Properties, and then click Advanced. Select Available from, and then enter the hours when you want the printer available (see Figure 11.11). Using this management tool is a good way to keep employees from printing out at 400-page game guide after work, or (conversely) keeping your kids from doing the same after they get home from school but before you get home from work.

Figure 11.11. Set the hours of availability for your printer.

The final gadget to help manage printers is the Priority setting. You can make different software print queues have different priorities, even when they go to the same print device. This feature ensures that the boss's reports are at the top of the print queue. The priority values range from 1, the lowest, to 99, the highest. The setting takes effect with the next print job you send through the queue.

Send and receive faxes

Fortunately, someone at Microsoft realized that PC faxing has become quite popular; otherwise this feature would probably have been forgotten or relegated to some dark corner of the operating system. If you are familiar with Windows XP, you probably remember that you had to actively go and install the fax program. Most users probably didn't know of the fax capability or simply gave up when they couldn't find it.

Windows Vista doesn't have this problem; it now proposes the Windows Fax and Scan program. This program is quite handy, especially for laptop users. You can run your office from pretty much anywhere off of a single computer, without having to have a bunch of bulky machines with independent phone lines. Of course, if you use the scan option, your mobility decreases.

As the program boasts, "Windows Fax and Scan allows you to send, receive, store, organize, and view faxes using your computer." It can also do much more than that; you can also use the scan feature to scan files and photos, or even scan a document and then fax it.

Configure the fax service

The first time you try to send a fax in Windows Fax and Scan, the Create Fax Account Wizard appears. Unlike in Windows XP, you cannot select this option from the Printers window.

1. The Create Fax Account Wizard asks you if you are interested in creating a fax modem connection or a Windows fax server connection (see Figure 11.12).

2. If you want to use your modem and phone line to send a fax, click the first option and click Next.

3. Vista asks you to create a name for the fax account and decide whether this account should be the default fax account.

4. Once you decide, click Create and the account is created.

Internet-based fax services

There are other options available for sending faxes from your computer. We like eFax, by j2 Global Communications (www.efax.com), as a fax service. This is both a free and fee-based service. If you use the free service, you are assigned a fax number and can receive faxes in either an image or PDF format. When someone faxes you, you receive an e-mail with the fax as a file attachment. The free service allows a limited number of incoming fax pages.

If you opt for the fee-based service like we do, you can pick your fax number from virtually anywhere in the world. You can receive faxes, but you can also send faxes from either a desktop application or through the eFax Web site.

This service has been very reliable for us, especially when doing business outside of the United States. If you are a SOHO user, you may want to consider this very cost-effective option!

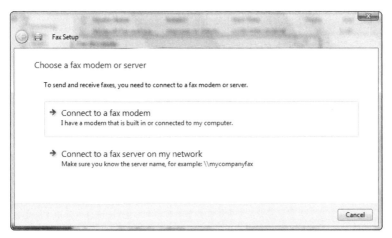

Figure 11.12. Setting up a fax account in Windows Fax and Scan.

If you change your mind or wish to add a fax server, you can

1. Go to Fax Accounts from the Tools menu in Windows Fax and Scan.

2. Click Add, select Windows Fax Server Connection, then click Next.

3. Add the address of the fax server and then click Next.

4. Enter a name for the account and set whether or not this account should be the default fax account.

5. Click Create, and the account is created.

In the Tools menu, select Fax Settings to configure send/receive settings (see Figure 11.13). Don't be surprised to see that the window is called Fax Properties; in Windows Vista, the names in the menus often do not match up with the names of the windows. If you click Allow the device to send faxes, you can use Windows Fax and Scan to send faxes. Likewise, if you select Allow the device to receive fax calls, you can then decide whether to answer automatically after a certain number of rings or to manually answer. By clicking More options, you can set a TSID (Transmitting Subscriber ID) and CSID (Called Subscriber ID) identity in the Additional Settings page; these IDs appear across the top of your

Watch Out!

You may need to unblock this service from the Windows Firewall in order for it to work. If this is the case, Windows Vista will definitely inform you of this fact.

faxes and usually consist of a company name and fax number. For more information on your fax, including status or when it was sent, right click the fax and select Properties.

Figure 11.13. Configure Fax settings for sending and receiving.

Figure 11.14. The Properties window provides useful information about your fax.

The Additional Settings window also lets you designate where you should print faxes as well as where a copy of the fax should be saved. Incoming faxes are stored in your inbox; however, you may want to store

Inside Scoop

The TSID and CSID fields are limited to 20 characters.

an extra copy in another location for safekeeping or if several people use the computer that receives faxes.

Send a fax

Once you've created an account using the Create Fax Wizard, you're ready to send a fax. However, if you plan on scanning a document and faxing it, you must first install the software for your scanner. You can do this from the Scanners and Cameras section of the Control Panel and then click Add Device. Once you install a scanner, it appears in the Windows Fax and Scan application.

1. To start a new fax, click the New Fax link in the application (see Figure 11.15) or select File, New, and Fax. A window strongly resembling that of an e-mail appears.

Figure 11.15. The e-mail editor-like New Fax window.

2. You can start by first selecting a cover page from one of the four options that appear in the drop-down box. (We discuss how to create or edit a cover page a little later in this chapter.)

3. If you select one of the available cover page templates, a text box called Cover page note appears. Here, you can add a quick note to the cover page of your fax.

4. The next step is to set a recipient. You can either manually enter a phone number or click the To: button (or click Contacts from the toolbar).

If you open up Contacts, please note that this is an address book for Windows Fax and Scan and it has its own interface, yet pulls information from either Windows Contacts or Microsoft Outlook. If you are using Microsoft Outlook, you may have established a dialing rule, which dictates how Windows dials phone numbers depending on your geographical location. You can use the Dialing Rule drop-down menu to either select an existing dialing rule or create a new one. Then you can add a subject line for your fax.

Before you send the fax, it wouldn't hurt to add the fax content. You may just want to send a note, in which case you can use the large text editor field to write your message. This is a basic text editor, but it still allows you to perform functions such as adding bullets, numbered lists, justification, and fonts. Or, perhaps you would like to add a picture or a file to your fax. You can use either the Insert menu or click the appropriate icon from the toolbar.

A new beginning

In Windows XP, Microsoft was roundly criticized for having millions of personalized folders (My Documents, My Music, My Pictures, and so on) but a rather arcane location for faxes.

This problem is now a thing of the past! As Microsoft dropped the adjective "My" from these folders, they also decided to restructure their use. In Windows Vista, faxes are now stored in the Documents folder for a given user in the Fax folder. This makes these documents much easier to find and manage, and they are easily accessible from the Documents folder.

One final step before we send the fax; go to Fax Options in the Tools menu (see Figure 11.16). You can request a delivery receipt or set a priority status for the fax. This window also lets you schedule the fax for delivery depending on the right balance of system resources, cost issues, and urgency of delivery. Click OK when you are done with this page.

To send the fax, click Send, or from the File menu, click Send Message. When you send the fax, it goes straight to the Outbox until it is sent. If you are concerned about the status of your fax, you can open the fax from the Outbox and then click File ⇨ Properties (you can also right-click the fax and select Properties). The current status of the fax is displayed (see Figure 11.17).

Figure 11.16. The Fax Options page lets you set fax receipt options.

Figure 11.17. The File menu Properties window.

You can also opt to send a fax from an application. Using the application necessary to read the file you wish to send, go to File ⇨ Print menu and select Fax from the list of printers. A Windows Fax and Scan new fax message opens up with the file as an attachment. You can then perform the steps listed above.

Receive and review faxes

If you have configured the fax service for manual answer, when the modem detects an incoming call, it will pop up to a notification asking if you want to answer the call as a fax call. Click the notification to "pick up" the fax. Windows Vista will then process the incoming fax. If you have configured the automatic answering, your incoming fax will be received without any further action on your part.

In each case, when the fax is complete, another notification appears showing you the sender's TSID (similar to caller ID). Click that notification to open Windows Fax and Scan. You can also open Windows Fax and Scan at any time by clicking Windows Fax and Scan from the Start menu.

If you read *The Unofficial Guide to Windows XP,* you may recall that we discussed the Fax Console extensively in Chapter 11. As you may have guessed, the Fax Console is replaced in Windows Vista by the Windows Fax and Scan application. You can still perform the tasks previously handled by the Fax Console, including viewing received, sent, incoming, and queued faxes with the Windows Fax and Scan application.

Create new fax cover pages

When you get a look at the four default cover pages provided by Windows Vista, you may want to create some new ones. However, like the Fax Console, the Fax Cover Page Editor that you may remember from Windows XP is no more, at least as a standalone application. Its functions are aptly handled by the Windows Fax and Scan application.

The good news is that this feature is found in Cover Pages of the Tools menu. The bad news is that you still cannot import personal cover pages, even if they are created in another Microsoft application!

To create a new fax cover page:

1. Open Windows Fax and Scan, go to the Tools menu, and select Cover Pages. The Fax Cover Pages window appears (see Figure 11.18).

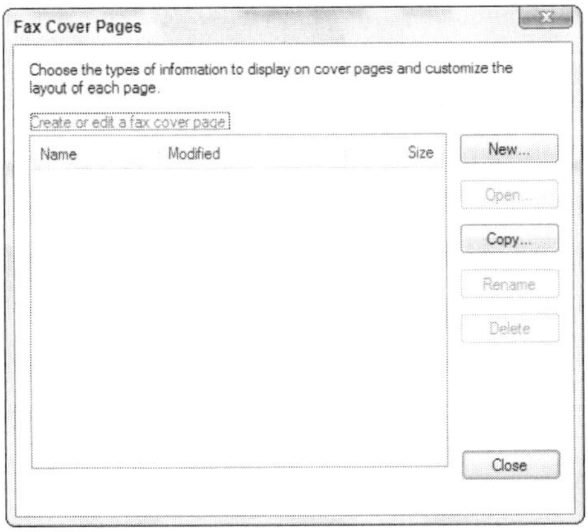

Figure 11.18. The Fax Cover Pages window.

2. Click New. The Fax Cover Page Editor appears.

3. Create your personalized fax cover pages in the text editor.

4. Save your cover page. By default, fax cover pages are saved in the user's Documents folder in the Fax subfolder called Personal Coverpages.

5. The new cover page appears in the Fax Cover Pages window. If you want to edit it, click Open.

6. Click Close when finished.

The next time you send a fax, the new cover page will appear in the drop-down menu. It has the label (Personal) after its name so that you don't mistake it for one of Microsoft's default cover pages (see Figure 11.19).

When creating a cover page, be sure to include important information, such as your name, address, telephone number, and fax number. Technology isn't perfect, and if your fax doesn't go completely through, it's important for the recipient to know how to get a hold of you. You can facilitate this task by entering the correct information in the supplied fields in the Fax Cover Page Editor (see Figure 11.19).

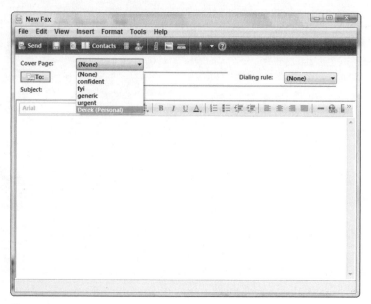

Figure 11.19. Your new cover page appears with the default cover pages.

Install and configure a Web server

Web servers are the workhorses of the Internet. They are the first point of contact between people and information of all kinds. Web servers can be portals to Web applications, database front ends, message boards, e-commerce sites, or just a list of personal pictures and links that you find interesting. Behind the scenes, Web servers are doing all the heavy lifting.

Though Windows Vista is a desktop operating system, you can run Microsoft's Internet Information Server (IIS) on it, which is Windows's Internet-based service for Web servers. Normally, you wouldn't want to run industrial-strength services on a desktop for two reasons. First, desktop hardware isn't designed for server loads and requirements; and second, your desktop applications introduce potential stability and security holes that would keep the server from running smoothly. But running a server can be handy, especially if you are developing a prototype Web site and want to see how it works before you deploy it on the actual Web server.

With those limitations in mind, Microsoft built in two significant restrictions to the desktop version IIS: You can have only ten concurrent connections, and you can have only one Web site running on your server. These limitations shouldn't be a problem; when you create a prototype you are designing the look and feel, or testing basic Web site functionality, and not testing capacity or server stability.

If you intend to run IIS on your desktop and make it a public Web site, you must do the following:

- Assign a static IP address to your computer. This allows others to use DNS to locate your new Web site. You may need to contact your ISP and change your account from dynamic to static addressing in order to do this.

- Convert any FAT driver partitions that will hold your Web files to NTFS. This shouldn't be an issue, since you shouldn't be running FAT32 on Vista anyway!

- Obtain a domain name, and have it point to your static IP address. Your ISP can usually handle the necessary paperwork and get you set up with this.

- Make sure your firewall allows inbound HTTP requests. This may involve creating an addition to its routing table so that HTTP requests are routed directly to your machine.

- Invest in, install, and use antivirus software.

- Prepare to be connected all the time. You don't need to invest in an uninterrupted power supply (UPS), but you will need to leave your computer on so that the public can find your Web server.

- Buy a good book on securing and running a Web server. Read it. Enjoy it. Work with your Web server prior to making it accessible to the public. You'll be glad you did!

Installing IIS, however, isn't as easy. Often, it seems that Microsoft really isn't interested in making life easier on users. One such example is their bad habit of hiding "big boy" components, such as IIS, from us mere mortals. One would expect that IIS would come installed out-of-the-box when you are running Windows Vista Ultimate. No such luck. In fact, you have to go on a wild goose chase just to find it.

Watch Out!

Want to be unemployed? Try installing a Web server on your work machine without first asking permission from the IT department. If you are a business employee, do not attempt to replicate this section on a work machine without explicit permission from your IT department.

In any case, here's how to install IIS on Windows Vista:

1. Open the Control Panel from the Start menu.

2. Open the Programs page.

3. Under Installed Programs, click Turn on or off Windows features.

4. Click Continue to authorize this request. The Windows Features window appears (see Figure 11.20).

5. Click the boxes for Internet Information Services, especially the Web Management Tools and World Wide Web Services.

6. Click OK to validate.

Figure 11.20. Setting up IIS 7.0.

Once Windows Vista installs the components, you're good to go. One nice aspect here is that you do not need to reboot your computer nor do you need to track down your installation DVD to install components not included with the initial installation.

A basic Web site is now running on your computer. Open Internet Explorer. In IE's address bar, type **localhost** and then press Enter.

A graphic that says "IIS 7" and "Welcome" in a wide variety of languages appears. You can manage your Web site using the IIS Manager, which is best accessible from the Start menu by typing **IIS Manager.**

The IIS Manager in Windows Vista looks considerably different than any previous version. This version is much cleaner and makes better use of screen real estate. This is the central point of your IIS served Web site. You can start by renaming the default Web site. In the typical Windows style, you can right-click the Default Web Site icon and select Rename.

Click the Basic Properties link under the Edit Site panel under Tasks of the IIS Manager. This is where you point to where your Web site's files will be kept on a hard drive. The default is set up on the same driver where Windows is installed, usually C:\inetpub\wwwroot, and you may want to change this to another partition or hard drive for security and ease-of-backup reasons. When you are done, click OK to close the dialog box and return to the IIS manager (see Figure 11.21).

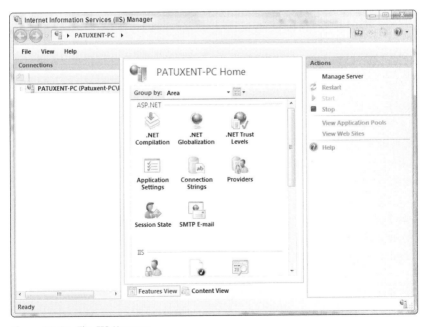

Figure 11.21. The IIS Manager.

When you return to the IIS Manager, you can view a file listing of what files are on your Web server. The files and folders that make up your Web site are listed in the left pane, under your Web site's name. You cannot edit them from this window, but you can delete them if they are no longer needed.

As a Web server administrator (doesn't that sound important!), you may need to pause, stop, or restart your Web site. For example, if you are updating files, you don't want anyone attempting to connect to a page when the contents are changing midstream. Select your Web site and then click one of the appropriate buttons in the Manage Site panel under Tasks. This is persistent over reboots — if your IIS service is paused and you reboot, your Web site service will still be paused when the server comes up.

Keep in mind that pausing your Web site only stops the server from serving; it doesn't stop IIS itself. If you need to stop the server completely, type **services.msc** in the Start menu search box and then press Enter. Scroll down the list for World Wide Web Publishing (see Figure 11.22) and then click the appropriate button in the toolbar. This setting is also persistent over reboots.

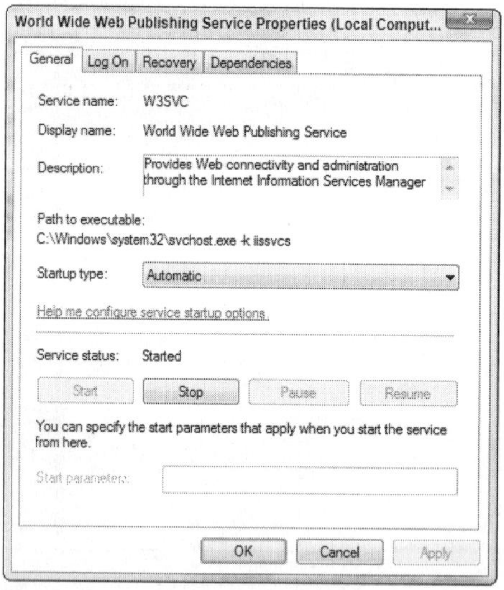

Figure 11.22. Start, stop, or pause your Web server.

Using Remote Desktop

Remote Desktop is a fantastic tool that allows you to view and control another computer's entire desktop and have access to all its programs, much as if you were sitting in front of its screen and keyboard. It is similar to commercial programs like Symantec's PCAnywhere or Laplink Software's Laplink Gold. You can run applications, work with files, print to printers, or do most anything to the remote PC. You don't have to be running Windows Vista on the remote computers; Windows Vista comes with client software that you can install on most recent versions of Windows. You should be able to use this on any computer running a supported Windows operating system.

The benefits of Remote Desktop multiply the more you use it. You can use it to access your office computer when you are on the road, or when you are at home and need to retrieve a report that was e-mailed to your work address. You can also use Remote Desktop as a help-desk tool. If people keep asking you to figure out what's wrong with their computer, you can connect to their desktop and work with it without leaving your own desk.

One good feature of Remote Desktop is that it is not enabled by default, and you must specifically add the names of people who will be allowed access. Otherwise it would be a gaping security hole, and even Microsoft thinks that giving anyone remote access to your computer isn't the best idea.

To use Remote Desktop, you first set up the remote computer so that you can connect to it remotely. Log on as a user with administrator privileges on the computer.

1. Right-click Computer from the Start menu and select Properties.

2. Click the Remote Settings link. The Remote tab of the System Properties appears (see Figure 11.23).

3. Click Select Users and then click Add in the Remote Desktop Users window.

4. In the Select Users window that appears, type in the domain and name for people you want to give access to the computer; click Examples to see the different ways you can grant access to people or computers.

5. Click Check Names to verify the names you've added.

Figure 11.23. The Remote tab for setting up Remote Desktop.

6. When you're done, click OK three times to return to the Windows desktop. You also need Terminal Services running.

7. Type services.msc in the Start menu search box; scroll down to Terminal Services and make sure it is set to Automatic (see Figure 11.24). If it is not, double-click it and change its setting; make sure that it is running. If it is, click Start and then click OK.

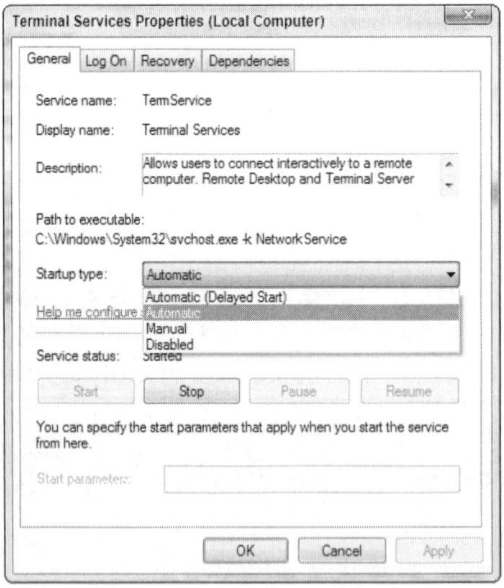

Figure 11.24. The Terminal Services entry in the Services window.

To connect to the remote computer:

1. Log on to your Windows Vista computer and select Remote Desktop Connection from the Accessories menu in the Start menu.

2. Click the Options button (see Figure 11.25) and the full set of available options for connecting to a remote desktop appears.

3. Select the remote computer name from the drop-down list box. Type the username and password for the account to which you granted permission on the remote computer.

4. If you are a member of a domain, enter the domain so the log on credentials can be verified. You can click any of the other tabs and adjust settings for your remote session, such as connection speed, desktop size, and various desktop effects.

5. Click Connect. The remote desktop appears.

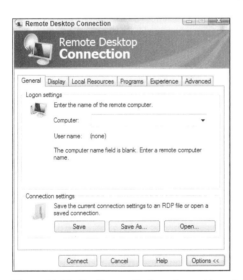

Figure 11.25. The Remote Desktop Connection window.

You can copy and paste information between the remote session and your local computer; or it both desktops are visible at the same time, you can drag and drop documents between them. To end the session, you can either click the Close button on the remote session's tab, or click Start and then Disconnect.

Inside Scoop

If you can't connect to a computer, your firewall is probably blocking inbound requests. Remote Desktop listens on port 3389, so you may need to explicitly open that port to allow incoming requests.

Note that if someone is connected to the computer when you attempt to log on, they will be notified that you are connecting and they will be logged off. If Fast User Switching is turned off, they won't even get a message, they'll be disconnected automatically.

Turnabout, as they say, is fair play. If you are logged on remotely and someone else logs on to the remote computer, you will be disconnected. So while Windows Vista claims to be a full-feature multiuser system, it doesn't allow two people to have an active session at the same time.

Using Remote Assistance

Remote Assistance is a specialized version of Remote Desktop. It uses the Terminal Services capability, but it does not allow you to automatically log on, even if you have an account on the machine. Instead, an invitation is sent out from one user, asking another user to connect to the machine. Both handle access through their respective firewalls.

To request help using Remote Assistance (see Figure 11.26), the most effective way is to type **Remote Assistance** in the Start menu Search box. You can also use the Remote tab in the computer Properties. If you want, you can set limits on how long the invitation is valid and whether the remote computer can control your desktop. For example, you may be more comfortable with another person viewing your desktop while they talk you through a troubleshooting session over the phone, rather than lose control of your computer.

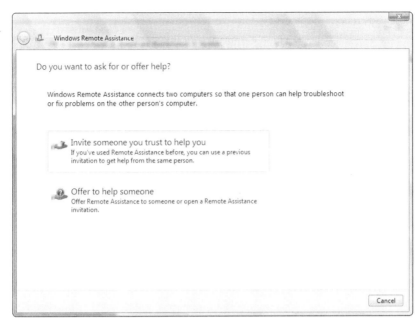

Figure 11.26. The Remote Assistance Wizard.

Click the Advanced button, and you can set either of these parameters for your remote session (see Figure 11.27). Click OK twice. To send a request, follow these steps:

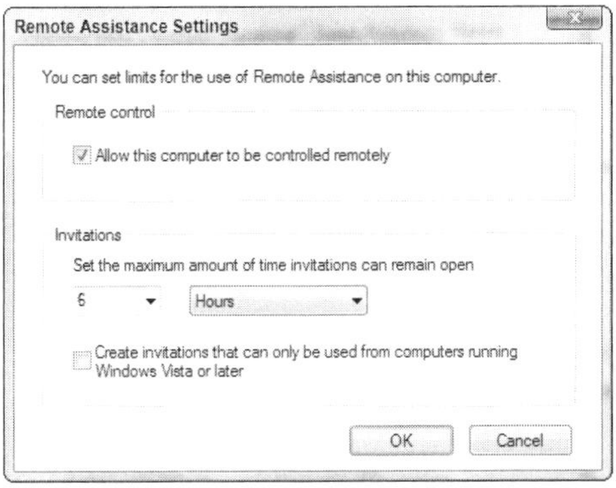

Figure 11.27. Remote Assistance Settings lets you determine how your computer handles invitaions and remote controls.

1. Choose Start ⇨ Help and Support.

2. Click the Remote Assistance link under Ask someone (see Figure 11.28).

3. Click Invite someone you trust to help you. You can use e-mail to send the invitation or save the invitation as a file.

4. If you select the e-mail option, type a password for the session and then type it a second time for validation.

5. Windows Vista opens your default e-mail editor. If you don't have one, Microsoft Mail is used.

6. Send the e-mail to the person you want to help you fix your problem.

Figure 11.28. The Help and Support Center.

Your friend receives this e-mail with an encoded attachment. He or she must follow the instructions contained in the attachment in order to help you. Don't worry; the other person doesn't automatically have control of your computer when he or she connects, even if you have granted remote control privileges. The remote helper must click the Take Control button on his screen, and then you must give explicit permission for him to share control. When this happens, you both can use the mouse and keyboard to control your computer; for this reason, you shouldn't use your mouse or keyboard at the same time. Use Windows Messenger or talk by phone to coordinate desktop actions.

At any time, if you get nervous about the way your remote session is going, or if you'd rather not share your desktop, press the Esc key, and the remote control is terminated. The other person can still see your desktop but must ask permission again to regain shared control.

If you're the person who is being asked for help and you receive an e-mail request for assistance, open the attached file to initiate the session.

Sync Center

Windows Vista now includes the Sync Center, which is a central location for synchronizing your devices with your computer. To access it, simply type Sync Center in the Start menu Search box; you can also find it from the Start menu Accessories menu.

The first thing you must do when you use Sync Center for the first time is to set up a partnership between your computer and your device. To do that:

1. Launch the Sync Centers.

2. Click Set up new sync partnerships, which appears in the Tasks pane of the window.

3. Click the desired device.

4. Click Set up.

Windows Vista syncs your device with your computer. You can view any existing partnerships, sync conflicts, and sync results from the Tasks menu in the Sync Center window (see Figure 11.29).

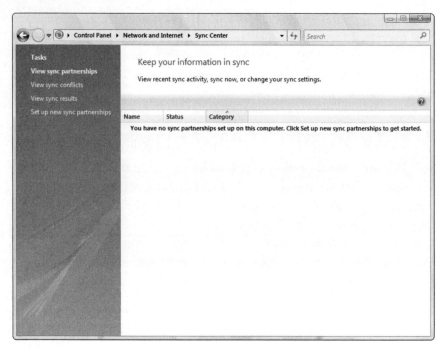

Figure 11.29. The Sync Center.

Just the facts

- Your printers can be set up with different settings to handle different print jobs.

- The Windows Fax and Scan application is one of the least talked about, and most useful, capabilities of Windows Vista, especially if you use a laptop.

- You can run a Web server on Windows Vista, though it's recommended more for internal development than for use as a public server.

- The Remote Desktop ability lets you connect with work PCs from home or vice versa.

- Remote Assistance is an easy way to help others fix desktop problems or to have others help you.

GET THE SCOOP ON...

Windows domains ▪ Working with objects ▪ Working with domains ▪ Using logon scripts ▪ Using IntelliMirror ▪ Searching for users and printers

Integrating with Active Directory

Chapter 12

This chapter introduces the Active Directory, which is an essential part of Windows server technology. You'll find that the Active Directory has less to do with Windows Vista than it does with Windows 2000 or 2003 Server products. The Active Directory is a central point for manageability, security, and interoperability.

Part of this manageability is the IntelliMirror feature; using this feature in either Windows Vista or Windows 2000/2003, administrators can intelligently manage user accounts and profiles, both of which are controlled by the Active Directory.

Set up a Windows domain

Understanding exactly what a domain is before trying to work with the Active Directory is important. A domain is essentially a group of machines that share a similar group of user accounts and security policies through a common database. The database for this domain is stored in what is called the Active Directory. Though the domain must follow certain common rules and procedures, it still has a unique name. Following this logic, an Active Directory is a group of computers that has been defined by the administrator of the Windows network. In Windows Vista, the Active Directory is managed using the Microsoft Management Console.

Watch Out!

The majority of this chapter deals with concepts and features that are only available in Windows 2000 or 2003 and can be used in conjunction with Windows Vista. If you do not use Windows 2000/2003, this chapter might not be for you.

Windows domains are set up using Windows 2000 or 2003 Server. This is not possible in Windows Vista because Windows Vista cannot be a domain controller; however, you can work with domains — for example, you can join a domain — in Windows Vista. The Active Directory is only available in domains containing Windows 2000 or 2003 domain controllers.

For more information on setting up a Windows domain, check out Microsoft's Windows 2003 Web site at www.microsoft.com/windowsserver2003/default.mspx.

About Active Directory Objects

The Active Directory is a database of object information; it lists every resource included in it — users, domains, or printers, for example. In basic Windows parlance, the term "objects" refers to users, computers, or groups. In Active Directory, these objects are controlled by a schema, or set of rules. The Active Directory generates a portion of the necessary values, or attributes, upon creation of an object. For example, if you are creating a user in the Microsoft Management Console (MMC), the Active Directory creates the globally unique identifier, or GUID, but it is up to the administrator to give a name to the user. These values, or attributes, will change depending on the nature of the object in the Active Directory; values are required to fill your object with data.

To create a user, for example, do the following:

1. Choose Control Panel ⇨ System and Maintenance ⇨ Administrative Tools ⇨ Computer Management. The Microsoft Management Console opens.

2. Under System Tools, expand Local Users and Groups, and then right-click Users.

3. Select New User from the menu that appears; the New User dialog box appears (see Figure 12.1), and you can enter the requested information to add a new user.

To work with these objects, such as the user created previously or any other resource, you need to use the Active Directory Users and Computers tool in Windows 2000 or 2003. This tool is for Domain or Enterprise administrators to handle standard object tasks, such as creating new objects or changing properties. Administrators can also apply policy templates to these objects. (A Domain or Enterprise administrator is the system-wide administrator who has full control over the Active Directory configuration — your company may use a different name for this administrator.)

Figure 12.1. The New User dialog box.

For more information on using the Active Directory Users and Computers tool or on defining Active Directory objects, please refer to Windows 2000 or Windows 2003 documentation.

Active Directory permissions and rights

Again, the Active Directory is simply a database. You can store any information you want in the Active Directory; some companies, for example, choose to store information such as positions and salaries within their Active Directory, and understandably they want to limit who is entitled to see this information. Even if your organization's Active Directory is only used to store basic information such as names, addresses, and phone numbers, company policy will probably still be to restrict who can edit it. Allowing users to update their own information, for instance when they move to a new office, is likely to be acceptable; giving the CEO a humorous new job title is probably not! That's where permissions come in.

Although setting and changing permissions for objects in the Active Directory is the work of an administrator, it may still be useful for you to gain a general understanding of how they work. In particular, you should be aware of four basic concepts that make up the Windows access-control model:

- **Security principal.** Any object in the Active Directory that can be assigned privileges and access control rights or permissions, including Computers, Services, Users, and Groups.

- **Security context.** The list of group memberships and the privileges and security identifier (SID) of the security principal that is attempting to access an object.

- **Security descriptor.** The security settings for any given object, including a Discretionary Access Control List (DACL), which indicates which users and groups have been explicitly granted or denied access to the object; an SID to identify the owner of the object; and a System Access Control List (SACL), which specifies the types of actions carried out on an object that will result in the generation of a log entry. Security descriptors can be inherited from the parent container, specified in the definition of the object, programmatically created and attached to the object at the time of creation, or replaced during the execution of some program.

- **Access check.** A security principal can only access an object if the security descriptor grants the rights requested. An access check is performed to confirm that this is the case.

Know your rights

There are two types of rights: permissions, which authorize you to carry out an action that affects a specific object (such as reading the object, or resetting a password), and privileges or user rights, which authorize you to carry out an action that affects an entire computer (such as logging on or adding users).

Configure Windows Vista to join a domain

On any network, computers can be part of a workgroup or a domain. Windows Vista is designed to work with both domains and workgroups. The difference between the two concerns mainly how network resources are managed; generally speaking, computers on home networks tend to be part of a workgroup, while computers on networks in companies are typically part of a domain.

In a workgroup:

- All computers are peers, and no computer has control over another. In other words, there is no server.

- Each computer has its own set of user accounts. To use any of the computers in the workgroup, you need to have an account on that specific machine.

- The number of computers in the workgroup tends to be quite small, generally no more than 10 to 20 machines.

In a domain, on the other hand:

- One or more computers on the network are servers. Servers control security and permissions across the entire domain, making it easy for administrators to make changes because these are automatically applied to all the computers across the domain.

- User accounts are centrally controlled, so you can log on to any computer in the domain without needing to have an account on that specific computer.

- Domains can include hundreds or even thousands of computers.

You can configure your machine to join a domain if you are running Windows Vista Business Edition, Windows Vista Enterprise Edition, or Windows Vista Ultimate. Otherwise, you are restricted to joining a workgroup only.

To join a domain, do the following:

1. Choose Control Panel ⇨ System and Maintenance ⇨ System. A summary page appears on which you can view basic information about your computer.

2. Click Change settings to open the System Properties dialog box, with the Computer Name tab selected (see Figure 12.2).

Hack

A quick way of accessing the System Properties window is to press the Windows logo key plus the Break key.

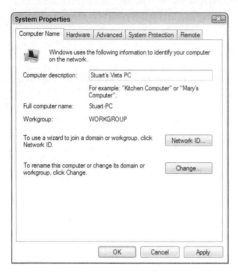

Figure 12.2. The System Properties dialog box.

If a name hasn't already been selected, add a name for your machine and validate your choice using the Apply button. Having a name is important for finding your machine on the network. Your company may have special rules for naming computers, or you may be free to choose whatever name you like.

Depending on whether or not you have TCP/IP installed, your desired computer name can be up to 63 characters long. If your machine does not have TCP/IP installed, you are limited to a paltry 15 characters. Note that if you are using Windows 2000 domain controllers, the administrator will need to allow longer names in the Active Directory domain account (for names over 15 characters).

If you want to change the name of your machine, simply click the Change button in the System Properties dialog box (see Figure 12.2) and keep the previously mentioned rules concerning the length of your name in mind. The Computer Name/Domain Changes dialog box appears (see Figure 12.3); this is also how you will join a domain. Before you attempt to join a domain, make sure you have everything you need — the sidebar a little later in the chapter will help you make sure.

Figure 12.3. The Computer Name/Domain Changes dialog box.

Once you enter the name of the domain at the bottom of the Computer Name/Domain Changes dialog box (in the Member of area — see Figure 12.3), one of two situations will occur: If everything mentioned in the following sidebar is present and functioning, a logon/password dialog box appears asking you to enter your details. (You can use any valid username here; however, it's best to choose a user who has administrator rights on the machine.) On the other hand, if there's a problem, a dialog box appears indicating the issue and providing a more detailed explanation of the problem and suggestions of how best to resolve it (see Figure 12.4).

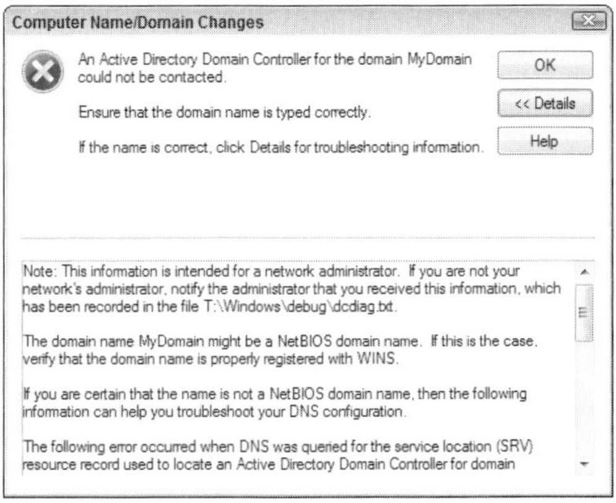

Figure 12.4. The error message with detailed description.

Get the gear

Before you attempt to join a domain, you should make sure your machine has all the necessary hardware and other bits and pieces to make this a success. If you are using an office machine, odds are that your system administrator has already taken care of this for you.

If you are the administrator, this information will seem second nature to you; if you are a home user (or even a guru who may be a little rusty), this quick crash course or refresher will help you through a relatively easy procedure.

If you are going to join a domain, you are going to need to have a network card (or at least wireless network capabilities), a working IP address (get it from a DHCP server or your system administrator), a LAN connection, a fully working DNS server, a permanent connection to the domain controller, and local admin rights. Also, knowing the domain name and the proper logon and password will help you achieve this goal.

Most of these things cannot be bought at your local electronics store; however, these are all basic components of a properly functioning server. If you are a regular user and have any questions, be sure to contact your system administrator.

If you click the More button in the Computer Name/Domain Changes dialog box (see Figure 12.3), the DNS Suffix and NetBIOS Computer Name window appears. There is no need to manually enter a Primary DNS suffix. Simply leave it blank; it will automatically be set to the DNS suffix of the domain.

Use the Network ID feature

Perhaps you are new to networking and worried about entering the wrong thing and dooming your machine for eternity. That's understandable — and the Network Identification Wizard is here to help you!

In the Computer Name tab of the System Properties window (see Figure 12.2), the Network ID button (just above the Change button) allows you to join a domain and create a local account. Click this button, and the wizard begins.

The Network ID Wizard (see Figure 12.5) starts by asking you a simple question: Is the machine part of a business network used to connect to other computers at work, or is it a home-based computer and not part of any business network? If you select the latter option, the response is swift: Click Finish to complete the procedure and the machine will restart. Why? This is because your computer has already been configured as a workgroup with a default name of WORKGROUP.

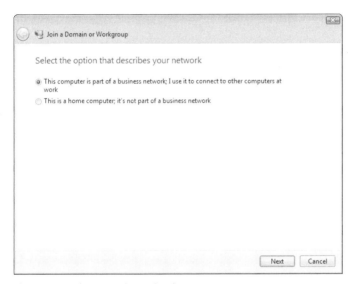

Figure 12.5. The Network ID Wizard.

On the other hand, if you selected the former option, you aren't getting off so lightly. The wizard then wants to know what kind of network you are connecting to, and specifically whether your network uses a domain. If you select "without a domain," the wizard tells you that you will be assigned to a workgroup and not a domain. The wizard will now let you select the name of your workgroup (though it is still WORK-GROUP by default, as shown in Figure 12.6). You will then need to click Next and then Finish and restart your machine.

If you told the wizard that you are indeed using a domain, the next screen will provide a list of necessary information before you can connect to a Windows network. The next screen solicits user account and domain information. This is where you finally enter your username, password, and the domain. The wizard then looks for your computer on the domain. If it cannot find it, it asks you for your computer name and domain again.

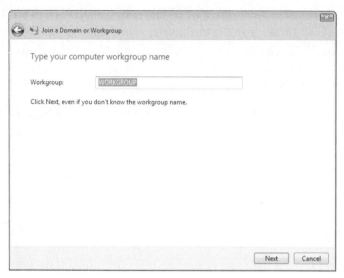

Figure 12.6. The Network ID Wizard Workgroup window.

Find the name of your domain

If your company or organization manages its network using Active Directory domains, you may need to check which domain your computer belongs to so you can access other computers and other network resources.

To do so, click the Start button, and then click Control Panel ⇨ System and Maintenance ⇨ System.

- If your computer is connected to a domain, you will see the name of the domain it is connected to under Computer Name, Domain, and Workgroup Settings.

- If your computer is connected to a workgroup, you will see the name of the workgroup it is connected to instead.

Create and deploy logon scripts

Logon scripts are locally stored scripts that tell Windows Vista what to do when starting up. These scripts can contain any valid command-line instruction. Usually in the form of a batch file, logon scripts can be

Watch Out!

Don't be fooled! Logon scripts can also be executable files or procedures (like VBScript or Java). They can also be command (.cmd) files.

added to user accounts and run automatically each time the user logs on to Windows Vista. Like many other features discussed in this chapter, this only applies to the domain-based versions of Windows Vista (Business Edition, Enterprise Edition, and Ultimate).

Write logon scripts

Writing logon scripts is similar to writing a regular program, though obviously not as involved.

Using a standard text editor (even a simple tool like Notepad will do), simply write out the valid instruction or command, and then save your file. You can name the file whatever you like; just remember to give it a .bat extension and to save it in the appropriate location (the \System32\ Repl\Import\Scripts folder). Note that this location is not created when Windows Vista is installed; you will have to create it yourself in the System32 directory.

Set logon scripts for a user

To set logon scripts for a user, you must access the Computer Management MMC. To do this, click Control Panel ⇨ System and Maintenance ⇨ Administrative Tools. The Computer Management MMC is accessible by double-clicking it in the Administrative Tools menu.

In the Computer Management MMC, you can click the Users subfolder in the Local Users and Groups folder to view the available users on your machine (see Figure 12.7). You must be the administrator or belong to the administrators group to do this.

By right-clicking the desired user account and selecting Properties, you can quickly assign a logon script to a user. In the Profile tab, simply add the name of your logon script (see Figure 12.8). Be aware that the name of the script may change; if you are not the administrator yourself, contact your administrator if you do not know the name of the script.

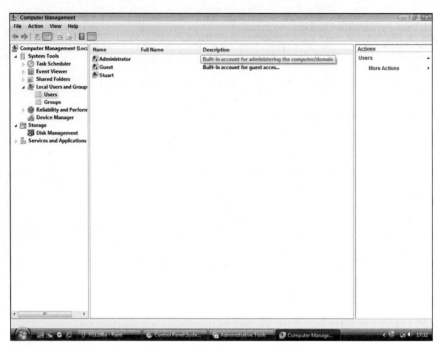

Figure 12.7. The list of users in the Computer Management MMC.

Figure 12.8. The Profile tab.

Once you have assigned your script, validate it by clicking OK. The logon script will be run when the user logs on to the machine locally, but not on the domain.

But hang on! We haven't quite finished with the logon script just yet. These scripts are stored in the \System32\Repl\Import\Scripts folder, which must now be shared. To share this folder, do the following:

1. Right-click the folder and select Share or Properties from the menu that appears.

2. Select the Sharing tab in the folder's Properties dialog box (see Figure 12.9).

3. Click the Advanced Sharing button. The Advanced Sharing dialog box appears (see Figure 12.10).

4. Check the Share this folder check box and enter **netlogon** as the Share name.

5. Click OK when you are finished.

Figure 12.9. Sharing a folder in the folder's Properties dialog box.

Watch Out!

You can share and apply "netlogon" to any folder that is accessible during logon. However, it must be applied before any logon script will work.

Figure 12.10. Sharing a folder in the Advanced Sharing dialog box.

Install programs using IntelliMirror

Back when Windows 2000 was released, Microsoft added IntelliMirror as a management system that was designed to lower the cost of desktop environment management and to increase productivity. This system is also available for Windows Vista.

IntelliMirror's benefits are basically divided into three different categories, each of which can be used independently or in combination: User Data Management, User Settings Management, and Software Installation and Maintenance.

It's the latter feature that interests us in this section. Software Installation and Maintenance handles basic tasks associated with installation: installing, repairing, configuring, updating, and removing the software from your machine.

What makes this unique is that instead of handling a single user installation or repair, IntelliMirror works in terms of groups of users and computers. It's essentially the Group Policy settings on a desktop level; IntelliMirror might dictate what software is available to a given user account regardless of what machine the user is logged onto. In a similar fashion, you might want to determine how applications are repaired and updated — for example, either by user or by computer. Using IntelliMirror, there are two types of applications: assigned applications and published applications.

If you are an administrator, consult your Windows 2000 or 2003 documentation for full details of how to configure IntelliMirror to assign and publish applications.

Use assigned applications

An assigned application is similar to those Windows update alert messages. How so? Let's say that the head of a documentation department in a large software company decides that her technical writers should all use Microsoft Word on their machines.

The manager will work with the administrator to make the application an assigned application. From now on, when any of the 15 technical writers logs on, he or she will find a Microsoft Word icon, perhaps named "Install me," in the Start Menu. The writer then has two choices: Click the icon and install the application, or disregard the file and delete it.

There's no point in a technical writer trying to be clever. If his manager or administrator wants Word installed, Word will be installed because it is an assigned application. Every time the writer logs on to his account, the icon will continue to appear until he gives in and installs the software. In other words, you can run but you can't hide — this is not an optional installation. An alternate installation method is for the writer to open an associated file (a Word document in this case), and the software will install prior to opening the file. In the event that the technical writer decides to delete the assigned application from his machine, the application is removed; however, it is replaced with the original icon on the desktop inviting him to re-install the application.

Use published applications

Published applications are slightly more "democratic" than their assigned counterparts. Unlike the former, which are required, one-click installations, published applications are installed voluntarily. The application is simply available to those following the Group Policy object; it is not actually installed, simply made available.

Inside Scoop

Our technical writer friend needn't worry about disk space; the icon on his desktop installs the bare minimum of files on his machine at this point. It's essentially an icon and file associations for the registry.

For example, suppose the same documentation manager thought it would be useful for the team to use Microsoft Digital Image. The next time a technical writer logs on to his account, he will notice that this software application is available for installation. If the team member doesn't install it, either because he didn't want it, or because he didn't notice it, he can ignore it or he can install the software by clicking a file associated with the software. The primary difference between assigned and published applications is that everyone must install assigned applications — a published application, on the other hand, is made available to specific users without any mandatory requirement to install it.

Search for users or printers

Windows Vista now comes with a special tool for searching the Active Directory, which can be useful if you need to connect to another computer or print to a network printer.

Before we look at how the Active Directory search tool works, it's worth remembering that the tool is like many things in life; what you get out is directly related to what you put in. This is because, when your administrator creates objects in the Active Directory, he usually has the opportunity to enter information describing many of the object's attributes. In the case of a user object, for instance, he must enter all the standard information such as username and password, but he also has the option of adding extra information such as address and phone number. The extent to which your administrator is conscientious in completing this information when she creates the object, and keeping it current, will determine how effective the search tool actually is.

To access the Active Directory search tool, do the following:

1. Click Control Panel ⇨ Network and Internet ⇨ Network and Sharing Center ⇨ View computers and devices. You will then see a page displaying all the computers in your domain.

2. Click the Search Active Directory button at the top of the window to launch the Active Directory search tool.

You can run a simple search query on the Active Directory from the search screen simply by entering a name or a description for the object you are searching for.

If you want specify the type of object you are looking for, click the Find drop-down list at the top of the window. By default, this is set to enable you to search for users, contacts, and groups, but you also have the choice of searching for computers, printers, shared folders, or performing custom searches.

To the right of the Find drop-down list, you can see that, by default, the tool is configured to search the entire Active Directory. Clicking the In drop-down list allows you to speed up the time it takes for your results to be returned by restricting your search to an individual domain.

Configure the Global Catalog

The Global Catalog is primarily a Windows 2000/2003 concern, but it does affect the Active Directory. It is essentially a domain controller with a replica of all the objects in the Active Directory; however, it only stores a few features of each object. The features "kept" in these replicas are features that are most likely to be used in a search and those needed to find a complete clone of the Active Directory object.

The Global Catalog is generated automatically based on a base model created by Microsoft. Obviously, this type of feature is only accessible to administrators, so it's not surprising that they can modify or add properties based on their requirements.

For information on configuring the global catalog on your Windows 2000/2003 server, please consult the Microsoft documentation.

Watch Out!

Don't overload your system with Global Catalogs because they can consume a great deal of system resources. One per domain per machine should be ample.

Just the facts

- The Windows Active Directory is primarily a Windows 2000 or 2003 feature; however, its influence and use extends to Microsoft Windows Vista's domain-based editions as well.

- The Microsoft Management Console (MMC) is a tool designed to help manage the Active Directory and its objects.

- Administrators can use logon scripts to configure your environment or influence your environment without having to get too close.

- IntelliMirror is a great feature of the Active Directory that allows administrators to assign or publish software for members of your team.

- Use the Active Directory search tool to look up computers, printers, or network users.

Manage the Hardware Environment

PART IV

GET THE SCOOP ON...
Using System Information and Device Manager to
manage your computer ▪ Using Task Manager ▪
Reviewing system errors ▪ Troubleshooting problems
and performance issues

Working with Windows Internals

Chapter 13

There is an inverse relationship between how easy technology is to use and the underlying complexity that makes it work. The telephone system is one example; everyone knows how to use a phone, but just try to explain call switching, inter-carrier exchanges, or even the billing system to someone.

Windows is no different; it is much easier to use Windows Vista than DOS or even earlier versions of Windows, but the underlying technology is exponentially more complex.

This chapter gives you a glimpse into the workings of Windows Vista, providing information on the services and components that make everything happen, and describing some of the many tools you have at your disposal for when things start to go awry.

Display system information

There is a lot going on under the hood of Windows Vista. The operating system has to keep track of all the hardware devices that are added and removed, all the device drivers and what versions to use, and even individual settings for those drivers, which change depending on who is logged on to the computer.

Whereas in older versions of Windows, accessing all of this information used to involve executing a series of tools from the command prompt or digging deep into the menu structure, much of it can now be obtained directly from the Control Panel. But as you may have realized, there often seems to be at least half a dozen ways of doing anything in Windows, so many of the old methods for accessing system information still work if you decide not to use the new Vista-style front end.

To access system information in the Control Panel, click Start ➪ Control Panel ➪ System and Maintenance ➪ System. This displays a page (see Figure 13.1) that summarizes important information about your computer such as basic hardware information, your computer's name, domain and workgroup settings, and which version of Windows your computer is running.

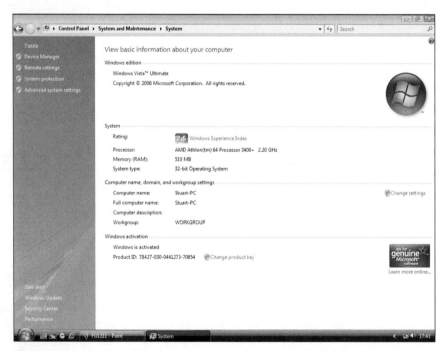

Figure 13.1. In the Control Panel, the System page lets you view basic information about your computer.

The information on this page is grouped under four headings:

- **Windows edition.** Find which version and edition of Windows you have running on your computer. When subsequent service packs are released, information about which service pack you are running will almost certainly be displayed here too.

- **System.** Discover how much random access memory (RAM) is installed, and learn your computer's Windows Experience Index Rating. The Windows Experience Index Rating is a number that describes the overall capability of your computer's hardware configuration — a higher performance rating means your computer will perform better and be more responsive, especially when carrying out resource-intensive tasks. You can also see a breakdown of your rating in Control Panel ⇨ System and Maintenance ⇨ Performance Information and Tools, and you can have Windows Vista help you address any specific performance issues it has identified.

- **Computer name, domain, and workgroup settings.** Find out information about the domain or workgroup to which your computer belongs. You can alter any of this information by clicking Change Settings.

- **Windows activation.** Find out whether your copy of Windows Vista is activated and view the Product ID. After installation, you must activate your copy of Windows within 30 days or certain Windows features will stop working.

The information provided on the summary page in Control Panel is useful but somewhat basic. Should you require more detail, you also have at your disposal the System Information utility, a one-stop center for information on your hardware, software, and some of the registry and domain settings that are affecting your computer. Most of the time this utility will help out people troubleshooting your computer, but it also proves useful for those moments when you need to know which version of modem you have or what version of drivers are being used with it.

Work with the System Information utility

Launch the System Information utility by clicking Start ⇨ All Programs ⇨ Accessories ⇨ Command Prompt, typing **msinfo32**, and then pressing Enter. You can also find it by typing **System Information** in the search box in the Start menu. It may take a few moments for System Information to collect and display the information, since it queries the hardware and software — and there is a lot of it to query.

When the dialog box appears (see Figure 13.2), you can browse through the different categories. These categories include

- **System Summary.** Provides general information about your computer and the operating system, such as the name, model and manufacturer of the computer, the version of BIOS your system is using, the location of the Windows Directory and the System Directory, the locale and time zone, and the amount of memory that is installed and available.

- **Hardware Resources.** Displays information about your computer's hardware that can let you determine if any devices are vying for the same system resource and perhaps causing you trouble, including details of hardware conflicts, and interrupt request (IRQ) and input/output (I/O) settings.

- **Components.** Displays information about the different components installed on your computer, such as disk drives and other storage devices, network adapters, modems, sound devices, and printers.

- **Software Environment.** Displays information about drivers, environment variables, running tasks, network connections, and other details relating to the software running on your computer.

At the bottom of the System Information dialog box is a search function that lets you look for particular system devices or manufacturer names. Type a name and then click Find. You can also specify whether to search the entire System Information database or a subcategory that you have clicked.

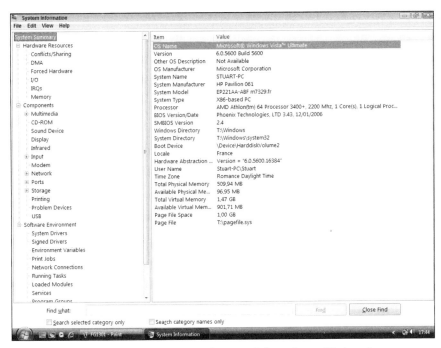

Figure 13.2. The System Information utility has more information on Windows than you may have thought existed.

Gone, but not forgotten

The version of the System Information utility that ships with Windows Vista has been slimmed down from previous versions. The System Restore utility, for example, is now found (as System Restore) in the System Protection tab of the System Properties window or in the Accessories' System Tools menu under the Start menu. The System Restore utility lets you turn back the hands of time and restore your system to its state at an earlier date. This tool is discussed in greater detail in the next chapter.

The File Signature Verification Utility doesn't exist anymore as a utility either; however, Windows Vista does inform you if driver software doesn't have a digital signature or if it has a digital signature that hasn't been checked and verified by a certification authority. You may have noticed Vista's tendency to tell you every little detail that might be wrong! That's not a bad thing, we suppose Microsoft is trying to make up for all the years of lax warning, but it can admittedly become annoying seeing all the pop-up warning messages.

The DirectX Diagnostic tool is still an integral part of Windows Vista, though you may have to exercise your search skills to find it. Like many "smaller" applications and features in Windows Vista, this one isn't found in the Start menu. To access the DirectX Diagnostic Tool, type **dxdiag** in the Start menu Search box. This tool is designed to help you work out any problems with multimedia-related applications. For example, if a game isn't displaying or working properly, or if you are having problems watching a movie, you may want to run the DirectX Diagnostic Tool to make sure everything is running smoothly. You can run tests on audio, video, and online play components of the DirectX component suite. While this tool is helpful for diagnostic and troubleshooting, it may not be the best choice for adjusting settings for enhanced performance. To do that, you may want to adjust hardware settings.

Dr. Watson, on the other hand, is no more. This dinosaur long overstayed its welcome; fortunately, someone in Redmond finally realized this and spread the word. If you need to analyze system issues, such as a crash, you can use the Problem Reports and Solutions tool instead. This replacement helps you troubleshoot both hardware and software issues on your computer. The Problem Reports and Solutions tool is found in the Maintenance menu of the Start menu. You can program a system scan or run it manually when necessary. Any problems detected in Windows Vista are logged by product, date, problem, and solution status.

In the past, we've always felt that Microsoft didn't offer serious troubleshooting or system protection tools. Even with improvements, trust is a big issue. While we might find ourselves using some of these tools, it's also highly likely that we'd use them in conjunction with a third-party application. The only difficult may be finding a third-party application that is tested and supported for Windows Vista.

Working with Device Manager

Device Manager is like a kindergarten teacher with 30 students. Most of the time the students obey the teacher and are well behaved, but when disruption breaks out it affects the whole class. Behind the desktop,

Device Manager is keeping track of all the hardware and device drivers, trying to keep conflicts to a minimum and isolating components that don't quite fit in the scheme of things.

In the days of Windows 95, Device Manager was one of the first stops for conducting any hardware troubleshooting. Older hardware used interrupt request (IRQ) or input/outing (I/O) settings that could only be changed using jumpers. If a conflict with other hardware popped up, users had to open the computer and either move tiny switches or replace pin jumpers — which often meant finding the hardware manual, or calling tech support, or . . . you get the idea.

Hardware and software manufacturers worked together to make hardware that could be changed using software interfaces. Plug and Play, FireWire, and Universal Serial Bus (USB) were all ways to make adding and removing hardware simpler, resulting in fewer conflicts. Today nearly all hardware lets the operating system change its settings so that conflicts are minimized.

However, conflicts do unfortunately still happen. If you constantly add and remove new hardware, you are likely to run into a case where a device isn't working, or another one stops working. This happens when Windows runs out of the assignable resources that are being requested by the new hardware.

To check the status of all your hardware, click Control Panel ➪ System and Maintenance ➪ System. In the left pane of the system information page that opens, click Device Manager to open the Device Manager (see Figure 13.3). If you prefer, you can execute the Device Manager from the Command Prompt by clicking Start ➪ All Programs ➪ Accessories ➪ Command Prompt, then typing **devmgmt.msc**, and then pressing Enter.

A yellow exclamation point next to a device means that there is a configuration problem and the device is not functioning. A red X next to a device means the hardware has been disabled. Right-click the device, and then click Properties. The Device Properties dialog box gives you some information about the device, including error codes if appropriate. You can do a search for the error codes in the Help and Support Center, which often has recommendations on how to resolve the issue.

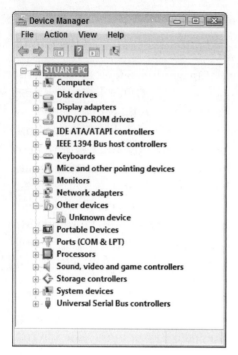

Figure 13.3. Device Manager alerts you to hardware conflicts that should be resolved.

The most common reasons to see a yellow exclamation point are a conflict with another device's resources or a missing driver. Sometimes you have to give Device Manager a little helping hand and pick an IRQ or I/O region that is not in use, and then the device will work. With a missing driver, you sometimes need to point Windows to the proper location for a driver (product CD, download from manufacturer's Web site, or other).

In some cases you may need to either disable some of your infrequently-used hardware (such as an infrared port), create different hardware profiles for laptops, or if you just can't get everything to work together, perform a new installation with all your desired hardware connected to the computer. This will let Windows start over with a clean slate and it will try to assign different combinations of resources so that all your hardware can work together.

Inside Scoop

With any hardware conflicts, it always pays to make a visit to the manufacturer's Web site for the latest device drivers and to check the FAQs and support forums. There may be suggestions for different hardware settings that will avoid conflicts.

The Device Manager also lets you add legacy hardware. This is a nice way of saying "ancient hardware" that is from the pre-Plug and Play days. In the Device Manager, select Add legacy hardware from the Action menu. The Add Hardware Wizard appears, assisting you in your quest to use old hardware on a new computer. The Device Manager can "refresh" itself if you select Scan for hardware changes from the Action menu. It scans the Plug and Play–compliant hardware for changes and refreshes the list of devices.

Use Task Manager

If Device Manager is like a kindergarten teacher, Task Manager is like a traffic cop. It monitors the various processes running on Windows, lets you see which ones are misbehaving, and lets you shut down processes that are not responding or are consuming all of Windows' resources. Open Task Manager by clicking Start ⇨ All Programs ⇨ Accessories ⇨ Command Prompt, typing taskmgr.exe, and then pressing Enter. You can also bring it up by pressing Ctrl+Alt+Delete (once if connected to a workgroup, twice if connected to a domain) and then clicking Task Manager, or from Control Panel by clicking Control Panel ⇨ System and Maintenance ⇨ Performance Rating and Tools ⇨ Advanced Tools ⇨ Open Task Manager, or even by right-clicking the taskbar and selecting it from the context menu that appears. The choice is yours!

One change to the Windows Vista Task Manager is that you are immediately presented with the choice between monitoring your own programs only or all programs running on your computer. After you make your choice, Task Manager opens.

Task Manager has six tabs, and each gives you a different view on Windows.

■ The Applications view shows you user-mode programs that are running on your computer — in other words, programs that you have started and currently have running (see Figure 13.4). From here, you have the option of ending a specific task, switching between programs, or opening a new program, folder, document, or Internet resource by clicking New Task, typing its name, and then clicking OK.

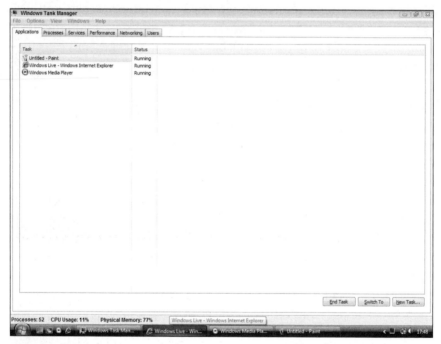

Figure 13.4. The Applications view shows you which programs are currently running on your computer.

■ The Processes view shows you the different processes, both kernel-mode processes being used by the operating system and user-mode processes such as Task Manager itself, that are currently running on

your computer, and what resources are being consumed by these
processes (see Figure 13.5). From this tab, you can also elect to end
certain processes, which can be useful if they are consuming too
many resources and causing your computer to freeze up.

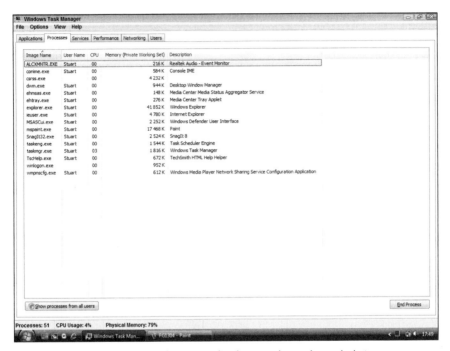

Figure 13.5. The Processes view shows you what is currently running and what resources are
being consumed.

- The Services view (see Figure 13.6) shows you the different services
  on your computer, and whether or not they are currently running.

- The Performance view (see Figure 13.7) displays the work being
  done by your processor (or processors, if you have a dual-processor
  motherboard), RAM, and page file usage.

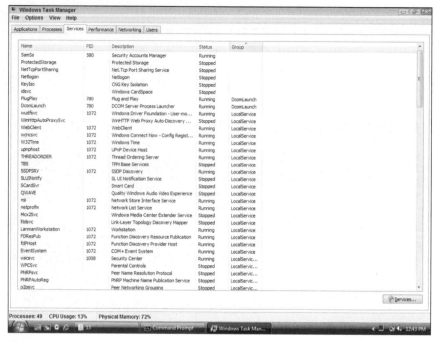

Figure 13.6. The Services view shows you the status of each service on your computer.

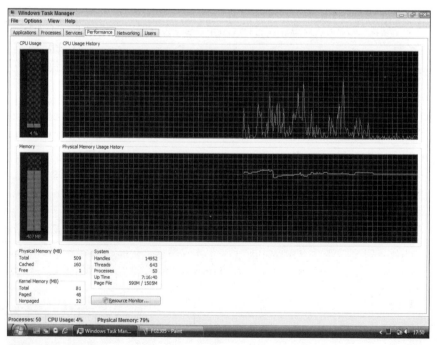

Figure 13.7. Task Manager's Performance view shows you CPU usage, page file usage, and RAM.

- If you have a lot of data moving on and off your computer, the Networking view lets you monitor which adapters are being used, to what extent, and at what speed (see Figure 13.8).

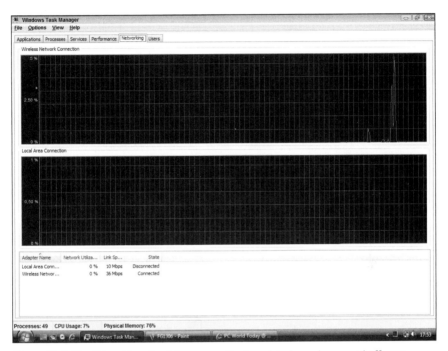

Figure 13.8. The Networking view lets you monitor how data is moving on and off your computer.

- Finally, you can see which users are connected to your computer with the Users view (see Figure 13.9). For example, you can obtain a listing of those users working with shared files on your computer, or disconnect certain users.

Task Manager remembers the last tab you select and opens to that one the next time you restart. You can customize what information is displayed on each tab by clicking View and then Select Columns. You can also change the refresh rate by clicking View and then Update Speed. Leaving it at Normal, which updates at roughly once every two seconds, gives you plenty of information without overloading Windows with refresh requests.

Figure 13.9. The Users view displays a listing of those users currently logged on to your computer.

Your viewing preferences can be changed under the Options menu. The two we prefer are Minimize on use and Hide when minimized. This puts Task Manager in the notification area, so if something is going wrong you can bring it up quickly with the mouse.

The tab we use most often is the Processes tab, typically to end a process that is consuming all system resources, or has stopped respond-ing. An application that isn't responding is displayed as such on the Applications tab; an out-of-control process displays 99% CPU on the Processes tab. To shut down a process, select it in the list and then click End Process. Windows attempts to end the process, and displays an End Process dialog box. You can wait for the process to time out or you can click End to force the process to end immediately.

Bright Idea

Add a shortcut to Task Manager in your startup group, or add it to the All Users startup group, so that it launches when you log on. It doesn't consume much in the way of resources, and you always have an indicator of your system's health where you can see it.

Deep in the heart of processes

Task Manager is a great general tool, but the more you know about Windows, the more likely you are to start to wonder which processes are linked to other processes, and sometimes you may want to end a process in spite of Windows telling you that you're not allowed to bump it off.

A freeware program called Process Explorer is available from www.sysinternals.com. It lets you end any process (whether you *should* end it is another question entirely) that you choose, displays a tree view of processes and associated DLLs, and does all this with an interface that is like Task Manager on steroids. If you are a tinkerer who really likes to get under the hood, Process Explorer is well worth checking out.

Some processes are so fundamental to Windows that you cannot end them using Task Manager. If your computer is completely out of control and Task Manager can't end your woes, your only real option is to restart your computer. You can then either try to duplicate the circumstances for the purposes of filing a bug report with Microsoft, or you can try not to duplicate the circumstances in the hope of avoiding another system lock-up.

Work with Event Viewer

Continuing with the theme of utilities as people, Event Viewer is like the town gossip — not a thing happens without Event Viewer seeing it. If a service is failing to start, an application is running out of disk space, or someone is trying to hack into the administrator account, you will find clues to all these happenings in the event logs. This makes Event Viewer a key tool when it comes to troubleshooting; Microsoft recognizes this fact and has made several major improvements to the tool in Windows Vista.

Event Viewer (see Figure 13.10) is a utility that lets you view events recorded in numerous log files so you can use this information to try and resolve problems with your computer. To open Event Viewer, click Start ⇨ Control Panel ⇨ System and Maintenance ⇨ Administrative Tools ⇨ Event Viewer.

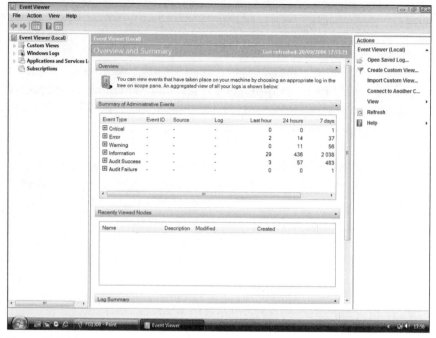

Figure 13.10. Important clues to your computer's health are found in Event Viewer.

Use panes effectively

One of the first changes you may notice in the new version of Event Viewer is the Actions pane on the right. This pane provides an alternative way of performing actions on the items you select by adding shortcuts to some of the most common tasks. All of these actions can also still be performed from the menus or by right-clicking.

In the scope pane on the left, new nodes have been added including Windows Logs, Applications and Services Logs, and Custom Views.

The information tracked in Windows Logs includes the following logs:

- **Application.** The Application log contains events logged by applications or programs. For example, a database program might record a file error in the Application log.

- **Security.** Security-related events are called audits and are listed as successful or failed. They can include such events as valid and invalid logon attempts, as well as events related to resource use such as creating, opening, or deleting files or other objects.

■ **Setup.** Computers configured as domain controllers have additional logs that are displayed in the Setup log.

■ **System.** This log contains events logged by Windows Vista system components and Windows system services. For example, the failure of a driver or other system component to load during startup is recorded in the System log.

Application and System logs contain three types of events: errors, displayed with a red X, indicate a significant problem such as loss of data or loss of functionality; warnings, displayed with a yellow exclamation point, are events that are not necessarily significant, but may indicate future problems; and information, displayed with a blue I, describes the successful operation of an application, driver, or service.

With Event Viewer, you can monitor four different types of event logs (which you see by clicking on a node or one of its subfolders): Administrative, Operational, Analytic, and Debug. Typically, system administrators will find Administrative and Operational logs to be the most useful, whereas Analytic and Debug logs tend to be of more interest to developers. In either case, event logs now have a far higher degree of granularity, allowing you to drill down and find information relevant to your specific issue more easily.

The center View pane contains all the information that has been gathered about each event. You can sort by any column simply by clicking it. In the bottom part of this pane, the information presented on the General tab (see Figure 13.11) should be familiar from previous versions of Event Viewer. Here, you can also find a link to Event Log Online Help. If you click this link, you are asked whether you agree to send your information across the Internet to Microsoft. Theoretically, you might get lucky and find some useful information in the Microsoft Events And Errors Message Center when you click OK; personally, we've only ever seen the message, "We're sorry. There is no additional information about this issue in the Error and Event Log Messages or Knowledge Base databases at this time." But you never know!

Inside Scoop

You can set up a task to launch whenever a specific event occurs by right-click-ing the event in the Event Viewer, and then clicking Attach Task To This Event in the context menu. This launches the Task Scheduler Wizard, which guides you through setting up the task.

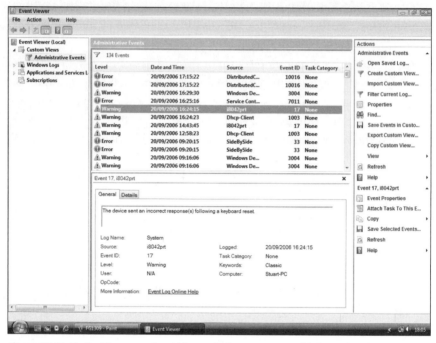

Figure 13.11. In the View pane, Event Viewer displays some general information about the event.

In Windows Vista, the properties of events in event logs are stored in XML format. Click the Details tab to see this information displayed in either the more human-readable Friendly View or the XML View (see Figure 13.12).

Introducing Views

Another important improvement to Event Viewer in Windows Vista comes with the introduction of Views. Views allow you to create power-ful, customizable queries across multiple event logs and save them for subsequent use.

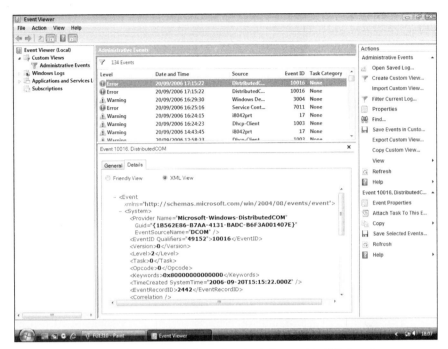

Figure 13.12. The XML View provides information about the event in XML format.

It's true that the previous version of Event Viewer also had a filtering capability that managed to do a fairly reasonable job, but this new version is much simpler to use. Right-click on the Custom Views Node and select Create Custom View to open a properties sheet where you can configure (filter) your View (see Figure 13.13) based on a range of criteria including level, date and time, user, event IDs, or even keywords.

Logs can sometimes be helpful in determining what failed and why. The System log, for instance, contains events that usually have an Event ID associated with them, and by searching in Help and Support, you can often find out more information about the problem and if any Windows Update has been issued for it.

Inside Scoop

Sometimes it's difficult to find information on particular event IDs. If Microsoft doesn't have information, take a look at www.eventid.net. It has links to other sites with information, as well as postings by others who have encountered the event in question.

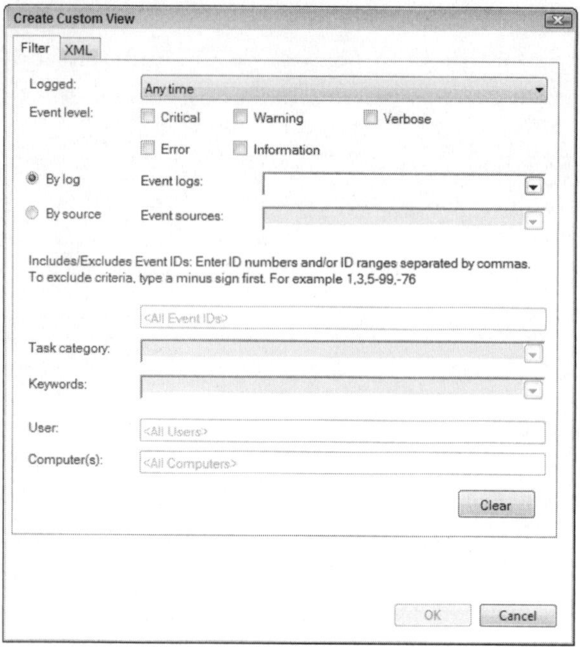

Figure 13.13. Create your own Custom Views.

Application events are somewhat different. The application manufacturer is responsible for writing an application that properly logs its events into the file. There may not be an event ID associated with it, or if there is, you will have to search the manufacturer's support forums to find it. The data may be meaningful only to the original programmers. Or in many cases, the application may write its own error log into its home directory or some other location. The bottom line: An application may crash, but there's no guarantee that it will show up in the Event Viewer.

The Security log contains different events: success audits, displayed with a yellow key, and failure audits, displayed with a yellow lock. Out of the box, Windows does not log many events to the Security log, not even log-on failures that you might see during a brute-force password attack. Audit events must be enabled separately. Fortunately, most of them can be quickly enabled by using the Group Policy Editor; see Chapter 7 for information on auditing security events.

Each event log can have a number of its properties changed from the default. Right-click a log in the left pane and then click Properties (see Figure 13.14). The default settings should be fine for nearly all cases except when you are running a Web server or checking particular error conditions; then you may want to point the log file to a different location, increase its size, or change the overwrite behavior for older events.

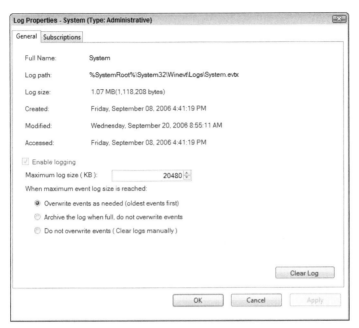

Figure 13.14. Each log file, in this case the System Log, can be configured for size and overwrite behavior when the log becomes full.

Viewing remote logs

If you have local administrator rights on other computers, you can use Event Viewer to connect to other event logs and view the contents remotely. Make sure Event Viewer (Local) is selected in the left pane, click Action, Connect to another computer, and then browse for the computer. You can also connect to another computer directly from the action pane, or by right-clicking on Event Viewer (local) and then selecting Connect to another computer. If the other computer is available, you will be asked to log on with your credentials. Once approved, you can view the event logs as needed.

Improve your performance

Windows Vista takes a new approach to managing performance issues. In fact, they've dedicated a whole new window to it, called Performance Information and Tools, that provides details of your Windows Experience Index score — the figure that measures how well your PC is capable of running Windows Vista — and provides links to commonly used features, such as Disk Cleanup, power settings, and indexing options. These features are all discussed in detail elsewhere in this book. You can access the Performance Information and Tools window by clicking Control Panel ⇨ System and Maintenance ⇨ Performance Information and Tools.

Other helpful features that Windows Vista offers to make your Vista ride smoother include a new Sleep state, the introduction of ReadyBoost™ technology, and the Windows System Performance Rating.

Monitor performance

Windows Vista comes with many new tools to help you troubleshoot problems and performance issues with your computer. One of these, Reliability and Performance Monitor, combines the functionality of several stand-alone tools from previous versions of Windows including Performance Logs and Alerts, Server Performance Advisor, Performance Monitor, and System Monitor. Featuring a greatly-improved graphical interface, this highly customizable tool can help you identify performance bottlenecks, and troubleshoot problems that may be slowing your computer down.

Performance is simply the measure of how quickly your computer carries out its tasks. Much of this depends on your computer's hardware: the amount of memory available to all the processes that may be running, the access speed of the physical hard disks, or the top speed of the processor. Let's not forget that performance, or at least our perception of it, is also fairly relative; whenever we upgrade to a new computer, we always spend the first few weeks being amazed at how fast everything seems to be, but it's never long before we begin to wonder how to shave a few seconds off here or there, and we always end up learning that there are certain tasks where we can safely go and have a cup of coffee while we wait for them to run.

On a day-to-day basis, there's not a lot you can do about your computer's hardware limitations, but you can monitor individual applications and processes to assess how much of the available resources they are using and identify potential bottlenecks. That's where Windows Performance Diagnostic Console comes into its own.

Open Reliability and Performance Monitor by clicking Start ⇨ Control Panel ⇨ System and Maintenance ⇨ Performance Information and Tools ⇨ Advanced Tools ⇨ Open Reliability and Performance Monitor, or execute it from the command prompt by clicking Start ⇨ All Programs ⇨ Accessories, right-clicking Command Prompt, selecting Run as administrator in the context menu, typing perfmon at the command prompt, and then pressing Enter.

The main view of Reliability and Performance Monitor provides a Resource Overview that displays graphically the real-time usage of CPU, Disk, Network, and Memory resources on your computer (see Figure 13.15).

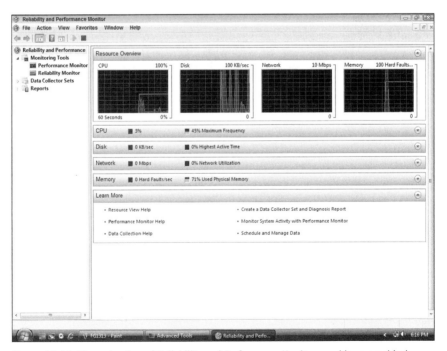

Figure 13.15. The main view of Reliability and Performance Monitor provides a graphical overview of how resources are being used on your computer.

Beneath these graphs are four sections that provide greater detail about each resource. To display or hide this additional information, click the arrow on the right side of each bar.

The CPU label displays a percentage showing the CPU capacity currently in use (see Figure 3.16). Its details include the following information:

- **Image.** The name of the application using the CPU resources

- **PID.** The process ID of the application instance

- **Threads.** The number of currently active threads from the application instance

- **CPU.** The number of currently active CPU cycles from the application instance

- **Average CPU.** The average CPU load from the application instance, shown as a percentage of the total CPU capacity

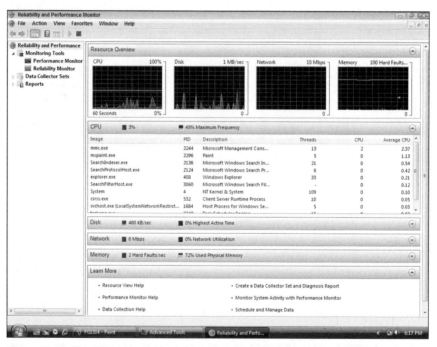

Figure 13.16. The CPU label provides information on the CPU capacity currently in use.

The Disk label displays the total current I/O. Its detail includes the following information (see Figure 13.17):

- **Image.** The name of the application using the disk resources
- **PID.** The process ID of the application instance
- **File.** The name of the file being read and/or written by the application instance
- **Read.** The speed (in Bytes/min) at which data is being read from the file by the application instance
- **Write.** The speed (in Bytes/min) at which data is being written to the file by the application instance
- **IO Priority.** The priority of the task for the application
- **Response Time (ms).** The response time in milliseconds

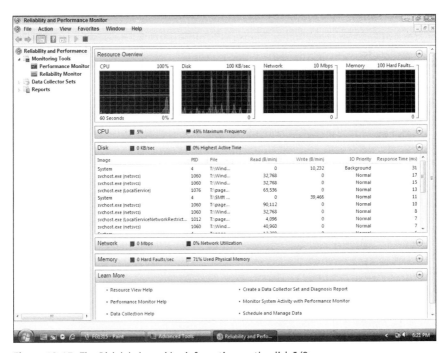

Figure 13.17. The Disk label provides information on the disk I/O.

The Network label displays the current total network traffic (in Kbps). Its detail includes the following information (see Figure 13.18):

- **Image.** The name of the application using the network resources
- **PID.** The process ID of the application instance
- **Address.** The network address with which the local computer is exchanging information, expressed as a computer name when referring to other computers on the same local area network, as an IP address, or as a fully qualified domain name
- **Send.** The amount of data (in Bytes/min) the application instance is currently sending from the local computer to the address
- **Receive.** The amount of data (in Bytes/min) the application instance is currently receiving from the address
- **Total.** The total bandwidth (in Bytes/min) currently being sent and received by the application instance

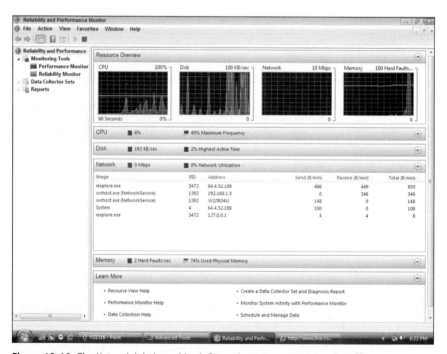

Figure 13.18. The Network label provides information on current network traffic.

The Memory label displays the current hard faults per second and the percentage of physical memory currently in use. Its detail includes the following information (see Figure 13.19):

- **Image.** The name of the application using the memory resources
- **PID.** The process ID of the application instance
- **Hard faults.** The number of hard faults per minute currently resulting from the application instance
- **Working Set.** The space (in KB) currently taken up in memory by the application instance
- **Commit (KB).** The maximum possible value for the working set
- **Working Set (KB).** The space currently taken up in memory by the application instance
- **Shareable (KB).** The number of kilobytes of the application instance's working set that is available for use by other applications
- **Private (KB).** The number of kilobytes of the application instance's working set that is dedicated solely to the process

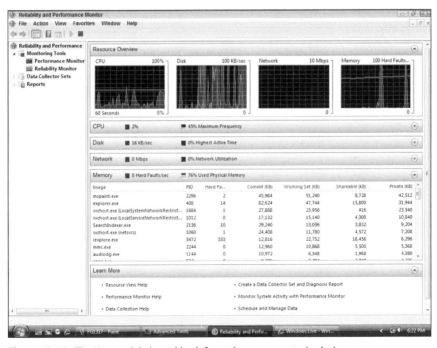

Figure 13.19. The Memory label provides information on current physical memory usage.

Use the Reliability Monitor

Reliability Monitor is another handy little utility included in Reliability and Performance Monitor. This tool provides you with a visual overview of the stability of your system over time (see Figure 13.20). The reliability of a system is the measure of how often it deviates from expected behavior over a period of time. Some events that might cause reductions in reliability include applications crashing, services freezing and restarting, drivers failing to initialize, or complete failures of the operating system.

As well as comparing your current system stability against a baseline, Reliability Monitor also tracks events to help you identify the causes of any reductions in reliability. It records not only failures, including application, driver, hardware, and operating system failures, but also key events relating to the configuration of your system, including the installation of new software, operating system patches and updates, and drivers. You can easily pinpoint exactly when the reliability of your system began to deteriorate and make the necessary changes to get your system performing optimally once more.

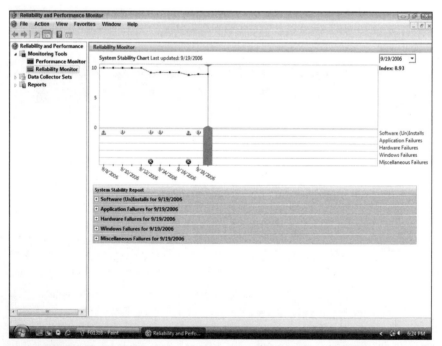

Figure 13.20. Reliability Monitor provides a visual overview of the stability of your system over time.

A generally better course

Windows Vista, overall, takes performance a lot more seriously than Windows XP did. A number of these enhancements are totally behind-the-scenes or low profile; marketing teams may not be singing the praises of these improvements, but we are!

Windows SuperFetch

Windows SuperFetch is a memory manager that makes sure that your applications have priority over background tasks. Vista rightly decides that you shouldn't be the one to suffer. Any background tasks still run as before; however, once they are finished, SuperFetch frees up the memory and replaces it with the data accessed just before the background task was executed. By doing so, applications continue to run as efficiently (and fast) as before.

SuperFetch also acts a little like Task Manager and Device Manager in that it monitors your system. It notes which applications your computer accesses the most and then stores them into memory. This feature is quite nice at startup, or if you switch users. SuperFetch is also smart enough to guess which applications you would most likely use during the week as well as which applications you would use over the weekend.

Windows Vista also introduces the concept of a low-priority I/O feature. Applications can be written to use low-priority I/O so that it has lower-priority access to the hard drive. By doing this, it can run at the same time as a user application without any decrease in performance.

Automatic disk defragmentation

Unlike Windows XP, where you had to think about actually defragmenting your computer, and then never got around to it because you simply didn't have time to wait an hour (or more) for your defragmentation to finish, Windows Vista automatically detects when it's time to defragment and then does it when necessary. Two big advantages of this enhancement are that it takes advantage of the new low-priority I/O feature, meaning that your performance isn't reduced due to defragmentation, and that the hard drive can be fragmented over several sessions and not in a single session as before.

Windows ReadyBoost™

The new ReadyBoost™ feature is definitely one of our favorite features in Windows Vista. In fact, we wonder why it wasn't developed sooner. Using this feature is a great way to speed up your machine at a relatively low cost. Let us be clear; this is not a memory upgrade. This feature lets you use space from a USB flash drive to act as virtual memory to be used in Windows Vista. Given the price of memory versus the cost of a flash drive, this option is very attractive. In addition to being an affordable way of increasing system performance, you can also remove the flash drive and use it elsewhere. It is also a great solution if you have limited memory expansion.

Using this feature is extremely easy — simply plug the flash drive into a USB port, and wait for the autoplay dialog box to load. Select the ReadyBoost™ option from the menu and set how much virtual memory you would like to create. We've noticed that 1.8GB is about the highest you would want to set this feature. If you already have a flash drive installed, you can set ReadyBoost properties from the flash drive properties.

Similarly, Vista will eventually work with hybrid drives using Windows ReadyDrive™. These drives are expected to be released around June 2007 and will become a laptop requirement for Vista at that time. Hybrid drives are hard drives that have an onboard flash drive with extensive flash memory. Windows Vista will boot from this flash memory, allowing for some of the fastest startup times ever. This also allows even faster Sleep recovery.

Go to Sleep already

Microsoft decided that Hibernate was for the bears, which leads us to another new feature: the Sleep power state. If you are familiar with Windows XP, you certainly remember how long it took to shut down your computer. Windows Vista feels your pain and proposes Sleep. The Sleep power state saves any open documents or other data and writes both it and open applications to memory and your hard drive. When you "wake

Watch Out!

If you remove the flash drive, your computer will go back to pre-ReadyBoost™ performance.

up" your computer, it loads much faster than in previous versions of Windows. Being the types that never sit for too long in front of our monitors, we regularly let our machines go to Sleep and are always impressed with how fast the machines comes back to life once we're ready to get back to work.

For people who are regularly called away from their desk and who usually use screen savers and reduce power to save energy, this is a very nice addition to the Windows Vista operating system. The best part is that you don't need to do anything to use it. Of course, you can always manually put your computer to Sleep from the Start menu.

Vista also offers a fast boot and resume feature that is similar in purpose to the Sleep function. Windows Vista reduces your wait time when starting your computer by running tasks and processes in the background. As a result, you can keep control of your computer instead of having to wait several minutes to use your machine like in XP days. We've also noticed that we've had to reboot Windows Vista far less than we do Windows XP; this is by design, not a fluke.

Editing the Registry

Throughout this book, references have been made to the Windows Registry (see Figure 13.21). The registry is a centralized listing of every setting Windows and its applications require for proper operation. It's a configuration file gone monstrously, horribly wrong. In Linux, each subsystem and application has its own text configuration file, stored where it can easily be found. Windows, on the other hand, requires that all settings be placed in the registry, using naming conventions that, it seems, could easily have been created by a committee of insane Scrabble players.

Windows Vista and Windows applications regularly make changes to the registry, even though you may not be aware of it. Whenever you change a setting in Control Panel, or alter your font choice in a word processing application, values are created or edited in the registry. This ensures that the proper keys are edited and the correct values assigned.

To get started performing your own surgery on the registry, click Start ⇨ All Programs ⇨ Accessories ⇨ Command Prompt, type regedit, and then press Enter.

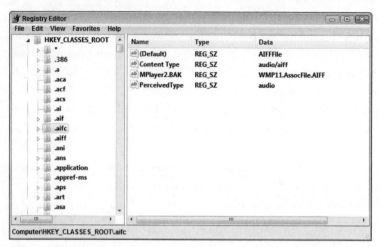

Figure 13.21. Windows Registry looks like Windows Explorer, but its contents are much scarier to work with.

The registry has five main collections of settings, called hives, which control different aspects of operations. These hives are

- **HKEY_CLASSES_ROOT.** This hive is a mega-glossary for Windows. It contains information on file types, objects, and how to handle them.

- **HKEY_CURRENT_USER.** This hive contains information on the user who is currently logged on. Technically, it's really just pointers to a subset of information from HKEY_USERS; any changes made here appear in both places.

- **HKEY_LOCAL_MACHINE.** All the information about your computer is contained here. It doesn't include any information that is specific to particular users.

- **HKEY_USERS.** This is the master hive for all user-related information, whether the users are logged on or not. When you log on, your information is copied from here to HKEY_LOCAL_USER.

- **HKEY_CURRENT_CONFIG.** This hive only contains pointers to other keys in other hives.

Click a plus sign next to a registry hive, or double-click its name. In each hive are keys that contain data in a particular format. The keys — Microsoft's term for "settings" — are determined by programmers, while the values are data that the program can use. For example, a key could be called "DefaultInstallation" and have a value of "C:\Program Files\ SoftwareInstalledHere." Values also have a particular data type, such as string, binary, and DWORD or double word length, referring to programming data types rather than English sentences jammed together.

When editing the registry, you must know three things:

- The registry key's exact name and location
- The value's data type
- The value or permissible values for the key

There are many places you can find suggestions of keys to edit for results that aren't otherwise available through Windows. If you are looking primarily for user interface changes, then install TweakUI (covered in Chapter 4), which has numerous settings you can edit without hacking into the registry. There are Web sites available with tweaks, some good, some indeterminate; with all edits, make sure you do some research first before changing registry values. One Web site that often has useful information is www.tweakvista.com. On this site, you can search different categories to find out if someone has figured out how to change a setting you're interested in.

As every reference on the subject will tell you, be careful! If you make the wrong changes in the registry, you can render your system inoperable. Don't say I didn't warn you!

Before editing the registry, you should make a backup of all or part of it. The two easiest ways are to create a system restore point and to export the current registry key and its value. To find out how to create system restore points, see Chapter 14. To export a registry key, open regedit and browse to the key you are about to change. Select the key (or, if you're especially paranoid, the parent key), click File ⇨ Export, type a name for your exported key (see Figure 13.22), browse to a location where you'd like to save the key, and then click Save.

Watch Out!

While editing the registry can often be the fastest way to fix or tweak Windows, making the wrong registry changes can render your system inoperable. Take your time, pay attention to what you're doing — and always make a backup.

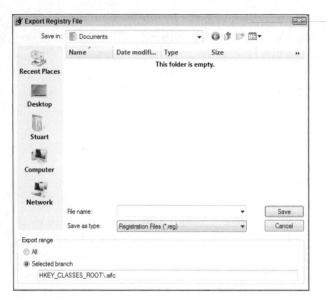

Figure 13.22. Give your exported key a useful name so you can later import it to the proper location without guessing.

To edit a registry key, double click the key. An Edit dialog box appears (see Figure 13.23). Select the base if necessary, type a new value in the box provided, and then click OK.

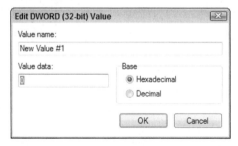

Figure 13.23. DWORD values can be entered in decimal or hex format; the dialog box automatically converts them if needed.

Sometimes you may need to create a new registry key, especially when you're tapping into undocumented settings that curious users have discovered. To create a new key, right-click anywhere in the right pane, click New, and then click Key. Type the key name you want to create and then click OK.

You can then enter a value for the key by right-clicking it, clicking New, and then clicking the data type for your new value. Enter in the data and click OK (see Figure 13.24).

Figure 13.24. New key values are easy to add.

Depending on the component, service, or application you are working with, your registry change may take effect immediately or it may require you to restart the service or application. Changing some keys may require a reboot of Windows itself.

In some cases there are exported registry key files available, usually ending in .reg, that contain the necessary keys and values. Importing the keys can be quicker than slogging through the registry, and you can feel more confident that the syntax and values are correct. To import a registry key (whether it is one you have found elsewhere, or one you backed up and want to restore), open regedit, click File ⇨ Import, select the file, and then click Open (see Figure 13.25). If all goes well, you should get an information dialog box stating the file was successfully imported into the registry.

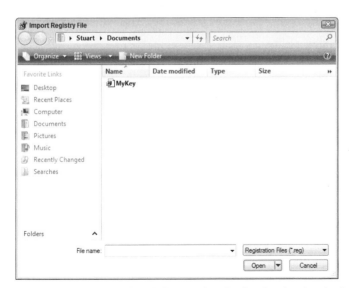

Figure 13.25. Importing keys is faster and easier than hand-typing the data.

Tracking down the elusive registry

With all the effort Microsoft put into creating a monolithic settings repository, logic states that it should also be a single file on the hard drive. However, the registry is actually several files, some of which may not even be present on the local hard drive! The two "real" registry hives are HKEY_USERS and HKEY_LOCAL_MACHINE; the other hives only contain pointers to those two hives.

HKEY_LOCAL_MACHINE has five subkeys: Hardware, SAM [security account manager], Security, Software, and System. All but Hardware are located at Windows\system32\config using the appropriate name in all capitals and without an extension (for example SAM). Hardware is dynamically generated at boot time and doesn't exist as a file on disk.

HKEY_USERS is a collection of pointers to user profiles, which are stored at Documents and Settings\%username%\ntuser.dat.

These files can only be backed up by registry-aware utilities, including Windows Backup; you cannot manually copy them to another location. The only exception is ntuser.dat files for anyone other than the logged-on user; you can back those up or copy them manually.

A quicker import method is to double-click the .reg file. Windows will ask if you are sure you want to import the data; if you are, click Yes. The data is then imported.

Configure and control services

At the most basic level, services are programs that need to run whether or not a user is logged on to the system. An example is the Print Spooler service that lets others send print jobs to the printer queue on your computer without your being logged on. Some services start after you log on, such as video card helper applications; there's no sense in having them consume resources when no one is logged on to the computer, so they load when a user logs on.

The Services snap-in (see Figure 13.26) is used to see which services are available, which are running, and whether they are set to start up or are disabled. To see the snap-in, click Start ⇨ Control Panel ⇨ System and Maintenance ⇨ Administrative Tools ⇨ Services. You can also execute the utility from the command prompt; click Start ⇨ All Programs ⇨ Accessories ⇨ Command Prompt, type services.msc, and then press Enter.

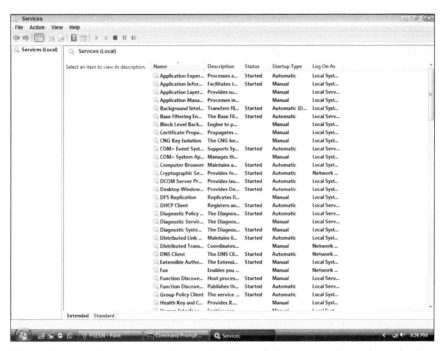

Figure 13.26. The Services snap-in is a lengthy listing of what is currently running under the hood of your computer.

In this window you can start, pause, stop, or restart a service. Highlight the service and then click the appropriate button on the toolbar. Pausing or restarting services may be needed if the service seems "stuck," as sometimes happens with print queues.

Somewhat more useful to know is the service's startup type. You can see the startup type listed in the Services snap-in, but it may not be set to the correct type for your computer. Double-click a service to open the service properties dialog box (see Figure 13.27).

Figure 13.27. You can change the startup type for each service depending on what you want running at boot time.

The most useful setting in this dialog box is the Startup type. The drop-down list box lets you set how you want the service to behave when the system reboots. The choices are

- **Automatic.** The service starts when the computer boots up. This is the setting for must-have services, or for services that would severely limit functionality if they weren't available.

- **Manual.** The service will start if it is called by an application, though this is not always the case.

- **Disabled.** The service is not available and cannot be started. You must change the status to manual or automatic before you can start the service.

To change a service's status, select the status from the drop-down list and then click OK. The startup type changes in the Services snap-in to the new startup type.

Hack

Services can be started and stopped at the command line. Type net start "service name" or net stop "service name" and then press Enter. "Service name" is the name found in the Services snap-in, such as Windows Image Acquisition. The quotes are needed if the service name contains spaces.

What are all these services for?

The services listed in the Services snap-in don't always tell you what they are for; and some are downright cryptic. A common phrase is "If this service is disabled, any services that explicitly depend on it will fail to start." Not much help when you don't know what a service does in the first place.

Fortunately there is a Web site dedicated to enumerating the Windows services and telling you what they do. Although at the time of writing, this site relates specifically to Windows XP, much of the information it contains is equally useful and valid for Windows Vista. Visit The Elder Geek's Web site at `www.theeldergeek.com/services_guide.htm` for guidance on what you can safely set to manual or even disable. Turning off services is one of the easiest, non-intrusive ways to reduce potential attacks.

If you have an account with local administration rights on another computer, you can connect to it and mange its services remotely. This can be extremely useful, especially when working to clear a print queue as mentioned previously. In the left pane of the snap-in, right-click Services and then click Connect to another computer. You can then type in the computer name or browse the network. You will be asked for log-on credentials; provide them, and you will be connected to the Services Manager on the other computer.

Work with Task Scheduler

Task Scheduler in Windows Vista greatly expands on the Scheduled Tasks tool available in previous versions of Windows. In particular, it overcomes certain limitations of the old Scheduled Tasks tool in the areas of reliability, security, and monitoring and control execution.

The purpose of Task Scheduler is to run services or applications when it's told to, as often as it's told to. Most operating systems have similar utilities or services so that things like system maintenance or periodic update checks can run. One major enhancement in the Task Scheduler MMC snap-in is that these tasks can now be prompted by specific events rather than being limited to having an administrator schedule them for a certain time, considerably increasing their usefulness when it comes to responding quickly and effectively to any problems that may arise.

To start Task Scheduler, click Start ⇨ Control Panel ⇨ System and Maintenance ⇨ Administrative Tools ⇨ Task Scheduler. You can also execute the tool from the command prompt by clicking Start ⇨ All Programs ⇨ Accessories ⇨ Command Prompt, typing taskschd.msc, and then pressing Enter.

When you schedule a task, the two key concepts to bear in mind are triggers and actions. A trigger is an event that causes the task to be run, and an action is how the task is set up to respond to this event. Actions can include running a specified program, sending an e-mail message to a predefined address, or displaying a message on-screen. Tasks can be triggered by a user booting up her computer (At startup), unlocking her workstation (On workstation unlock), or whenever the computer becomes idle (On idle). As in previous versions of Windows, you can also simply schedule a specific time when you want the task to be run.

Set up a new task

When setting up a new scheduled task, you have the option of either creating a basic task using the Task Scheduler Wizard or creating a task manually in the Create Task dialog box.

To create a basic task using the wizard, do the following:

1. Find and click the task folder in the console tree where you wish to create the task.

2. Click Create Basic Task in the actions pane.

3. Follow the instructions in the wizard.

To schedule a new task manually, do the following:

1. Click Create Task in the actions pane. (You can also click Create Task in the Action menu, or right-click Task Scheduler (Local) and then click Create Task.)

2. In the Create Task properties sheet that appears, define the criteria under which your task will run (see Figure 13.28).

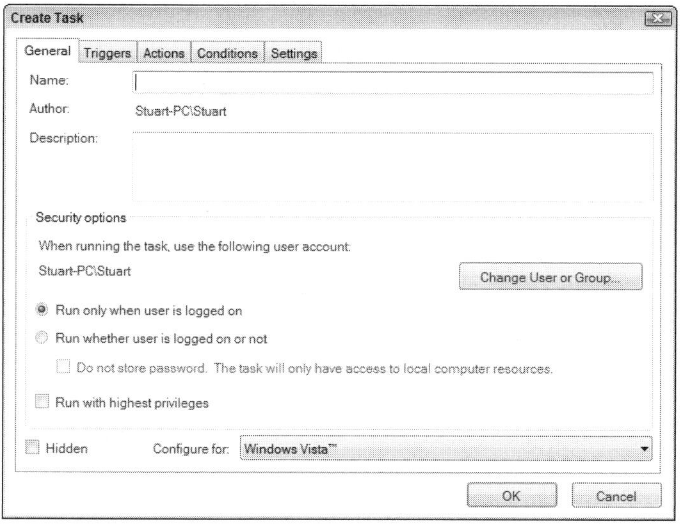

Figure 13.28. In the Create Task properties sheet, set up the trigger that causes your task to run, and the Action you want to take.

First, you need to provide some general information about your task, including a name and description. You then specify the circumstances under which the task begins and ends under the Triggers tab, and provide details about what action or actions you want to take place in response to the triggers under the Actions tab. You also have the option of defining additional conditions and settings (under the Conditions tab and the Settings tab), such as whether the task should still run if the computer is on battery power or only if the network is available, or how to respond if the task fails or runs for too long. Click OK when you're done, and your new task appears in the scope pane on the left. Double-clicking your new task opens the properties sheet for the task, where you can fine-tune or adjust any settings without having to delete and re-create your task.

Create complex schedules

In previous versions of Windows, tasks were launched based on a single trigger (nearly always the time) and each task was limited to just one action. Happily, the Windows Vista Task Scheduler now allows you to create more complex scenarios. For instance, Task Scheduler might wait for three separate events to occur before sending an e-mail alert to a support technician. Equally usefully, it also allows you to define sequences of actions, whereby multiple actions can be set up to run as a series of single tasks, one after the other, or where events prompted by one task are used to launch the next task in line. This does away with the need for guesswork; in the past, administrators who wanted to run tasks in sequence had to estimate how long one task would take to ensure that it was completed before the next one began.

Security and reliability improvements

In addition to these improvements in flexibility, the Windows Vista Task Scheduler also increases its reliability in a number of ways. It can retry tasks in case of failure (with options for you to specify both how many times to retry and how long to wait between each attempt). It can wake your machine from standby or hibernation to ensure that tasks run even if the machine is asleep. It can also let you specify that a task should run when the machine becomes available, for example, as soon as it is switched on if a scheduled task has been missed. Each of these enhancements ensures that the tasks that are supposed to run do run, making the automated administration of your computer all the more efficient.

As is the case with many other areas of Windows Vista, security in the Windows Vista Task Scheduler has also seen some major changes. If passwords are required, these are stored in the new Credentials Manager (CredMan) using encryption interfaces that prevent them from being easily retrieved by malware and other rogue programs. Additionally, Task Scheduler supports a security isolation model, which means that each set of tasks running in a specific security context starts in a separate session, in isolation from both the current user and from system services.

Options

Task Scheduler also features options which ensure that background operations remain unobtrusive and do not interrupt critical work. You can set Task Scheduler to activate tasks only if the computer is idle for a specified length of time (and to stop them as soon as the computer ceases to be idle). You can save power if you are working with a laptop by starting tasks only if the computer is on AC power. You can also prevent tasks that require a network connection from starting needlessly if you are not connected to the network, and even specify which network you need to be connected to before the task will run.

Task Scheduler keeps a log of its status using a set of predefined events in the Event Log. On the Summary page (see Figure 13.29), you are presented with a quick overview of all the tasks that have run in a specific period of time (which you can select), whether their status was success or failure, and what time they started and ended.

Figure 13.29. The Task Scheduler Summary page provides an overview of recently run tasks.

What to do when tasks won't run

When you create a task, you should always try to run it before relying on Task Scheduler to do the work for you, in order to ensure that it is working correctly. If it doesn't run, check the following:

- **Use the correct command-line options.** Many Windows applications use command-line options, also called switches, at startup to control how they run. Some applications have switches to fully automate them, others don't. Check the documentation (or search the Help and Support Center) for the options your program uses. Double-click the task and add the options to the end of the Run box.

- **The task isn't running.** You may have specified the task to run under another user's account. If that user logs on, then Fast User Switching is in effect, and the task is running under his name, not yours.

- **The task didn't run when scheduled.** Your computer may have been turned off, in hibernation mode, or low on battery power. Check the Event Log to see if the task is listed as a Missed Task, and try running it manually.

Work with the command prompt

Back in the days when text-based operating systems such as UNIX and DOS ruled the roost, those who didn't know their way around the command prompt would have had real difficulty in getting a computer to perform anything other than the simplest of tasks. But one fine day, along came the graphical user interface (GUI) to open up the power of various versions of the Mac and Windows operating systems to novice users, and the world was never the same again.

But still, GUIs may well do away with the need to memorize dozens of arcane commands just to find your way around your computer, but they also reduce the flexibility of the operating systems that lie beneath them because, by their very nature, they are designed to cater for less-experienced users. The command prompt, on the other hand, still present at the heart of Windows Vista, provides expert users with a range of options they would find it hard to live without. Learning even a handful of the most common commands is an important step on the road to feeling that you are fully in control of your operating system, rather than the other way round.

To open the command prompt, click Start ⇨ All Programs ⇨ Accessories ⇨ Command Prompt. (If you want to run the command prompt with additional privileges, click Start ⇨ All Programs ⇨ Accessories, right click Command Prompt, and then select Run as administrator instead.)

Where am I?

Whenever you arrive somewhere new, the first thing you usually want to do is get your bearings. With command prompt, it's no different. To find out which directory you are working in, type **cd**, and then press Enter. (Note that the command prompt is not case sensitive; cd, CD, cD, and Cd are all the same.) If you also want to display a list of all the files and folders in your current directory, type **dir**, and then press Enter. You should see something like Figure 13.30.

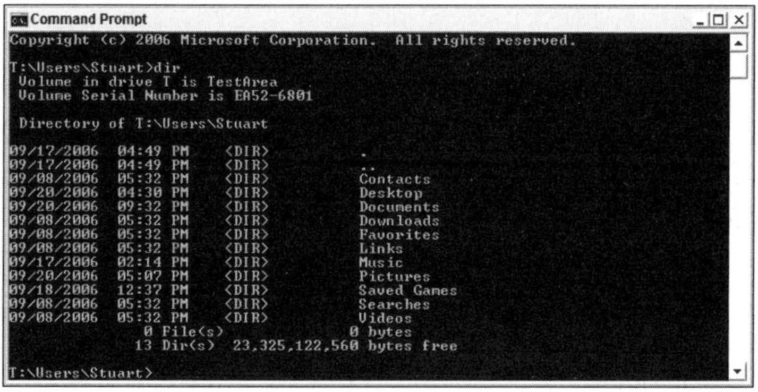

Figure 13.30. The dir command displays a list of files and folders in your current directory.

You also use the cd command to move around from one directory to another; it stands for "change directory." To get to the Windows folder from the c:\ prompt, for instance, type **cd windows**, and then press Enter. The prompt will now read C:\WINDOWS>, indicating that you are in the Windows folder on the C:\ drive.

Typing `cd..` and then pressing Enter takes you back to the parent folder or drive of the folder you are in. On our current journey, this would take us back to the root of the C:\ drive. You can also jump directly to the root directory from deeper within your folder structure by typing `cd\`, and then pressing Enter.

If you know the full path of the folder you want to navigate to, you can move through several directories at once by typing the full path after the `cd` command. For example, typing `cd windows\system32\config`, and then pressing Enter, will take you directly to the folder you want to reach.

As mentioned previously, typing `dir`, and then pressing Enter, displays all the folders and files in your current directory. It's the command prompt equivalent of clicking a folder to examine its contents. Note, however, that the order in which folders and files are displayed is slightly different to what you might see in Windows Explorer; while Explorer puts folders before files, the `dir` command simply lists all items alphabetically, irrespective of their type.

Switches

Now might be a good time to mention switches. Switches are optional settings that you add to command prompt commands to modify their behavior. You probably noticed that the `dir` command produces a list that is often too long to be of much use, since it only fills more than one screen and you only get to see the bottom of it. However, with switches, we can improve the readability of this output. Typing `dir /p`, and then pressing Enter, causes the list to pause after every screenful of information. Alternatively, typing `dir /w`, and then pressing Enter, lists the contents of the folder in several columns.

To obtain instructions for any command prompt, type the command followed by `/?`, which is the help switch. For instance, if you want to find out more about the `dir` command, type `dir /?`, and then press Enter (see Figure 13.31). The help switch displays a description of each command and provides details of its syntax.

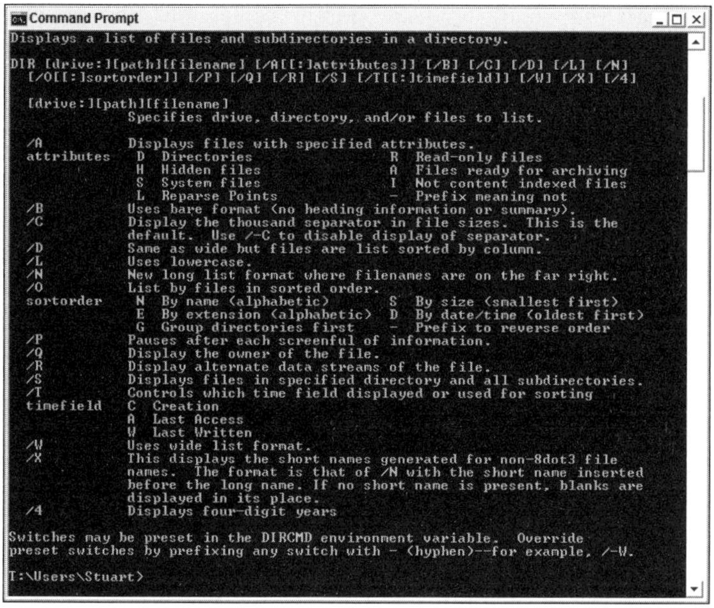


```
Displays a list of files and subdirectories in a directory.

DIR [drive:][path][filename] [/A[[:]attributes]] [/B] [/C] [/D] [/L] [/N]
  [/O[[:]sortorder]] [/P] [/Q] [/R] [/S] [/T[[:]timefield]] [/W] [/X] [/4]

  [drive:][path][filename]
              Specifies drive, directory, and/or files to list.

  /A          Displays files with specified attributes.
  attributes   D  Directories                R  Read-only files
               H  Hidden files               A  Files ready for archiving
               S  System files               I  Not content indexed files
               L  Reparse Points             -  Prefix meaning not
  /B          Uses bare format (no heading information or summary).
  /C          Display the thousand separator in file sizes.  This is the
              default.  Use /-C to disable display of separator.
  /D          Same as wide but files are list sorted by column.
  /L          Uses lowercase.
  /N          New long list format where filenames are on the far right.
  /O          List by files in sorted order.
  sortorder    N  By name (alphabetic)       S  By size (smallest first)
               E  By extension (alphabetic)  D  By date/time (oldest first)
               G  Group directories first    -  Prefix to reverse order
  /P          Pauses after each screenful of information.
  /Q          Display the owner of the file.
  /R          Display alternate data streams of the file.
  /S          Displays files in specified directory and all subdirectories.
  /T          Controls which time field displayed or used for sorting
  timefield   C  Creation
              A  Last Access
              W  Last Written
  /W          Uses wide list format.
  /X          This displays the short names generated for non-8dot3 file
              names.  The format is that of /N with the short name inserted
              before the long name. If no short name is present, blanks are
              displayed in its place.
  /4          Displays four-digit years

Switches may be preset in the DIRCMD environment variable.  Override
preset switches by prefixing any switch with - (hyphen)--for example, /-W.

T:\Users\Stuart>
```

Figure 13.31. The help switch /? displays a description of any command and an explanation of its syntax.

A few other commands

Other commands that you may find useful for managing your files and folders are the make directory command `mkdir` and the remove directory command `rmdir`. Just type `mkdir [directory name]`, and then press Enter to make a new directory. Note that the new directory will be created relative to your current location. To delete an empty directory, type `rmdir [directory name]`, and then press Enter. Similarly, the `del` command lets you delete both directories and files. With all of these commands, you can add directories to the path to execute the command in a location other than your current directory, for example `del windows\mydir\myfile.exe`.

When you're finished working with the command prompt, type `exit`, and then press Enter to return to the Windows Vista GUI. Try to resist the temptation to simply click the X in the top-right corner of the Command Prompt window. Remember, you've just taken your first steps towards harnessing the power of the command prompt.

Ping

The `ping` command has justifiably been called the killer app of the command prompt. It queries a remote (or local) IP address by sending four groups of data packets to it at regular intervals and listening for a response. If a response is received, you know that the two systems are able to communicate over a network. If you receive no response, this indicates that the target computer is either not receiving the ping or is failing to respond. As a result, `ping` is the first port of call for any network troubleshooter, and can only be accessed from the command prompt.

---

ipconfig

As an example of how powerful command prompt commands can be, let's end by looking at one in more detail: `ipconfig`. The `ipconfig` command provides you with information about your system's network setup.

At the command prompt, type `ipconfig`, and then press Enter. You will see how this command displays a short list of the network interfaces available on your system and their corresponding IP addresses. Useful as this may be, and perhaps quicker to obtain from the command prompt than through the GUI, it is hardly earth-shattering stuff. Use the command with the `/all` switch, however, and you move onto a whole new level of detail (see Figure 13.32).

And there's more. As well as providing a wealth of information about your network setup, much of which is difficult to come by elsewhere in Windows Vista, the `ipconfig` command also has other switches that perform functions that are only available from the command prompt. These include the `/release`, `/renew`, and `/flushDNS` switches.

The `ipconfig /release` and `ipconfig /renew` commands, respectively, instruct your network adaptor to drop and renew its current IP addresses, which can be useful if you are attempting to solve certain network problems in a network that uses the Dynamic Host Configuration Protocol (DHCP) to assign IP addresses, as is the case with many broadband Internet providers.

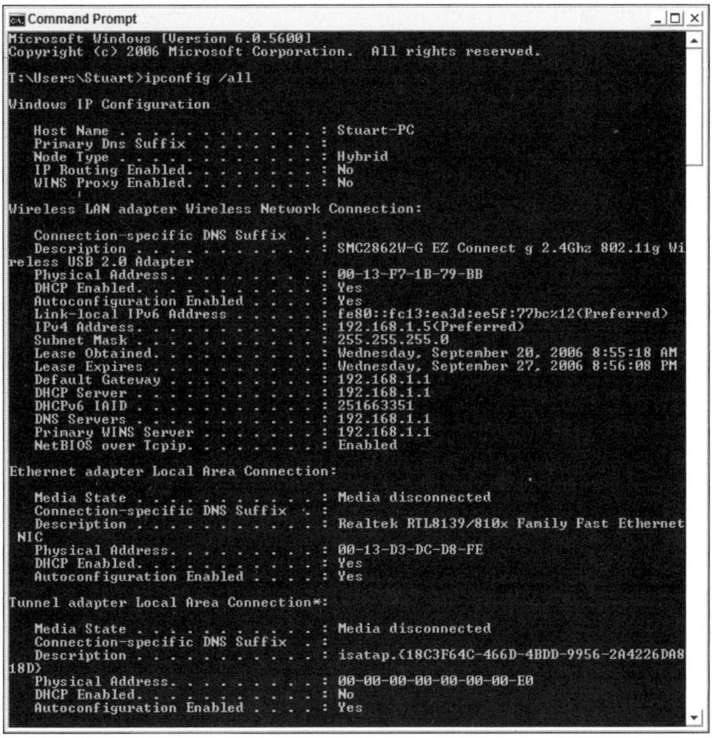

Figure 13.32. The `ipconfig /all` command provides a wealth of information about your network setup.

The `ipconfig /flushdns` command serves an equally useful purpose, that of clearing out the DNS resolver cache in which your computer stores the IP address for frequently accessed DNS names (which is basically the same as saying URLs). Again, this is useful in dealing with certain network problems because it forces your system to recheck its settings instead of relying on potential out-of-date information in the cache.

Understand Windows PowerShell

The command-line experience in Windows Vista is about to take a great leap forward. Windows PowerShell, formerly known as Microsoft Shell (MSH), is a command-line interface shell and scripting language that, at the time of writing, is still under development. While its interface is similar to UNIX shells, it is based on object-oriented programming and the Microsoft .NET framework. It marks a change in philosophy on the part of Windows; GUIs such as the Exchange Server 2007 user interface are now built on top of PowerShell, rather than the command-line interface shell simply providing access to functionalities that were also available elsewhere. This is the Unix way of doing things.

PowerShell was originally intended to ship with Windows Vista, but Microsoft subsequently decided on a separate release schedule for the product, taking it beyond the scope of this book.

Just the facts

- System Information and Device Manager contain everything worth knowing about your computer's hardware and its operation.

- Task Manager can be your first indication that something is going wrong with your computer.

- The significantly upgraded Windows Vista Task Scheduler enables you to automate many common administration tasks.

- Windows Reliability and Performance Monitor combines the functionality of several stand-alone tools from previous versions of Windows to help you troubleshoot problems and performance issues.

- Event Viewer, another significantly enhanced tool in Vista, helps you see if something is failing, or is about to.

- The command prompt lets expert users harness the power of a range of tools that are inaccessible from the graphical user interface.

GET THE SCOOP ON...
Improving system performance ▪ Backing up data ▪
System recovery ▪ Creating disk partitions ▪
Creating dynamic and RAID disks ▪ Setting
quotas ▪ Dual monitors ▪ UPS

Working with Hard Drives

Windows Vista, just like earlier versions of Windows, offers a number of system tools to keep your computer — hardware and software — running smoothly. This chapter illustrates how you can manage your hard drives and make them into more than a simple storage space. Important activities such as spanning, extending, quotas are all discussed in this chapter.

This chapter also details the use of backup devices or UPS to protect your data, as well as how to properly back up your data. Finally, we show you how to maximize your screen space by using multiple monitors for a single computer!

To be perfectly honest, this isn't the chapter with the greatest amount of new features. In fact, improvements are largely restricted to the new Backup and Restore feature. (Microsoft calls it new; however, we recall having a similar feature in Windows XP.) Hard drives work basically the same in Windows Vista as they did under Windows XP. One major difference is the support of hybrid disk drives (HDD) for laptop computers.

Monitoring system performance

Managing your machine's performance is a job unto itself; in fact, it's almost like being a parent. If you'd like a better analogy, maintaining your machine is similar to taking care

Chapter 14

of your car: both must be cleaned, regularly maintained, inspected, checked for aging parts, and so on.

Fortunately, keeping on top of your system performance is largely a routine, automated task nowadays. There are a number of excellent programs that monitor your system and repair errors, including Norton SystemWorks or McAfee Office. However, let's not discount Microsoft Vista's offering. While it's hard to say if the tools have actually improved over the years, it's easy to tell that Microsoft hasn't increased the number of tools.

Windows Vista has a virtually identical offering to Windows XP. What has changed? Security Center is no longer accessible from System Tools menu, nor is Activate Windows. The Vista System Tools now lets you access Computers and the Control Panel; while Scheduled Tasks is now Task Scheduler, and File and Settings Transfer Wizard is now Windows Easy Transfer.

To that end, Windows Vista System Tools (see Figure 14.1) are

- Backup Status and Configuration
- Character Map
- Computer
- Control Panel
- Disk Cleanup
- Disk Defragmenter
- Internet Explorer (No Add-ons)
- System Information
- System Restore
- Task Scheduler
- Windows Easy Transfer

Using the System Tools Menu

If you've decided to use the tools on hand, you have about half the items you need to keep your machine running smoothly.

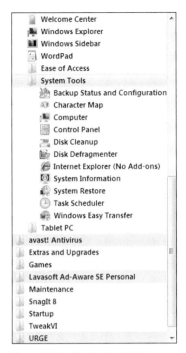

Figure 14.1. The System Tools menu.

Character Map

The Character Map doesn't do much in the way of improving system performance, but it is a helpful little utility that may prove invaluable for out-of-the-ordinary characters such as foreign currency symbols and math symbols; for drawings; for different characters from languages such as Arabic or Japanese; or for accents for Spanish or French words. The Character Map (see Figure 14.2) lets you simply select and copy the character to the Clipboard, and it provides the ASCII code as well.

Inside Scoop

You may have noticed that Windows Vista still doesn't have a bundled anti-virus program. Microsoft has made strides in that department; effective with Windows XP, you can use Microsoft Live OneCare's subscription service that includes an antivirus application. This is supposed to be released for Windows Vista around the time of release; in the meantime, there are third-party antivirus programs available for Vista. Let's review the tools that are available for Microsoft Windows Vista.

Inside Scoop

Use ASCII codes to quickly apply foreign language accents or other special characters. ASCII codes involve holding the Alt key and entering a three digit numeric code.

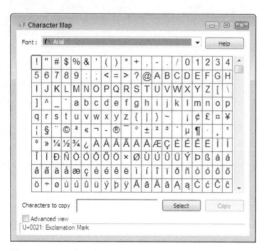

Figure 14.2. The Character Map is helpful for adding foreign characters.

Disk Cleanup

The Disk Cleanup feature lets you clean up temporary files, Internet files, Web Client files, Office Setup files, or the Recycle Bin in any combination. Unfortunately, this has always been one of the weaker links in the Windows operating system. In Vista, you can choose whether you want to clean up just your account, or files for all users on your computer, which is a nice option. While it may have the new Vista look and feel, the speed (or lack thereof) hasn't improved any in this release. Just like in past Windows versions, you have enough time to go have a glass of water and make a phone call before it completed its calculations.

There are some positives to this utility, though. The Disk Cleanup tab (see Figure 14.3) contains considerably more file categories to delete than in Windows XP. Using the More Options tab allows you to lighten your hard drive by uninstalling little-used applications by launching the Uninstall or change a program window. By clicking the Clean up button, you can delete all but the most recent restore point.

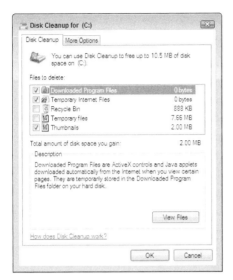

Figure 14.3. The Disk Cleanup feature lets you perform spring cleaning on your computer.

Disk Defragmenter

The Disk Defragmenter (see Figure 14.4) is a valuable tool that analyzes your hard drives to check for file fragmentation. If this number is too high versus the percentage of free space, the Disk Defragmenter will defragment your hard drive. The utility provides a very detailed report on the status of your hard drive and individual files.

You should run this utility fairly regularly, depending on how often you use your machine. A good sign that your machine is fragmented is when your machine and applications run markedly slower for no apparent reason. Incidentally, if you have a Microsoft Live OneCare subscription, you can also defragment your disk there.

Watch Out!

If you must defragment a drive, it is best to do it when you have downtime. For example, good times would be late in the evening (letting it run during the night) or on the weekend. Depending on the size of your hard drive and the fragmentation rate, this procedure can take a long time — in some cases, well over an hour.

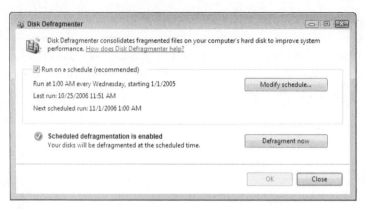

Figure 14.4. The Disk Defragmenter is a great way to speed up your computer.

This is an overall improved version of Disk Defragmenter for two reasons:

■ You can program when it should be run.

■ You can enable automatic defragmentation.

Unlike Windows XP, you can determine the right time to defragment your computer. After you program it using the Modify Schedule window, the Disk Defragmenter window tells you the last time it defragmented your disk and when the next time is scheduled. Compared to Windows XP, this is a perfect example of a small application that was greatly improved. Now, you can actually run the defragmenter without having to shut everything else down because it eats all of your machine's resources.

Backup Status and Configuration

The Backup feature (see Figure 14.5) is modernized in Windows Vista. In addition to an improved interface, it also offers a different way of achieving a system backup. If this is your first time performing a backup, you will first have to select Set up automatic file backup from the Back up Files option in the Backup and Restore Configuration window.

Your first step is to decide where you want to save your backup files. By default, Windows selects your local hard drive. We recommend not using this as a backup option; ostensibly, you'd want to protect your data from a total system crash, which means that you could lose your hard drive. There's no point in saving information to your hard drive if you could potentially lose it. It's best to store the backup on a movable device, such as a thumb drive, a removable USB flash drive, or a floppy disk. You could even save it to your hard drive and then burn it to a CD or DVD.

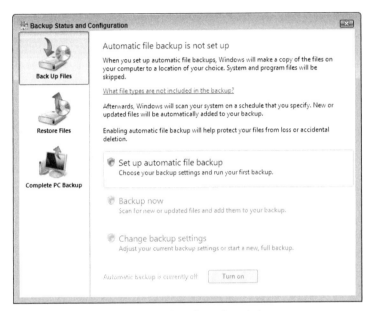

Figure 14.5. The Backup Status and Configuration window.

The next step is to determine which file types to back up. After you click Next, a list of eight different file types appear as check boxes. By default, they are all selected. To get a better idea of what is included in each file type, simply mouse over the category and descriptive text appears in the Category Details window.

Watch Out!

System files and temporary files are not included in the backup.

After you decide which information to back up, you must decide how often you want to perform a backup (see Figure 14.6). By default, Windows suggests every Sunday at 7 p.m. Depending on what you are backing up and how sensitive it is, you may want to program it more or less often. Once you have set your backup frequency, click Save settings and start backup. Once you confirm the backup, it starts in the background. During the backup, the Backup Up Files window indicates that the backup is in progress.

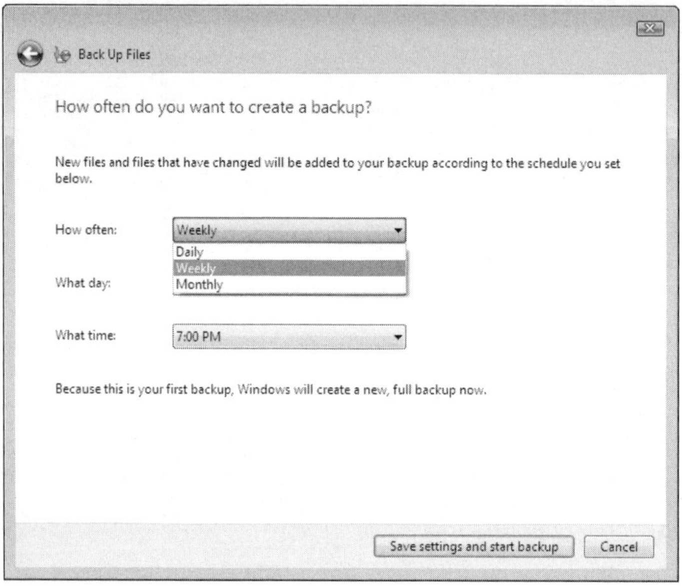

Figure 14.6. You can program how often you should perform a backup.

If you have already run a backup, you can go back to the Backup Status and Configuration window and select either Backup now or Change backup settings. You can also disable the automatic backup, which is activated once you set up a backup schedule.

You can also restore from backup using the Restore Files option in the Backup Status and Configuration window. The Restore files window (see Figure 14.7) presents you with two options:

■ Restore a backup from another computer, provided you have administrator privileges

■ Restore one or more files

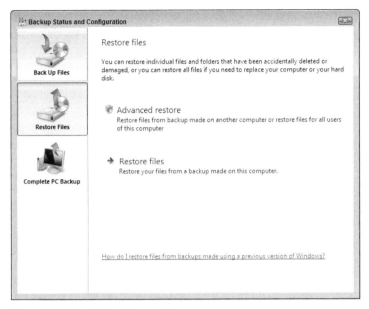

Figure 14.7. The Restore files option.

If you click Advanced restore, you have three different restore options from which to choose (see Figure 14.8):

▪ Restore files from the latest backup on your computer.

▪ Restore files from an older backup on your computer.

▪ Restore files from a backup made on another computer.

To restore a backup, you should:

1. Select the type of restore that you want to perform and click Next. This window also lets you repair Windows (a system restore) or view recently deleted files.

2. Select a file or folder to restore from the corresponding button, or use Search to find what you want to restore.
   Click Next.

3. Choose where you want to restore the recovered file; you can either restore to the original location or use Browse.... If you choose the latter, you can restore the file(s) to the original subfolder or create a subfolder for the driver letter.

4. Click Start Restore.

5. Click Finish.

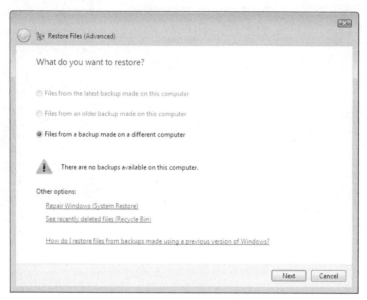

Figure 14.8. The Restore Files Advanced options.

For whatever reason, Microsoft decided to link the Backup feature from the System Tools to a Backup and Restore Center in the Control Panel (see Figure 14.9). The Backup and Restore Center lets you back up or restore files, create a restore point or change its settings, and use the System Restore. It also lets you use a new feature called the CompletePC Backup. This feature makes a backup image of your entire computer in case you have hardware failure.

Hack

You can restore previous versions of files that have been accidentally modified or deleted using shadow copies. These earlier file versions are saved as part of a restore point that you can search for restoration purposes.

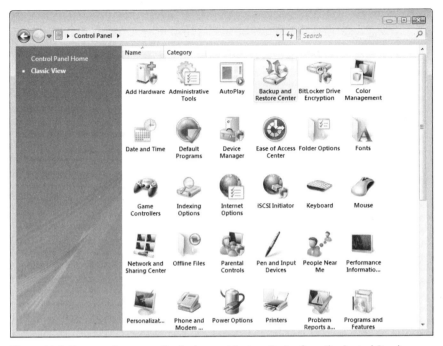

Figure 14.9. You can also access the Backup and Restore Center from the Control Panel.

The CompletePC Backup works a lot like the standard backup; you must pick your target drive (either an NTFS hard drive or a DVD). After you select your target, Vista confirms the disks that are backed up and to where they are backed up.

Making the case for backups

Windows Vista provides a backup tool for the obvious task of backing up your data in the event of catastrophic hard drive failure or some other unthinkable event whereby you could lose the entire contents of your machine. For information on using this feature, please refer to the Backup Status and Configuration section.

Backing up your machine (on a regular, if not daily, basis) is important. This is one area where you certainly don't want to get caught unprepared.

Okay, I can't take it anymore! What is a thumb drive? What is a removable drive?

It's true; this chapter tends to refer to these little gadgets quite a bit.

Not so long ago, computer-friendly people faced a dilemma; how to store or transport data with the least amount of risk.

At the time, the options were a 5.25" floppy disk (literally, a floppy disk) or a 3.5" diskette. Iomega brought out the Zip disk which could hold 100MB of data in an oversize blue drive. That led to the upgraded version, called a Jazz drive which could hold 1GB. These eventually faded away as hard drives held more data making these storage device sizes (especially Zip) obsolete. Iomega lost its luster (perhaps in part to the literal size of the disks, the price, or the legendary click of death — a familiar term for the clicking noise that Iomega drives would make before breaking).

Finally, a legitimate solution to data storage for the ever-increasing hard drive arrived. External hard drives, connected to your computer using a SCSI bus and SCSI cable, hit the market. These drives were the founding fathers of our current external drives, which are now connected via an IEEE 1394, or FireWire, connector or even using USB ports. Plug and play was finally something more than a mouse or a keyboard! These external drives are great for enhancing your data storage capacity, but they're also great if you are often on the road or often need to use the same files over several computers. Finally, many of these drives are designed to be a backup system where you can perform a one-touch system backup.

This is also the time that companies such as SanDisk put out the Cruzer Mini flash drive. These devices are named for exactly the reason you think — they are literally the size of a thumb and easily plug into an open USB port. Despite the size, they offer storage sizes from 128MB to 4GB. Despite the ever-increasing storage size, these drives have come down in price. These devices are excellent for transferring files or backing up mail folders, applications, or even entertainment files. In Windows Vista, they are also great for increasing virtual memory!

The Windows Backup utility is fine, but it's not Microsoft's specialty or a flagship product or feature. This is another situation where it may be best to use more specialized, third-party software or, quite simply, a removable USB drive that has proprietary software and is designed to easily perform system backups.

How often should you back up? It depends on how much you use your computer as well as the sensitivity of your data. Your average home user should back up at the very minimum once a month. Your computer configuration and layout can greatly change over a short period of time — you may have a new operating system, new applications, new documents, and so on. You certainly do not want to be in the position of losing your hard drive and then finding that your last backup was from six months ago and does not have any of your files or applications on it. If possible, try to schedule a system backup once a week.

Sensitive data/files are another matter. If you have sensitive data on your computer, not only should it be backed up on a daily basis, but you should also consider encrypting this data, especially if you use a laptop or a computer that is frequently accessed by other users. Get in the habit of using a thumb drive to back up important files, such as the Documents folder.

Using System Restore

Things are done a little differently in Windows Vista, as you may have noticed. For example, the Automated System Recovery is now known as the System Restore feature.

The first time you launch the application, System Restore (see Figure 14.10) indicates that you haven't created any restore points and suggests that you open System Protection. The System Protection feature is part of the System Properties window. By clicking Create, you can create a restore point.

The System Restore feature creates a snapshot of 	computer at a particular point in time. This is helpful if you later in	software or update a driver and find that you need to	ous state due to malfunction or performance issues.

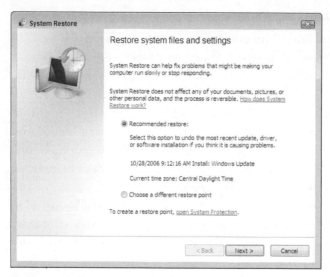

Figure 14.10. The System Restore menu.

To create and use a system restore point:

1. Open System Restore from System Tools in the Start menu.

2. Open System Protection if you need to create a restore point.

3. From the System Properties page, click the Create button in the System Protection tab.

4. Type in a name or description for your restore point.

5. Click OK in the System Properties window.

6. Close System Restore and open it again to make sure the restore points refresh.

7. Select the desired restore point and click Next.

8. Click Finish.

9. Click Yes to start the restore (see Figure 14.11).

Watch Out!

This is a very simplistic, bare-boned method to backing up your machine. It provides a "skeleton" backup of your machine in case of disk failure. Files, such as those in the Documents folder, are not backed up in this process.

Figure 14.11. Restoring from a restore point.

Windows Easy Transfer

Previously referred to as the Files and Settings Transfer Wizard, the Windows Easy Transfer is a helpful utility available in Windows Vista (see Figure 14.12). Its purpose is to help you transfer files and settings from an old computer to a new computer.

The utility lets you transfer a number of settings including Internet Explorer and Microsoft Mail settings as well as desktop and display settings and internet dialup connections.

Microsoft recommends using a direct cable connection or a network for transferring files. In fact, Windows even offers you a help topic on the main page of the wizard so that you can brush up on connecting computers. That said, in the interest of time and hassle, you may simply want to consider another option such as a removable drive (for example, a thumb drive) or save to your local hard drive and then burn it to CD.

What is the rationale for this? Why not just directly transfer data between two machines via a cable? One reason for this is that using one of the suggestions listed above means that you now have a backup of these files. Should your computer crash or a file become corrupt, you have an accessible replacement, which is especially important if you use a laptop and are on the road.

Once you start the wizard, you must first select if you are the "new" or "old" computer (see Figure 14.13). In other words, are you transferring the files and settings or receiving them? Let's choose "Old computer." Select it and move on to the next menu, which lets you decide on one of four transfer methods.

Watch Out!

In order to use this utility, you must be running Windows 95 or later (Windows 98, Windows 98SE, Windows ME, Windows NT 4.0, Windows 2000, Windows XP, or Windows Server 2003) on the old machine.

Figure 14.12. The Windows Easy Transfer.

Figure 14.13. Preparing your transfer.

Watch Out!

Unfortunately, this utility is an all-or-nothing utility; even though there is a Back button, it is dimmed. Should you need to go back to a previous screen, your only option is the Cancel button.

You may transfer files by:

■ **Direct cable.** This option is exactly what it sounds like. Using a PC to PC serial cable. The first page of the wizard provides a help topic on this option.

■ **Home or small office network.** This option is only available if you have a home or small office network. If not, it is dimmed.

■ **Floppy drive or other removable media.** This option allows you to use any removable media such as thumb drives, USB/FireWire drives, or even floppy disks. Given the propensity of floppy drives to go wobbly (corrupt), try using one of the removable media types. CD-ROM or DVD-ROM drives cannot be used here.

■ **Other.** This option lets you save settings and files to a hard drive or network drive. This option is good if you use a network drive as a backup or an archive. It's also a good option if you wish to save it to your desktop and then burn it to CD-RW.

The next window lets you choose between saving settings, files, or both. Depending on your selection, a box on the right side of the window displays the specific file types as well as which program settings will be transferred. Of course, you can select the corresponding check box on this page and customize your list. In this event, the next screen lets you add, modify, or remove items.

Once you move on to the next page, the wizard may remind you (if necessary) to install certain software programs on your new machine. The old computer then saves and compresses your files and settings.

Watch Out!

If you decide to use the third option, the removable media must be plugged-in and turned on in order for it to appear in the drop-down menu. If you plug in the drive after the wizard is open, the drive will not appear as an option. You will need to quit the utility and start over.

Importing the settings to the new computer is quite similar; go back to the wizard, select "New computer," and then get ready for an odd question. The wizard reminds you that it also needs to be run on the old computer. It offers to create a wizard disk to use on the old machine or use the wizard on the Windows Vista DVD. Eh? Option four on this page — "I don't need the Wizard Disk. I have already collected my files and settings from my old computer" — ideally will be the right option for you. If not, you should cancel and go back and collect the files and settings. Of course, Windows does give you an easy way out. You can create a Wizard Disk on a floppy or removable drive; or create one using the wizard on the Windows Vista DVD, or indicate if you already have a Wizard Disk.

Task Scheduler

The Task Scheduler utility (see Figure 14.14) lists various bits of information for programmed third-party tasks. These may include programmed antivirus software tasks or firewall-related tasks that often occur unnoticed. This is a very helpful utility, especially if you are someone who is busy and would otherwise forget to manually run important tasks like antivirus or adware. It is also helpful for people who are not regularly on the computer and would not think to perform such tasks.

Select the Add Scheduled Task button to open a wizard that lets you program a task for Windows to run (see Figure 14.15). You can then select an application from the list of programs, or you can use Browse to pick the desired program.

Once you've picked your program, you must decide the frequency (Windows Vista offers seven options, varying from daily to monthly to whenever you log on). The wizard then lets you set the time and frequency (daily, weekly, monthly, once, on startup, or on logon) with a specified start date. Select a username and add the appropriate password (twice). Once you've done that, the wizard confirms the details all over again.

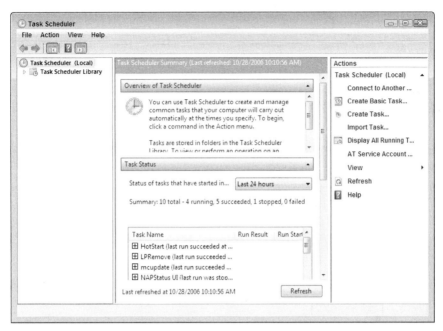

Figure 14.14. The Task Scheduler utility.

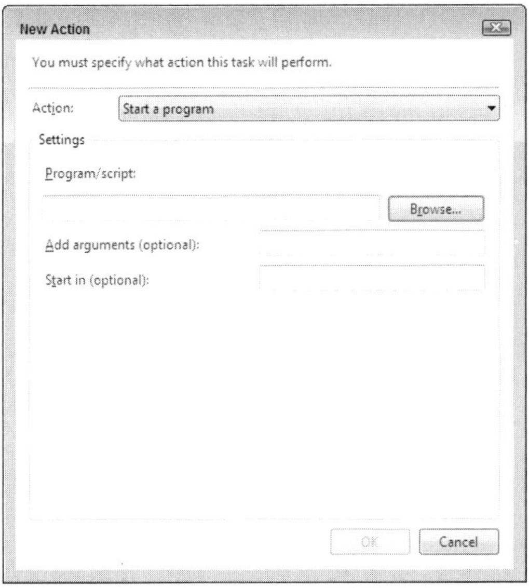

Figure 14.15. Preparing your scheduled task.

> **Watch Out!**
>
> Keep in mind your computer's usual activity when you program a task. For example, if you want to schedule a system-wide maintenance, set it for Friday evening when you're likely to have more system resources available. If you run too many tasks at the same time during prime working hours, your system may slow down.

Security Center

The Security Center (see Figure 14.16), which is also available in the Control Panel, is the central location for working with security settings, including malware protection and the Windows Firewall. For complete information on the Security Center, please refer to Chapter 7.

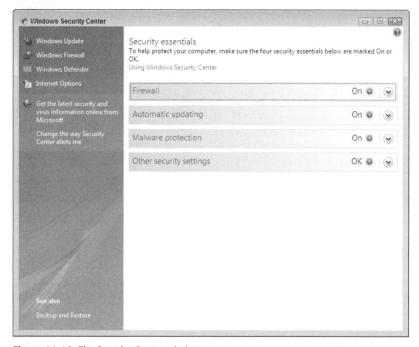

Figure 14.16. The Security Center window.

System Information

The System Information window (see Figure 14.17) is largely informational and doesn't necessarily contribute to improved system perform- ance, but it is still an invaluable system tool. This is helpful if you need to verify your computer's stats in comparison with the minimum requirements for a software program.

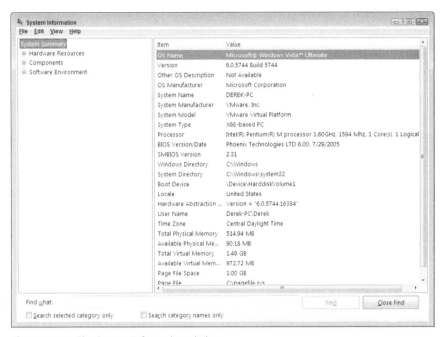

Figure 14.17. The System Information window.

This window contains summary information for hardware resources, components, the software environment, Internet settings, and Office applications. You can also perform a search for a particular item in the submenus.

The bottom line

Windows has increased its offering of utilities that make your system run smoother and take advantage of your powerful processor. Unfortunately, most of them are still poor or nothing to get excited about. Unfortunately, the existing utilities that we discussed above have not evolved. Another problem is that some essential features, such as Backup, are only available in higher-end editions. One big change that makes us hope that Microsoft will reconsider their tool and utility offering is the integrated Windows Firewall.

All things being equal, it is still better to use Microsoft Live OneCare or to use third-party system performance software such as Norton SystemWorks or McAfee Office. These tools are somewhat pricey — Norton System lists for about $70 on many sites — but worth looking into. The primary advantages of these applications are that they fully integrate into your system, they consistently monitor your machine, and they run well in the background. Finally, an automatic update feature lets you quickly update your software with updates or patches, or update virus definitions as long as you are connected to an active Internet connection. Windows System Tools seem to wait to be found and don't "play well with the other kids on the playground." The tools do their job, but they simply aren't powerful enough to cover features offered by Microsoft Live OneCare, Norton, or McAfee.

Creating new partitions

Hard drives are decreasing in physical size but ever increasing in data size. For serious hard drive hogs — users running multiple operating systems on a home machine, or gamers, or developers who need extra space for their projects — this is great news, especially as the price of drives decreases proportionately with the decrease in size.

There are, however, some drawbacks. Once these disks become fragmented, it takes forever and a day to defragment them. It's also no picnic to reformat a disk. One way to deal with these types of problems is to partition your hard drive; in other words, divide your disk into several drives.

This is a huge benefit if you wish to keep data separate on your hard drive. For example, if you use your machine for both home and professional purposes, you might keep personal information on one partition and professional information on a second partition. If you decide to make your machine a dualboot machine (in other words, run two different operating systems on your machine), running Linux on your machine side by side with Windows, for example, creating a second partition (essentially dividing the disk in two or more "sections") helps you achieve this. You can also reformat a single partition without losing the content of an entire disk each time you format the partition. You may want to partition your hard drive if you decide to run more than one operating system (in the example above), or if you have a large hard drive (to increase performance) or if you plan on doing any type of testing or development that would require frequent reformatting.

Unfortunately, creating a partition can be a confusing task using the Microsoft Windows Vista method. This area is where Windows Vista unfortunately (still) falls short; creating and managing a partition is much better handled using Norton PartitionMagic.

How low should I go?

How to partition your hard drive is not always an easy or obvious answer. First, you must decide if your disk is reasonably worth partitioning. Frankly, it may not be worth partitioning a hard disk that is less than 40GB.

Remember, the primary partition will still "host" your operating system and its files, which will eat up a large chunk of drive space. So, cutting a 20GB drive into two 10GB partitions might not be a wise idea — one partition will be dedicated to the operating system and everything that comes with it (Documents, Music, and so on), while the other partition will be limited to the remaining 10GB for your applications and files. This space fills up very quickly, especially if you store a lot of audio or video files.

Determine the size of your partition based on how you plan to use your machine. If you intend to install a second operating system, you'll most likely want to halve the disk, depending on the secondary operating system's requirements. Remember that you can create multiple partitions, so make the sizes reasonable and not random numbers. Never make a drive too small, because you never know when you may unexpectedly need more. For example, 30/70 percent or 25/75 percent is a decent partition example.

Watch Out!
If you have a large hard drive, you should consider partitioning the drive as mentioned earlier. Larger drives take longer to defragment and experience decreased performance as the drive is filled.

There are two ways of using Windows Vista to create a new disk partition: via the command line (prompt) or using the Windows interface.

Use the command line

If you are logged in as an Administrator or at least belong to the Administrator group, you can create a new partition using the command line (see Figure 14.18).

Figure 14.18. The command line in Windows Vista.

However, this is the more complicated of the two Windows Vista options; if you're looking for something simpler, by all means, use the Windows interface, which is covered in the next section.

Creating a partition is done through the use of the Diskpart utility. The Diskpart utility lets you handle objects, for example, and disk partitions through the use of scripts from a command line.

 Watch Out!
If you are used to using other versions of the Windows operating system, such as Windows 2000 Server, please note that the Diskpart utility is not the same as the Diskpart utility found in Windows 2000 Server.

The details surrounding the inner workings of this command inter-preter are beyond the scope of this book but are detailed by Microsoft at `www.microsoft.com/technet/prodtechnol/windowsserver2003/library/ServerHelp/ca099518-dde5-4eac-a1f1-38eff6e3e509.mspx.`

Use the Windows interface

The Windows interface is the easier of the two methods for creating a new partition, especially if you're not a Windows Vista power user.

This is done through the use of the Computer Management console, which is one of the pre-installed Microsoft Management Consoles (MMC).

In the Disk Management part of the console, you can see a "sketch" of the drives available on your machine, including CD-ROM drives and external/USB drives (see Figure 14.19).

By right-clicking the desired drive, you can format it, delete parti-tions, change drive letters, and so on.

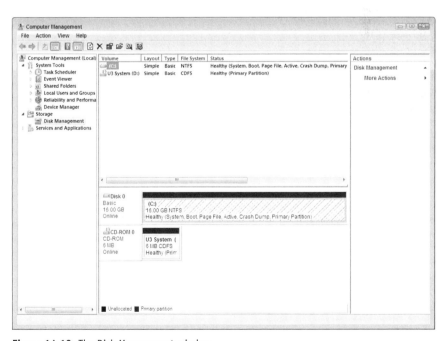

Figure 14.19. The Disk Management window.

The bottom line

Creating a new partition can be a cumbersome task in Windows Vista. Frankly, it seemed much easier when home computing was in its infancy, before Windows. If you are an advanced Windows Vista user, use the Windows options that are presented in previous sections of this chapter. It's important to attentively read all available instructions in this book or in the Microsoft Windows Vista before attempting to create a partition. Should you inadvertently format your hard drive, there is no undo feature to bring it back.

If you're lacking in confidence when it comes to delicate maneuvers such as this, invest in a third-party application designed for managing disks, drives, and volumes. Norton PartitionMagic is a perfect example of such an application; it uses a wizard format to walk you through hard drive and partition management. For more information on Norton PartitionMagic, please visit www.symantec.com/partitionmagic/.

Creating dynamic disks

Dynamic disks are actual physical disks that can only be accessed using Windows 2000, Windows XP Professional, and Windows Vista. Unlike basic disks, dynamic disks can be used to create volumes than span multiple disks or to create fault tolerant (hardware or software that guarantees data integrity in case of hardware failure) volumes.

Before you consider a dynamic disk

There are a couple of hard and fast rules that Windows Vista requires you follow before you can even consider using a dynamic disk over a basic disk.

You cannot install Windows Vista on a dynamic disk; however, you can extend the volume in order to do so. Extending a volume is simply incorporating unused disk space into the volume without losing or compromising data.

Dynamic disks cannot be used on portable computers (laptops), on USB or FireWire (IEEE 1394) disks or other removable disks, or disks using SCSI busses. In other words, you need to use a desktop computer with a standard hard drive.

If you are using a dual-boot machine (a machine that has more than one operating system; the desired OS is selected as the machine boots up), the secondary operating system must not be MS-DOS, Windows 95/98, Windows Me (Millennium Edition), Windows NT 4.0, or Windows Vista Home. The secondary operating system could be Windows Vista or something else, such as Linux Red Hat, Debian, or a UNIX operating system.

Convert a basic disk to a dynamic disk

When we say "Creating a dynamic disk," basically we mean converting a basic disk to a dynamic one. Assuming your system meets the criteria, it's a straightforward process. Remember, however, that this is a definitive process. What does this mean? It means you cannot convert your disk back to a basic disk unless you delete every volume on the disk. In other words, the entire hard disk — for example, the data on all drive letters associated with the disk (such as C, D, and F) — will be erased.

In the Disk Management window of the Computer Management console, which is found in the Administrative Tools page of the Control Panel, right-click the disk on the right side of the window. The disk has a small icon next to it (see Figure 14.20).

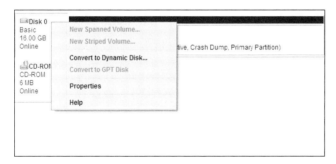

Figure 14.20. Preparing for disk conversion.

Watch Out!
Be sure to save any data and then close all open applications that are running on the drive about to be converted.

> **Inside Scoop**
>
> The above procedure is not a perfect science; it is possible that you may encounter an error. One common error we found was a missing or corrupt "hal.dll" file. To combat this problem, use the Recovery console on the Windows Vista installation CD; select the Recovery console to try and repair the current Windows installation. Press Return when it asks for your administrator password. At the prompt, type **bootcfg /list** and then type **bootcfg/rebuild**. Select Y (Yes) and add a name. Once you validate, you can reboot and select this new "operating system" and Windows will load.

Select the Convert to Dynamic Disk command from the menu that appears, you will be asked to select a basic disk(s) for conversion. The mini-wizard will ask you to confirm your selection twice before converting your basic disk to a dynamic disk and confirm that you understand the file systems on the disks will be dismounted. Once you do this, it's as simple as clicking OK. However, do realize that if you convert to Dynamic Disk, you will not be able to mount any other operating systems from any other volume on the disk.

So, what is the benefit of creating a dynamic disk or converting a basic disk to a dynamic disk? It's a great feature for spanning hard drives and creating a combined logical drive. In other words, if you have some smaller hard drives, say 5GB each, around the house, you can create a dynamic drive of 20GB using the four drives. Keep in mind that Windows Vista will allow you to "combine" up to 32 hard drives.

Work with dynamic disks

Now that you've got your disk converted to a dynamic disk, there is still quite a bit you can do as we will demonstrate next! You can create or extend a simple or a spanned volume. If the dynamic disk isn't working out for you, you can even delete it (in most cases).

Create a simple or spanned volume

This is similar to the first step necessary for converting a basic disk to a dynamic disk. You may want to keep a simple volume if you do not plan on installing a second operating system, plan on doing any type of development or testing, or if you have a modest hard drive capacity. Spanned disks are ideal if you have multiple hard drives installed on your machine, all of which have modest capacity and you'd like to string them together to make one large virtual disk.

Back in the Disk Management window of the Computer Management (see Figure 4.21) console, which, as discussed earlier, is in the Administrative Tools page of the Control Panel, right-click the disk on the left side of the window (with the icon next to it) and select New Volume from the menu that appears.

The wizard lets you decide between creating a simple (one disk) or a spanned (multiple disk) volume. If you opt for the former, select the disks you want to use to install a simple volume from the "Selected dynamic disks" menu. If you opt for the latter, make sure the desired disks appear in the "All available dynamic disks" area.

You can then select a size and a drive letter, if desired, before moving on to the formatting options. Whether you choose to format the partition is up to you. Formatting the partition is ideal if you wish to start fresh with a "new" drive. For example, if you decided to span three 10GB hard drives to make a "single" 30GB hard drive, you may want to format it before trying to install a complete installation of Windows Vista.

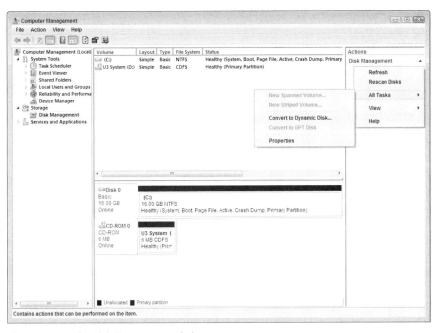

Figure 14.21. The Disk Management window.

Extend a simple or spanned volume

Once a volume is created on a dynamic disk, you may want to extend it. If you are working with a simple volume, you can extend it to include unused space on your that disk or another disk without having to lose any of your data. To do this, the simple volume must be either unformatted or formatted as an NTFS drive (and not FAT32). Why would you want to extend a volume? Let's say you have two drives — one is 25GB and the other is 50GB. On the smaller drive, the capacity is reached and you require 5GB to complete a software installation. You can extend this drive by "borrowing" it from the larger disk without losing data on either drive.

Of course, not all volumes can be extended. For example, if you are running the boot volume on a simple volume, you cannot extend it. Also, the simple volume must have been created after the conversion from basic to dynamic disk. If it was created prior to the conversion, the volume cannot be extended.

Extending a spanned volume is essentially the same, including the use of unformatted or NTFS formatted volumes.

For both types of volumes, this is done similar to the creation procedure. However, in the size box, you can now enter a new volume size and then validate.

Using RAID disks with Windows Vista

We haven't found any official documentation discussing RAID (Redundant Array of Independent Disks) configurations and their "official" compatibility with Windows Vista. However, we assume that they must be supported because there are RAID drivers available for Windows Vista. RAID is a commonly-used way to standardize and categorize disks. It is similar to a spanned disk; the difference is that spanned disks are not fault-tolerant and RAID is fault-tolerant. In other words, RAID guarantees the integrity of your data in case of hardware failure; spanned disks do not. However, if you are using Windows Vista, you have the alternate workaround of using dynamic disks as discussed earlier in this chapter.

The next best thing!

So you cannot really use a true RAID disk on Windows Vista Professional (or Home for that matter). There are still some fun RAID-related things you can do with your Vista box. For example, you can create a RAID-5 volume on a remote Windows 2000 machine.

To do this, it is assumed that you will first know how, and be able, to access a remote computer using the Computer Management module.

In the Disk Management module (not to be confused with the Computer Management module above), select a part of the dynamic disk where you will create a new RAID-5 volume. You can then set it up the same way you set up a dynamic disk (detailed earlier in this chapter), and once you're finished, simply disconnect from the Disk Management module.

Understanding disk quotas

Windows Vista allows the use of disk quotas. Disk quotas are limits assigned to a given user account limiting the amount of disk space they can use. Disk quotas allocate resources among different users. You can assign 20 percent of disk space to four users, for example. Quotas can be both a blessing and a curse; a blessing if you are a fair administrator with a realistic sense of how to divide disk space when faced with the realities of your machine's hardware. They can be a curse if you are a non-administrator user and you find yourself locked out.

Using disk quotas can be a good way of regulating your disk resources among various users. For example, if you're in college and your roommates use your computer, it's a great way to prevent the gamer from using up all your disk space with a 6-CD game that eats up 4GB on your machine. If the gamer has a quota of 1GB, the game can't be installed.

Watch Out!

The minimum disk quota should be 2MB, which is the amount of space required for user policies on Windows Vista. Any less than this and the user will not be able to use Windows properly.

Remember, only the administrator or computer owner can set these quotas. Keep in mind that with this privilege comes responsibility. How so? It's important to be realistic when setting quotas. As the computer administrator, don't shortchange yourself on the disk quota — you need some of the space you've allotted to other accounts. Also, it's important to decide whether all accounts will have quotas or just specific ones. If all accounts are subject to disk quotas and have received a certain amount of disk space, what will you do if you need to add more accounts later? You may be forced to divvy up the pie again.

Disk quotas are set using the Computer window. There are two distinct ways to modify default disk quotas (and this may sound familiar): using the command line or the Windows interface. As in previous examples, the Windows interface is the easier option for most users.

Set up disk quotas

If you right-click a volume from the Computer page and then click Properties, you will see a tab called Quota (see Figure 14.22). This tab will not be visible if you're not part of the administrators group or if your disk is formatted as FAT32. Only NTFS-formatted volumes can have disk quotas. Click Show Quota Settings.

Most likely, the status is set to "Disk quotas are disabled." This is easily changed by checking the "Enable quota management" check box. This window allows you to deny disk space to users exceeding the quota limit. Before you enable this option, keep in mind that one day the user that goes over the account allocation and is locked out may be you!

Inside Scoop

Don't forget to delete a user's account or disk quota when you are sure that the account will not be used again. Freeing up unnecessary disk space provides more space for other users.

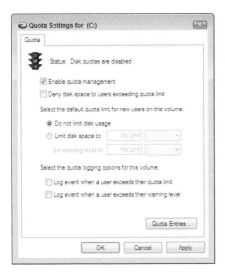

Figure 14.22. The Quota tab of the selected volume in Computer.

Surprisingly enough, you can opt to enable quota management, yet decide to not limit disk usage for new users. It seems odd that Windows would allow you to not limit disk usage for new users, yet still allow denial of disk space to previous users in excess of their limit.

The limits can be set up to 1 Exabyte (you read that right — 1,000 terabytes or 1,000,000 gigabytes) with a corresponding warning level set at your discretion that will gently remind users that they are nearing the quota limit. Windows Vista also logs any time a user exceeds a quota or warning level.

There is one more important feature on this tab — the Quota Entries dialog box (see Figure 14.22). For this example, opening the Quota Entries dialog box reveals a single entry for the administrator indicating the Status (OK), Amount Used (0 bytes), Quota Limit (No Limit), Warning Level (No Limit), and Percent Used (N/A).

You can easily add a new entry from the Quota menu or by clicking the blank page icon (first icon on the left). In the text box, add the user as directed (for a sample of proper nomenclature, click the Examples link above the text box). Use the Check Names box to validate your selection if necessary. The Advanced button provides the Select Users menu that can help you locate users in a given location. Click OK to finalize your choices.

Watch Out!

Don't forget that you can set disk quotas for removable drives (USB or FireWire), but not for thumb drives.

Once the new entry appears in the Quota Entries window (see Figure 14.23), double-clicking it (or right-clicking it and selecting Properties) opens the Quota tab, where you can set a disk limit or warning level (or to not limit usage). The quota used and amount remaining also appear on this page.

The Quota Entries dialog box also allows you to export quota settings by right-clicking an entry and selecting Export from the menu. Simply save the settings as desired.

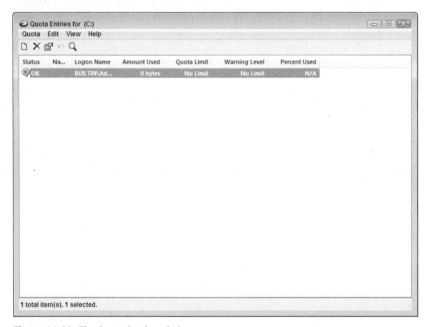

Figure 14.23. The Quota Entries window.

Inside Scoop

If you've decided that disk quotas are not helping out, simply open the Quota tab in the Computer volume and deselect the "Enable quota management" option. This may be the case if you are the lone user, or you find that you have to constantly re-adjust your quota limits.

Assign default quotas via the command line

From the command line, you can assign or modify default quota values for a user. Access the command prompt by choosing Start ⇨ All Programs ⇨ Accessories ⇨ Command Prompt, or by choosing Start ⇨ Run and then typing cmd in the Run dialog box.

Again, make sure the volume is NTFS. From the command line, simply type:

```
fsutil quota modify [volumepathname] [threshold] [limit]
[username]
```

The first value, volumepathname, is simply the drive letter where you wish to set the quota. The second value is the warning level limit in bytes (not megabytes or gigabytes, but plain old bytes). The limit is just that, the limit. It too is measured in bytes. The final value is the username, which must respect the domain\username format in order to work.

The fsutil value is a versatile command that is very helpful when managing disk quotas. Consult the Windows Vista online help (using "fsutil" as a search term) for more information on the use of this command, which includes disabling, tracking, enforcing, and querying disk quotas.

Assign default quotas via the Windows interface

As stated earlier in this section, assigning quotes is done through the Quota tab of the selected volume in Computer. The "Limit disk space to" field is the appropriate place to assign or modify default quotas.

Watch Out!

You must be logged on as the administrator or be part of the administrators group in order to use this feature.

Work with dual monitors

If you work in Information Technology or in the graphic arts, you can certainly appreciate the need for dual monitors. Windows Vista continues the Windows tradition of allowing such a configuration. In fact, you can connect up to ten monitors for a single field of vision.

In this setup, a single monitor is designated as the primary display. This is the monitor hooked up to the first video out port. If you have a laptop, you have a feature called Dualview, which is essentially the same as what we describe earlier, with the exception that you cannot select your primary display. The primary display is always the LCD display.

The monitors are set in the Display Settings either in the Control Panel or by right-clicking Personalize on the desktop and then clicking the Display Settings option (see Figure 14.24).

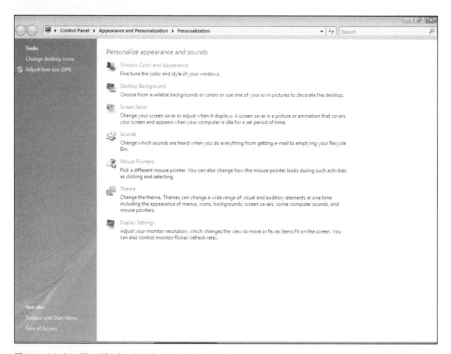

Figure 14.24. The Display Settings window.

Watch Out!

Visit the Microsoft Web site at http://support.microsoft.com/ default.aspx?scid=kb;en-us;307397 and make sure your display adapter is compatible with the multiple monitor feature.

The list of available monitors (displays) appears in a drop-down menu in the middle of the window. To find which display is currently active, click the Identify Monitors button. The monitor icons appear illustrating which monitor is number one, number two, and so on. Displays appear in a preview area toward the top of the page. You can arrange the monitors depending on how you want to drag items across your screens. If you'd like to move desktop items from top to bottom, place the second display below display number one. If you wish to move items from left to right, place the second display next to the right of the first display. Once you have orchestrated the positioning of the multiple monitors, you are set to go.

Configure a UPS

Windows Vista allows the use of Uninterruptible Power Supplies (UPS). A UPS is a device that sits between your machine and the electrical socket. In the event of a power outage, the UPS guarantees a continuity of power for a limited amount of time.

The UPS also protects your machine against potentially fatal enemies such as power surges. At the very minimum, if you cannot afford a UPS device for your home system, or you think it will not provide enough value to justify the cost, make sure you have a quality surge protector to protect your machine. Personal experience makes this worth repeating: At the very minimum, buy a proper surge protector for your computer equipment — make sure it says surge protector, because not all multiple socket plugs actually protect against surges or brownouts.

One last thing, please consult the product documentation for your UPS device before attempting installation.

Once you have installed your UPS, you can manage its properties in the Power Options menu in the Control Panel. The Power Options Properties dialog box has a UPS tab that features device status (as well as device estimates) and details about the device, such as the manufacturer or model.

Watch Out!

You must be logged on as the administrator or be part of the administrators group in order to use with UPS Configuration.

Watch Out!

Do not, at any time, attempt to change these settings before consulting the user documentation provided with your UPS device. The warning even appears at the top of the Power Options page with a large warning icon. Heed it.

To configure your UPS device, simply go to the Power Options Properties dialog box and click Select in the Details section. The UPS Selection window appears. None appears by default: select Generic. Once Generic appears as the selected manufacturer, click Custom in the Select model area. Select the port where the UPS is installed. Once you go on to the next page, you can configure the signal polarities for your device and then click Finish.

Once installed, it may be a good idea to test your device. However, do not test it on the key computer in your network. Try it on the weakest link of your computer collection. If you only have a single machine, you're not in luck: you can only test your main computer. There is always the potential of shorting out your machine.

To test, simply unplug the UPS device and wait until the UPS battery is almost flat, then plug it back in (this will simulate a power outage). Your device most likely has some power. If all is right with the world, everything will be working normally.

If you wish to remove the device, go back to the Power Options Properties dialog box and click Select and then select None from the list of manufacturers. The device is now safe to remove from your machine.

Just the facts

- No matter how often you use your computer, it is essential that you back up your data and system files. Windows Vista offers some on-board tools to help get this done.

- Windows Vista helps you maximize hard drive space by allowing you to extend or span disk drives.

- Keep track of your users and disk usage by using Windows Vista's disk quota feature.

■ Windows Vista works with UPS devices to protect your machine and data in case of a power outage.

■ The dual monitor feature allows you to connect several monitors to a single computer, making your work area larger. This is an excellent feature for graphic artists or anyone else who spends their day working in front of a single monitor.

Chapter 15

Managing Portable Computers

Portable computing has come a long way since Windows XP came out. Of course, laptops have long been a popular option for business people and others who require portability or simply don't have the room for a desktop system. Over the years, laptops have continually improved their power while becoming increasingly smaller and lighter.

This chapter is specifically dedicated to you, the laptop user. We will discuss important laptop issues, such as hardware profiles, setting appropriate levels of power management, improving remote capability, the new Windows SideShow, and improved features for Tablet PC. Windows Vista contains improvements for making all of the above easier.

Goodbye hardware profiles, hello Mobility Center

Windows Vista has dropped hardware profiles from its line. According to Microsoft, this was a rarely used feature in Windows XP, and so it has made its swan song and is relegated to the dustbin along with items such as WinFS, EFI support, and Windows PowerShell. It's unfortunate that more users didn't use this feature; however, it apparently wasn't practical. If user feedback indicates that users weren't using it, Microsoft did the right thing by removing it from Vista.

Out with the old, in with the new; let's take a look at the Mobility Center, which lets you handle many of the features in the Power Options window (see Figure 15.1). This new feature is the central location for mobile users. The Mobility Center is available in Home Premium, Business, Enterprise, and Ultimate editions of Windows Vista.

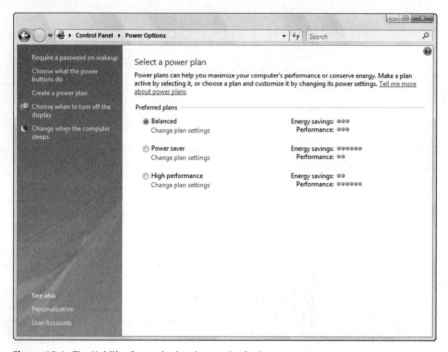

Figure 15.1. The Mobility Center is the place to be for laptop users.

The Windows Mobility Center is located in the Control Panel, assuming you are working on a mobile computer (for example, a laptop). To open it, there are three options:

- Double-click Mobile PC and then Windows Mobility Center.
- Click the battery meter icon in the notification area and click Mobility Center.
- Use the Windows button + X.

Watch Out!

The Mobility Center is only available on mobile computers. If you are using a desktop computer, this feature is not installed, and thus, does not appear.

By comparison, the hardware profile manager adjusts hardware settings for different locations, while the Mobility Center helps adjust Control Panel settings for different locations.

The Mobility Center is a series of frequently used Windows computer settings arranged in rows of squares that each contain different information. By default, the Mobility Center lets you set the following:

- **Brightness (Internal LCD Display).** Using the slider, you can set the desired brightness of your laptop monitor.

- **Volume (PC Sound).** Using the slider, you can adjust the speaker volume of your laptop or even mute it.

- **Battery Status.** You can view your battery status or select a power plan from the drop-down list.

- **Wireless Connection.** You can view information on your wireless network connection or turn it off.

- **External Display.** You can set up a secondary display (for example, a projector) for presentation purposes.

- **Sync Center.** You can sync information between your laptop and another computer or view the status of an existing sync.

- **Presentation Settings.** You can adjust settings for a presentation; for example, speaker volume or desktop background.

Depending on the manufacturer of your computer, it is possible that manufacturer-specific panes are added to the Mobility Center to facilitate management of unique features.

Exploring power management options

If you're a laptop owner, it doesn't take long to realize how precious, and fleeting, battery life is. Frankly, it's quite a hassle to find the right balance between performance and longevity. In a perfect world, it's easier to just whip out your flat battery and pop in a fully charged replacement. The reality, unfortunately, is that all batteries have a relatively short life span, especially if you are using multiple applications or multimedia. Also, a secondary battery can be quite costly and not an option for everyone.

The truth about Windows Vista is that it guzzles battery power; in fact, it currently has less favorable results than benchmark results for Windows XP. If you are using the Aero theme, you can expect even shorter battery life. Microsoft hopes to improve upon this, especially when hybrid disks hit the shelves in 2007. If you run Windows Vista on a laptop with a hybrid drive (which Microsoft strongly recommends you do), you can theoretically reduce power consumption by 70–90%, thereby reducing overall computer energy consumption by up to 12%. This is because the ReadyDrive feature (discussed in Chapter 13) puts the hybrid drive into a power save mode.

All of this is not to say that Windows Vista doesn't have a better, more streamlined power management feature. This feature is actually quite nice and users will appreciate the simplicity (see Figure 15.2).

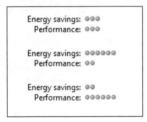

Figure 15.2. The square pegs of Windows Mobility Center.

There are a number of ways of accessing power management settings:

- Click Power Options in the Control Panel.
- Type **Power Options** in the Start menu Search box.
- Type **powercfg.cpl** in the Start menu Search box.

The whole notion of a desktop versus laptop configuration is out the window in Windows Vista. In fact, Windows Vista's power management options (see Figure 15.3) are based on power plans, which are shown in Figure 15.1 and 15.4. Power plans are a "package" of hardware and system settings that you can apply to your laptop/mobile computer. This isn't really a new concept; in previous versions of Windows, power plans were referred to as power schemes.

Vista lets you select from one of three power plans (Balanced, Power saver, and High performance), or lets you mix and match to create your own power plan. That's not all the Power Options window lets you do; you can choose how power buttons behave, create a new power plan, and schedule when a display should be turned off or when the computer goes to Sleep.

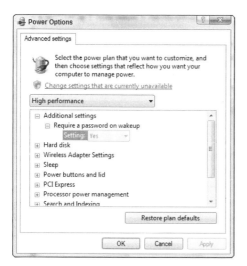

Figure 15.3. The Power Options Advanced window lets you set the minutiae for a longer life.

As we mentioned earlier, there are three different power plans. The Balanced plan gives you all the power you need when necessary and conserves battery power during inactivity. The Power saver plan puts the priority on maximizing battery power. The High performance plan goes for broke! It uses full processor speed and enhanced performance; on the other hand, you have a considerably shorter battery life.

A key appears next to each of the preferred plans, illustrating the balance between energy savings and performance. As you can see, balanced has a true equilibrium between the two criteria; conversely, the other two are heavily tilted towards one of the two criteria.

If you want to customize a plan, you have two choices: edit a power plan or create a new power plan. If you just want to edit a plan, click the Change plan settings link. The Edit Plan Settings windows appears, allowing you to set when to turn off the display and when to put it to sleep. There are a number of advanced settings that you can configure for the power plan (see Figure 15.4). If at any time you wish to restore the initial settings (default), you can do it from either the Advanced settings page or the Edit Plan Settings page.

Bright Idea

If you'd prefer not to work with the Control Panel, you can click the battery meter in the notification area to switch individual power settings.

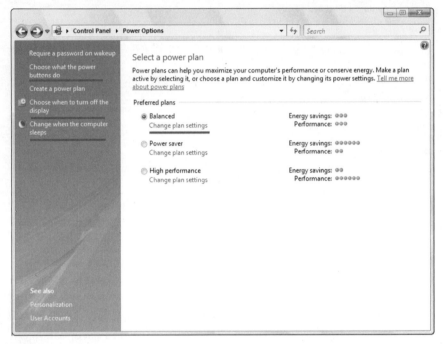

Figure 15.4. There are a ridiculous number of ways to change a plan; choose one.

If you create a new plan, do the following:

1. Click the Create a power plan link in the Power Options window.

2. Select the preferred power plan closest to your ideal plan.

3. Enter a name for your new plan. Click Next.

4. Change settings for when to turn off the display and when to put the computer to sleep.

5. Click Create.

The Power Options page displays your power plan in place of the power plan that you selected to modify. The original plan that you copied over is relegated to the Additional plans section just below the Preferred plans. If you decide that you no longer when to use your customized plan, you must first select a plan other than the one you wish to delete. Then, you click the Change plan settings link of the plan to delete; click the Delete this plan link. A dialog box asks you to confirm this; click OK if you are ready to confirm.

Using the first two links on the left pane of the Power Options window, Require a password on wakeup and Choose what the power buttons do, lets you manage your plans accordingly. Both of these links open the System Settings page (see Figure 15.5), which lets you define power buttons and password protection.

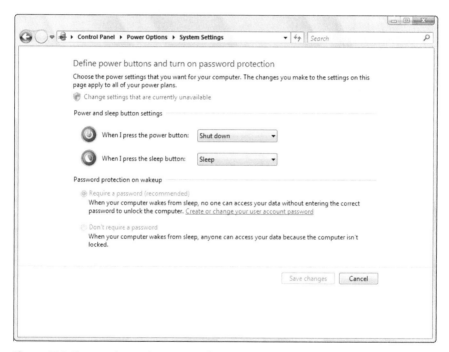

Figure 15.5. You can change the purpose of power buttons and require a password to wake up.

Inside Scoop

You cannot delete any of the original power plans, which do not feature the Delete this plan link.

The Power and sleep buttons let you define the action performed when you click each respective button. By default, the choices are rather logical; the sleep button puts your computer to sleep and the power button turns off your computer. You can change the power button to sleep, shut down, or hibernate. The sleep button can be set to sleep, hibernate, or do nothing.

To be honest, we're not quite sure why you'd want to change the behavior of either button. If you're not comfortable with the sleep feature, or wish to maintain Windows XP–like behavior, you may want to change how the sleep button behaves.

The other option on this page lets you set whether or not to require a password when your computer wakes up from Sleep. We recommend that you enable this feature to prevent someone else from "waking up" your computer and accessing your data. If you don't have a password set up for your account, you can do this using the User Accounts section from the Control Panel.

The Choose when to turn off the display link is exactly the same thing as the Change plan settings link. This link displays the settings for whatever radio button is selected in Preferred plans. Quite frankly, it seems rather pointless to have the same feature listed twice in the same window. Pick your poison, both options provide the same feature.

We'll let you guess what the Change when the computer sleeps feature does. In fact, the previous paragraph applies verbatim. This is a perfect example of bad interface design. A link to User Accounts, so that you can set an account password, would be more helpful here than the same window presented in three different ways in the same window.

Picking the right settings

Only you can determine what the best settings are for your laptop. It's important to take into account what kind of work you will be doing and for how long you will be running on battery power.

Bright Idea
Pay attention to the low-battery notification (new to Windows Vista) to make sure that you haven't reached a critically low battery level.

Bright Idea

Reduce the brightness of your laptop display to help reduce battery consumption. Many laptops automatically decrease brightness when running on battery power. Reduce yours to the lowest level that is still comfortable for you.

If you are working with an AC adapter, you might as well just select High performance and not look back. However, if you are using battery power, you'll certainly want to spend a little more time thinking about this. We usually use Power saver so that we can maximize energy savings; of course, we use our laptops conservatively when operating off battery power. For example, watching a DVD is off limits when on battery power. We tend to limit our activities to the Microsoft Office or Internet applications when running on battery.

We recommend setting the display to turn off in 15–20 minutes and then put the computer to sleep after 25–30 minutes. Your needs will certainly vary, so you should spend time becoming familiar with the Power Options page and see what works best for you.

Understanding power states

Windows Vista has made a couple of changes to the list of power states. In the new power button found in the Start menu (see Figure 15.6), you have several states or system options from which to choose. Options such as Switch User, Log Off, Lock, Restart, and Shut Down are quite obvious in function.

Figure 15.6. The new power button in Windows Vista is the literal BRS (Big Red Switch), though it's black in Vista.

However, you may be less sure about the Sleep and Hibernate functions. First, let's talk about the missing Standby option that you may remember from Windows XP days. In short, it's gone. The Standby option has joined forces with the Hibernate feature to form Sleep. The Sleep feature is discussed in Chapter 13, but we will give a quick refresher of its purpose here.

Inside Scoop

The Sleep feature is not available on all mobile computers; some video cards do not support the Sleep state. If you are unable to go to Sleep, update your video driver. If the feature is turned off, check your BIOS settings.

The Sleep state is like Hibernate in that it greatly reduces how much power is used during this state and also protects your data by saving your files and applications and putting them into memory if you are on a desktop. Using a laptop, it protects your data's integrity. Using the Sleep feature on your laptop is a great way to reduce the number of times you restart and shut down your laptop. It has the added benefit of being fast like Standby. In fact, we've found Vista's Sleep function to be considerably faster than XP's Standby feature.

The Hibernate feature uses less power, but it still uses more power than the Sleep state. The other downside is that the hibernation file can be quite large, depending on the amount of RAM installed on your laptop. If your laptop is running out of disk space and you find that you don't use Hibernation mode, we recommend disabling hibernation and getting some disk space back. Be careful, you cannot disable hibernation in Windows Vista like you could in Windows XP. This involves a little more typing! To disable hibernation:

1. Open a command prompt from the Accessories menu in the Start menu.

2. Type **powercfg –h off**.

3. Press Enter.

Hibernation has other downsides too; for example, some services and activities don't work when you come back out of hibernation. If you are connected to a Web server for a transaction and you go into hibernation, the session won't be available when you come back. Similarly, if you are connected to a wireless access point, then hibernate and return from hibernation, your wireless connection is gone. You will need to re-establish your wireless connection or reboot the system so it starts clean without any services in a frozen or pending state.

You can also change what happens when you close your laptop (Figure 15.7). In the Select a power plan page, click Choose what closing the lid does. You can then set the desired behavior on the Define power buttons and turn on password protection page. We recommend setting this option to Sleep; once you make your decision, click Save Changes.

Figure 15.7. Windows Vista lets you decide what happens when you close your laptop.

Work with Tablet PCs

Tablet PCs have become increasingly common in the past few years. Microsoft realized this trend and created a Tablet PC version for Windows XP. Windows Vista continues where Windows XP left off, notably by including Tablet PC features in Windows Vista instead of creating a completely separate operating system.

While we won't cover Tablet PCs themselves, we will discuss some of the new features available for these users in Windows Vista. There are a number of new features and improvements for the pen, input panel, and handwriting configuration.

Tablet PC applications are found in the Tablet PC menu in Accessories in the Start menu. From here, you can access the Input Panel, Sticky Notes, and the Windows Journal.

Building a better pen

In order to improve precision, Windows Vista offers a new cursor for Tablet PC. This makes pen strokes easier to read and easier to recognize. It also makes such maneuvers as targeting scroll bars, small menu items, and notification area icons easier.

You can also write with more confidence in Windows Vista. If you worked with Windows XP Tablet PC, you may have noticed that the lack of feedback made it easier to wonder if the system was just slow or if you don't tap the screen well enough. Vista provides discreet, yet helpful, feedback.

The pen in Windows Vista makes selecting multiple files easier. To select multiple files, simply pen over a set of files with the pen; you can select the files and then perform a group action, such as move, copy, or cut.

Another new pen-related feature in Windows Vista is Pen Flicks. You can use Pen Flicks to navigate or perform shortcuts. These are helpful for scrolling up and down or going back or forward a page. Literally flick a pen to scroll down instead of dragging the scroll bar down to the end of a page. There are also editing pen flicks that let you copy, cut, and paste a body of text using pen flicks. Windows Vista lets you customize pen flicks to perform other important shortcuts or actions.

Does your Tablet PC support touch-screen functions? If so, here's some good news: so does Windows Vista. Vista has a new feature called the touch Pointer, which is a drag area, a pointer area, and a left and right click button.

The final pen tool is the snipping tool. The snipping tool lets you capture a screenshot or part of any item on your screen. You can also write comments for the snipped selection and then e-mail it or just save it. This isn't a totally new feature; it first appeared in Windows XP Tablet Edition 2005; however, this is a much improved version.

The new and improved Input Panel

The Input Panel lets you create notes using an on-screen keyboard or by using the handwriting feature. Windows Vista reads and translates your input into text. This is a great feature if you're in a location where using your laptop's keyboard to type would be inappropriate, like in a classroom lecture or an important meeting at work.

The Input Panel now supports Auto Complete. This feature is exactly the same as the auto complete features that currently exist in Microsoft Office Outlook and Internet Explorer. Based on words you've previously entered into the Input Panel, it suggests any eventual matches to save you time and effort.

Erasing errors (hey, we all make typos) is a lot easier in Windows Vista. If you used the XP version for Tablet PC, you may remember how you had to make that Z-like sketch to erase a word. If you have a Palm Pilot, you probably remember this too. Fortunately, Windows Vista is a little more understanding and allows other options for erasing mistakes.

For example, you can use strikethrough, and circular and angles scratch-out sketches. You can even make M-like sketches to erase words. Of course, you can also use the "eraser" at the end of your pen if it has one!

Making writing legible

Some of us, including us, have handwriting that may be less than legible. Windows Vista understands our predicament and even lets people like us create writing samples (see Figure 15.8). No, it's not to impress a publisher; these writing samples are to help Windows Vista recognize your writing style. The Handwriting Personalization tool lets you enter upper- and lowercase letters as well as a sample sentence. You can also teach it to go after specific recognition errors.

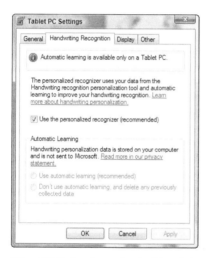

Figure 15.8. Input your handwriting style so Vista better understands you.

Windows Vista also provides an automatic learning feature that can study your writing style. To maximize its chances of successful writing recognition, Windows Vista collects data about the words you employ and how they are written. If you are writing in English, this feature creates a dictionary based on sent e-mail messages. Any new words found are added to this dictionary,

Finally, you can send recognition errors as a report to Microsoft. If you decide to do this, be sure that you consult Microsoft's Web site and read their privacy policy before you send any information to them. If you are one of the many users that doesn't trust Microsoft, you may want to reconsider sending such information. Of course, if the Microsoft trust issue is a tempest in a teapot to you, send away!

Understanding ClearType

Microsoft continues the use of ClearType technology in Windows Vista. First introduced in Windows XP, this feature is now turned on by default (unlike in XP).

What is it all about? Laptop users, as well as desktop users with LCD (Liquid Crystal Display) screens, have long complained about how fonts appear. Fonts appear perfectly well at certain resolutions, but are horrible at order. Many monitors work well at 1024 x 768; however, pricier monitors can support greater resolutions. What is essential is that you find a resolution that is comfortable for your vision and where the icons don't appear fuzzy.

The problem with LCD screens wasn't the fonts, but the technology. Liquid crystals are larger than CRT (Cathode Ray Tube) display pixels, and are square-like in shape instead of round. As a result, screen objects can appear blurry because some of the crystals try to display only part of each image.

Fortunately, CRT monitors are becoming less and less the norm, while LCD is increasingly popular. These types of screens are found in laptops, Tablet PCs, and in flat-panel screens (for computer and television). As we mentioned earlier, ClearType has been around since the Windows XP days. Microsoft wisely opted not to activate it by default because, at the time, CRT monitors still ruled the day. Since the average Windows user probably uses the out-of-the-box configurations, many people either didn't know it was there (Microsoft's fault) or didn't bother to enable this feature.

Inside Scoop

Read your computer or monitor's documentation to see the list of supported and recommended resolutions. If you select an unsupported resolution, your screen will go black and you will be unable to see what you are doing to get your old resolution back.

Things are different now in Windows Vista; ClearType is turned on by default regardless of your screen type! To help make things clearer, we have seven new fonts in Windows Vista:

- Constantia™
- Cambria
- Corbel
- Calibri
- Candara™
- Consolas
- Segoe UI

The first five fonts are ideal for e-mail, Web design, and writing documents. The Consolas font is ideal for developers who are writing code. There is also a new font called Segoe UI, which is the new Windows Vista interface font.

If you use Far East languages, ClearType has been optimized to accept bold characters and provides better horizontal text display through the use of a new font, called Meiryo.

If you decide that you still prefer not to use ClearType to improve the appearance of screen fonts, open the Appearance Settings from the Control Panel (Appearance and Personalization, Personalization, Visual Appearance). If you click Effects..., click the Use the following method to smooth edges of screen fonts check box so that it is no longer checked. You can also leave this box checked and select Standard from the drop-down list. We recommended enjoying the improved font display and sticking with ClearType (see Figure 15.9).

Figure 15.9. Though we don't recommend it, you can still disable ClearType fonts.

Work with Windows SideShow

Windows Vista offers another new feature; however, most users probably won't be able to use it. If you have a secondary screen on your laptop (literally a screen that is on the lid of your laptop; they are probably no more than a few inches by a few inches in size), then Windows Vista supports this new platform.

Windows SideShow uses small applications from third parties that allow you to view information in this secondary screen without having to turn on your computer (see Figure 15.10). This can be helpful if you need to consult information in a hurry, but don't have the time or means to turn on your laptop. For example, you could pull up an e-mail message (Outlook Inbox), consult Outlook Tasks, Contacts, and Calendar, or even access Windows Media Player. There are even gadgets that can alert you in real-time of a new message or phone call.

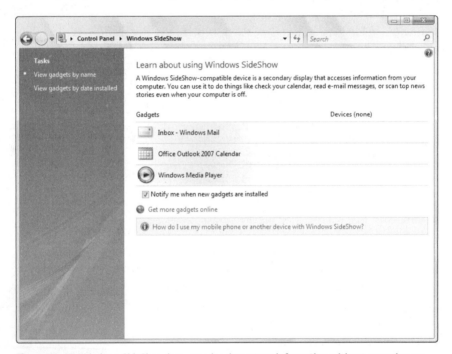

Figure 15.10. Windows SideShow lets you view important information without powering up.

Through the use of these devices and gadgets, Windows SideShow lets you save time and battery life. Most information can be pulled up in the same amount of time it would take to consult such information on a PDA. The way it works is that Windows SideShow writes copies of your e-mails into the secondary screen's memory cache.

Using the Windows SideShow menu from the Control Panel (see Figure 15.10), you can set preferences for any installed devices, including when your computer should update your installed gadgets.

We really like the concept of this feature, though it seems highly unlikely that many users will take advantage of it, at least at the time of Windows Vista's launch. These types of secondary displays simply haven't saturated the market yet. When they do, Vista users will really appreciate this new feature, especially if they are always on the go.

Setting up VPN

Virtual Private Networks, also known as VPN, are ways of connecting remote computers to an office network so that your remote computer takes on the appearance and behavior of your network computer operating on a LAN. This lets you act exactly as if you are in the office; you can use the Exchange server or even print to network printers.

You can use the Remote Desktop (see Figure 15.11) feature in Windows to do this; for more information, we discuss the Remote Desktop feature in Chapter 11.

Remote Desktop aside, there are other methods of remote access found in larger companies; these often require large amounts of hardware, specialized software, and a full-time IT staff to manage the VPN.

VPN still remains one of the cheapest and easiest ways to give employees access to internal resources while on the road. As a laptop user, you may find that a VPN client is all you need. It sits between your operating system and a network adapter, and as such does not consume large quantities of hard drive space or processing cycles. Setting up your computer to work over a VPN connection is detailed in Chapter 11.

Inside Scoop

Check with your IT department before attempting to connect to a VPN. Your company may have preconfigured software for you to install and quickly access the network. Some companies may require additional permissions before your account can access the VPN.

Figure 15.11. The Remote Desktop is a great feature that's been around for awhile.

Configure offline files

Windows Vista, like its predecessor, allows you to keep a copy of files stored on the network locally so that you can work with them when you are offline.

If you decide to use offline files, there are two very important pieces of information to keep in mind. First, Fast User Switching is not possible when using offline files. Secondly, be careful when synchronizing folders. Windows Vista checks timestamps to see which version is the most recent and uses that. If someone modified the network version since you last updated your copy, you will lose your work. Either make the network file off limits to other users, or save a copy of your file to the desktop for safe keeping.

To access this feature, type Offline Files in the Start menu Search box.

1. In the General tab, make sure Offline Files are enabled.

2. In the Disk Usage tab, make sure the disk space limits are to your liking.

3. In the Encryption tab, click Encrypt... to make sure your files are protected.

4. In Network, set the On slow connections, automatically work offline option to your liking.

Back in the General tab (Figure 15.12), you can view your offline files by clicking the so-named button. This opens the Offline Files folder, which displays the list of files currently available offline. Once you're ready to sync your folder with your network, go back to the General tab, and click Open Sync Center.

Figure 15.12. The Offline Files window lets you work with network files offline.

This feature probably isn't much help to home users that aren't working on office files from their machine. If you do regularly work from home on your machine, it may still be a good idea to check with your IT department to make sure that any internal IT policies forbid the use of offline files.

Just the facts

- The Mobility Center lets you adapt your Control Panel settings to various locations.

- Use power management power plans to create a strategy for maximizing laptop battery power.

- Use the Sleep state to let your computer conserve energy, while protecting your data.

- Windows SideShow lets you view important Outlook information without having to turn on your laptop.

- VPN is a great, easy way to connect to your corporate servers while on the road.

Troubleshooting Windows Vista

I n a perfect world, Windows Vista would work perfectly and never have problems. In that same world, we wouldn't have to work either. Unfortunately, you may find yourself in a bit of a dodgy situation with Vista every now and then.

Every operating system has its faults and bugs; it's true that Windows Vista is a new operating system and it may take a service pack or two before it really hits its stride. Nevertheless, Windows Vista is much more stable than previous versions of Windows. However, problems may occur. In this chapter, we provide some tips to help you combat those issues.

Using the User Assistance platform

We'll be honest with you — most online help systems are garbage. We feel well placed to say that, having almost 20 years of technical communication experience between us. That said, the Windows Vista User Assistance platform (also known as Windows Help and Support) is a very nice support system that actually helps users.

In the interest of full disclosure, we should mention that at the time of writing this book, the help system is not 100 percent complete. However, it is complete enough to recognize that Microsoft has totally changed how they help customers with Windows Vista.

In the past, the Help and Support system has been quite principled; in other words, it spent a lot of time describing how features should work. Windows Vista is a huge shift from that mentality; the Help and Support Center (HSC) now helps you accomplish tasks. It's a much more pragmatic approach to online help. To open the online help, click Start ⇨ Help and Support (see Figure 16.1). There is also contextual help in certain menus and folders (for example, Documents); this is represented by a blue circle with a question mark (see Figure 16.2).

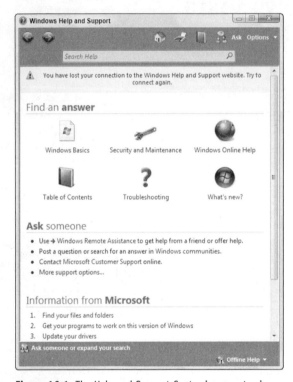

Figure 16.1. The Help and Support Center is a great primary resource.

The HSC in Windows Vista makes far better use of screen real estate than the Windows XP help. It is a single pane, rather than a main page with various panels. The HSC is broken into three sections: Find an answer, Ask someone, and Information from Microsoft.

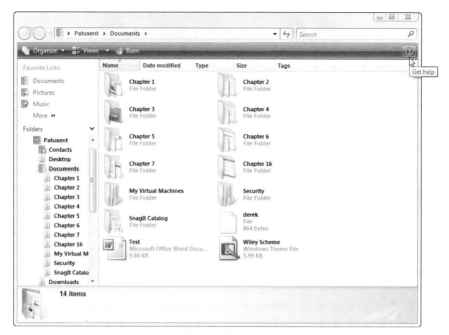

Figure 16.2. Yes, contextual help is still available in Windows Vista.

Find an answer

The Find an answer section displays six different icons that are designed to answer the most frequently asked topics or concerns (see Figure 16.3). We really like this approach because the six sections aren't necessarily links within the traditional online help structure. We detail these icons in the following paragraphs:

■ The Windows Basics page is a list of introductory topics that teach you important rudimentary information and concepts, such as learning about your computer, desktop fundamentals, working with programs, files, and folders, working with the Internet, using the Help, and so on.

■ The Security and Maintenance page provides important information and links to Vista features that help you keep your computer running smoothly.

■ The Windows Online Help page takes you to an online Web site that has the latest in help and support. It is like an expanded online help that picks up where the current HSC leaves off.

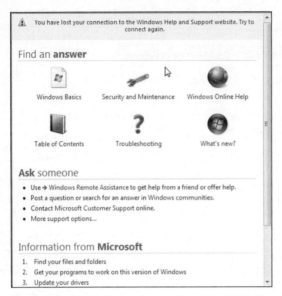

Figure 16.3. The Find an answer section of the HSC is like a beginner's manual.

- The Table of Contents page takes you to a traditional online help table of contents.

- The Troubleshooting page offers troubleshooting tips for handling networking, Web, e-mail, and hardware and driver issues.

- The What's new page provides a quick overview of the new features in your particular edition of Windows Vista.

Because Microsoft has traditionally not included user documentation with their operating systems (or software, for that matter), we recommend starting your Windows Vista experience using the HSC.

Ask someone

If you're still stuck, Microsoft offers a lifeline of support using the Ask someone section (see Figure 16.4). This section has four different options for obtaining additional support. These include

- **Remote Assistance.** Discussed in Chapter 11, the Remote Assistance feature lets you contact a friend to help you out or lets you help a friend out.

- **Windows communities.** A Web-based forum where you can post questions and reply to queries from other users with support issues. This option requires a live Internet connection.

- **Microsoft Customer Support.** This feature takes you to the Microsoft Support Web site; it provides information on available support options. This too requires a live Internet connection.

- **More support options.** The weakest link of the section, it rehashes the above, plus offers a link to the Knowledge Base, the Microsoft Web site for IT professionals, as well as Microsoft support phone numbers.

Microsoft does offer a rather extensive set of support options in Vista. Between these multiple options, you should hopefully be able to solve any troubleshooting issues quickly. It's also nice to see an expansive help and support system online. If your computer is completely KO'd, you can always use another computer to visit the Web-based help and support Web site to get answers for the other computer.

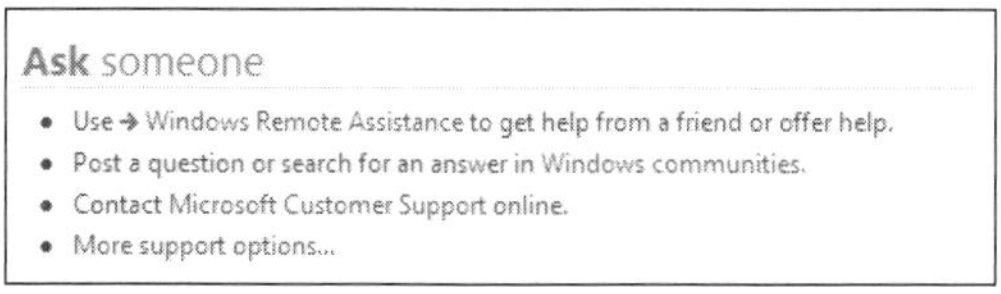

Ask someone

- Use → Windows Remote Assistance to get help from a friend or offer help.
- Post a question or search for an answer in Windows communities.
- Contact Microsoft Customer Support online.
- More support options...

Figure 16.4. The Ask someone section of the HSC lets you do just that.

Information from Microsoft

The final section contains a short list of presumed frequently asked questions. These questions appear as links that display an online help page that acts more like a user manual or an article than traditional online help. Microsoft has suddenly become expansive in the Windows Vista HSC, and it's quite welcome. These articles feature extensive information on how to realize a particular task; they also provide other references, including a See also section.

A traditional online help system

Don't worry; there is still a traditional online help system! At the top of the HSC, there is a colored toolbar with a number of icons and a Search box (see Figure 16.5).

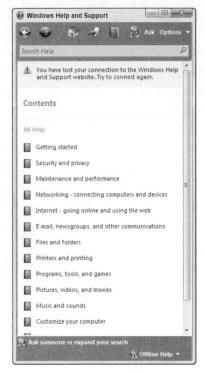

Figure 16.5. The more traditional aspects of the HSC.

Directional arrows let you jump a page forward or backwards, while the icons provide basic options, such as return to home page, print, browse help, access the Ask someone page, and set HSC options. The Help Settings page (see Figure 16.6) from the Options menu lets you include online resources (Windows Assistance Online) when consulting help. This feature should definitely be checked if you are a broadband user; it means that you are sure to have the most up-to-date online help information available since your help queries consult both the local and Internet-based online help.

The Search box acts as a traditional online help search box. You can type in one or several search terms and then press the green arrow. Windows will run your search and return results, if any, in the same window. Although the Set search options feature no longer exists in Windows Vista, you can click the Ask someone or expand your search link for setting additional parameters for your searches (see Figure 16.7).

Figure 16.6. The HSC Settings page.

Figure 16.7. The Ask someone or expand your search link.

General Windows troubleshooting techniques

Throughout this book, there have been suggestions and recommendations for taking care of problems related to a specific area. If your printer isn't printing, check the obvious (is it on? is there paper?) and then proceed to more complicated solutions, such as pausing and restarting the printer queue.

Other times you may be totally in the dark as to what has gone wrong. Your well-mannered, polite computer suddenly becomes a hooligan and spits out some weird error code or message. Even worse, you may be introduced to the legendary Blue Screen of Death (BSOD). When this happens, polish your badge and your boots and play detective. Computer errors fall into three categories:

- **Hardware.** The inside of a computer case is an unfriendly environment. High heat, poor ventilation, dust bunnies, and mysterious radiation from extraterrestrial visitors can cause your hardware to fail sooner or later. Sometimes, hardware failure is obvious; for example, a hard drive failure. Other times, things like bad memory or faulty converters are harder to diagnose because they cause many different types of problems.

- **Software.** Sometimes it really isn't Microsoft's fault; software can be badly coded. For example, an application might crash and take your files along with it. Some software bugs are hardware-related, such as when bad device drivers cause your video card to run in VGA, or 640x480 resolution, mode. That is really annoying, especially if you just dropped an entire paycheck on a nice LCD panel!

- **Human.** To paraphrase, never underestimate the ability of a human to screw up. Sometimes we do the darndest things, like trying to erase the C: drive or move the operating system to a server.

Unfortunately for you, it's possible that any issue could be a combination of the three! For example, you spill your syrupy beverage onto your keyboard and now your "e" key won't work and you suspect that your motherboard is about to fail because of it. When troubleshooting, the best thing you can do is back up, breathe deeply, and think clearly about what could possibly be the cause of your problems.

There isn't a magic formula or direct path to solving problems. A lot of it is thinking soundly and remaining calm. The more time you spend around the blasted machines, the more comfortable you will feel diagnosing and repairing them (just like if you are a car buff).

There are a number of seemingly silly questions (but in reality, these aren't silly at all) that you should ask yourself before tinkering with your computer:

- **What happened just before the problem occurred?** Bad things just don't happen out of nowhere. Most are the result of a specific action that triggered the problem. Think back over the previous few minutes. What were you trying to do? What did you press? What was open? Determining the conditions for a crash is a good first step.

- **Can you repeat the problem? If your computer still works, are you able to repeat this problem?** Try doing the same series of steps and see if it happens again. A repeatable bug is more likely to be fixed than an intermittent one. Also, if you contact technical support, the tech-support staff will ask you this as well.

- **Any new hardware, software, or Web gadgets installed recently?** More often than not, it's a new addition to your computer that causes problems. This could be a new video card, a new game, or a new plug-in that triggers a crash. Even patches or service packs have been known to be the culprit in these cases.

- **Is the problem reported elsewhere?** Thanks to the Internet, you can get online and within minutes see if anyone else has had such a problem. A quick Google search can reveal forums or columns that may discuss your issue.

Check the manufacturer's Web site for updated drivers, patches, FAQs, or forums where other users can chat and swap stories. We recommend checking out third-party forums and not manufacturer forums, because users may be more likely to be honest in their assessment.

There are a few obvious techniques that you can use to diagnose or try to cure your ills:

- **Reboot.** When in doubt, reboot. You can either try and do this the proper way, from the power button in the Start menu, or just turn the machine off at the base, if the power button isn't an option. Wait a minute or so before rebooting.

- **Remove.** Remove any new piece of hardware that could have potentially caused the crash. Anything that was installed prior to the crash is generally fair game in this case.

- **Reinstall.** Remove any recently installed applications, such as hotfixes or a service pack. Sometimes an installation doesn't "take" the first time around; sometimes the second time is the charm.

- **Restore.** Use the System Restore feature to go back to a previous state. If you haven't used it yet, we bet you wish you had right about now!

When you troubleshoot your computer, be sure to only change one thing at a time. Doing so allows you to individually rule out hardware or software changes. If you still aren't able to solve your problem, you have two choices: computer repair or wipe your system. If you're an old pro with Windows, you are probably comfortable with wiping your system and reinstalling Windows. It's a hassle, but you know how to get it done. If you're not very comfortable with your computer, you may want to consider sending it in to the shop for repairs. However, this option can be both costly and time consuming. Every time we've considered sending a machine in, we've been told it would take 3–4 weeks to diagnose and repair it.

Using the Startup Repair Tool

The Startup Repair Tool, formerly known as the Recovery Console, is an easy-to-use tool that fixes a number of problems, such as corrupted or missing system files. The tool scans your computers for problems and does its level best to fix them. If Startup Repair Tool is unable to fix your problems, it provides a summary of the problem and provides links to support contacts. For example, the tool cannot fix hardware failures and some virus attacks, nor can it help you recover lost files.

To repair your system:

1. Boot your computer with your Windows Vista installation DVD.
2. Click Repair your Computer.
3. Select the desired operating system to repair.
4. Click Load Drivers if your operating system doesn't appear in the list. This will let you load disk drivers.
5. Click Next.
6. Pick one of the diagnostic tools from the list.

- **Last Known Good Configuration.** Not nearly as useful as it sounds. When Windows shuts down properly, it writes out registry information to this setting as being "good." Of course, if you were having problems and decided to reboot, and do so successfully, it still considers your session as "good." A more accurate description would be Last Known Complete Shutdown Configuration.

- **Start Windows Normally.** Windows Vista throws caution to the wind and boots as it normally does.

Troubleshoot network problems

If we had a dollar for every time Windows wasn't able to connect to a network, we'd be wealthy. Most of the time, this involves trying to figure out why your expansive broadband connection keeps returning error messages.

The default reaction is to reboot the computer and reboot your router or modem. Most times this is sufficient, but not every time. Don't worry, it's not always you! Many times, it's the remote Web site, your ISP, and then your computer.

The easiest test is to try and connect to the Web site with another computer on the same network. If it works, try again on the misbehaving computer. If it still doesn't work, focus your time on the non-connecting computer.

If both computers cannot reach the first Web site, try another Web site. If they both fail again, it's most likely your ISP, or possibly your router, firewall, or hub that is being bad. Try connecting to your ISP; if this doesn't work, then it's your broadband provider, your modem, or your router.

The Windows Vista toolbox contains a number of tools: ipconfig, ping, and tracert. These are all command-line tools; you simply time them in using a command prompt from the Accessories menu in the Start menu.

Use ipconfig

To use ipconfig, type **ipconfig** at a command prompt and press Enter. Information about your computer's adapter (IP address, subnet mark, and local gateway) appears. If you want more information, type **ipconfig /all** and press Enter. This utility includes information about DNS servers, the MAC address, and details about all adapters installed on your system (see Figure 16.9).

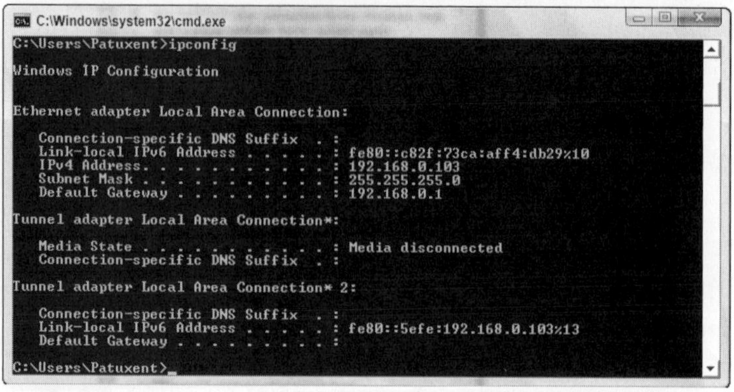

Figure 16.9. The ipconfig utility reveals all sorts of useful information.

You can release and renew your IP address by typing **ipconfig /release** and then **ipconfig /renew**. This is tantamount to rebooting your Internet connection by rebooting your adapter.

Use ping

Ping is a network utility that sends out a series of packets to a destination IP address. The utility basically asks if anyone is home. The destination machine sends back a packet in reply. Ping reports on how many packets made it back, and how long it took.

At the command prompt, type **ping** followed by an IP address or a host name such as **myisp.com** (see Figure 16.10).

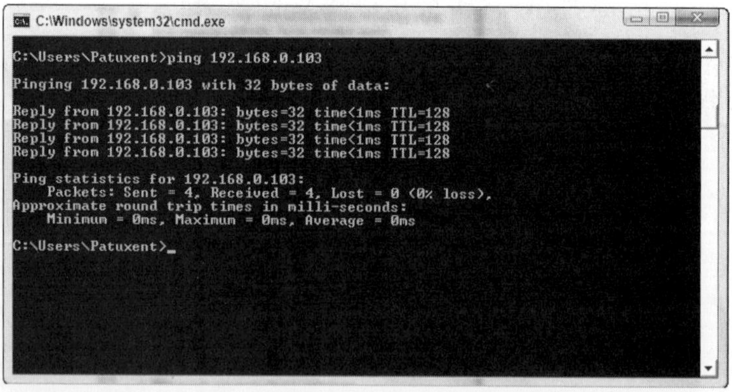

Figure 16.10. Ping lets you see if anyone is home at an IP address or host name.

Inside Scoop

Most large Web sites do not respond to ping requests, so lack of a response doesn't necessarily mean that the server is unavailable. Because too many ping requests can flood a server, many administrators of large Web sites disable ping.

Ping is a quick and easy way to tell if a network connection is working. If you are getting ping responses, the network connection is doing its job. You can also ping your own router or gateway to see if it works. Anything that doesn't reply to the ping request is a suspect, but not necessarily guilty.

Try the tracert utility

The last utility is the tracert utility. This feature lets you know where a break in the system is happening. It asks for a reply from each router along the path to the destination. A very long reply time, upwards of one second, and timeout messages show a router that is not working, keeping your service request from reaching its destination.

Open a command prompt and type **tracert** followed by an IP address or a host name and then press Enter (see Figure 16.11).

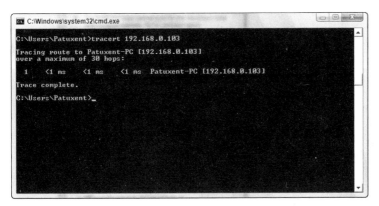

Figure 16.11. The tracert utility traces the route your packets take and reports back on the health of the routers along the way.

Tracert prints out the IP address and reply from each step, showing you where there may be problems. It's a quick way of determining if it's your ISP's equipment or yours that is at fault.

You can perform other quick inspections. Try the following:

- Check for any loose or disconnected network cables.

- Make sure that the network connection isn't accidentally set to Disabled.

- Look for firewall or antivirus software that somehow appeared on the machine.

- Look for changed or missing network connection settings.

- Check new network connections that somehow appeared on the computer, such as a wireless connection to your neighbor's Wi-Fi access point.

As you can probably tell by now, it's pretty rare for a computer's own networking adapters to fail without some other intervening agent or cause. Network adapters can fail, but it's easy to run the Help and Support Center troubleshooter to diagnose potential problems.

Just the facts

- The Windows Help and Support Center is a very good primary resource to check when things go wrong.

- Take a step back, relax, breathe, and then determine what was happening when your computer started to malfunction.

- The Startup Repair Tool can help you fix basic problems with your computer.

- Windows Safe Mode can help you rule out potentially corrupt device drivers.

- Network diagnostic tools are available to help you figure out whom to blame.

Appendixes

PART V

Supported Video Cards

O ne of the most difficult aspects of Windows Vista upgrading is the type of video card you will need. At the time of writing, the video cards listed here are supported in Windows Vista for the Aero theme.

The following list is the product support list for Windows Vista 32-bit video cards by manufacturer. Please note that this list only contains Aero-compatible video graphic cards; other cards not on this list may work with Vista Basic. To be sure, use the Upgrade Advisor before installing or upgrading to Windows Vista.

Nvidia

- GeForce FX 5100
- GeForce FX 5200
- GeForce FX 5200SE
- GeForce FX 5200 Ultra
- GeForce FX 5500
- GeForce FX 5600
- GeForce FX 5600 Ultra
- GeForce FX 5600SE
- GeForce FX 5600XT
- GeForce FX 5700
- GeForce FX 5700VE

593

- GeForce FX 5700 Ultra
- GeForce FX 5700LE
- GeForce FX 5800
- GeForce FX 5800 Ultra
- GeForce FX 5900
- GeForce FX 5900 Ultra
- GeForce FX 5900XT
- GeForce FX 5900ZT
- GeForce FX 5950 Ultra
- GeForce PCX 5300
- GeForce PCX 5750
- GeForce PCX 5900
- GeForce 6600 GT
- GeForce 6600 LE
- GeForce 6600
- GeForce 6800
- GeForce 6800 GT
- GeForce 6800 LE
- GeForce 6800 Ultra
- GeForce 7800 GTX
- Quadro FX 540
- Quadro FX 1000
- Quadro FX 1100
- Quadro FX 1300
- Quadro FX 1400
- Quadro FX 3000
- Quadro FX 3000G
- Quadro FX 3400
- Quadro FX 4000 SDI
- Quadro FX 4400
- Quadro NVS 280 PCI

ATI Radeon

Desktop

- All-In-Wonder® X600 Series
- All-In-Wonder® X800 Series
- All-In-Wonder® 2006 Edition
- All-In-Wonder® 9600 Series
- All-In-Wonder® 9800 Series
- Radeon® Xpress 200
- Radeon® Xpress 200 CrossFire
- Radeon® X300 Series
- Radeon® X550 Series
- Radeon® X600 Series
- Radeon® X700 Series
- Radeon® X800 Series
- Radeon® X850 Series
- Radeon® 9500 Series
- Radeon® 9550 Series
- Radeon® 9600 Series
- Radeon® 9800 Series

Mobile

- Radeon® Xpress 200M
- Mobility™ Radeon® X300 Series
- Mobility™ Radeon® X600 Series
- Mobility™ Radeon® X700 Series
- Mobility™ Radeon® X800 Series
- Mobility™ Radeon® X800 Series
- Mobility™ Radeon® 9500 Series
- Mobility™ Radeon® 9600 Series
- Mobility™ Radeon® 9700 Series

- Mobility™ Radeon® 9800 Series
- Mobility™ FireGL V5000 Series
- Mobility™ FireGL V3100 Series
- Mobility™ FireGL V3200 Series
- Mobility™ FireGL T2-128 Series
- Mobility™ FireGL 9000 Series
- Mobility™ FireGL 7800 Series

Workstation

- FireGL V3100 Series
- FireGL V3200 Series
- FireGL V5000 Series
- FireGL V5000 Series
- FireGL V7100 Series
- FireGL T2-128 Series
- FireGL X2-256 Series
- FireGL X3-256 Series

For more information on these video cards, or for the latest list of supported video cards, please visit the following manufacturer Web sites:

- `www.ati.com/developer/windowsvista.html`
- `www.nvidia.com/object/winvista_32_supported.html`

Upgrade Checklist

Upgrading to Windows Vista doesn't have to be a difficult task. The following checklist will help you ensure that you are ready for the transition to Windows Vista with your current machine.

Did you . . .?

General questions

1. Visit the Windows Vista Get Ready Web site at www.microsoft.com/windowsvista/getready/default.mspx?

2. Install and run Microsoft's Windows Vista Upgrade Advisor Beta?

3. Decide on the most appropriate edition of Windows Vista for your needs?

4. Verify if your current operating system qualifies for an upgrade or requires a custom installation?

Hardware

1. Verify your current onboard memory?

2. Upgrade to at least 1GB?

3. Consider a 1–2GB USB flash drive for DriveBoost™?

4. Buy a supported graphic card for Aero?

Appendix B

597

5. Verify that your computer has an AGP or PCI-Express x16 slot for use with a high-end video card?

6. Verify that your power supply has sufficient wattage to support your video card?

7. Verify available disk drive space?

8. Verify that your motherboard supports ACPI?

Mobile computers

1. Consider buying a hybrid drive (HDD) for upgrading to Windows Vista?

2. Verify that your video card is Aero compatible?

3. Verify available disk space?

Differences between Windows Vista and Windows XP

Perhaps you're reading this book and aren't quite sold on whether or not you should upgrade. This appendix compares some key features of the two operating systems. Of course, this list is non-exhaustive.

Table C.1. Comparing Windows features

Windows Vista	Windows XP
Vista claims to install in 35-minutes	XP requires close to an hour to install
Vista uses the Startup Repair Tool	XP uses the Recovery Console
Vista uses the Mobility Center	XP uses hardware profiles
Vista has a bidirectional firewall	XP has a one-way firewall (inbound only)
Start menus open and close using single-click	Start menus expand to three columns
Vista has a power button to shut down the operating system	XP has a shutdown menu
Vista uses the Window Switcher button to view folders in 3D	XP has nothing like this

continued

599

Table C.1. *continued*

Windows Vista	Windows XP
Personal folders are called Computer, Pictures, Music	Personal folders are called My Computer, My Pictures, My Music
Address bar appears as a breadcrumb bar	Address bar appears as a hierarchical folder menu
Vista folders use "look inside" to reveal actual content	XP folders display a generic icon
Search menus are a mix between search and library features	Search menus only handle search capabilities
Public folder lets you share data with other users	There is no Public folder
Windows Media Player 11 has URGE, an online music store	Not available in XP
Internet Explorer 7	Internet Explorer 6
Windows Defender installed	Windows Defender manually downloaded
Windows Calendar	Not available in XP
Windows Mail	Outlook Express
BitLocker application	Not available in XP
Windows Welcome Center	Not available in XP
Network diagnostic tool	Not available in XP
Windows Vista Aero/Vista Basic	Not available in XP
Windows Live Messenger	MSN Messenger
Windows Media Center	Not available in XP (except Media Edition)
Windows DVD Maker	Not available in XP
Windows Meeting Space	Not available in XP
User Account Control	Not available in XP

Windows Vista	Windows XP
Windows SideShow	Not available in XP
People Near Me	Not available in XP
Problem Reports and Solutions	Not available in XP
Pen and Input Devices	Not available in XP

Appendix D

Keyboard Shortcuts

Without a doubt, one of the most important advances in personal computing came with the invention of the mouse by Douglas Engelbart in 1968. With the mouse, computers changed from being a specialist tool that only scientists could use to a user-friendly device accessible to all.

Nonetheless, there are times when it is quicker and more convenient to use a keyboard shortcut than to point and click in a series of menus. This appendix provides a few of the more common shortcuts in the Windows Vista operating system.

Table D.1. Windows Vista keyboard shortcuts

To Do This	Press
Select all	Ctrl+A
Copy an item to the Clipboard	Ctrl+C
Cut an item to the Clipboard	Ctrl+X
Paste an item from the Clipboard	Ctrl+V
Undo your last action	Ctrl+Z
Delete	Delete
Cancel the current task	Esc

continued

Table D.1. *continued*

To Do This	Press
Switch between open items	Alt+Tab
Display or hide the Start menu	Ctrl+Esc
Display or hide the Start menu	Windows key
Carry out a command or select an option in a dialog box	Alt+[Underlined letter]
Highlight a block of text	Ctrl+Shift+[any arrow key]
Move the insertion point to the start of the next paragraph	Ctrl+Down Arrow
Move the insertion point to the start of the previous paragraph	Ctrl+Up Arrow
Move the insertion point to the start of the next word	Ctrl+Left Arrow
Move the insertion point to the start of the previous word	Ctrl+Right Arrow
Select more than one item in a window or on the desktop, or select text within a document	Shift+[any arrow key]
Delete selected item permanently without placing it in the Recycle Bin	Shift+Delete
Open the Task Manager	Ctrl+Alt+Delete
Lock your computer if you are connected to a domain, or switch users	Windows Key+L
Display the System Properties dialog box	Windows Key+Break
Display the desktop	Windows Key+D
Open My Computer	Windows Key+E
Search for a file or folder	Windows Key+F
Minimize all windows	Windows Key+M
Restore minimized windows	Windows Key+Shift+M
Refresh the active window	F5

Online Resources

Much as we would like to think otherwise, this book that you hold in your hands does not constitute the only resource when it comes to obtaining information on the Microsoft Windows Vista operating system.

Table E.1 points you to some useful resources on the Web that will help you extend your knowledge of Windows Vista, many of which have proved invaluable to us in the writing of this book.

Table E.1. Online resources

Address	Description
www.unofficialvista.com	The companion blog to this book
www.microsoft.com/ windowsvista	The official Microsoft site
www.microsoft.com/technet/ windowsvista/	Windows Vista: Resources for IT Professionals
msdn.microsoft.com/ windowsvista	Microsoft Vista developer center

continued

Appendix E

605

Table E.1. *continued*

Address	Description
www.winsupersite.com/vista/	Paul Thurrott's SuperSite for Windows: Windows Vista Activity Center
www.longhornblogs.com	"The Source for Windows Vista News and Experiences"

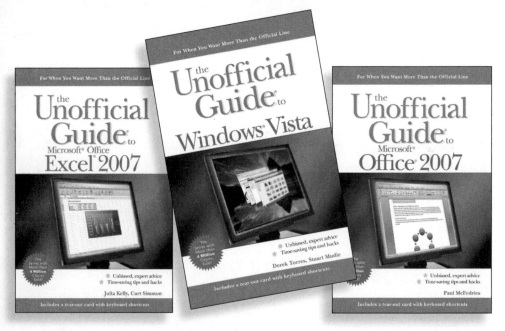